WORDPRESS® 24-HOUR TRAINER

Continues

WordPress®

24-Hour Trainer

WordPress®

24-HOUR TRAINER

Second Edition

George Plumley

WILEY

John Wiley & Sons, Inc.

WordPress® 24-Hour Trainer, Second Edition

Published by
John Wiley & Sons, Inc.
10475 Crosspoint Boulevard
Indianapolis, IN 46256
www.wiley.com

Published simultaneously in Canada

ISBN: 978-1-118-06690-4

Manufactured in the United States of America

10 9 8 7 6 5 4 3 2

Library of Congress Control Number: 2011930318

This book is dedicated to my family: to my wife, Kim, and daughters, Grace and Ella, for putting up with my absences a second time around — "Didn't you already write this book, Daddy?", and to my parents, Adelaide and Stan, and my sister, Patricia, as well as my in-laws, Gord and Carole — your support and encouragement mean the world to me.

ABOUT THE AUTHOR

GEORGE PLUMLEY is a web developer living on Vancouver Island, Canada. After doing graduate work in philosophy at York University, Washington University in St. Louis, and Rutgers, he went on to web development in 1993. He's been working with various content management systems ever since, and then, in 2006, discovered the joys of WordPress. He also runs the WordPress help site `www.seehowtwo.com` and is the author of *Website Design and Development: 100 Questions to Ask Before Building a Website* (Wiley, 2011).

ABOUT THE TECHNICAL EDITOR

MIKE LITTLE is the cofounder of WordPress, and founder and CEO of zed1.com ltd, a WordPress specialist web development consultancy. He has developed many websites for his clients (WordPress-based, of course), including a number of prominent UK government websites.

His background is in software development and he has more than 25 years under his belt, many at the most senior levels. He is a member of Mensa, a published author, a technical editor, and a member of the Usability Professionals Association.

He lives with his family in Stockport, England.

CREDITS

EXECUTIVE EDITOR
Carol Long

PROJECT EDITOR
Ed Connor

TECHNICAL EDITOR
Mike Little

PRODUCTION EDITOR
Rebecca Anderson

COPY EDITOR
Kim Cofer

EDITORIAL MANAGER
Mary Beth Wakefield

FREELANCER EDITORIAL MANAGER
Rosemarie Graham

MARKETING MANAGER
Ashley Zurcher

BUSINESS MANAGER
Amy Knies

PRODUCTION MANAGER
Tim Tate

VICE PRESIDENT AND EXECUTIVE GROUP PUBLISHER
Richard Swadley

VICE PRESIDENT AND EXECUTIVE PUBLISHER
Neil Edde

ASSOCIATE PUBLISHER
Jim Minatel

PROJECT COORDINATOR, COVER
Katie Crocker

PROOFREADER
Paul Sagan, Word One New York

INDEXER
Johnna VanHoose Dinse

COVER DESIGNER
Ryan Sneed

COVER IMAGE
© Mike Bentley

DVD TECHNICAL PRODUCER
Focal Point Studios LLC

ACKNOWLEDGMENTS

I WANT TO THANK Carol Long for sending the tweet that got this all started years ago and for being a great Acquisitions Editor/hockey mom through the entire process of all of my projects with Wiley; the whole Wiley team, in particular the editorial staff headed by Ed Connor, who kept it all running smoothly even when I made the road a bit bumpy, Kim Cofer, who made sure my that's and which's were right way 'round and my voice was active, and Mike Little for his indispensable technical editing; Doris Michaels for pointing me to my wonderful agent, Carole Jelen, who's been so supportive; friends like Karen Hollowell, who got me addicted to 3 × 5 note cards and was my Canadian/American cultural attaché, Ann Douglas for running the mother of all author support lines, Peggy Richardson for her insights into the art of writing books and for doing some research, Angela Crocker for all her support, and Julie Winkel for the use of the MacBook when mine suddenly "retired" from doing videos, the programmers who make WordPress possible, and the WordPress community, from whom I've learned and continue to learn so much; and finally, I want to thank all my clients over the years and the readers of the first edition, who, by asking great questions, have helped me learn to explain things more clearly.

CONTENTS

SECTION XI: TAKING WORDPRESS EVEN FURTHER

INTRODUCTION

ALTHOUGH WORDPRESS is currently the world's number-one blogging software, this is not a book about blogging. In *WordPress 24-Hour Trainer*, you learn how to use this open-source software to build and maintain a website, whether it's a blog, has a blogging section, or has nothing at all to do with blogging. WordPress is a content management system — a system you can customize in a number of ways to make it do exactly what you need.

Whether you're building a website for yourself or for someone else, you want it to be:

- Easy to set up
- Easy to maintain
- Easy to grow and adapt

This book shows you how WordPress fulfills all these needs.

This last quality — ease of growing and adapting — is particularly important on the Web, where technological change is fast and furious. WordPress is nimble for reasons I'll go into later, and that makes it well suited to fast-paced change. For example, when Facebook introduced "like" buttons, a number of WordPress plugins were released by members of the community almost immediately, making it simple for site owners to use this new feature right away.

Since I began building websites exclusively with WordPress, I've noticed an important change in my clients: they look forward to updating and expanding their sites. When changing some text, let alone adding a new page, is like pulling teeth, you're less likely to do it. With WordPress, not only are my clients making their own changes, but they're excited about it and that's also made them more involved in their sites. Instead of having a site built and then sitting back, my clients are actively thinking about what they can change or add to make their sites better because they can go in and do it themselves when the thought strikes them.

That's the real power of WordPress: putting more control in the hands of the website owner.

WHO THIS BOOK IS FOR

This book is for beginners at two levels: those who've never built a website and those who've never built or used a WordPress website.

You should be aware that there are two versions of WordPress:

- The free hosted version at WordPress.com
- The open-source downloadable version from WordPress.org, which you then install on your own server (commonly referred to as the self-hosted version)

The important difference between the two is that the hosted version is primarily meant for blogging and offers few choices to customize your site. For example, you have a very small, fixed number of plugins to choose from and you can't do things like create different page layouts or other theme customizations.

Though this book deals with the self-hosted version of WordPress, much of it — how to enter content, how to upload photos and documents, how to lay out content, and so on — still applies to the hosted version.

WHAT THIS BOOK COVERS

Since the first edition of this book, WordPress has undergone significant changes, all of which make it even easier to use and even more flexible for managing any type of website. This new edition includes features up to and including Version 3.1, with indications of some changes expected in 3.2.

You'll learn how to set up a WordPress website from scratch, using the default features of the software. Each lesson covers a specific set of topics, so you can follow the lessons in order but you can easily dip into any one of them to refresh your memory. Later in the book, I cover some customization of the look of the site as well as the addition of plugins, which are bits of code that add extra features to WordPress.

Keep in mind, this book is not what I call an extended manual. It does not aim to cover every feature of WordPress. Instead, it focuses on the key tasks you need in day-to-day use, and covers them in great detail. I do that by showing you not just the basics, but the tips and tricks that make things as simple as possible. The addition of video for key points helps make things clearer and reinforce the concepts.

HOW THIS BOOK IS STRUCTURED

This book consists of short lessons covering tasks you'll typically need when building and maintaining a website with WordPress. This means that not every feature of WordPress is covered — I'll provide links to places on the Web where you can get that kind of detailed reference material. The goal here is to show you the key skills you'll use every day.

The 39 lessons are grouped into themed sections:

- **Section I: Before You Start** — Get to know how WordPress thinks about content and what planning you need to do before starting your site.
- **Section II: Firing Up WordPress** — Instructions for installing the software, an overview of the administration interface, and the basic settings you'll need to get going.
- **Section III: Working with Written Content** — Entering your content and publishing it.
- **Section IV: Working with Media Content** — The ins and outs of uploading images, video, documents, and so on and using them on your site.

- **Section V: Managing Your Content** — Navigating through various types of content, editing it, moving it around.
- **Section VI: Making Your Site Social** — Dealing with links, comments, RSS feeds, social networking, and multiple users.
- **Section VII: Choosing and Customizing Themes** — How to choose from the astonishing array of themes, and some basics for making the site look exactly the way you want using WordPress features and Cascading Style Sheets (CSS).
- **Section VIII: Becoming Search Engine–Friendly** — Basic techniques for optimizing your site so that you get indexed in the best possible way.
- **Section IX: Housekeeping Chores** — Keeping an eye on your site statistics, making sure your software is up to date, and getting into good backup habits.
- **Section X: Added Functionality Using Plugins** — Using these add-ons to let your site do even more and remain flexible.
- **Section XI: Taking WordPress Even Further** — Running multiple websites from a single installation, customizing your site with templates, and creating even greater flexibility with custom post types.

When you're finished reading the book and watching the DVD, you'll find lots of support in the p2p forums, as you'll see in a moment, but there's also the WordPress community on the Web. Hundreds of thousands of people around the world are using this software and a lot of them give back in so many ways. It's a spirit that's reflected in the quality of WordPress and its continued improvement.

From the people who created and maintain WordPress, to the people who make plugins and themes, to the people who write about WordPress on their blogs or contribute to the official and unofficial forums, there are thousands of bright minds giving back to the community with code, ideas, fixes, and more. You never have to feel you're alone when you're using WordPress. I like to think of it as a worldwide 24-hour help line. Whether you need help or can offer help, you're welcome any time.

INSTRUCTIONAL VIDEOS ON DVD

Learning is often enhanced by seeing in real time what's being taught, which is why most lessons in the book have a corresponding video tutorial on the accompanying DVD. And, of course, it's vital that you play along at home — fire up WordPress and try out what you read in the book and watch on the videos.

CONVENTIONS

To help you get the most from the text and keep track of what's happening, we've used a number of conventions throughout the book.

> *Boxes like this one hold important, not-to-be-forgotten information that is directly relevant to the surrounding text.*

> *Notes, tips, hints, tricks, and asides to the current discussion are offset and placed in italics like this.*

> *References like this one point you to the DVD or to the website, at* `www.wrox.com/go/sp2010-24`*, to watch the instructional video that accompanies a given lesson.*

As for styles in the text:

- We *highlight* new terms and important words when we introduce them.
- We show URLs and code within the text like so: `persistence.properties`.

We present code in the following way:

```
We use a monofont type for code examples.
```

ERRATA

We make every effort to ensure that there are no errors in the text or in the code. However, no one is perfect, and mistakes do occur. If you find an error in one of our books, like a spelling mistake or faulty piece of code, we would be very grateful for your feedback. By sending in errata, you may save another reader hours of frustration and, at the same time, you will be helping us provide even higher-quality information.

To find the errata page for this book, go to `www.wrox.com` and locate the title using the Search box or one of the title lists. Then, on the Book Search Results page, click the Errata link. On this page, you can view all errata that has been submitted for this book and posted by Wrox editors.

> *A complete book list, including links to errata, is also available at* `www.wrox.com/misc-pages/booklist.shtml`.

If you don't spot "your" error on the Errata page, click the Errata Form link and complete the form to send us the error you have found. We'll check the information and, if appropriate, post a message to the book's errata page and fix the problem in subsequent editions of the book.

P2P.WROX.COM

For author and peer discussion, join the P2P forums at `p2p.wrox.com`. The forums are a web-based system for you to post messages relating to Wrox books and related technologies and interact with other readers and technology users. The forums offer a subscription feature to e-mail you topics of interest of your choosing when new posts are made to the forums. Wrox authors, editors, other industry experts, and your fellow readers are present on these forums.

At `p2p.wrox.com`, you will find a number of different forums that will help you not only as you read this book, but also as you develop your own applications. To join the forums, just follow these steps:

1. Go to `p2p.wrox.com` and click the Register link.
2. Read the terms of use and click Agree.
3. Complete the required information to join, as well as any optional information you wish to provide, and click Submit.
4. You will receive an e-mail with information describing how to verify your account and complete the joining process.

> *You can read messages in the forums without joining P2P, but in order to post your own messages, you must join.*

Once you join, you can post new messages and respond to messages other users post. You can read messages at any time on the Web. If you would like to have new messages from a particular forum e-mailed to you, click the Subscribe to this Forum icon by the forum name in the forum listing.

For more information about how to use the Wrox P2P, be sure to read the P2P FAQs for answers to questions about how the forum software works as well as many common questions specific to P2P and Wrox books. To read the FAQs, click the FAQ link on any P2P page.

SECTION I
Before You Start

1

Thinking Like WordPress

WordPress provides you with the tools to organize your website content, but those tools function in specific ways, just as one type of word processing software has its specific buttons for creating, say, lists. But there's a difference between knowing which button to press to create a list and thinking about ways you can use lists in your documents. That's what this lesson is about: learning to think like WordPress so that you can organize your content in an efficient and flexible manner right from the start, and be able to use it in new and useful ways later.

DYNAMIC VS. STATIC WEBSITES

When you open a website in your browser, you see a single page filled with text and media (graphics, photos, video, and so on), as a page in a magazine or newspaper is a single entity made up of text and images. But what you see in a browser window is created from a series of instructions: the HTML code. So ultimately, the HTML is the single entity behind what you see onscreen: the equivalent of the printed page.

However, there's an important difference between an HTML page and a printed page. The HTML that's fed to your browser may be a single entity when it arrives at the browser, but it may or may not be a single entity sitting on the server waiting for browsers to retrieve it, like a magazine on a newsstand waiting to be purchased. The HTML may be made up of chunks of code that get assembled into a whole in that split second when the browser pulls it off the shelf.

That's the difference between dynamic and static web pages. Static pages are complete sets of HTML waiting to be retrieved, whereas dynamic pages are chunks of HTML that are assembled at the moment of retrieval into a single entity that's displayed in your browser (some systems store the most recent static version of a dynamically created page to keep the server from being overworked, but ultimately, the browser pages were created dynamically).

What I want you to take away from this lesson in particular, but the book in general, is to reject static thinking in favor of dynamic. You might have a vision right now for the content of a particular page on your website, but if you learn to view the content in chunks, there may be ways to use part of that content on another page as well. *Dynamic thinking* means you want to keep that chunk of content separate and reusable, not welded to the other content.

CONTENT MANAGEMENT SYSTEMS

Creating HTML pages dynamically is one half of what a content management system (CMS) does: it takes chunks of code (your content) and pieces them together into a single HTML page. The other function of a CMS is to provide an easy way for you, the user, to manage all those chunks of content.

Managing content does not just mean allowing you to enter text or upload images; it also means making it easy for you to determine the relationships between chunks of content. Selecting a category for the article you're working on, for example, tells the CMS to assemble that chunk in a particular way when someone on the Internet requests a page on your website.

Everybody understands the role of a CMS when it comes to managing content: it saves having to know HTML coding. But why not just have the CMS manage the content of individual HTML pages? All this assembling business seems like a lot of extra work. If you had a five-page website that never changed, that might be true. But suppose, even on a five-page website, that you decided you didn't like the top section or header that appears on all the pages of your site. Although a CMS for static pages would make it easy to change, you'd still need to change the graphics on all five pages separately, because they're all individual, physical pieces of coding. Now imagine that task on a site with 500 pages or 5,000! Even with search-and-replace capabilities, you would need to upload all 5,000 pages back onto the server to replace the old version, then do it all again for the next change. Ouch!

By separating the content of individual HTML pages into chunks, a CMS offers tremendous flexibility. Say you wanted 3,000 of your pages to have a different kind of header than the other 2,000. Easy, with a CMS! What if your business partner decides that your line of 500 different wuzzbuzzes should be categorized under buzz instead of wuzz? Easy, with a CMS!

We're always being told to embrace change, and one of the advantages of a website over print is that it allows you to change things as much as you want, as often as you want. The advantage of using a CMS instead of manually creating static or dynamic web pages is that the managing of change is much easier and more flexible, which is exactly what WordPress does.

WordPress as a CMS

In the first edition of this book, I explained that, although WordPress was developed as blogging software, it could be manipulated to be used as a CMS for any type of site. With the latest versions of WordPress, it has become a full-fledged CMS. But the question still remains: why use WordPress for your website? Lots of other content management systems are out there — good ones — that are also open source. I think the answer is twofold:

- The simplicity and flexibility of WordPress's design make it easy to learn, easy to expand, and easy to customize.
- The WordPress community is so large and so vibrant that you have excellent support, and will have for years to come.

The fact is, every CMS requires creative thinking, sometimes add-on software, and sometimes customization of the coding, because every site owner will have specific needs. No one CMS can fulfill everyone's requirements right out of the box.

All websites have a lot of common elements that may have different names and different functions, but from the standpoint of HTML coding, they operate in basically the same way. For instance, I need a page full of testimonials whereas you need a page of all your current specials. If a testimonial and a special are the chunks of content, all we need the CMS to do is assemble our chunks into whole pages. Your header and footer may be very different in look and content from mine, but we both need a header and a footer. A good CMS couldn't care less which is which — it just assembles and manages, easily and efficiently. As WordPress does.

HOW WORDPRESS ASSEMBLES PAGES

Three basic structures in WordPress interact to create HTML pages: the *core*, the *theme*, and the *database* (where content is stored). The core is the set of files that you download from `WordPress.org` and that perform the tasks of storing, retrieving, and assembling content. The database is where the content is stored and the theme is made up of template files that provide instructions to the core about what to retrieve and how to assemble it, as I've tried to illustrate in Figure 1-1.

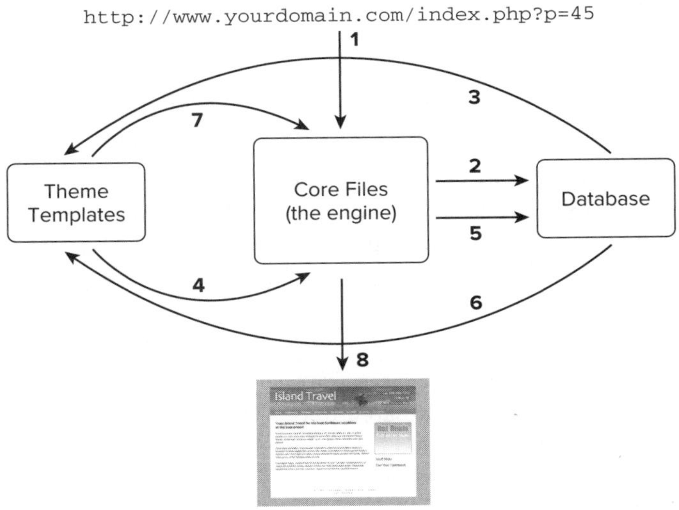

FIGURE 1-1

The web address you type into a browser window goes to the WordPress core, which then checks with the database to determine which template file to look for in the theme. The core then reads the template file and follows the instructions about what chunks of content to retrieve. Depending on the complexity of the template, there may be dozens of chunks to be located in the database where they're stored (technically, not all chunks are physically stored in the database, but at least the information on how to find them is stored there). Having found the content, the core then assembles the chunks according to the template's instructions and you see the result as the HTML page in your browser. And, of course, all of this has happened in a split second (or two).

Why Separate Is Good

You saw earlier why it's important that a CMS keep form (design and structure) and content (text and media files) separate, and now you're seeing the particular power of the way WordPress achieves this. Remember that earlier example of wanting 3,000 pages to have one header and 2,000 pages a different header? Depending on exactly how WordPress generates those pages, you might have to add only one template file to your theme to accomplish the change.

If you want to see a dramatic example of how the separation of form and content works on the Web, visit a site called CSS Zen Garden (`www.csszengarden.com`). You can instantly switch between dozens of incredibly different looks, all presenting exactly the same content.

But separating form and content isn't the only useful kind of separation that WordPress employs. It also separates the form from the core — the set of files that do the actual assembling and managing. That core is completely separate from the theme and the content, which is a good thing from a number of standpoints, the most important of which is the ability to easily update the core.

Software of any kind is constantly being given new features, strengthened for security, made more efficient, and so on. If you had to completely redo your theme every time the core needed an update, it would be very inefficient, just as having to redo your website content because of a new structure or look would be inefficient. As I said earlier, WordPress at its heart is a set of three separate structures — the core, the theme, and the content (in a database) — each of which can be tweaked, updated, or completely replaced, all independently.

There's a fourth separate structure to WordPress that is entirely optional: plugins. These are bits of extra code that you literally plug into the WordPress system and they provide additional functionality, from letting people rate the content on your site to automatically creating tweets on Twitter.

Sometimes, people ask why they don't just incorporate the plugins into the core, but that would be defeating the whole purpose of this elegant and flexible system. To begin with, plugins are meant to address specific needs. Why clutter the core with features that not everyone uses? Sometimes, a plugin is so useful to everyone that it is eventually incorporated into the core, but most plugins aren't like that. Also, the more complex the core, the better the chance things will break down. Keep the core simple and add on extras as you need them. I have some WordPress sites with only two plugins, and others have dozens.

Another reason for keeping extra features as plugins is that there can be many variations of a plugin, each one serving the needs of a group of users. A good example would be plugins for photos — some are very simple, some are very complex, some work better than others. Having a choice of those plugins, rather than being stuck with only one, is another important advantage.

HOW WORDPRESS MANAGES CONTENT

Very easily, thank you. Like any CMS, WordPress stores the chunks of content it uses to assemble HTML pages in a database. Getting that content into the database, letting you edit that content, and then storing instructions about how that content relates to other content is really what managing the content means. All databases work pretty much the same way, and though part of WordPress's simplicity and flexibility stems from the way its creators built the database and the files to run it, what ultimately matters to users is the interface that's used to do the managing. It's this administrative interface (a sample screen is shown in Figure 1-2) that my clients and hundreds of thousands of users around the world find so easy to use — for them, it *is* WordPress.

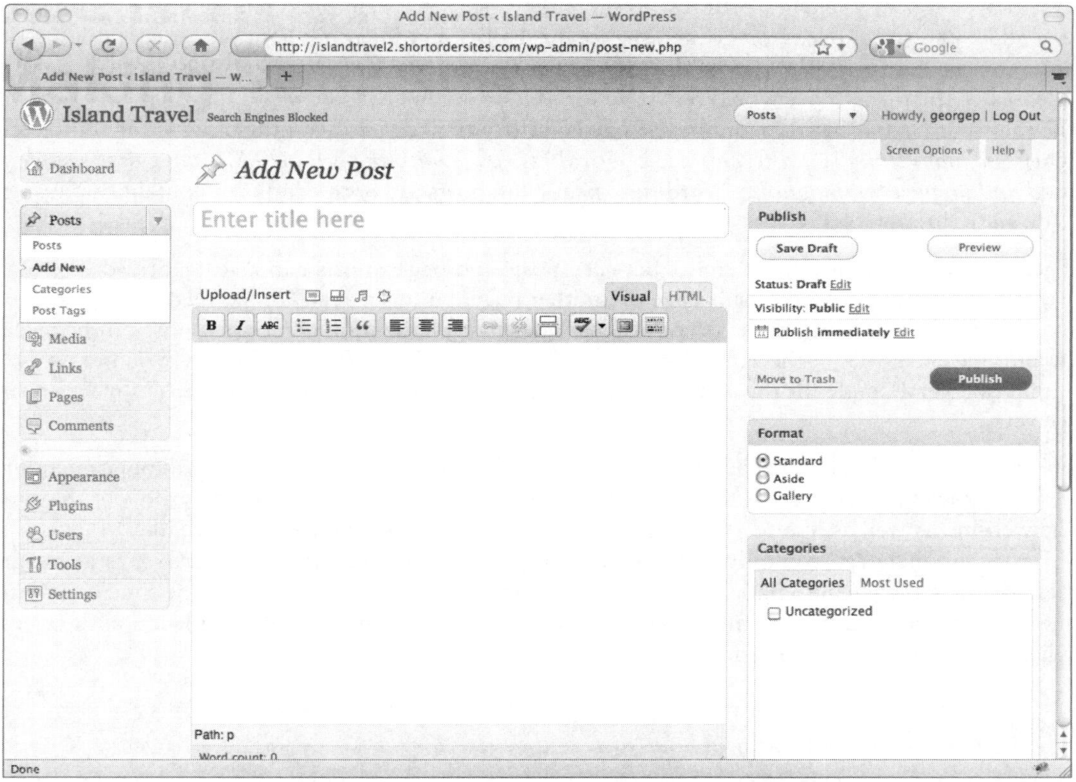

FIGURE 1-2

Every CMS has its particular way of dealing with content and though WordPress is extremely easy to use, you still need to understand how it refers to content and the methods it uses to organize content. Take *posts*, for example. In the world of blogging, people refer to the act of creating a new blog entry as posting. So it's not surprising that the primary kind of content chunk in WordPress is called a post, but that doesn't mean we have to use WordPress posts exclusively for a blog. A post is just a block of text and some instructions stored in a database. They could just as well have called them *chunks*. We don't want to get tied to how we use posts simply because they were originally intended for and named after an element within blogs.

WordPress has another type of content chunk called a *page*, but not the HTML pages you see in your browser. Like posts, WordPress pages are essentially blocks of text and accompanying instructions stored in a database. They're different from posts, though, in several ways. For a start, you can put only one WordPress page at a time into the final assembled HTML page. On the other hand, you can have dozens or even hundreds of posts displayed on a single assembled HTML page.

Suppose you set up WordPress so that each press release for your company is entered as an individual post. Then, you tell WordPress to show the five most recent press release posts. Whenever you add a new press release, it goes to the top of the list. On the other hand, the content describing your company's mission statement doesn't change that often — it's static in comparison to press releases — so you set up a WordPress page for that content. That's how you'll hear people describe the difference between posts and pages: one is for dynamic content and the other is for static content. *The main thing is not to confuse a WordPress page with the final HTML page that gets generated and viewed by the public.* WordPress pages and posts are both chunks of content that just get utilized in different ways.

There's another important difference between posts and pages: posts can be categorized whereas pages cannot. Pages can be a sub-page of another page, but it's a very limited relationship. There's a lot you can do with categories, as you will see later, but I'll mention one here: a post can be placed in multiple categories at the same time. That has enormous consequences for how you use posts. It makes it very simple for the content of a post to appear in several or even dozens of places on a website.

For instance, if I don't go to the press release area of your site, I won't see your announcement of a new wuzzbuzz for kids. But if the post for that press release also appears in the products section of the website, as well as in a section on helpful tips for keeping kids busy, it's more likely I'll notice this new product. Yet, you only had to enter that press release once and assign it to several categories. WordPress then automatically displays it in multiple locations, saving you the time of entering the same information two or more times, let alone having to remember all the places on the website where that information is needed.

> *OK, having just told you how posts and pages differ in WordPress, I'll be using the term* posts *throughout this book to mean both posts and pages. Partly, it's to avoid potential confusion over the term* page, *but mainly, it's for the sake of simplicity. The way you enter and edit content for posts and pages is virtually identical, because they both share the majority of content management features. Where necessary, I'll distinguish between them but unless I do, you can assume that when I say* posts, *I mean both posts and pages.*

Now that you're thinking like WordPress, it's time to take an actual website plan and see how it can be organized using WordPress, which is what you do in the next lesson.

TRY IT

There isn't anything specific to try based on the material in this lesson, but one thing you could do is examine your favorite news website and count how many different chunks of content are on one page. Then go to another page on the site and think about what's common with the previous page and try to imagine how the builders have divided up the structure of the page — map it out on paper.

There is no video to accompany this lesson.

2

Planning Your Site for WordPress

It's beyond the scope of this book to go into the entire planning process for a website; rather, the goal is to take a plan for a website and make it work using WordPress. If you're setting up a blog and nothing more, WordPress has done much of the structuring for you and you can skip to the next chapter. For everyone else, this is a very important step because with the right kind of planning up front, not only will you save yourself lots of time and energy down the road, but it also will help you think about ways to make your website even more useful and easier to navigate. To build a site in WordPress, you have three key things to consider:

- How are various kinds of content going to be entered in WordPress?
- What categories are needed to organize that content?
- What do the layout and design roughly look like?

The sample site you'll be working on is for a company called Island Travel, a small travel agency with two locations that specializes in vacations to the Caribbean. Its primary goal is to have a website that provides a very personal touch, with information largely written by its staff, and of course, the company wants it to be as easy as possible to update and expand.

What I've learned over the years from my clients is that "easy" doesn't just mean having a WYSIWYG (what you see is what you get) text editor. It also means being able to clearly understand how what they see on the administrative side fits with what's seen on the site — how the various parts of the site fit together.

HOW CONTENT WILL BE ENTERED

I've talked about how WordPress assembles chunks of content into HTML pages, and one of the most important tasks of the planning process is to develop a useful and straightforward organization for those chunks. Another important task is to decide how to break down the content into the smallest logical chunks. It's easy to assemble those chunks in different ways later on (perhaps in ways you can't even envision at the moment); it's costly to break apart chunks later when you figure out that they're too large. As a simple example, it's better to have each testimonial as a separate chunk than to have one single chunk of all testimonials. With that in mind, look at one potential site map for Island Travel shown in Figure 2-1.

FIGURE 2-1

You can see the sub-pages for each of the vacation companies Island Travel deals with and sub-pages for the various destinations for which they book vacations. Then, the rest of the site is a series of individual HTML pages, all linked, of course, through a common menu, and there would be various links between them within the content of the pages.

Now, keep in mind that this is a plan for how the site will be organized when you view it, but as you saw in the previous lesson, that's not the same as how it might be organized in a content management system like WordPress. Of course, you could build the exact structure shown in the plan using WordPress pages and sub-pages. But remember that example about testimonials? If you just create a single WordPress page and keep adding testimonials to it, you can't do anything more with the individual testimonials. You can't reuse them in any way. But if you enter each one as a post in WordPress, the sky's the limit.

For example, you could create a category called Testimonials, and then a series of subcategories corresponding to each of your vacation destinations. When a new testimonial is added, it would be assigned to the subcategory for the destination the testimonial is about. Now, if you want to show all testimonials at one time, it doesn't matter how many subcategories there are; they're all under the parent category, so you could show all testimonials as a group. At the same time, on the Jamaica destination page, for example, you could have a link saying Read Testimonials About Jamaican Vacations and it would connect to all the testimonials in the Jamaica Testimonials subcategory.

Suppose the testimonial concerns Jamaica and The Dominican Republic. Simply categorize it under both destinations and the same testimonial will show up in three places automatically — the Testimonials page, the Jamaica page, and the Dominican Republic page. That's the power of keeping your content in the smallest chunks possible.

It's really the same thinking that led to the original site map showing suppliers and destinations as sub-pages. You could put all the suppliers on a single page, but not only might that make for a very large page (not very friendly for visitors), it just wouldn't be as flexible, such as having a link to a specific supplier. So, suppliers were broken down into their smallest possible chunks — same with the vacation destinations. You're applying that principle even further when you're thinking about how to use WordPress.

Another way to think of this process is to look at content and ask whether it can be used in multiple ways across the site. If it can be or even if you think it might be in the future, it's better to enter the content as a post now.

Coming at it from yet another direction, enter your base products or services as WordPress pages and supporting information as posts. That's not a hard and fast rule by any means, but it's a starting point. For example, Island Travel has vacation suppliers, each of which has many products, has ever-changing company news, and has customers giving testimonials about them, and so on. The supplier's basic information (logo and so on) does not belong anywhere else, whereas its products could be listed in several places on the site, as could its company news, testimonials, and so on. So keep the supplier as a WordPress page, the rest of the information as individual posts, and then just link those posts to the page through categories.

Going back to the site map, then, here's a list of how you're going to enter various types of content into WordPress:

Suppliers — individual sub-pages

Destinations — individual sub-pages

Specials — individual posts

Staff Picks — individual posts

Travel News — individual posts

Testimonials — individual posts

Staff — single page

About — single page

Contact — single page

Customer Deals — password-protected single page

You could, of course, deal with the content in other ways, but I think this is a logical approach and leaves a lot of room to get even more creative later on.

HOW CATEGORIES WILL BE ORGANIZED

Now, it's time to give some thought to the category structure for posts and how that structure will relate to your primary types of content chunks: suppliers and destinations. Consider two approaches you could take:

TWO APPROACHES TO CATEGORIZING

SUBJECT-BASED	TYPE-BASED
Jamaica	**Testimonials**
Jamaica Specials	Jamaica Testimonials
Jamaica Testimonials	Sun Worship Testimonials
Jamaica Travel News	Cancun Testimonials
Sun Worship Holidays	**Travel News**
Sun Worship Specials	Jamaica Travel News
Sun Worship Testimonials	Sun Worship Travel News
Sun Worship Travel News	Cancun Travel News

At first glance, it might look as if the Subject approach is nicely geared to your primary content chunks. The parent categories — Jamaica and Sun Worship Holidays are the examples shown — correspond to sub-pages on the site. The problem is, other than linking the Sun Worship Holidays category to the Sun Worship Holidays page, how would you easily use the posts in that category?

Let's go back to the example of testimonials for a moment. If you choose the Subject approach, it wouldn't be easy to have a single testimonials page displaying all testimonials at one time. You'd need to figure out some way to gather together the various testimonials categories rather than letting WordPress's parent-child category structure do the work for you. Same problem if you want to have a random testimonial from the list of all testimonials appear on the site's sidebar; unless they're all under one parent category, there'd be some customization work needed.

But with the Type approach, not only can you easily have an "all testimonials" page, but you simply link the Sun Worship Holidays testimonials category to the Sun Worship Holidays page. Keep it simple; keep it flexible; that's the motto in this planning process. So let's go with a category structure based on content type and not on the destination or supplier.

HOW THE SITE SHOULD LOOK

Part of the planning process for any site is to determine the layout of the pages and the way they'll look. As you saw in Lesson 1, WordPress assembles and delivers HTML pages through a group of template files called a theme, so all you need to do is choose a theme that will give you the look you want, or at least something very close to it. You can, of course, get a customized theme created for you, but there's very likely an existing free theme that will give you something close to what you want.

The best place to look for a theme is the WordPress.org theme directory at `http://wordpress.org/extend/themes/` or you can search it directly from the administration screen, which I cover in Lesson 27. Not only are the themes in this directory free, but more importantly, they've been checked to make sure they function properly. Right now, however, you're simply planning what you want in a theme.

A word of warning as you browse through the themes: don't get caught up in what I call the *magpie effect* and be dazzled by all the bright, shining objects. That directory contains a lot of very nice looking designs, but you need to follow some guidelines. As I say, it's highly unlikely that any theme in the WordPress directory is going to be exactly right for your travel site or any particular site — at the very least, you're going to want to add your own logo — but the better idea you have of the layout and the look, the less you're going to have to do to make that theme work for you and the less likely you are to be a magpie.

Site Layout

When it comes to the overall site layout, conventional and safe is not only good, it's essential. People have come to expect certain things in certain places — why mess with their minds? Besides, you want them to focus on your content, not on the fact that your main menu sits sideways on the right-hand side of the screen and does a cool slide-out when you mouse over it. You want people to find things easily, and the best way to do that is to follow conventions. Let your individuality come out in the header and the content, but for the basic layout, follow the path well-worn for a small business site, as Figure 2-2 illustrates.

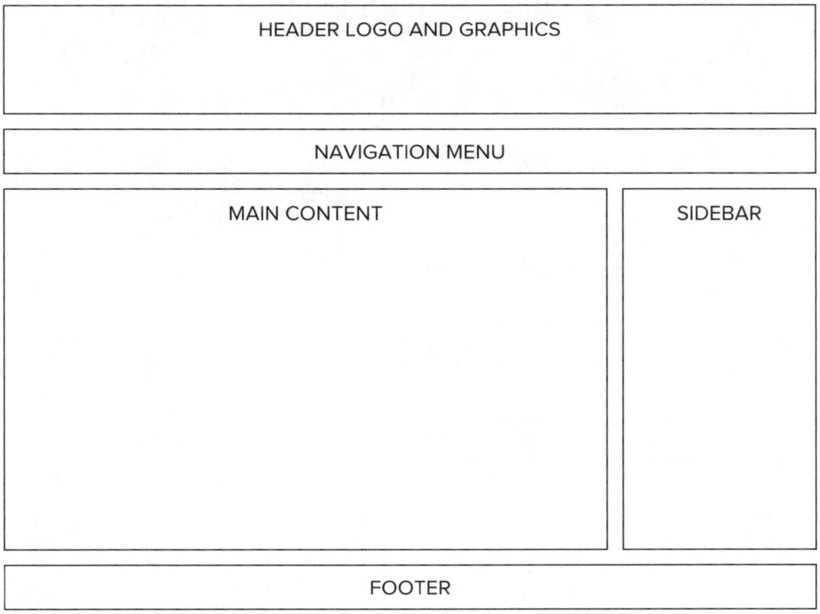

FIGURE 2-2

You start with a header area across the top, including the menu of all your pages. On the left-hand side, you have any secondary navigation plus additional information such as random testimonials, important specials, and so on. Your content will fill the rest of the page and then at the bottom, you have your footer, including a reduced menu with just key pages listed. Simple, easy to follow, and no surprises. Now you know what you're looking for in a theme's layout.

Site Design

This is a far more individual issue than site layout, but you still need to think of your visitors, and from that standpoint, simplicity of design is always better. It's just easier to find your way around a simple design because it's less cluttered and visitors are more likely to focus on the content. Of course, if the point of your site is to show off design skills, that's another matter. For the Island Travel site, you're concerned about creating the right mood (fun, relaxation, sunshine, and so on) but at the same time making it clutter-free and easy to see content on the page.

To capture the right mood, I think something light — no thick lines, fancy graphics, or strong areas of color — with light browns and sky blues could be one way to go. If you have a graphics program, even a basic one, it's worth creating a simple mockup of your site design, like the one in Figure 2-3 for Island Travel, or simply sketch out a design on paper, making notes about colors.

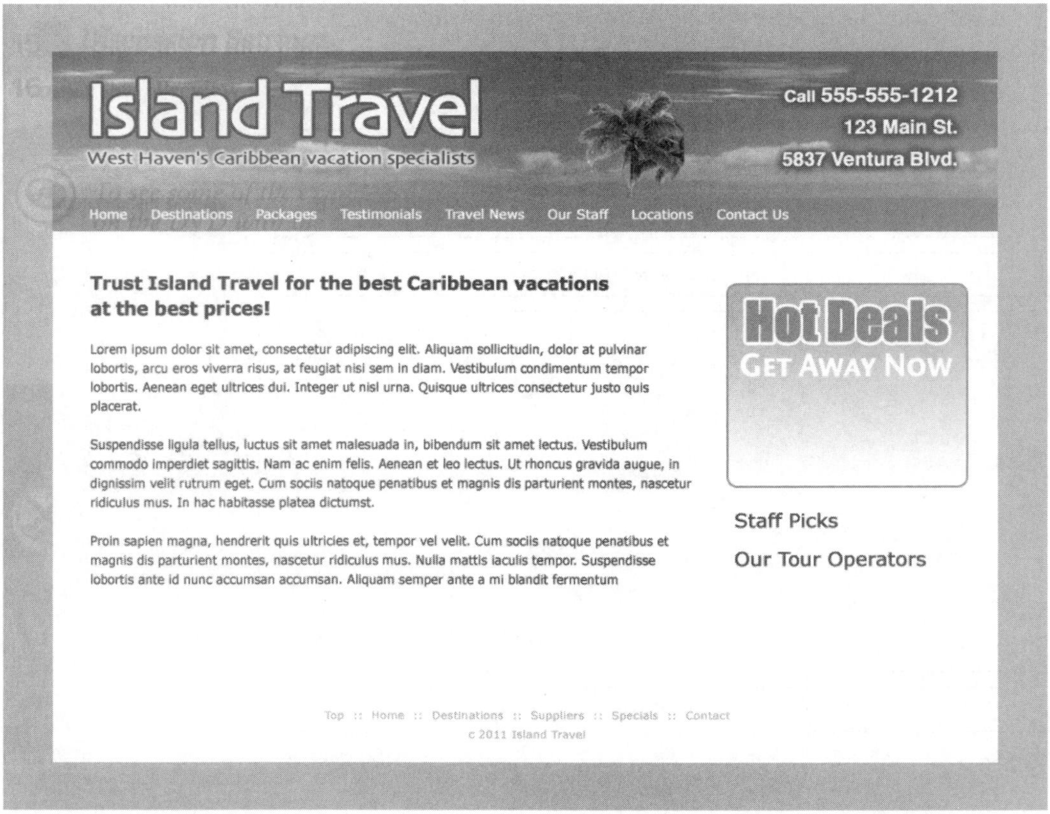

FIGURE 2-3

This mockup will be useful for whoever is going to do the customizing of your WordPress theme — the topic of Lesson 28 and Lesson 39. I'm leaving the look of the site until later in the book because getting content entered and organized is the most important task and as that process unfolds, new ideas for the design may come to mind. But at least for the moment, you have a good idea of where you want that design to go.

If you need design inspiration, the official WordPress theme directory I mentioned earlier is a great place to start. If you find something very close to what you want, all the better because it will be simpler to modify and get exactly the look you want. For the purposes of this book, you're going to work with the Twenty Ten theme that's automatically installed with WordPress. And speaking of installing, that's the subject of the next lesson.

TRY IT

This lesson does not have a step-by-step instruction you can follow, but it would be good for you to create the kinds of planning documents discussed in the lesson for your own site:

- Site map
- List of types of content and whether they will be pages or posts
- Category structure you think you'll want for posts
- Site mockup

> *There is no video to accompany this lesson.*

SECTION II
Firing Up WordPress

3

Installing WordPress

The WordPress website talks about its famous five-minute install. It's no idle boast — everything in this lesson can be done in five minutes, but it took me quite a few WordPress installations to get it down to that time. If it's your first install, and you're handy with an FTP program and familiar with database installs using a hosting panel like Parallels/Plesk or cPanel, I would count on about 10 to 15 minutes. If you're relying completely on this lesson to lead you through the steps, it could be 30 minutes or more.

What the five-minute install really refers to is the fact that once you have files in place and a database created, clicking the Install button will have you up and running in less than five minutes. This lesson is mostly about what comes *before* clicking the Install button.

Because this book covers the self-hosted version of WordPress, I'm assuming that you have a hosting account on a web server. This is different from having a domain name. Domain names point to servers where the files for a website are stored and having a place to put your website files is what I mean by a hosting account.

> *Some hosts offer auto-installation of WordPress, so check for that. They don't always use the latest version, so once you install, you may see a message to update (but that doesn't take long).*

There are a few software requirements for hosting WordPress, but most hosting packages these days — even the most basic — should meet them. Still, it's best to double-check the host you're planning to use or your existing account for the following (important changes are coming to WordPress requirements in mid-2011 so I've included those here):

VERSIONS 3.1 OR EARLIER	VERSIONS 3.2 OR LATER
MySQL database Version 4.0 or greater	MySQL database Version 5.0.15 or greater
PHP Version 4.3 or greater	PHP Version 5.2 or greater
(Quality hosts have been offering PHP 5+ for quite some time so look elsewhere if the host is using 4.3.)	

Almost all servers meet these new requirements already or can easily upgrade your account to meet them. WordPress has said that the updater function in Version 3.2 will automatically check to see if your hosting account meets these standards.

If you're not sure how to word your question to your hosting company, the WordPress site provides you with the text for an e-mail you can send: `http://wordpress.org/about/requirements/`. *You'll notice that the letter adds a third item to the list: the mod_rewrite Apache module. This module is needed for the custom permalinks feature in WordPress and, though there is a way to use custom permalinks without it, it just makes life a bit easier. Most Linux servers have the module installed.*

Once you've confirmed that these requirements are met, you're ready to begin the installation process.

UPLOADING THE WORDPRESS FILES

The first thing you're going to need is a copy of the latest version of WordPress, and you can easily get that from the official WordPress website at `http://wordpress.org`, where you'll see a big orange button at the top right called Download. That takes you to a page where the latest release is always available. Click the large button that says Download WordPress 3.1 (or whatever the current version is).

If you have your browser set to ask you where to save downloaded files, find your My Downloads (Windows) or Downloads (Mac) folder and create a new folder called WordPress, then save the `.zip` file there.

If your browser just starts downloading the file, you may need to do some hunting around to locate it (hopefully, it's just on your Desktop). Create a folder called WordPress in your My Downloads or Downloads folder and move the `.zip` file there.

All the WordPress files are zipped up or packed into a single file, so you'll need to "unpack" it. If you right-click the `.zip` file, you should see an option in the popup window to open the file. If you don't, it means your computer does not have a program capable of unzipping the file; for Windows, try 7-Zip at `http://www.7-zip.org`; for Mac, try Stuffit Expander at `http://my.smithmicro.com/mac/stuffit/expander.html`.

The unpacking process will leave you with a new folder containing all of the WordPress files, which now need to be uploaded to your server. For that, you'll need an FTP program and the following information:

- Hostname
- User/login name
- Password

You would have received a username and password from your hosting company or the person who set up the account for you. The hostname is usually just `ftp.yourdomain.com`, but you'll need to check that's the case. If you don't have an FTP program, lots of choices are available for Windows and Mac. An excellent free FTP program for both platforms is FileZilla at `http://filezilla-project.org` or you can go to `www.downloads.com` and search for FTP.

In your FTP program, you create a new connection and enter the hostname, user/login, and password. When you click the Connect button, the program logs in to your server. Virtually every FTP program operates by showing you a screen like Figure 3-1, which is split between your computer on the left and the server on the right.

You can see the WordPress files you downloaded over on the left. Virtually all have `wp-` at the beginning, which is very useful because it makes it extremely unlikely that they'll have the same name as existing files on your server, so there's little chance of overwriting something you shouldn't. The important exception to this is `index.php`, so check to see if the directory already has a file of that name.

The decision you need to make now is exactly where you want to put WordPress on your server. If WordPress is going to run your entire website, the decision is simple — it goes in the root folder of whatever is the web directory on your server. This directory will have different names depending on your server — like `public_html` or `httpdocs` or `www` — and you'll need to check that out with your hosting company. In Figure 3-1, the web directory is public_html, so you would open that and put your WordPress files in there.

If you have an existing website and you're going to be using WordPress as an add-on, put WordPress in its own directory. If you're replacing the existing site with WordPress, it's still useful to create a separate directory where you can work on the new site "behind the scenes." When you're ready to launch the new site, there's no need to move WordPress as long as you follow the instructions on the WordPress site: `http://codex.wordpress.org/Giving_WordPress_Its_Own_Directory`. Once you've decided where to put WordPress and you're in that directory on the right side of the FTP screen, you simply highlight all the files on the left side and click the button that goes the direction you want. Typically, FTP programs use arrow buttons, and as you can see in Figure 3-1, it's an up-arrow button (top left of the screen), indicating that you're uploading to the server. Other programs use left and right arrows to indicate you're transferring from one side to the other.

In a short time, you'll see all of the files on the left copied over to the right. You're one third of the way to completing your installation. Now you just need to set up a database and configure one file before you're ready for the Install button.

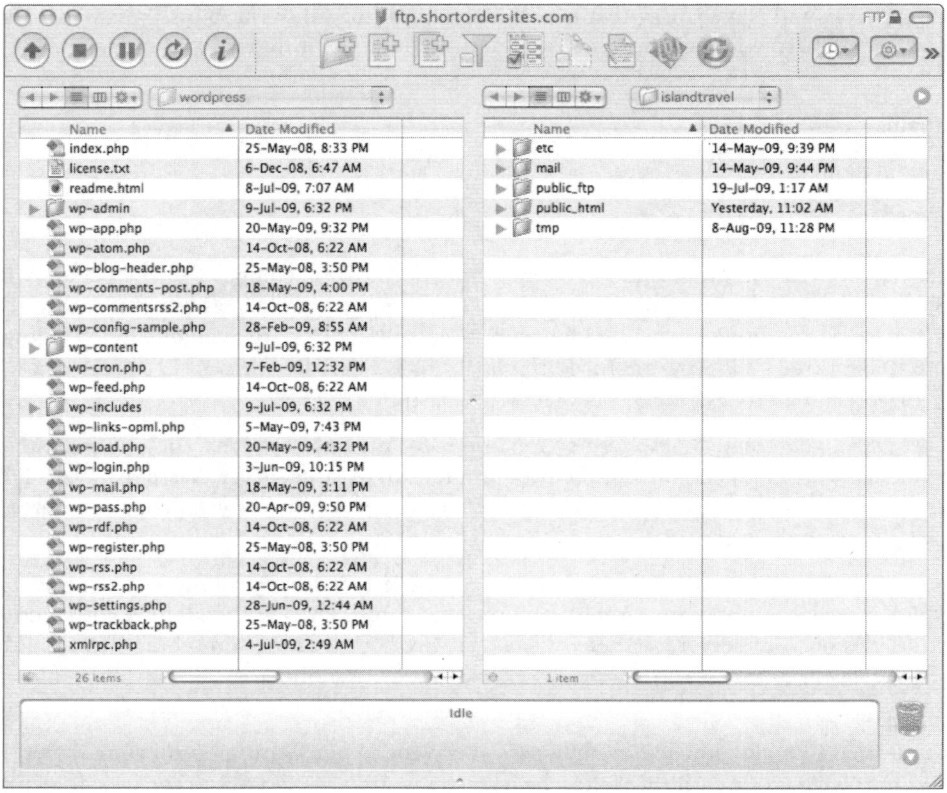

FIGURE 3-1

SETTING UP YOUR DATABASE

One of the requirements I mentioned for WordPress was that your hosting package include a MySQL database. That's where WordPress is going to store not only what you write, but all the details about your categories, preferences, passwords, and so on. However, having a database included with your hosting still means you need to set it up, and for that, many hosting companies offer an interface, usually as part of a hosting control panel such as Parallels/Plesk or cPanel. Other hosts may require you to submit a request for creation of a database and they'll do it for you.

I can't cover all the possible ways of setting up the database, but you need to do three things:

1. Create/name the database.
2. Create a user — a username and password.
3. Assign that user to the database.

When assigning the user to the database, make sure she has "all privileges," which means she can read and write to the database, alter its structure, and so on. If someone else is setting up the database for you, make sure to let them know this.

Make sure the user's password is a strong one — no names of pets or numbers based on birthdays. If your system doesn't have a password strength indicator, use at least nine characters with a mix of upper- and lowercase letters and numbers in it.

For the installation of WordPress, you'll need the following information (keep track of it as you set up the database or make sure you get it from whoever does the install):

1. Full name of the database
2. Username
3. User password
4. Host or server name for the database (usually it's "localhost")

Most of you will be hosted on what's called a shared environment, which simply means a whole lot of websites on a single server. Typically in a shared environment, the name you enter for the database is combined in some way with your username to make sure the database's name is unique.

So, if you call your database "mydb," the actual name could be "mydb-myhostloginname." At the end of the database creation process, hosting panels like Parallels/Plesk and cPanel will display these complete names, so be sure to write them down and not just the name you entered when you created the database.

DOING THE INSTALLATION

With all the WordPress files uploaded to your site, your database set up, and your database details by your side, it's time to do the installation.

If you're planning to use the multisite feature of WordPress — the ability to run multiple sites from a single installation — you can find specific installation instructions in Lesson 38. There's also information about how to take an existing WordPress site (Version 3.0 or greater) and convert it to multisite functionality.

In your browser window, enter the address `www.yourdomain.com/wp-admin/install.php` (if you uploaded the files to a subdirectory, you'll need to include that as well) and hit Enter.

The resulting screen tells you that WordPress can't find the configuration file, but that's OK because there isn't one included in the files you downloaded from WordPress.org — it has to be created. You have two options at this point:

1. Continue and let WordPress try to create the file for you.
2. Manually edit the sample configuration file included with the WordPress files you downloaded.

Option 1 is the simplest way to go, so I'll be demonstrating the automated creation of the configuration file. Sometimes, a server won't allow WordPress to create the file and you'll need to use Option 2. I cover the manual creation of the configuration in this lesson's video.

After clicking Create a Configuration File, you'll see a screen like the one in Figure 3-2 outlining the information that you'll need to proceed (the four items I told you to write down when you created your database).

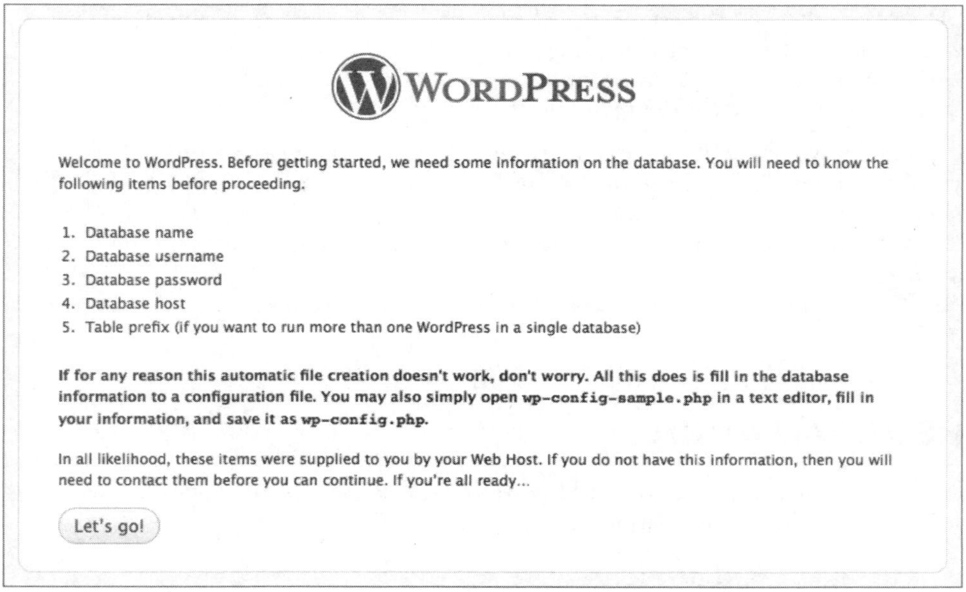

WordPress
Welcome to WordPress. Before getting started, we need some information on the database. You will need to know the following items before proceeding.
1. Database name
2. Database username
3. Database password
4. Database host
5. Table prefix (if you want to run more than one WordPress in a single database)
If for any reason this automatic file creation doesn't work, don't worry. All this does is fill in the database information to a configuration file. You may also simply open wp-config-sample.php in a text editor, fill in your information, and save it as wp-config.php.
In all likelihood, these items were supplied to you by your Web Host. If you do not have this information, then you will need to contact them before you can continue. If you're all ready…
Let's go!

FIGURE 3-2

The screen in Figure 3-2 also explains about manually creating the configuration file if the automated process doesn't work. When you click Let's Go, you're taken to the screen shown in Figure 3-3.

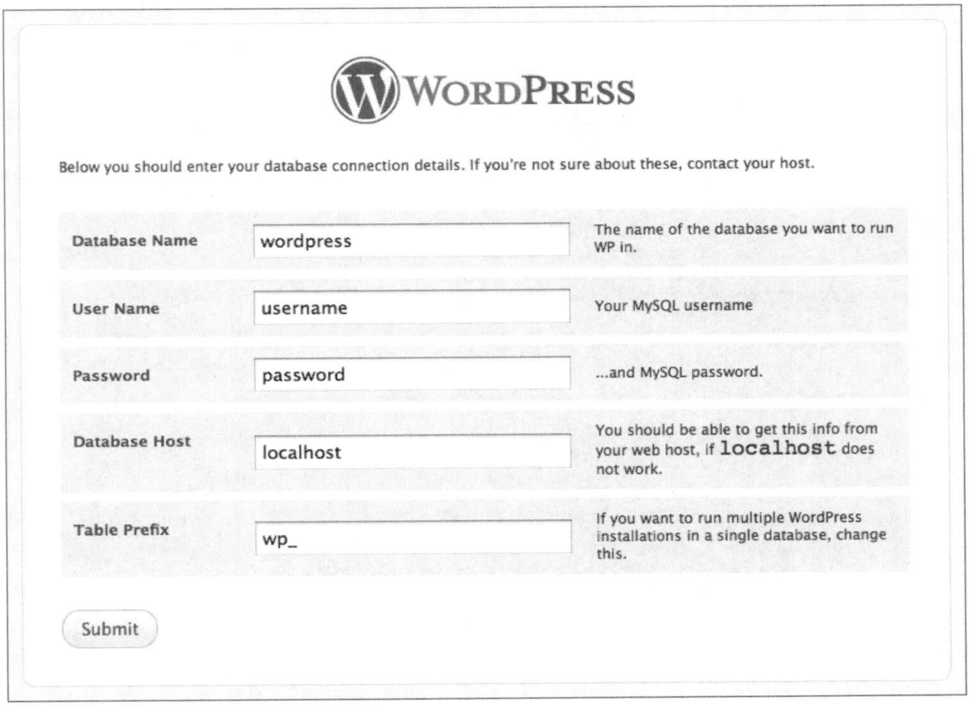

FIGURE 3-3

This is where you'll enter the information about your database. As the screen says, it's extremely rare that you'll need to change the value for Database Host. The default Table Prefix is wp- but you can increase the security of your database data by changing this to something else, such as your initials or an acronym of your site: it- (for Island Travel). Once you have all the information copied into the correct box, you can click Submit. The next screen tells you that WordPress and your database are on speaking terms and that it's time to install, so click Run the Install.

This is where the famous five-minute install really begins, and the first thing WordPress wants is a bit more information, as shown in Figure 3-4.

You can change this information later if you need to, but go ahead and enter the title of the website and your e-mail address (that's where a copy of your password will be sent). For the username, the default is admin, but it's useful for security purposes to choose your own. I typically use a word relating to the website, but not in the domain name or title, plus a few numbers. Make sure to choose a secure password (at least nine characters long, with a mix of upper- and lowercase, numbers, and symbols).

I recommend leaving the checkbox at the bottom ("Allow my site to appear...") unchecked for the moment — you don't want search engines looking at your site until it's ready. Don't worry about forgetting and leaving the search engines blocked later — WordPress has a very obvious warning at the top of admin screens to let you know if they're still being blocked. Now you're ready to click the Install WordPress button. In the blink of an eye, the install is done and you're given the option of going to the WordPress login screen, which is exactly what you'll need to do for the next lesson.

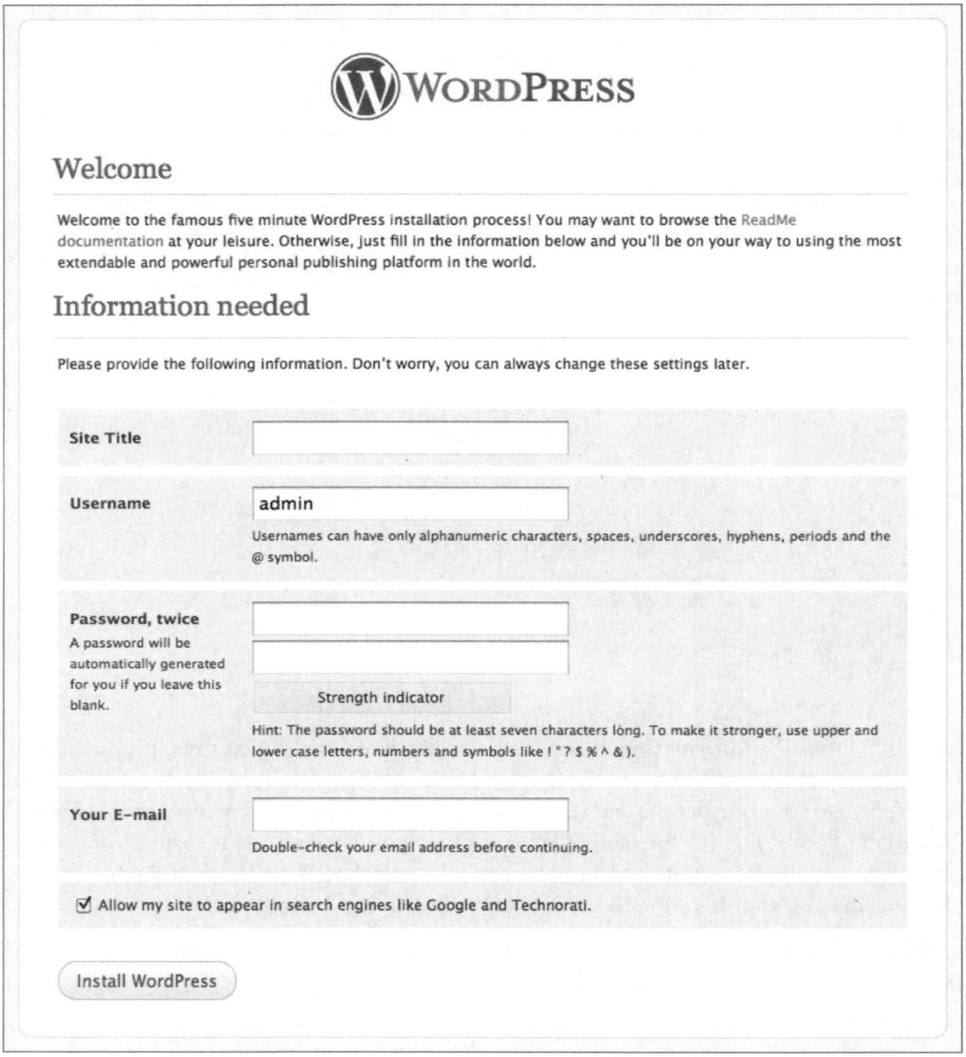

FIGURE 3-4

TRY IT

There's nothing additional to try in this lesson — hopefully, you completed the installation using these instructions. If you don't plan on doing the installation right now, you could always set up an FTP program if you don't have one or download WordPress for use later.

> *You can see more details, such as creating a configuration file by hand, under Lesson 3 on the DVD with the print book, or watch online at* `www.wrox.com/go/wp24vids`.

4

Admin Area Overview

One of WordPress's greatest strengths is the user-friendliness of its administration interface. From both an organizational and a design standpoint, it's laid out in a way that's pretty intuitive. As with any system, of course, you need to take some time and learn how it works, where things are, and so on, and that's what this lesson is about: helping you familiarize yourself with the WordPress administration area.

LOGGING IN

At the end of the installation process, you're given the opportunity to log in to WordPress with the administrator username and password that you set, using the default login page shown in Figure 4-1.

FIGURE 4-1

> *If you don't log in right after installation, you can get to the login page later by going to your site and looking for the login link. Most WordPress themes include a login link, usually on the sidebar or in the footer, but if not, you can still get to the login screen using the address* `www.yourdomain.com/wp-admin`*. If you installed WordPress in a subdirectory, you would need to add that before* `/wp-admin`*, of course.*

The login page also contains a link for recovering your password should you forget what it is, but that only works if the e-mail address in your profile is up to date (I show you how to do that in Lesson 5).

> *When you log in to WordPress, a cookie is created in your browser so that the program knows you're logged in. If you close your browser or tab without logging out, and then come back in a few hours, you'll find that you're still logged in. Always log out when you leave WordPress, especially if there's any chance other people might access the machine.*
>
> *Often, people will return to their WordPress site later and notice Edit links everywhere. They panic and think that the world can access the admin area. What's happened is that they never logged out and the cookie is still active.*

NAVIGATING THE ADMIN AREA

When you first log in to WordPress, the most important place to start is the left-side navigation menu. It shows you all the pages you can access in the admin area, so it's crucial to know how it operates.

By default, the submenus for each area are not visible, but the headings for each area are, as shown in Figure 4-2.

FIGURE 4-2

I've circled a small down arrow at the right side of the Dashboard section in Figure 4-2. This is visible when you mouse over a closed menu or when the submenu is showing. When you click that down arrow, the submenu appears or disappears. If you click a section whose submenu is closed, you're taken to that section and the submenu is automatically opened.

Once you've become familiar with the menu, you may find that you don't need to see the names of each section. In that case, you can reduce the footprint of the side menu by clicking one of several lines that appear throughout the menu, as highlighted in Figure 4-3A. You can see the collapsed menu in Figure 4-3B.

You can open any submenu at any time. Your browser will remember that and keep it open until you decide to close it again. I keep frequently used submenus open all the time, such as Posts and Pages.

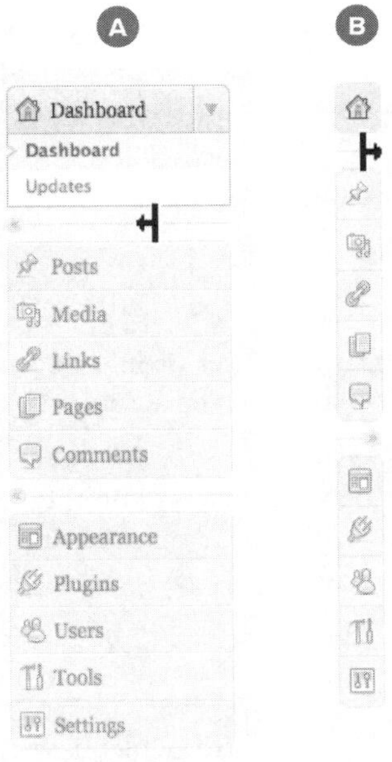

FIGURE 4-3

In addition to this side menu, there is a small drop-down menu at the top right of the screen, known as the Favorites menu — though you can't control what's on it. As shown in Figure 4-4, it contains links to some key pages in the administration area: New Post, Drafts, New Page, Upload, and Comments. The menu is contextual, so you'll notice it changing based on which admin page you're viewing.

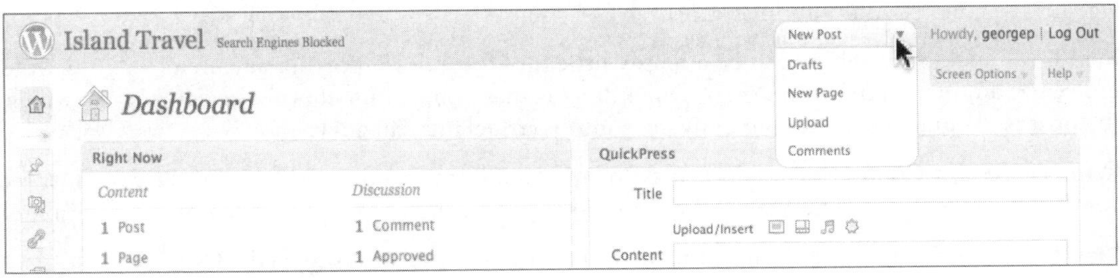

FIGURE 4-4

A new feature in Version 3.1 is the Admin Bar. Often, your admin screens can be quite long and accessing the side menu or the Favorites menu takes a lot of scrolling. The Admin Bar, on the other hand, remains in place while you scroll, as shown in Figure 4-5.

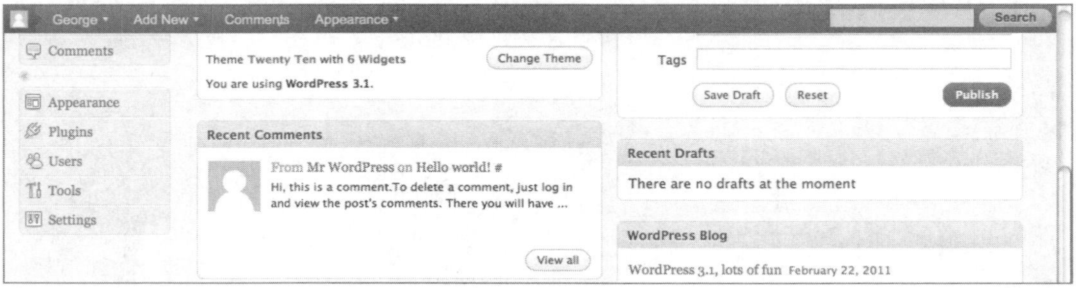

FIGURE 4-5

By default, the Admin Bar is not visible but you can turn it on and off in your user profile screen (User ➪ Your Profile). You can also decide whether to have the bar displayed on the actual website, though only, of course, if you're logged in.

As of this writing, WordPress does not provide any interface for altering what displays on the Admin Bar, but it can be done with custom coding. No doubt, plugins will appear that provide a user-friendly interface for such modifications.

THE DASHBOARD

Whenever you log in to WordPress, the first screen you get is called the Dashboard, which is the homepage for the administration area. The top half of the Island Travel Dashboard is shown in Figure 4-6.

There's a lot going on in the Dashboard, so I'll only cover the main functions here.

Item A is the Right Now box, where you'll find a quick overview of your WordPress installation: how many posts, pages, drafts, and comments you have, with links directly to each of those areas of the admin section. You'll also see what version of WordPress you're running, and if you don't have the latest version, an Update button automatically appears (or if you're not an administrator, a warning to contact your administrator).

Item B is QuickPress, which can be a handy little tool for quickly posting new items to your website. However, an important limitation of QuickPress is that you cannot choose the category to which the post is assigned — it automatically goes into your default category.

Item C is Recent Comments and it displays a couple of lines and the author from the five most recent comments on your site. The View All button takes you to the Comments screen of the admin area.

Item D is Recent Drafts and it lists the most recent items you've saved as drafts.

Item E is Incoming Links. It shows you what blogs are linking to your site. The default feed comes from Google Blog Search, but you can customize this and I show you how in Lesson 32.

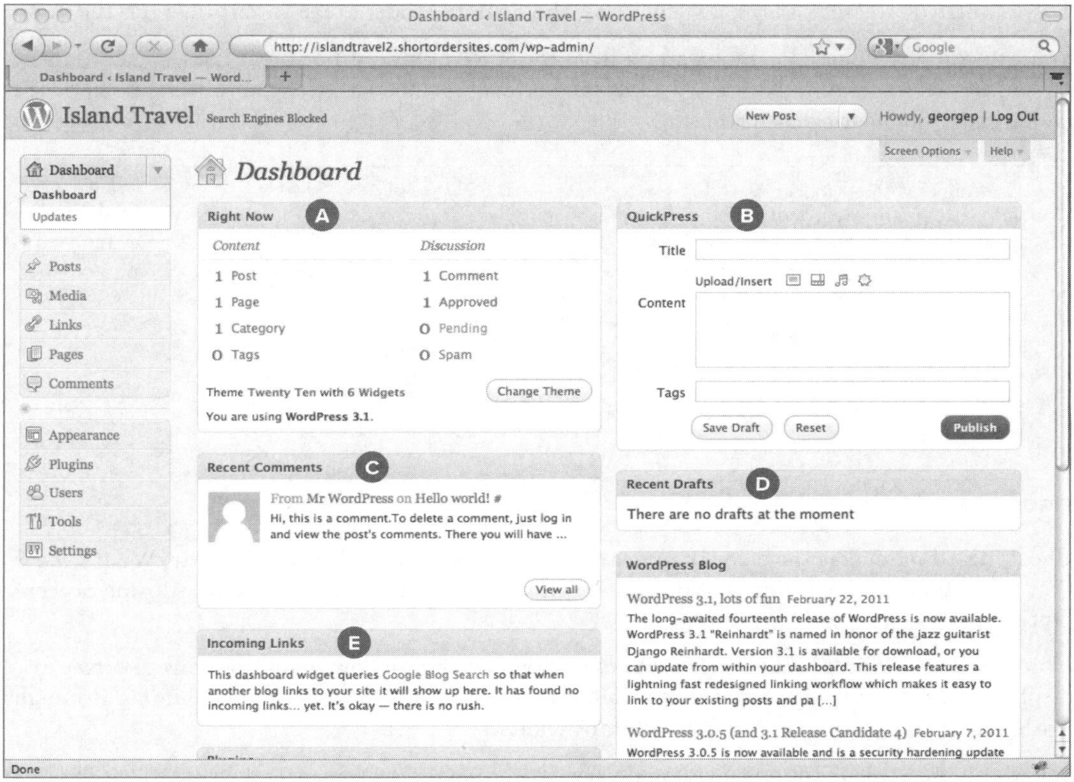

FIGURE 4-6

The rest of the Dashboard contains the latest news about WordPress, the latest plugins available, and your recent drafts.

I must admit, I don't make a lot of use of the Dashboard in day-to-day maintenance of sites, except in the case of blogs, where knowing at a glance where comments stand can be very useful. Still, it's good to be able to have your finger on the pulse of your website and the WordPress community whenever you log in.

CUSTOMIZING ADMIN SCREENS

You can customize the boxes on WordPress admin screens in four ways:

- Minimize a box
- Show or hide a box on the page
- Move boxes around the screen
- Change the number of columns containing boxes

To minimize or collapse a box, just click anywhere on its header area. To restore it, do the same.

You can completely hide (or show) a box from the Screen Options button at the very top right of the screen, shown in detail in Figure 4-7. Dropping down this menu allows you to pick and choose from the boxes available for that screen.

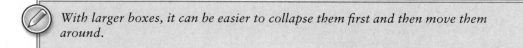

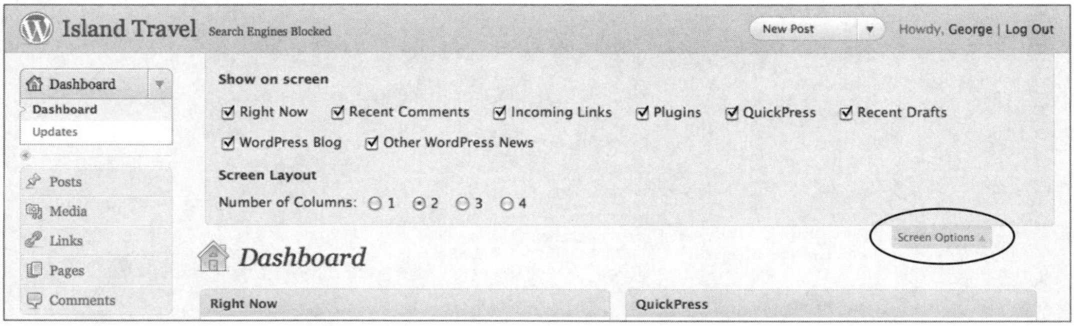

FIGURE 4-7

Checking a box makes the element appear and unchecking it makes it disappear. What's nice is that this happens in real time so you can see what the change looks like before closing Screen Options.

In addition to deciding what boxes are shown, you can choose how many columns of boxes to display. The default is two, and for most admin screens, that's the maximum columns, although the Dashboard is able to expand to four columns wide.

What's on the Screen Options menu will vary depending on the screen, so be sure to check out what's available on any particular one. The options may make your life a bit easier.

The third way to customize the display of boxes is to physically move them around the page. For example, if I don't use the QuickPress feature so much, but I do read the development blog info, I can switch places by moving them around.

All you do is place your mouse over the dark gray header bar of the box and you'll see it change to the hand cursor. At that point, you can click and drag. As the box moves, it disappears from its original location, and a blank box inserts itself between existing boxes wherever you point the mouse, as shown in Figure 4-8.

When you see that blank box in the spot you want, you just release the mouse button and the screen has been rearranged.

> *With larger boxes, it can be easier to collapse them first and then move them around.*

The fourth way to customize the admin screen is to change the number of columns available to display boxes. On most screens, the only choice is between one or two columns, but some offer up to four columns. You'll find this under Screen Options.

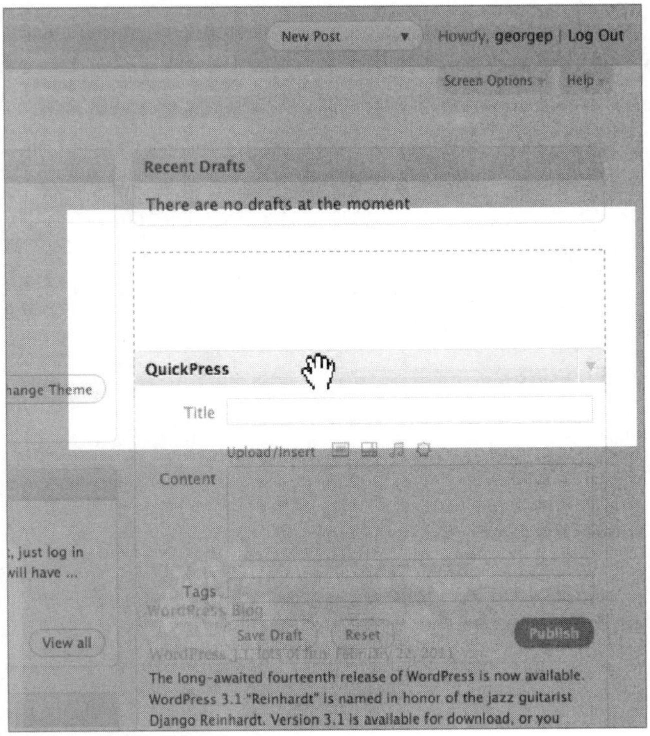

FIGURE 4-8

TRY IT

In this lesson, you try reorganizing your Dashboard and collapsing your side menu.

Lesson Requirements

WordPress installed.

Step-by-Step

To reorganize the Dashboard, follow these steps:

1. Click and drag the header of the QuickPress box downward.
2. When you get below Other WordPress News, stop and let go.
3. Go back up and double-click the header of the WordPress Development Blog box (which should be at the top of your right-hand column). The WordPress Development Blog should now be collapsed.
4. Do the same for Other WordPress News. You should now be able to see QuickPress without having to scroll.

5. Go to Screen Options and click it.
6. Uncheck Recent Comments and you should see it disappear.
7. Close Screen Options by clicking the button again.
8. Return the Dashboard to the way you want it.

To collapse the side menu, follow these steps:

1. Move your cursor over the light gray line below Dashboard on the side menu.
2. Click when the cursor changes to a double-ended arrow (Internet Explorer — Windows) or a left arrow and upright line (Firefox — Windows and Mac).
3. You should now see only icons and no titles.
4. Mouse over an icon to view the submenu.
5. Restore the full menu if you prefer, using the same method.

> *To see some of the examples from this lesson, watch the video for Lesson 4 on the DVD with the print book, or watch online at* `www.wrox.com/go/wp24vids`.

5

Basic Admin Settings

WordPress has dozens of administrative settings at your disposal, but you'll probably use most of the default settings for as long as you run your site. So, the good news is you don't need to mess with more than a few settings as you begin to build your site.

This lesson familiarizes you with the Settings menu and shows you how to change those truly important few settings. I deal with other admin settings as they're needed in later lessons.

SETTINGS TO GET YOU STARTED

The Settings heading on the admin menu is where you control various site-wide parameters for WordPress, and its submenus are divided by functions, as shown in Figure 5-1.

FIGURE 5-1

> *This is the menu when you first install WordPress. If you add plugins (those extra pieces of software that enable WordPress to do even more), this Settings menu may show more choices depending on the plugins.*

The first of the crucial settings to be changed are under Settings ➪ General, where you'll get the screen shown in Figure 5-2.

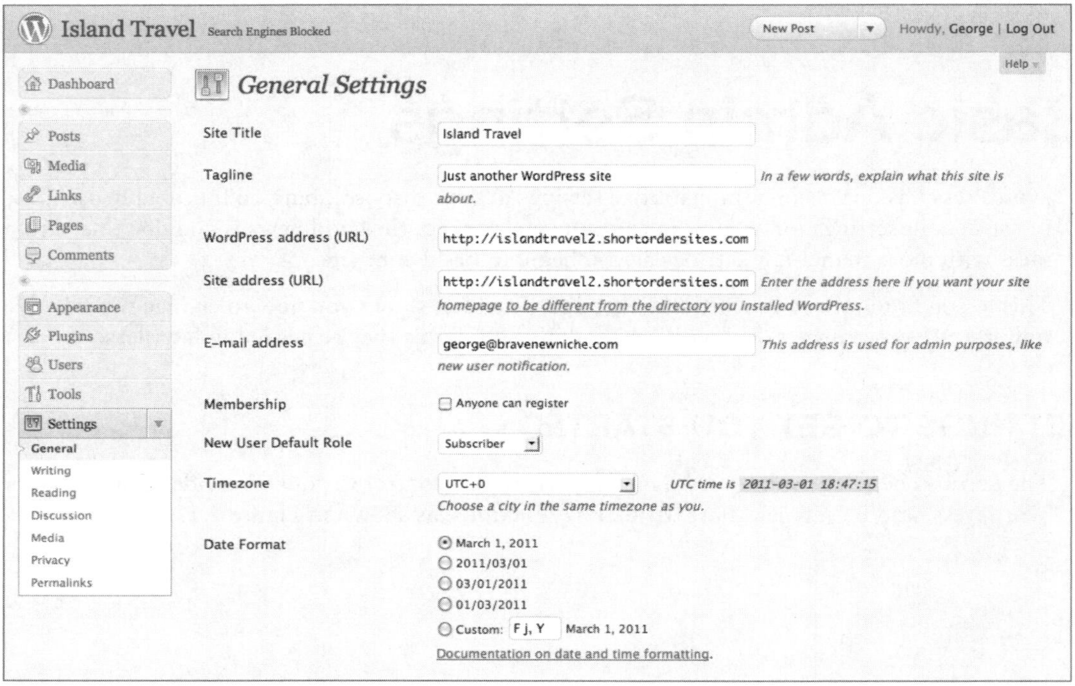

FIGURE 5-2

Tagline

The Tagline is meant to be a more descriptive phrase about your site and is often displayed by themes somewhere near the Site Title (in the Twenty Ten theme, it's opposite the title on the right-hand side).

The default Tagline in a new installation is "Just another WordPress site" and, obviously, you'll want to change that. Figure 5-3 shows the new Island Travel tagline as it appears on the site after saving the changes.

FIGURE 5-3

> *You'll sometimes see the default Tagline still showing on people's sites — they neglected to check their General Settings!*

WordPress Address (URL)

This is the web address of the directory where you actually installed WordPress. It tells WordPress where to look for its files. Usually, this is already filled in, but you should check to make sure it's right. If you installed WordPress in the root directory on your server, the URL is simply `www.yourdomain.com`. If you put WordPress in a separate folder, it would be `www.yourdomain/foldername`.

Site Address (URL)

This is your website address so it would be `www.yourdomain.com`, and again, it's usually already filled in, so you're just making sure it's right.

Don't be concerned if this is the same as the WordPress address; they're used for different purposes, and often are one and the same. The real value of having the two addresses becomes clear when WordPress is installed in a folder or subdirectory.

E-mail Address

Double-check that this is the address you entered when you installed WordPress. You can change it, of course, but whatever e-mail you use, remember, this is the one where notifications are sent having to do with administrative tasks, such as new users being created.

> *Keep in mind that some plugins will use this e-mail address as a default as well. For example, plugins that create forms may use this as the mailing address where the form is sent.*

Timezone

You'll want to change the time zone to match your region, so that dates and times are accurate when you're publishing or scheduling content on your site. WordPress makes this easy by providing a drop-down menu of major cities around the world (if your server is still using PHP4, you won't see a cities list, just the numerical offsets for the various time zones). Just find a city in your time zone, click Save Changes, and the correct date and time should show up in the Timezone setting area.

> *The Save Changes button is at the very bottom of the page and it's easy to forget to scroll down and click it each time you make a change.*

That does it for the General Settings screen.

A couple of other administrative settings are worth checking at this point. The first is under Settings ➪ Discussion. This controls the settings for the comments system of WordPress.

At the top of the screen shown in Figure 5-4, you'll see a setting to "Allow people to post comments on new articles."

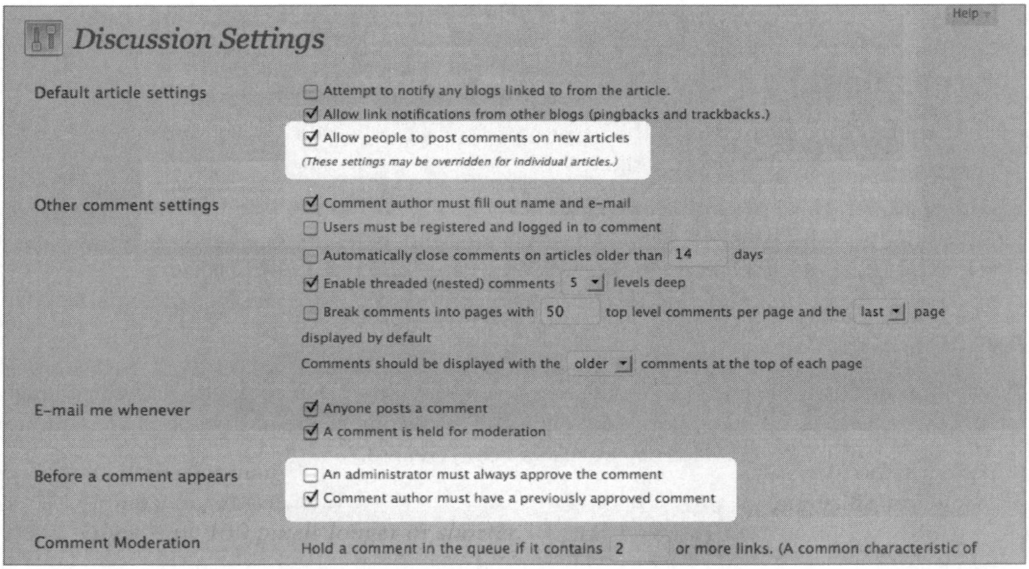

FIGURE 5-4

By default, this box is checked because, typically, people want visitors to be able to comment on their blog posts. However, when you're creating a website, of which blogging may only be a part, you likely won't want people commenting on pages or even some posts. In that case, I would uncheck this box (remember to save at the bottom of the page).

Whichever setting you choose, comments can be turned on or off in each individual post or page, so you're never stuck. What you want to ask yourself is which scenario is going to be most common on your site, and choose this setting accordingly; that will save you some time when you start creating posts and pages.

One other setting to check under Discussion Settings is "Before a comment appears." By default, the "Comment author must have a previously approved comment" should be checked off. If it's not, make sure it is. This is an important line of defense against spam comments.

The other setting — "An administrator must always approve the comment" — is unchecked by default and is OK to keep that way unless you're particularly worried about spammers and don't mind that regular commenters may not like having to wait for approval or that it means some extra work for you if you have a lot of regulars.

The final setting worth a triple check is your Settings ➪ Privacy screen. I say triple check because you were asked during installation whether you wanted your site blocked from search engines. Plus, WordPress tells you at the top of your admin screens — beside your site title — whether search engines are being blocked.

Still, before you begin entering content, it's worth asking yourself again if you're ready or will shortly be ready for search engines to index your site. I say keep the robots at bay and then change the setting when you're definitely ready for indexing.

And that's it for administrative settings at this point. We'll come back to adjust other settings as needed, but except for completing your personal profile, there's nothing stopping you from publishing content to your site.

SETTING YOUR PERSONAL PROFILE

This is where you enter your personal preferences and provide information about yourself that's used in various ways throughout WordPress. For example, if your posts display the author's name, this is where you set that name. Access to the Your Profile screen, shown in Figure 5-5, can be found under the User menu at the side or on the Admin Bar if you have that activated (which you can do from your profile).

> *If you create more users to access WordPress, you'll be entering their information in exactly the same screen as this.*

Working through this screen in order, the first setting allows you to disable the Visual Editor when writing content. Visual Editor refers to WordPress's Text Editor in Visual mode as opposed to HTML mode (I cover the Text Editor in Lesson 7). In Visual mode, you work with your text in "what you see is what you get" format rather than having to deal with HTML coding. That's why many users will want to leave this box unchecked.

However, if you prefer working in HTML, and in particular if you're writing code that the Visual Editor may change, you'll want to disable Visual mode to prevent any accidents.

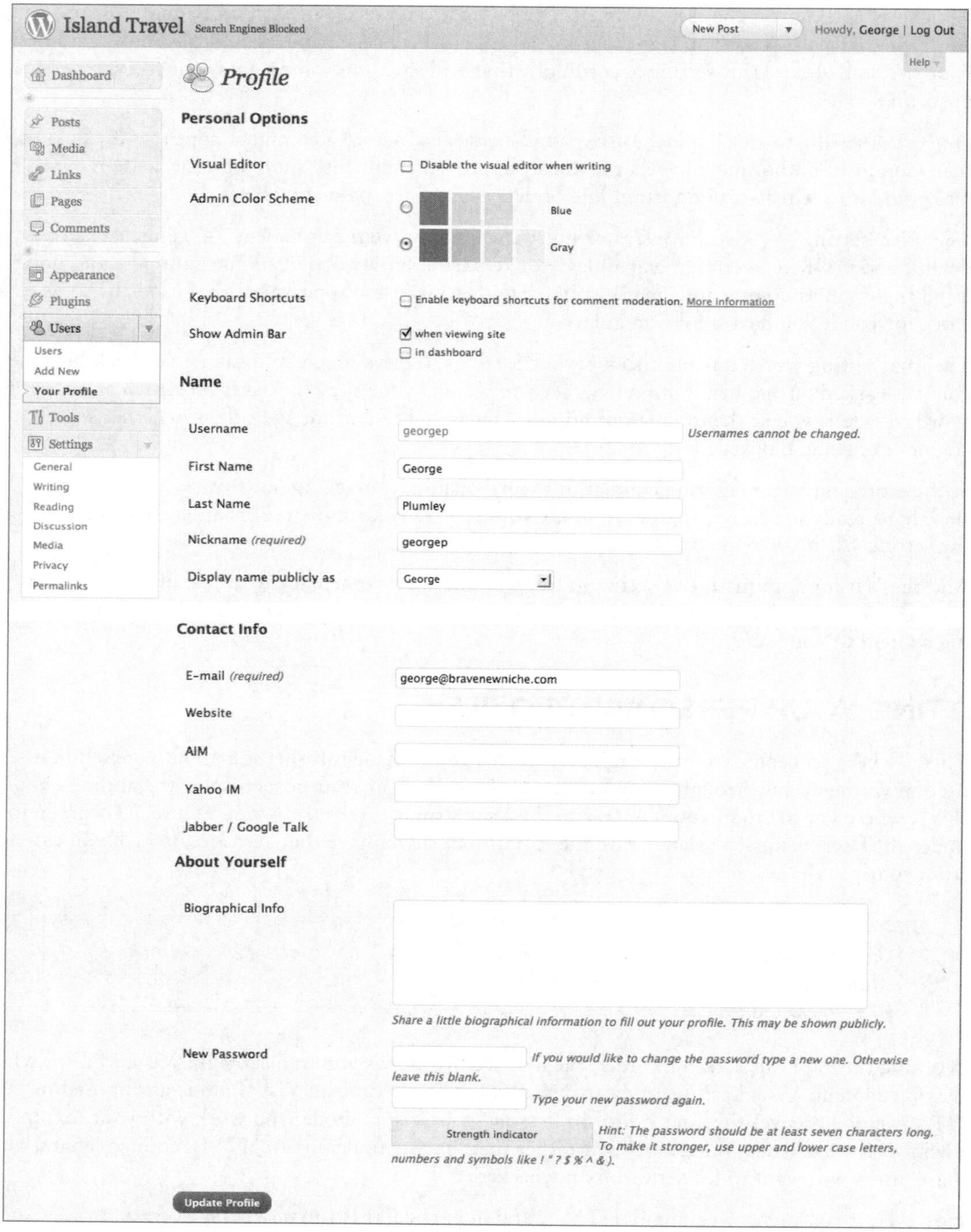
Island Travel
Search Engines Blocked
New Post
Howdy, George | Log Out
Help
Dashboard
Posts
Media
Links
Pages
Comments
Appearance
Plugins
Users
Users
Add New
Your Profile
Tools
Settings
General
Writing
Reading
Discussion
Media
Privacy
Permalinks
Profile
Personal Options
Visual Editor
Disable the visual editor when writing
Admin Color Scheme
Blue
Gray
Keyboard Shortcuts
Enable keyboard shortcuts for comment moderation. More information
Show Admin Bar
when viewing site
in dashboard
Name
Username
georgep
Usernames cannot be changed.
First Name
George
Last Name
Plumley
Nickname (required)
georgep
Display name publicly as
George
Contact Info
E-mail (required)
george@bravenewniche.com
Website
AIM
Yahoo IM
Jabber / Google Talk
About Yourself
Biographical Info
Share a little biographical information to fill out your profile. This may be shown publicly.
New Password
If you would like to change the password type a new one. Otherwise leave this blank.
Type your new password again.
Strength indicator
Hint: The password should be at least seven characters long. To make it stronger, use upper and lower case letters, numbers and symbols like ! " ? $ % ^ &).
Update Profile

FIGURE 5-5

The next option is to choose the color scheme of the administration area. Two schemes are available — gray and blue — and the gray one is selected by default. Plugins are available for WordPress that allow you to have even more choices. I'm a fan of the default gray, but some prefer the blue because it provides more contrast with the gray background of the admin screens.

Next is the setting for keyboard shortcuts when dealing with comments. There's a link here that explains more, but basically, these are single-key shortcuts that let you deal more efficiently with comments. Unless you receive a lot of comments all the time, there's no point in turning this on.

The Admin Bar setting was first introduced in WordPress 3.1 and it turns on a menu bar that remains at the top of the screen as you scroll, giving you access to some of the most important links for administering your site, as shown in Figure 5-6.

FIGURE 5-6

The bar is quite handy, especially on long screens, so you don't have to keep scrolling up or down to use the side menu. You can set it to be visible when in admin screens or when you're logged in and viewing the actual site, or both.

Next comes a sometimes confusing array of names that you can fill in: First Name, Last Name, and a Nickname. By default, the Nickname is the same as the username, but you can change it (you can't change the username). Once you've entered whatever names you want, they're available in various combinations under the drop-down menu Display Name Publicly As. If your posts display an author name, this is where you choose what name will be displayed.

Under Contact Info, the most important item is your e-mail address — make sure this is always up to date. When you first log in, you'll see the e-mail address you entered during installation and which appeared under General Settings as the site e-mail address. The two can be different, but the main thing is that your profile e-mail be, and continue to be, a functioning e-mail address or else you won't be able to recover your password if you ever lose it.

The other contact information here can be filled out if you wish. Some themes make use of this information and it can be handy if you have a number of different authors and you want to provide contact information. The details here can also be accessed if you ever create your own custom theme template that displays user contact info.

The same is true of the biographical field — it may be accessed by some themes (in fact, the Twenty Ten theme shows author bio information at the bottom of a post if this field is filled in) or you could make it accessible to public view through a customization. This field does accept some basic HTML tags.

Finally, if you want to change your password, you can do that in the final area of the Profile page, using the strength indicator as your guide to a secure password. Many people recommend changing your password every few months, as long as you continue to choose something tough to crack.

As always, remember to scroll to the bottom of the page to update your profile settings. There is no warning that you're leaving this screen without saving changes.

> *There is no provision for uploading a photo to your profile. By default, WordPress uses the gravatar.com system — sign up for free and the image you upload there is tied to an e-mail address, which may also be used by many different programs around the Internet. However, some plugins give you the ability to upload user photos.*

TRY IT

In this lesson, you practice changing the most essential data under General Settings.

Lesson Requirements

WordPress installed.

Step-by-Step

The following is the process for entering important general settings.

1. Drop down the Settings area of the admin menu.
2. Click General.
3. Find the Tagline box and change it to your new tagline.
4. Find the WordPress Address (URL) box and make sure it's correct.
5. Find the Site Address (URL) box and make sure it's correct.
6. Find the E-mail Address box and make sure it's correct.
7. Find the drop-down menu for Timezone and choose a city in your time zone, or if you know your time zone, choose that.
8. If the changes look good, you can click Save Changes at the bottom of the page.

> *To see some of the examples from this lesson, including the Admin Bar, and to see the setting of a personal profile, watch the video for Lesson 5 on the DVD with the print book, or watch online at* `www.wrox.com/go/wp24vids`.

SECTION III
Working with Written Content

6

Adding a New Post — Overview

In this lesson, you learn the basics of creating a new post, tagging it and categorizing it, and then publishing it to your website. Virtually everything I talk about here applies to writing pages. When I use the term *post*, then, I'm also talking about pages. I'll point out important differences as they come up and then, in Lesson 10, I cover the elements unique to pages.

ANATOMY OF A NEW POST

A new post can be started from three locations on the admin screen: the Add New link on the left-hand menu under Posts (or Add New under Pages), from the drop-down menu at the top right of the screen, or from the Admin Bar (if you have it displayed), as shown in Figure 6-1.

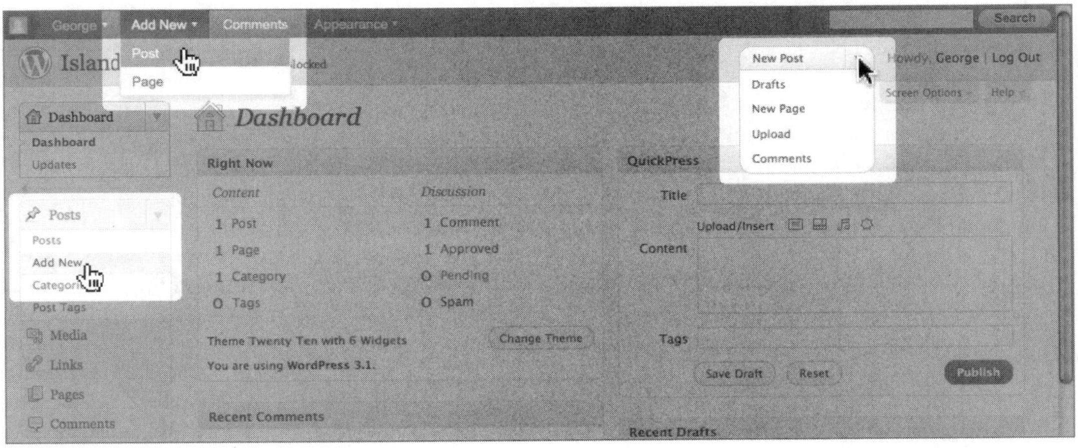

FIGURE 6-1

> *Bloggers and others in a hurry should note that posts (but not pages) can also be added from the QuickPress section of the Dashboard as well as from a Press This bookmarklet, if you have it installed in your browser.*

Any of these links take you to the Add New Post screen, the default version of which is shown in Figure 6-2.

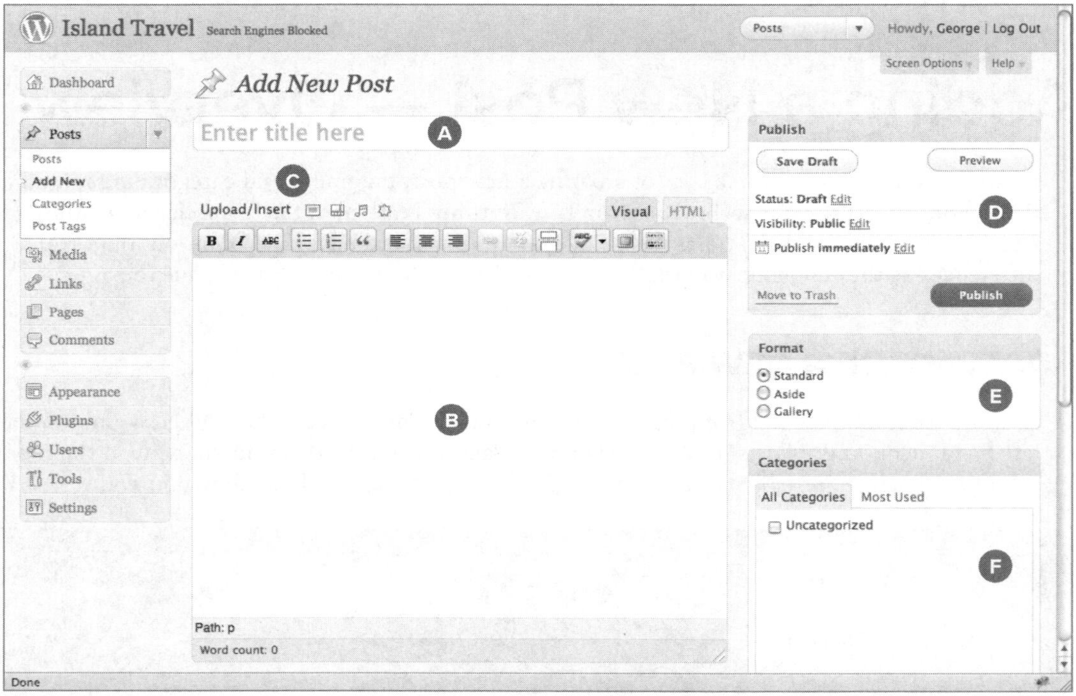

FIGURE 6-2

The meta boxes in this figure, which I've labeled for ease of reference, are the ones you'll work with the most. Additional meta boxes exist but are not displayed by default, and I'm leaving them until Lesson 9.

You can move meta boxes around by dragging them by the title bar or you can choose to remove them by using the Screen Options at the top right. In all the installations of WordPress I've done, though, I've rarely moved or removed any of the boxes in this top area of the screen because I'm always using them.

Item A is the *Title* box. The area below the Title box is blank when you first open the screen, but after you've entered a title, you'll see the Permalink area, as shown in Figure 6-3.

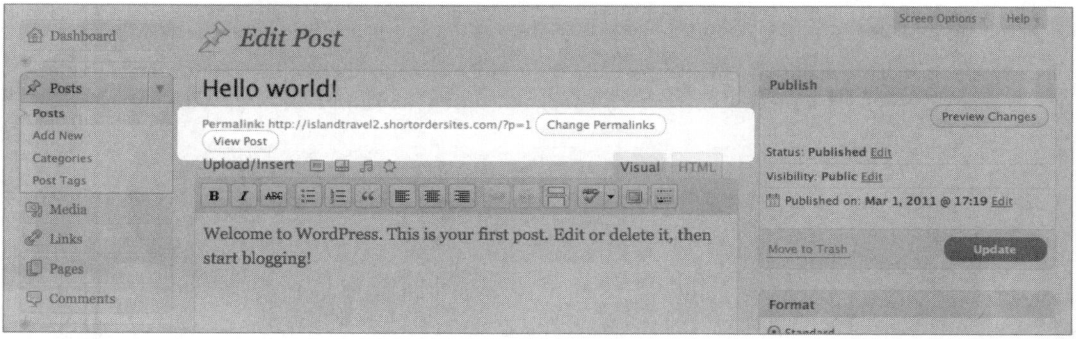

FIGURE 6-3

Item B is the primary work area for entering content: the *Text Editor* or Post Box as it's sometimes described. I'm going to use the term Text Editor partly because it's used mostly for editing and laying out text, but also because it's used for both posts and pages.

By default, the Text Editor displays in Visual mode, which means that text is displayed in a WYSIWYG format, like a word processor — there's even a row of function buttons like on a word processor. You can see the two tabs on the right of the Text Editor header bar and they allow you to switch between Visual and HTML mode. It's handy to be able to see the HTML coding, but for the most part, you'll likely work in Visual mode.

Just above the header bar over on the left is Item C — a small menu called *Upload/Insert*. These icons are for working with images and other media you may want to include in a post. I cover this menu in Lesson 11 when I talk about media content — for the moment, we'll stick with written content.

At the top right of the Add New Post screen is Item D — the *Publish* box. Publishing a post means making it go live so the world can see it, and from this box, you control when and how your content is published.

A recent addition to WordPress is Item E — the *Format* box. You'll see this only if your theme has specified one or more post formats. In the case of the default theme, there are three: Standard (the default), Aside, and Gallery. Choosing something other than Standard allows the theme not only to style the post differently, but even to create special layouts. I talk more about post formats in Lesson 9.

Next is Item F, *Categories*, and off-screen below it are *Post Tags* and *Featured Image*. I come back to these three after covering the actual writing of a post.

WRITING A POST

In this part of the overview, I touch on the very basics of using the Text Editor, then in Lessons 7 and 8, I go into more detail about all the functions.

The Button Bar

The heart of the Text Editor is the button bar, from which you access all the functions. By default, WordPress displays a single row of buttons in Visual mode, as shown in detail in Figure 6-4.

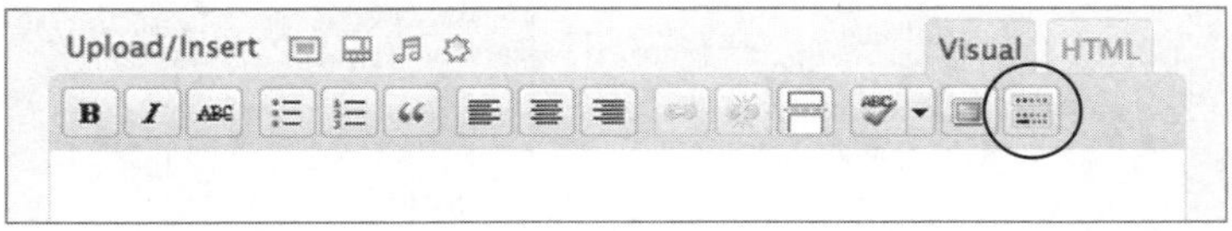

FIGURE 6-4

Some of these will be familiar from using word processing programs. Most are used for formatting text, but the one at the far right that I've circled is called the Kitchen Sink button and clicking it reveals a second row of buttons, as shown in Figure 6-5.

FIGURE 6-5

> *If you log out of WordPress with the second row of buttons displayed, it will still be there when you log in again and until you toggle back at some point to a single row. There is no setting for defaulting to one or two rows of buttons — it's determined by each user's actions.*

Before getting to a few of these functions and actually entering some text, it's important to say something about the realities of Visual mode.

What You See Isn't Quite What You Get

On the surface, it seems like Visual mode is supposed to show your content as it's going to look when you publish it, just as word processing programs show you what your page will look like when it's printed. However, there are two key ways in which the WordPress Text Editor is not WYSIWYG and I think it's important to get these out of the way early to avoid confusion and disappointment.

1. The Text Editor is not necessarily controlled by your style sheet.

   What you see on your live site is formatted by the style sheet of your WordPress theme, but it may or may not control what you see in the Text Editor. That will depend on whether your theme has an editor style sheet that mirrors the live site. The default WordPress theme does incorporate this feature.

Whether or not your theme supports styling for the editor, it's important that you use the Preview button. It will show your post exactly the way your style sheet is going to display it to visitors, and in the context of the rest of the site layout.

2. The Text Editor thinks of spacing very differently than you.

   You're used to hitting your Enter or Return key on a word processor and getting extra space between paragraphs — the more you do, the more space you get. Not so with the Text Editor.

   Put as many spaces as you like between paragraphs, but when you click Publish or Update, they all disappear. There's a method in this apparent madness, and I explain more in Lesson 8. I also show you some ways to add that extra space if you're desperate to do so. For the moment, it's enough to know that you can avoid frustration by hitting the Enter key only once per paragraph.

Another way of putting these warnings is to say that the role of Visual mode is not to give you exactly what you're going to get, but to make basic formatting obvious and to simplify functions like creating links. For instance, it's much clearer to see that **this is going to be bold text** on my website than to decipher the actual HTML: `<strong>this is going to be bold text</strong>`. And for tasks like creating links or making lists, it's much easier to click a button than to learn HTML coding. So, Visual mode is still very useful to most users despite its limits.

Working with Text

To enter text, of course, you just start typing in the Text Editor box. As you type, the box scrolls down as needed (the default size of the Text Editor is fairly small, but you can change that in a number of ways — see Lesson 7). You can keep track of your word count at the lower left of the box, while on the right, you'll see the last time you saved the current material and the last time the post was edited.

I'm going to create a new post with the title Seven Day Capital Package and enter text about a vacation package in Kingston, Jamaica. When you want to format text, you simply highlight the words, press the appropriate button, and you'll see the change. For example, I'll go in and make the name Kingston bold, as shown in Figure 6-6.

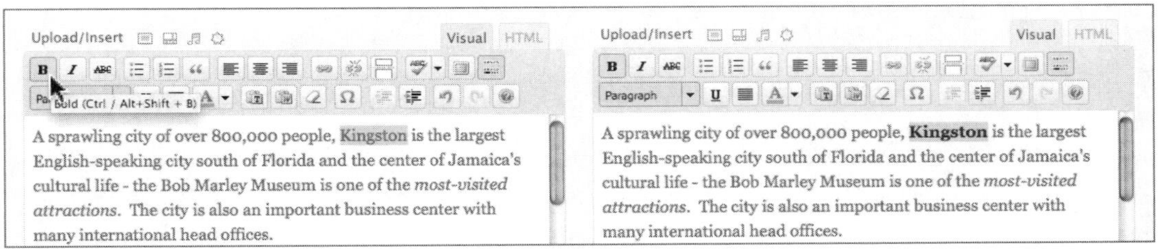
Upload/Insert
Visual
HTML
Bold (Ctrl / Alt+Shift + B)
A sprawling city of over 800,000 people, Kingston is the largest English-speaking city south of Florida and the center of Jamaica's cultural life - the Bob Marley Museum is one of the most-visited attractions. The city is also an important business center with many international head offices.
Upload/Insert
Visual
HTML
Paragraph
A sprawling city of over 800,000 people, Kingston is the largest English-speaking city south of Florida and the center of Jamaica's cultural life - the Bob Marley Museum is one of the most-visited attractions. The city is also an important business center with many international head offices.

FIGURE 6-6

When you want to start a new paragraph, you hit Enter on your keyboard. To cut, copy, or paste text, you'll need to use the standard keyboard commands — Ctl+x, Ctl+c, Ctl+v — because there are no buttons for these functions.

For those who like to use keyboard shortcuts, most of the old standbys work in the Visual mode Text Editor, including undoing and saving. You can also access any non-standard function on the button bar using the keyboard. To find out the keyboard commands, just mouse over the button or, on the second row, click the rightmost button to bring up a window with details about the Visual Text Editor, including all keyboard commands.

Before leaving the Text Editor, I make sure I save my work. Because this is a new post but I don't want to publish it yet, I click Save Draft at the top of the Publish box. I would keep using that button until I publish, and at that point, Save Draft disappears and the Publish button changes to Update Post. There is autosave built into WordPress, but you never know what might interrupt you and cause unsaved changes to be lost, so it's just a good habit to save regularly.

CATEGORIES AND TAGS

You can organize posts (but not pages) in two ways: by categorizing and by tagging them. Each fulfills a special role even if they seem quite similar. One way to think of the difference is that categories are like a table of contents whereas tags are like an index — categories are general and tags are specific.

Categories

Categories are the primary way of organizing posts, so I'll begin with them. The Categories box shown in Figure 6-7A displays all the existing categories for your site and allows you to add new categories without leaving the screen.

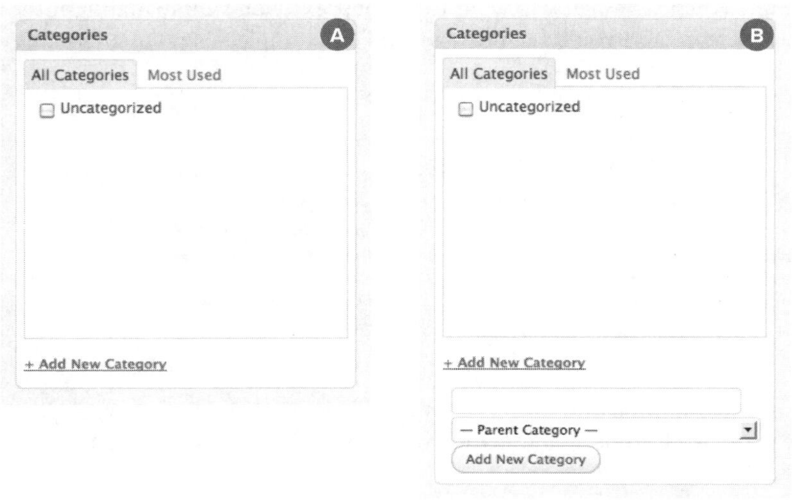

FIGURE 6-7

Right now, there's only one category, called Uncategorized. Because posts must be in at least one category, WordPress comes with a category that cannot be deleted. So, if you save or publish a post and forget to choose a category, you'll find that WordPress has automatically placed it in the Uncategorized category.

> *Be sure to change the name of this default category — you'll often see WordPress sites with an "Uncategorized" category. I go into renaming categories and choosing a different default category in Lesson 20.*

The post I'm working on here is about a vacation package, so I'll add a new category called Packages. Click the Add New Category link and you'll see a text box appear like the one in Figure 6-7B.

You enter the name of your category here. Just below the text box is a drop-down menu called Parent Category. This is used if you want your new category to be a subcategory of something else (you want it to be the child of a parent category). In this particular case, I don't want Packages to be a subcategory of anything else, so I don't touch Parent Category.

When you click Add, you'll see a yellow bar flash at the top of the categories list and your new category appears with a check mark beside it, as shown in Figure 6-8A.

However, I don't want this post in the Packages category, I want it in a child or subcategory of Packages, but because Packages did not exist yet, I had to create it. So, I uncheck Packages, go back to the Add New Category link, and enter Jamaica Packages in the new category box. Packages appears in the Parent Category list, so I choose that and click Add (Figure 6-8B). The results are shown in Figure 6-8C (I've added a couple of other child categories under Packages to illustrate a point).

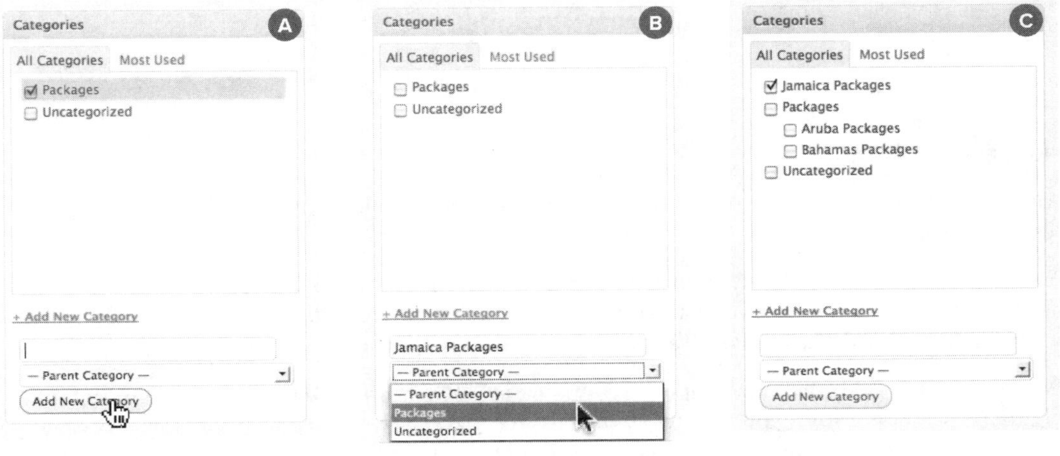

FIGURE 6-8

Normally, categories are shown in alphabetical order, with child categories nested below parents, but notice that Jamaica Packages is listed at the top, out of order. When you have a lot of categories, it can be time-consuming to scroll through to find the ones that your post is connected to, so WordPress moves those categories to the top of the list.

Remember, too, that adding categories, even though they're checked off, does not mean they've been assigned to the post yet — that only happens when you click Save Draft or Publish or Update Post.

> *Something I mentioned in Lesson 2 is worth repeating at this point: posts in child categories automatically are members of their parent categories. So, in the case of my post, I don't need to check Packages — my post is automatically included in that category by being in Jamaica Packages. This is very useful because on the website, I could have a listing that shows all Packages, including those for Jamaica, while also showing a list just for Jamaica.*

Tags

Earlier, I used the term *specific* to describe tags. In the case of the current post, I categorized it under Jamaica Packages, but in the body of the text, it talks about Kingston and all-inclusive resorts. Those are terms for which people might be interested in seeing all similar posts. One option would be to create a Kingston category, but there are so many cities in the Caribbean that the category structure would become bloated. However, if I make Kingston a tag — using the Post Tags box in Figure 6-9A — visitors could still see all posts tagged with "Kingston" just as if it were a category.

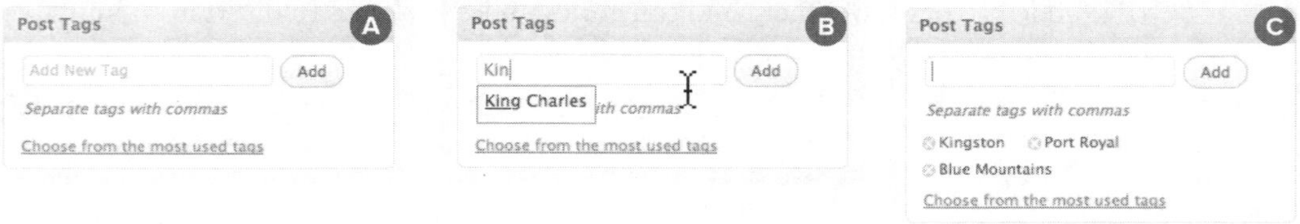

FIGURE 6-9

All I do is enter the tag in the text box. If you want to enter more tags, WordPress reminds you to separate them with commas.

As you enter a word or phrase, WordPress checks existing tags and displays possible matches in a popup window, from which you can choose, as shown in Figure 6-9B. You can also click Choose from the Most Used Tags in Post Tags to get a list of popular tags on your site.

When you click Add, the tag(s) appear below the text box, with a small x beside them — see Figure 6-9C. This allows you to remove tags from a post later on. As always, remember to click Save Draft, Publish, or Update Post, because even though the tags appear under the text box, they're not saved in the system until you click one of those buttons.

PUBLISHING A POST

Once you have your post entered, categorized, and tagged, you need to decide what to do with it, and that's where the Publish box comes in. The name is a bit misleading because publishing is only one of the options you have, but because it's the most important of all the options here, it makes sense to use that title. Figure 6-10 shows the Publish box in detail.

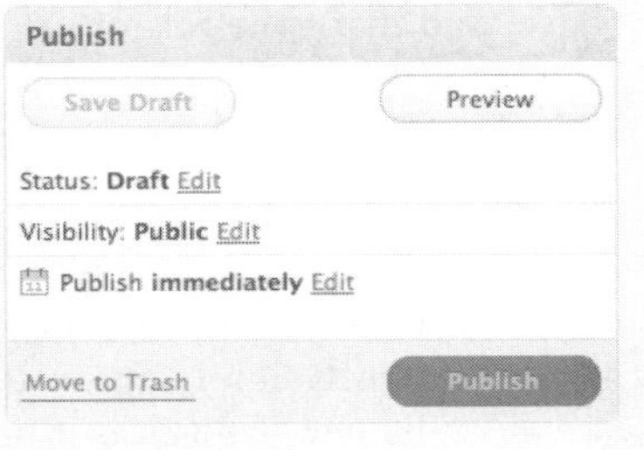

FIGURE 6-10

What jumps out at you first is the large blue button, which will say Publish, Update, or Schedule, depending on the context. For instance, once you've published a post, the button will say Update Post, or if you change the date of publication to one in the future, the button will say Schedule.

Starting at the top of the Publish box, there are two white buttons. Save Draft keeps a copy of your post, if you're not ready for the world to see it just yet. The Preview button, of course, allows you to see the post exactly as it would look on the live site.

Status

The Status menu allows you to move your post from one state to another depending on the post's current state. In other words, it's a contextual menu. But to see that menu, you need to click the Edit link beside the current status, and you get what's shown in Figure 6-11.

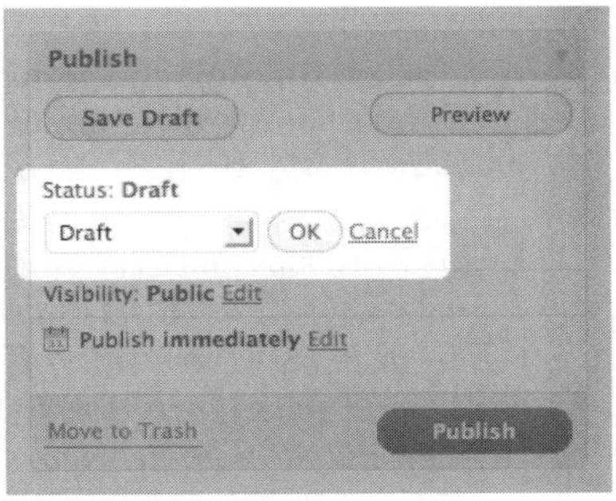

FIGURE 6-11

Once you've chosen the new status, click OK and the menu disappears. If you decide not to change anything, just click Cancel.

A post has four different states. Not all of these are shown at once — as I mentioned, this is a contextual menu — so only the relevant choices are open to you at any particular time:

- **Draft:** This means that the post is still in its early stages and not ready for any eyes, public or otherwise.
- **Pending Review:** This is a state used when you have multiple authors and there's an editor who will review the post before it's published. When the post is ready for review, you simply switch it from Draft to Pending Review. Items that are Pending Review are listed separately so, for example, someone who's editing posts knows that those ones are ready to be checked over.
- **Scheduled:** This means the post will be published at a certain date and time in the future. You cannot change the status of a scheduled post to Published by using this drop-down menu. You must change the publication date and then the big blue button will switch to Publish.
- **Published:** This means the post is live on the website. Depending on the visibility settings, it may not be visible to all visitors, but it's available to whomever has permission to see it.

Visibility

When publishing a post, you can decide who can see it when it's live, and that's the role of the Visibility menu. The current visibility is displayed, but to see other choices, you'll need to click the Edit link to display the menu shown in Figure 6-12.

FIGURE 6-12

- **Public:** This is the default setting and it means that anyone on the Internet will be able to see the post. You also have the option of making a public post *sticky*, which simply means that it does not get bumped down by newer posts as it normally would (by default, posts are shown in reverse chronological order — newer ones first). This stickiness applies only to the front-page blog posts, if you've chosen that as the content of your homepage.
- **Password Protected:** As the name implies, this means visitors will need to enter a password if they want to see the content of that particular post. You'll need to select Password to see the entry box for the password. Enter it and click OK.

> *Password-protecting a post is a very handy feature because you might want to provide some exclusive content but don't want to go to the trouble of creating a password-protected directory on the server for a single item or an item you only need protected for a short time. A good example would be a document you want to offer only to subscribers of a newsletter. You simply upload the document to a post, password-protect the post, and then send out the URL and password in the newsletter. After a specified time, you just unpublish or delete the post.*

- **Private:** This can be a confusing setting because it actually relates to the administrative end of WordPress rather than the public website. Making a post Private simply means that only Editors or Administrators can see the post listed in the admin screen. Other levels of users wouldn't see it displayed. If you're looking to make material on the live site visible only to certain people (for example, if you had memberships to your site), you'll want to explore WordPress plugins that can do that, and I cover some of those in Lesson 37.

When you're finished choosing among these, be sure to click the OK button and the new state will display beside Visibility. Remember that although it looks like you're done, *you must click Update Post (or Publish or Save Draft) for the change to actually be made.*

Publish

This setting determines when the post will be published, and the default is immediately. If you want to schedule the post to publish automatically in the future, click the Edit link and you'll see the date display, as shown in Figure 6-13.

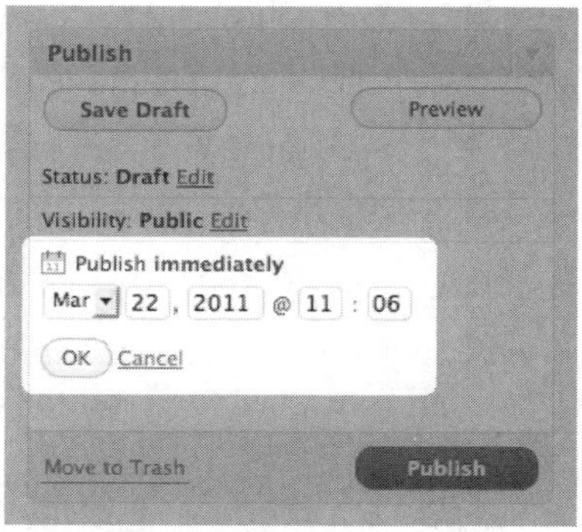

FIGURE 6-13

You can even set things up to publish at a specific time of day. For instance, I often set press releases to publish the morning of the day I'm sending out e-mail notices about the release.

Once you've set the date and time, just click OK and the new time appears next to Publish. And again, *remember to click Schedule or Update Post* (depending on what the big blue button says) or else your change won't be saved.

> *Because you can set any date you like, it's possible to date a post in the past, but why would you want to do that? Suppose you have a press release that had been missed and you want it to appear in your archives in the proper order by date. Simply backdate the post and hit Publish.*

TRY IT

In this lesson, you create a new post, then schedule it for publishing at a later date.

Lesson Requirements

WordPress installed.

Step-by-Step

Steps for creating and scheduling a post:

1. Click Add New under the Post section of the admin menu.
2. Enter a title for the post.
3. Check that the Text Editor is in Visual mode.
4. Enter some text — try making it bold, italicizing it, or changing its alignment.
5. In the Categories box, click Uncategorized.

6. In the Publish box, under Visibility, click Edit.
7. Click Private and then OK.
8. Still in the Publish box, click Edit beside Publish Immediately.
9. Choose a date and time in the future.
10. Click OK. The blue button in the Publish box should now say Schedule.
11. Click Schedule. When the screen refreshes, you should see a message at the top saying "Post scheduled for" and the date/time, along with a preview link.

> *To see some of the examples from this lesson, such as adding tags and categories or password-protecting a post, watch the video for Lesson 6 on the DVD with the print book, or watch online at* `www.wrox.com/go/wp24vids`.

7

Working with the Text Editor

In Lesson 6, you learned the basics of using the WordPress Text Editor — now, it's time to examine its capabilities in detail. You'll learn the functions of each of the buttons on the button bar, including plenty of little tricks to help make it easier to use this powerful tool. Mostly, you'll be working in Visual mode, but this lesson also covers a bit of HTML mode.

ANATOMY OF THE TEXT EDITOR

As you've seen, the Visual Text Editor has two rows of buttons. By default, only the first row is displayed and you have to access the second row by clicking the Kitchen Sink button (the very last button on the default row). I've created a visual directory of each row, so let's begin with the default one.

> *You may have more buttons on your Text Editor if you have plugins installed on WordPress. If you install the TinyMCE Advanced plugin, you'll also have more rows of buttons and the ability to move buttons around. Some plugins give you a different text box altogether. For the purposes of this lesson, however, I'm only covering the default Text Editor.*

Figure 7-1 shows the functions of the primary button bar.

Figure 7-2 shows the secondary button bar.

Finally, Figure 7-3 shows the single row of buttons for HTML mode.

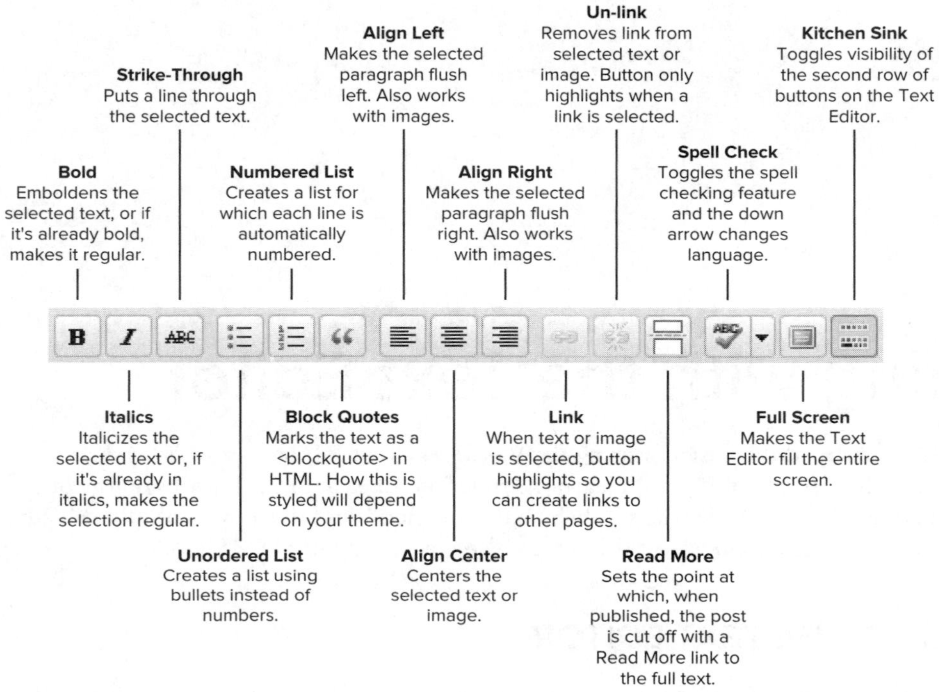
Bold
Emboldens the selected text, or if it's already bold, makes it regular.
Strike-Through
Puts a line through the selected text.
Numbered List
Creates a list for which each line is automatically numbered.
Align Left
Makes the selected paragraph flush left. Also works with images.
Align Right
Makes the selected paragraph flush right. Also works with images.
Un-link
Removes link from selected text or image. Button only highlights when a link is selected.
Spell Check
Toggles the spell checking feature and the down arrow changes language.
Kitchen Sink
Toggles visibility of the second row of buttons on the Text Editor.
B
I
ABC
Italics
Italicizes the selected text or, if it's already in italics, makes the selection regular.
Unordered List
Creates a list using bullets instead of numbers.
Block Quotes
Marks the text as a <blockquote> in HTML. How this is styled will depend on your theme.
Align Center
Centers the selected text or image.
Link
When text or image is selected, button highlights so you can create links to other pages.
Read More
Sets the point at which, when published, the post is cut off with a Read More link to the full text.
Full Screen
Makes the Text Editor fill the entire screen.

FIGURE 7-1

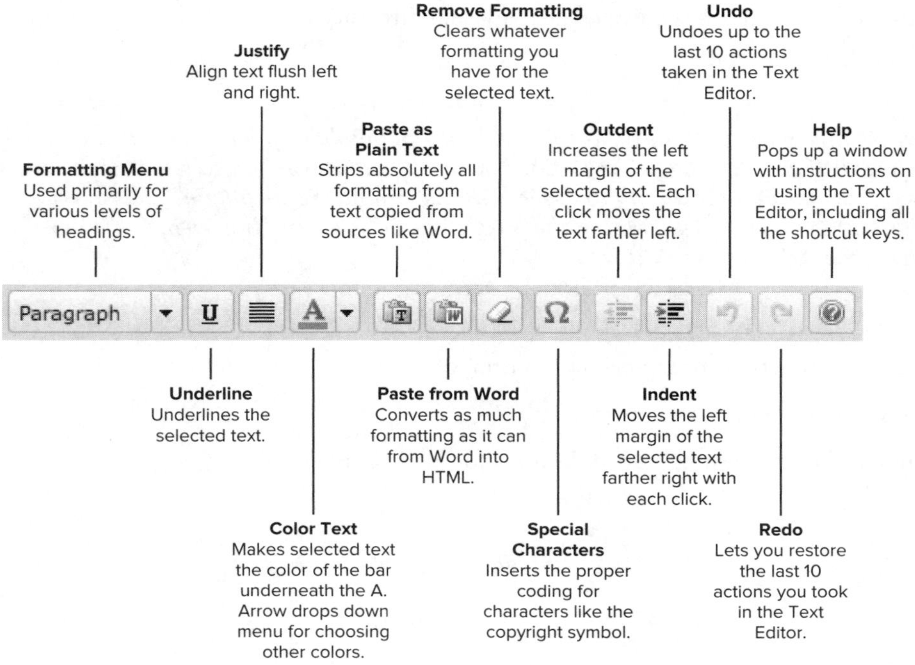
Formatting Menu
Used primarily for various levels of headings.
Justify
Align text flush left and right.
Paste as Plain Text
Strips absolutely all formatting from text copied from sources like Word.
Remove Formatting
Clears whatever formatting you have for the selected text.
Outdent
Increases the left margin of the selected text. Each click moves the text farther left.
Undo
Undoes up to the last 10 actions taken in the Text Editor.
Help
Pops up a window with instructions on using the Text Editor, including all the shortcut keys.
Paragraph
U
A
Ω
Underline
Underlines the selected text.
Color Text
Makes selected text the color of the bar underneath the A. Arrow drops down menu for choosing other colors.
Paste from Word
Converts as much formatting as it can from Word into HTML.
Special Characters
Inserts the proper coding for characters like the copyright symbol.
Indent
Moves the left margin of the selected text farther right with each click.
Redo
Lets you restore the last 10 actions you took in the Text Editor.

FIGURE 7-2

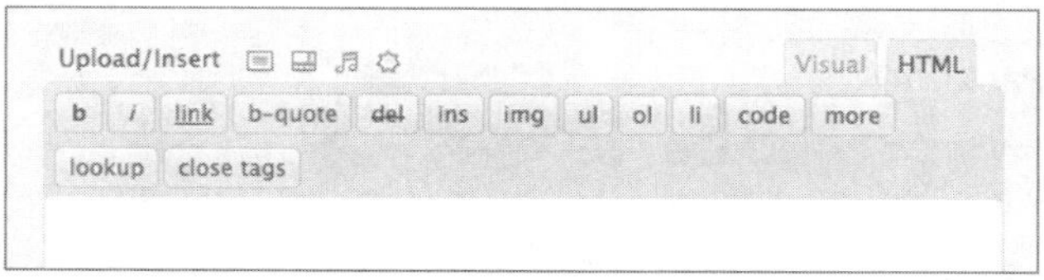

FIGURE 7-3

SIZING THE TEXT EDITOR

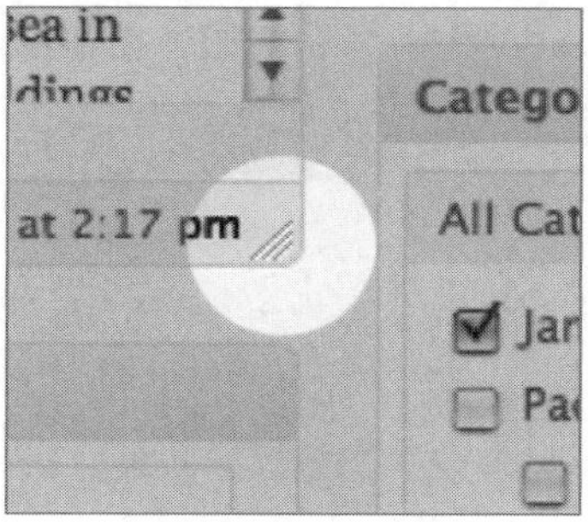

FIGURE 7-4

The default size of the Text Editor gives you a fair bit of room to work, but you may want more. One way to change its size is to drag the lower right-hand corner of the box downward. To do this, look for the three faint lines on that corner — shown in Figure 7-4 — then click and drag the box downward (this does not work in HTML mode, so you may need to switch to Visual mode, resize, and then switch back).

WordPress will remember the new height, but only for you. If you want all users to see a larger text box by default, you can change that under Settings ➪ Writing as shown in Figure 7-5 (the Size of the Post Box setting).

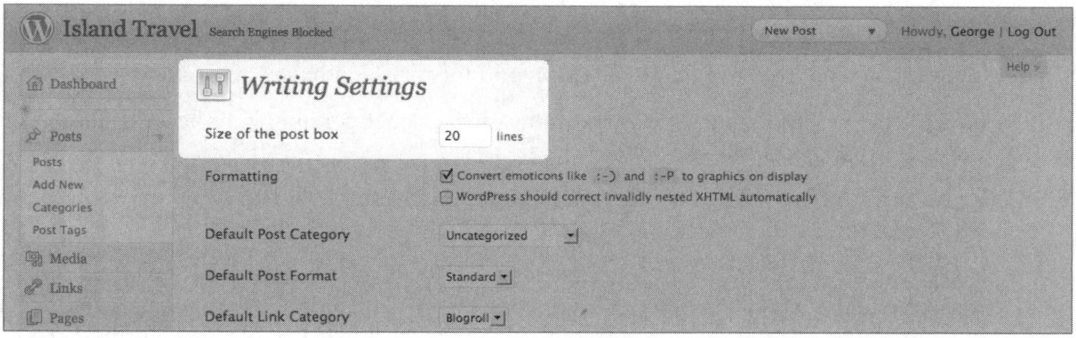

FIGURE 7-5

Users will still have the ability to resize the box to their liking.

However, height isn't always the only issue you may have with the size of the Text Editor. You could find the other boxes on the screen overlapping the Text Editor, as shown in Figure 7-6 (possible causes: as you add plugins to WordPress, they may place more buttons on your Text Editor, or perhaps you've increased the text size of your browser and the button bar gets larger as a result, pushing the Text Editor to the right).

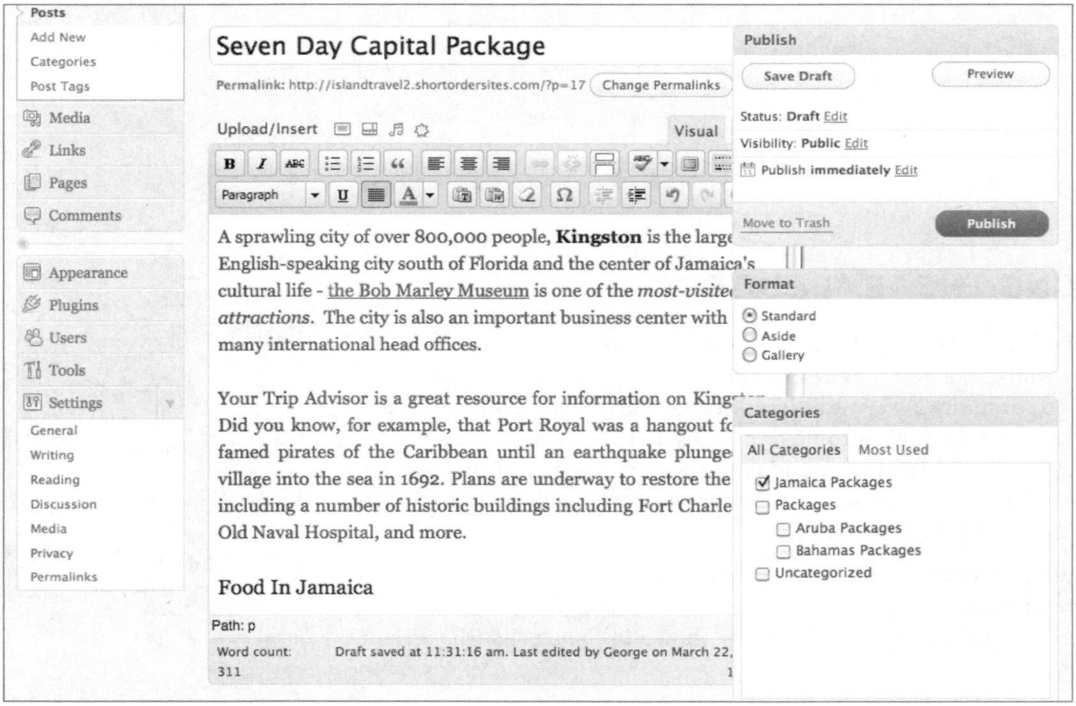
Posts
Add New
Categories
Post Tags
Media
Links
Pages
Comments
Appearance
Plugins
Users
Tools
Settings
General
Writing
Reading
Discussion
Media
Privacy
Permalinks
Seven Day Capital Package
Permalink: http://islandtravel2.shortordersites.com/?p=17
Change Permalinks
Upload/Insert
Visual
Paragraph
A sprawling city of over 800,000 people, Kingston is the large
English-speaking city south of Florida and the center of Jamaica's
cultural life - the Bob Marley Museum is one of the most-visite
attractions. The city is also an important business center with
many international head offices.
Your Trip Advisor is a great resource for information on King
Did you know, for example, that Port Royal was a hangout fo
famed pirates of the Caribbean until an earthquake plunge
village into the sea in 1692. Plans are underway to restore the
including a number of historic buildings including Fort Charle
Old Naval Hospital, and more.
Food In Jamaica
Path: p
Word count: 311
Draft saved at 11:31:16 am. Last edited by George on March 22,
Publish
Save Draft
Preview
Status: Draft Edit
Visibility: Public Edit
Publish immediately Edit
Move to Trash
Publish
Format
Standard
Aside
Gallery
Categories
All Categories
Most Used
Jamaica Packages
Packages
Aruba Packages
Bahamas Packages
Uncategorized

FIGURE 7-6

Whatever the cause, you need to find more width, and for that, you have a few options:

- Increase the width of your browser window — the center column with the Text Editor is fluid and will expand with the window.
- If you're already at your screen's limit, another option is to collapse the admin menu on the left side of the screen, as shown in Lesson 4.
- You can set the Text Editor to full-screen mode. When you click the Full Screen button, the editor expands to take over the whole of your screen. The button bar remains visible at the top, along with the buttons for the Upload/Insert menu. To get back to the normal screen, just click the Full Screen button again.
- Finally, you could specify that the Add New Post page have only one column instead of two. To change the columns, open up Screen Options at the top right and select Number of Columns: 1. All the boxes on the Add New Post screen will still be there; they're simply moved into a single column with the Title and Text Editor at the top.

> *If you do change to a single column and then change back to two columns, WordPress does not automatically restore your screen. Instead, it makes space for the second column and you'll need to drag back the boxes you want to appear on the right-hand side. Also, the change in columns will affect your Edit Posts pages as well.*

STYLING TEXT

Whenever you're thinking about styling some text, keep in mind these two points:

- Does the styling help visitors understand what you're saying in the post or is it simply adding clutter to what they see, no matter how "pretty" it looks?

  Take the example of making text bold, which was covered in the preceding lesson. If you use too much bold text on a page, the purpose begins to get lost. Everything becomes important so nothing stands out properly. Like that.

- Is this styling needed for this post alone or is it something that might better be handled by your theme's style sheet because you want to develop a standard style across multiple posts?

  I often see people create special styles for a section heading on a post. Those headings are already controlled by your theme. Creating a style for a particular heading overrides what's in the style sheet, and that's okay, but maybe what you really want to do is change the style sheet so that all headings of that type look the same.

There isn't time to go through all types of text styling here, and I cover the styling of large bodies of text in the next lesson, so I'll just mention a few common issues.

Underlining

I'm not a fan of using the Underline function at all, at least not on the Web. I think it's just too confusing to your visitors because underlined text spells "link" in their minds. They try clicking the underlined text and you either disappoint or confuse them.

I know some uses of underline are actually required, such as in scholarly documents, but for cases like that, the visitor has some context and is familiar with the underlining. If you need to emphasize text, it's usually best to stick to bold and italics, or perhaps color.

Coloring Text

Having mentioned coloring text, remember a few things before you start doing it:

- Don't use the same or a similar color as the one you use for your text links — that's going to confuse visitors.
- If you have colored headings in your theme, using the same color for pieces of text can also be confusing, though a shade of that color maybe isn't so bad.
- Always think about the background color behind the text. You don't want anything that's going to blend in too much with the background, especially when people are printing the page in black and white.

How, then, do you color text? It's the button with the letter A on the second row of the Text Editor button bar. If you highlight some text and click that button, the text will turn the color of the small bar displayed on the button. If you want to change that color, click the down arrow and you get some preset choices. Click More Colors and you get a popup window where you can choose from any color.

> *Changing color this way bypasses your theme's style sheet. If you change your theme, this kind of coloring remains, so if it clashes with the new look, you'll have to manually go in and change it.*

The Formatting Menu

The drop-down menu on the left-hand side of the second row of buttons (shown in Figure 7-7) can be a bit confusing at first. It seems to be, as the name suggests, a way of formatting text in different ways, but here's what's really going on:

- Changes affect blocks of text as a whole, and not simply individual words or phrases within the block. If you highlighted five words in the middle of a paragraph and tried to switch them to Heading 2, the entire paragraph would become a Heading 2.
- Headings are not just about formatting or styling; they're completely different from paragraphs and each heading level has different semantic properties in HTML (different meanings). So, choosing Heading 3 for a paragraph is actually changing the paragraph into a Heading 3, not styling or formatting the paragraph.

I talk more about paragraphs and headings in the next lesson, but the main point here is: do not use the formatting drop-down for styling text.

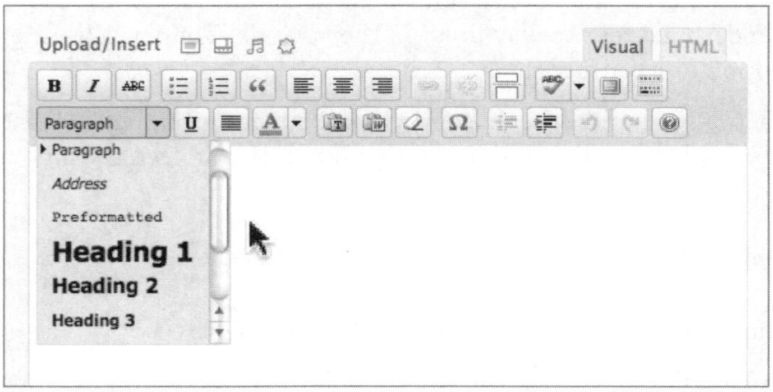

FIGURE 7-7

WORKING WITH TEXT LINKS

Creating links within the body of your text is important for leading visitors to more information — it's one of the greatest strengths of web-based material. But it's easy to mess up the HTML formatting of links, so thankfully, the WordPress Text Editor makes linking very simple. It's not quite as straightforward as, say, bolding, but you're led through every step with an easy-to-use form.

> *Much of what is said here applies to creating links using images. Details about linking images are covered in Lesson 13.*

The first thing to do is highlight the text that's going to be linked. Sometimes, deciding which text to link is fairly obvious: "I was reading an article in People magazine today and...." But the best rule of thumb is to link as much of the text as relates to where you want to take your visitor.

Once your text is highlighted and you click the link button, you get a popup window like the one in Figure 7-8.

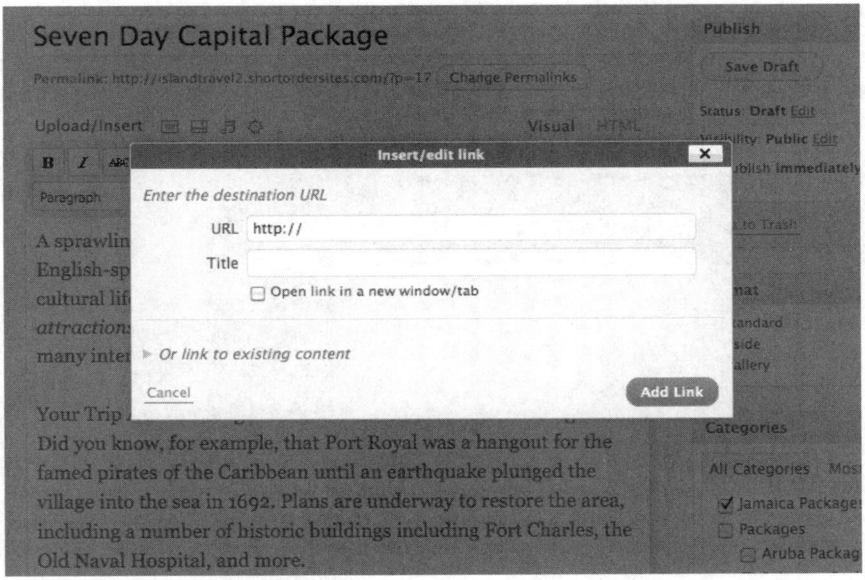

FIGURE 7-8

As the name Insert/Edit Link suggests, this window is not only for adding new links, but also editing existing ones.

URL is obviously where you're going to put the address of the web page you're linking to. WordPress automatically puts in the `http://` so you're not wondering whether it's required. It's also highlighted so that if you're like me and paste URLs copied from your browser address bar, you'll automatically erase the default text and not end up with `http://http://`.

Next, you can give your link a Title, which is what people will see when they mouse over the link. This can also be helpful in search engine optimization, which I talk about in Lesson 30. The key is to make the title clear and descriptive of where you're taking visitors if they click the link.

Finally, there's a check box for making the link open in a new browser window or tab. If the box is left unchecked, the link will automatically stay in the current window and replace its contents.

Either way of handling this has pros and cons. I personally like it when a link opens in a new window or tab — I'm not a big fan of using the back button (which may explain why I have dozens and dozens of tabs and windows open at any one time). Others will say it's confusing for new windows or tabs to be open, particularly when visitors end up with a whole raft of them. Do what you think best.

Once you have everything entered, click Insert and you'll see your text underlined and colored. Remember that this link format is just to help you distinguish the link in the Text Editor. How your links look on the website depends on your style sheet. And of course, before leaving the screen, click Update Post or your nice new link will not be saved.

Internal Linking

A new feature starting in WordPress 3.1 is found at the bottom of the Insert/Edit Link screen, and this allows you to easily link to your existing content. If you click Or Link to Existing Content, the window expands to show a search box and a list of recent posts, as shown in Figure 7-9.

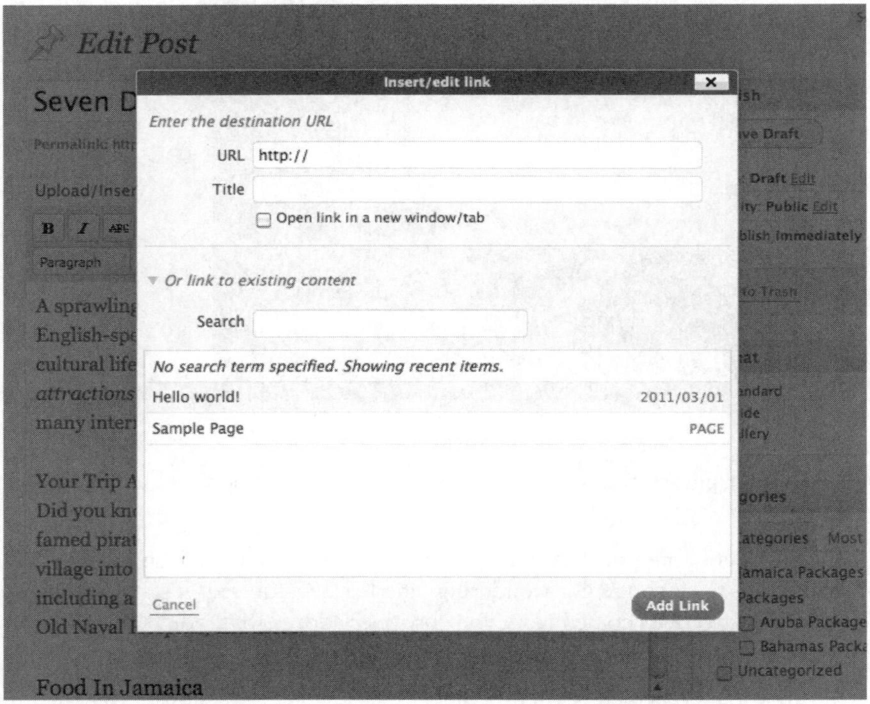

FIGURE 7-9

After finding the content you want to link to, just click the row for the post or page and WordPress will populate the URL field with the address and the Title field using the title of the post or page. Finally, click the Add Link button.

Not only does this make it handy to reference your own material without having to go hunting for it on your live site, but internal linking like this is useful for improving search engine ranking, as I discuss in Lesson 30.

Creating E-Mail Links

You can use the link button popup screen to create an e-mail link. Clicking this kind of link automatically opens the user's e-mail program and places the e-mail address in the To: box of a new message. So, instead of a website address, put the following in the URL field of the Insert/Edit Link screen: `mailto:myemail@mydomain.com`.

However, this is not a good plan. It leaves your e-mail address exposed to spammers who have robots running around the Web gathering up such addresses. Your best bet is to have visitors e-mail you by way of a form. WordPress has lots of plugins that make it very simple to create forms, and I talk about those in Lesson 36.

You'll hear people say you can get around the e-mail harvesters by tricking them with things like writing your e-mail like this: `myemailATmydomainDOTcom`. Problem is, robots easily learn to get around these tricks, and it's not very convenient for your visitors. Scripts are available that may do a slightly better job, if you're comfortable with setting them up, but the simplest answer is to use a form.

Editing Links

To edit an existing link, just click it and you'll see the two link buttons highlighted. Click the solid link button (the left one) to get the popup window you saw earlier. You can change any of the options in the window and then click Update to save those changes and be taken back to the Text Editor.

If you want to change the highlighted link text, you simply erase words or insert words, and the link remains in place. If you want to change all of the wording, highlight the entire link and begin typing the new text. Be careful not to highlight anything beyond the link or else you'll break it and you'll need to create a whole new link.

If you want the link moved to new text elsewhere in the post, just copy the URL from the old link, remove the link from that text, and then create a new link using the copied URL.

Removing Links

I've been careful to use the phrase "remove a link" rather than "delete a link" because removing a link means you're keeping the words that were linked. Deleting a link could mean that you want to get rid of the words as well as the link.

To delete a link, you simply highlight the words and delete them, but to remove a link, you need to click anywhere on the link itself and then choose the broken link button (the right-hand one). You'll see the underlining and the coloring removed from the words — then you know the link is no longer functioning.

When editing or removing links, remember that you need to click Update Post for the change to take effect.

IMPORTING TEXT

Nobody likes typing when you're just reentering things into a post, so copying and pasting is a popular sport. Quite often, though, you're copying from a source that can cause you problems by carrying hidden coding with it.

I often have clients say to me that they can't change a certain part of their text, no matter what they try to do in the Text Editor. A look behind the scenes in HTML mode quickly reveals the problem: hidden coding that's controlling the look of the text. In Figure 7-10, compare the text on the left — what the person saw in her word processor and wanted to copy — with the actual coding that got pasted into the WordPress Text Editor.

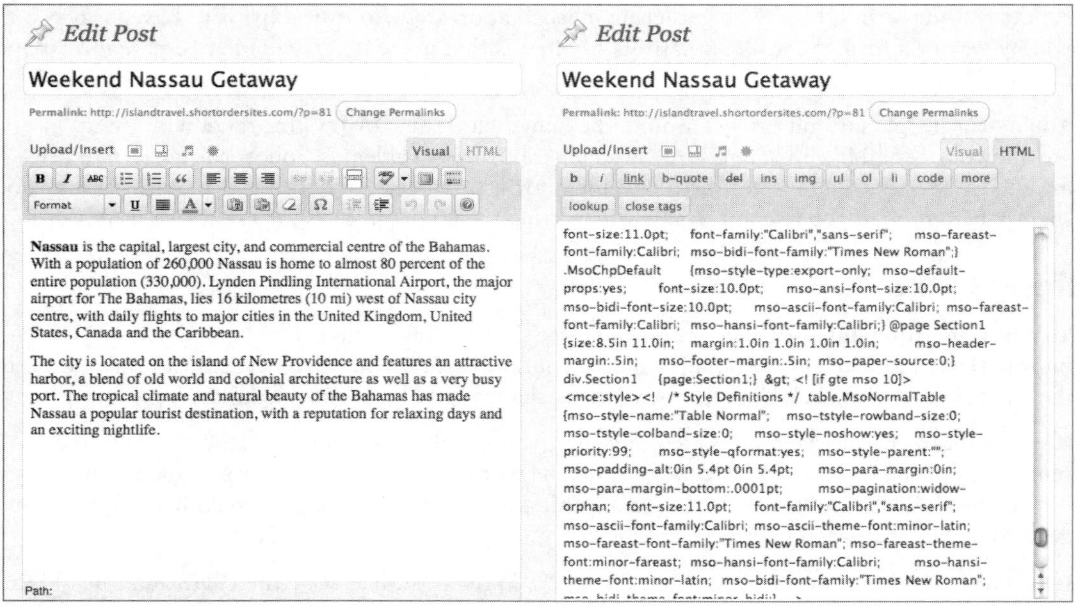

FIGURE 7-10

Because of the way style sheets work, this coding takes precedence over anything in your style sheet. Then, there's the problem of excess coding — you get a few of these on a page and it can make your HTML bloated and slower to load.

One way around the problem is to put any text into a simple text editor program first (such as Notepad on Windows or TextEdit on Mac) and then copy and paste from there. The excess coding will be stripped off in the process, and that includes all formatting, even bold and italics.

If you want to try to preserve some basic formatting, so you don't have to reconstruct it in the Text Editor, you can try using one of the paste buttons — they're the two buttons on the second row of the button bar that look like little clipboards. There's one for text copied from Word (it has the Word logo on it) and one for pasting text from other sources. The Word button is most commonly used and reports vary on what formatting will be preserved from your document, so it's really a matter of trying it out. Basic things like bold text usually make it through the process, but complex layouts like tables and so on typically do not.

If you want all formatting stripped from the text you're trying to insert, then use the other clipboard button with the T on it.

TRY IT

In this lesson, you practice creating a new link.

Lesson Requirements

A post with text.

Step-by-Step

Practice creating a link using Visual mode.

1. Make sure you're in the Visual mode of the Text Editor.
2. Highlight the text you want to be linked.
3. Click the link button (the unbroken chain icon on the top row) and the Insert/Edit Link window pops up.
4. Copy the URL from the address bar of your browser window or wherever you have the full URL you want to link to.
5. In the popup window, paste the URL into the URL box.
6. Enter a Title for the link.
7. Check the box if you want the link to open in a new window or tab.
8. Click Insert.
9. Verify that the text is linked the way you planned.
10. Click Update Post.
11. Click Preview to see how the link looks on the live site.

> *To see some of the examples from this lesson, including how to import text from a Word document, watch the video for Lesson 7 on the DVD with the print book, or watch online at* `www.wrox.com/go/wp24vids`.

8

Laying Out Text

Now that you know how to style bits of text, it's time to look at styling larger blocks using the Text Editor and laying out entire posts. In this lesson, you learn more about how the Text Editor behaves and tips for how to arrange your written content effectively. In the end, it always comes down to what's easiest for your visitors to read.

STYLING PARAGRAPHS

I'm using the term *paragraph* to refer to any block of text that you've separated in the Text Editor by using the Enter/Return key. That's because in HTML terms, the Text Editor sees any text separated in that way — even a single sentence — as a paragraph.

Aligning

To change the alignment of a paragraph, you simply need to click anywhere in the paragraph (there's no need to highlight the whole paragraph, though you can) and then click the appropriate alignment button — left, center, and right appear on the top row of the button bar.

There's a fourth alignment button that's only visible on the second row of the button bar, and that's for justified alignment. This is when text lines up flush on the left and the right, as shown in Figure 8-1.

Though the symmetry of this look pleases one part of my brain, there's another part that says things like, "Isn't the gap between those two words the same gap that indicates the end of a sentence?" The problem is that browsers aren't as sophisticated as print typesetting programs, in particular with respect to hyphenation, and the real-time nature of browsing does not allow for manual control of things like word spacing and letter spacing. These are some of the reasons I never use justification, but if you're considering it, think about how your desire for symmetry is getting in the way of readability for your visitors.

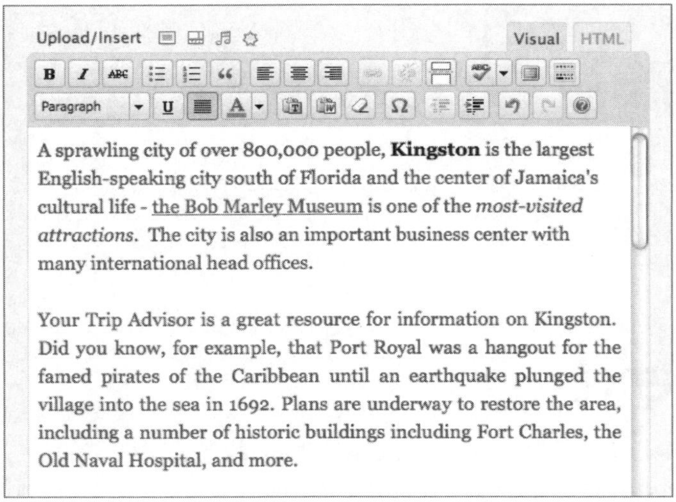

Upload/Insert
Visual
HTML
Paragraph
A sprawling city of over 800,000 people, Kingston is the largest English-speaking city south of Florida and the center of Jamaica's cultural life - the Bob Marley Museum is one of the most-visited attractions. The city is also an important business center with many international head offices.
Your Trip Advisor is a great resource for information on Kingston. Did you know, for example, that Port Royal was a hangout for the famed pirates of the Caribbean until an earthquake plunged the village into the sea in 1692. Plans are underway to restore the area, including a number of historic buildings including Fort Charles, the Old Naval Hospital, and more.

FIGURE 8-1

A common misconception is that if you have a paragraph aligned right, center, or justified, to return it to the standard left align, you have to click the Align Left button. However, the default alignment in HTML is to the left, so all you need to do is click the same alignment button — that turns off the alignment — and the text will go back to the left.

Blockquotes

A *blockquote* is an HTML tag for designating a section of quoted text. They're typically used for quoting more than a sentence or two from printed matter or other websites and so on. Blockquotes are displayed in the WordPress default theme indented from both the left and the right, but it all depends on the style sheet for your theme. Some creative blockquote styles are shown in Figure 8-2.

Creating a blockquote is easy. You simply place your cursor in the paragraph you want or highlight multiple paragraphs, and then click the Blockquote button. On the Jamaica page of Island Travel, I have a quote from a travel guide website. Rather than simply putting quotes around the two paragraphs, I want to really set them apart from the other text, so I use a blockquote — you can see the difference on the live site in Figure 8-3.

Notice, too, that I created a link to the site where I got the quote. I want to give them credit and it also allows visitors to easily get more information. The other site will also appreciate the link and not just the fact that you quoted them.

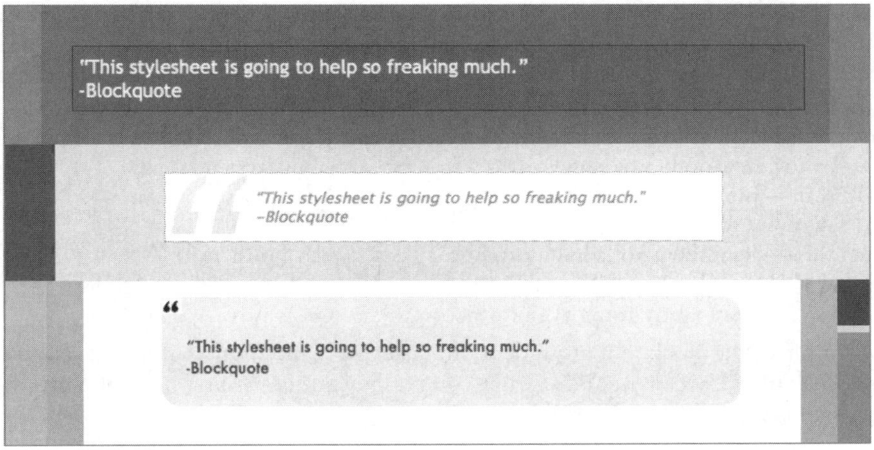
"This stylesheet is going to help so freaking much."
-Blockquote
"This stylesheet is going to help so freaking much."
-Blockquote
"This stylesheet is going to help so freaking much."
-Blockquote

FIGURE 8-2

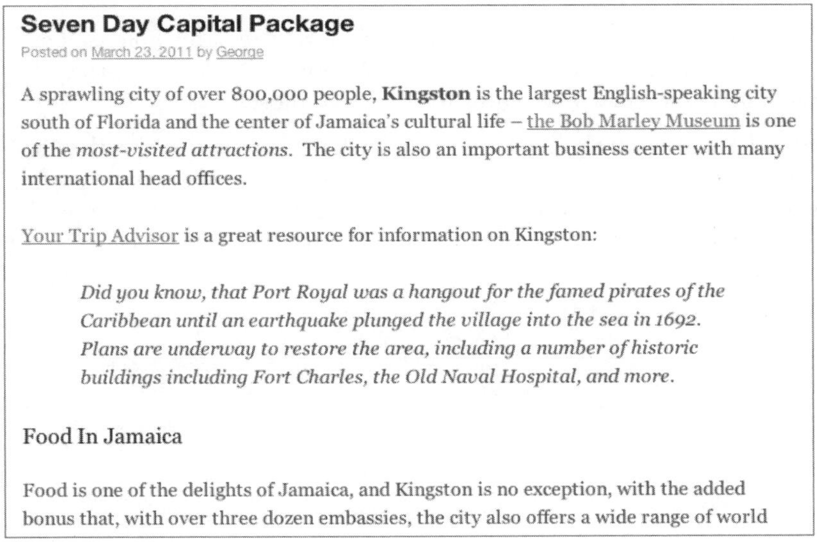
Seven Day Capital Package
Posted on March 23, 2011 by George
A sprawling city of over 800,000 people, Kingston is the largest English-speaking city south of Florida and the center of Jamaica's cultural life – the Bob Marley Museum is one of the most-visited attractions. The city is also an important business center with many international head offices.
Your Trip Advisor is a great resource for information on Kingston:
Did you know, that Port Royal was a hangout for the famed pirates of the Caribbean until an earthquake plunged the village into the sea in 1692. Plans are underway to restore the area, including a number of historic buildings including Fort Charles, the Old Naval Hospital, and more.
Food In Jamaica
Food is one of the delights of Jamaica, and Kingston is no exception, with the added bonus that, with over three dozen embassies, the city also offers a wide range of world

FIGURE 8-3

Indenting

You might think the indent button produces an indented first line of a paragraph, but, in fact, it moves the entire paragraph to the right. Click the button a second time and it indents the paragraph farther to the right.

I'm not sure what you'd use this for other than for quotes, and as you just saw, they're handled with the Blockquote button. But, you say, a blockquote is indented both left and right, so if I don't want a quote indented from both sides, then it would make sense to use the Indent button. In many themes, it's true that blockquotes are indented from both sides, but you can change the style sheet to just indent from the left. And that's the key to choosing between Blockquote and Indent.

To achieve the left indent effect, WordPress uses what's called *inline styling*: <p style="padding-left: 30px;">. This means the style is controlled in the HTML instead of in your theme's style sheet, the way that blockquotes are. If you want the indent to be 20 pixels instead of 30, you'll need to go in and change every single one of them by hand in the HTML. Much easier to change a style sheet once.

There's another reason for using Blockquote to indent, and that's because it also indicates a semantic difference in the language of HTML. Oh, and if what you really want is the first lines of paragraphs to be indented, there's a CSS style sheet rule for that.

CREATING LISTS

Lists are very useful because they help break up information into more manageable pieces. On the Web in particular, people have become used to seeing information not only in smaller pieces, but in visually helpful structures, and lists are one of the most important of those.

In HTML, lists are either ordered or unordered, which means each list item is set off with either numbering or with bullets. If you delete an item in an ordered list, the remaining items are automatically renumbered, whereas an unordered list has the same bullet beside each item and nothing changes if an item is deleted. Figure 8-4 shows an example of each type of list, with its corresponding button highlighted.

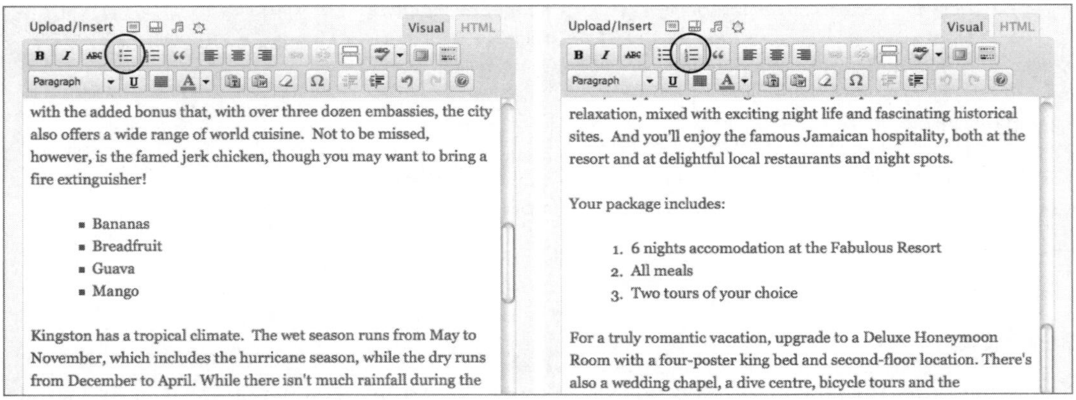

FIGURE 8-4

If you're not keen on the heavy square bullet of the unordered list, rest easy, I talk about how to change that and other kinds of styling in Lesson 28. If your theme does not style the Text Editor, you can always check how your list will actually look on your site by clicking Preview.

Beginning a New List

To begin either type of list, start a new paragraph (hit Enter or Return) and then click the appropriate button on the button bar. You'll see the cursor indent with a round, black bullet for unordered lists (the bullet styling may be different if your theme styles the Text Editor) or a number 1 for ordered lists.

> *If you click a list button while you're at the end of a paragraph (or anywhere inside a paragraph), that paragraph becomes the first item in the list. To return the paragraph to normal, just click the same list button (it'll be highlighted).*

After you've entered the first item on your list, simply hit Enter and you'll begin a new list item. Keep doing that until you've entered all the items on your list. To end the list, simply hit Enter after the final list item, as though you're starting a new item, and then hit Enter again. The new item bullet or number disappears and your cursor returns to the far left of the Text Editor, ready to begin a new paragraph.

Working with Existing Text and Lists

If you want to turn existing text into a list, you need to make sure that each item in the list is a paragraph, which really means that each item has to be separated by hitting Enter after it. For example, if I have a paragraph describing the features of a resort, I can't simply highlight the paragraph and click a list button. The entire paragraph would become a single list item. What I need to do is go through the paragraph and hit Enter after each sentence, then highlight all these "paragraphs" and click a list button.

Converting an existing list to the other type of list is even simpler. Just highlight all the list items and click the other list button. Your ordered list instantly becomes an unordered list, or vice versa.

> *Unlike regular paragraphs, for which you can place the cursor anywhere in the paragraph and apply certain styling to the whole (such as alignment or making it a blockquote), you must highlight the entire list to convert it. If you just place your cursor somewhere in the list, you'll convert only the list item you're on.*

If you want to de-list some or all items in a list, highlight the ones to be converted and click the appropriate list button. Each list item becomes an individual paragraph. If you've de-listed only some items, the rest remain in list format and, if it's an ordered list, they automatically renumber. If the de-listed item(s) is in the middle, you end up with two independent lists, one above and one below, and if the original was an ordered list, the two remaining lists will renumber themselves separately.

TIPS FOR LAYING OUT POSTS

My first tip for laying out the text in a post is to ask yourself whether you might not be better off with one or more smaller posts. I say this because often, when people are asking about layout, it's because they have a lot of material to deal with and they're not sure how to break it up visually. And sometimes, the answer to that is to break it up into separate posts or pages.

In the case of posts, for example, I talked about testimonials when I was planning the Island Travel site in Lesson 2. Instead of having all the testimonials on a single page in WordPress, I said it would be useful to put each individual testimonial into a post. Part of that usefulness is that I don't have to figure out how to lay out a giant page of testimonials — the work is done for me when I call up the Testimonials category, and all of the testimonials are displayed as individual posts with headings and other visual separators.

In the case of pages, when there's a lot of content on a single page, ask yourself whether your visitors wouldn't be better served by breaking it up into separate pages, each with its own focus. The goal here is not to save yourself the trouble of laying out a lot of text on a page — that's just a side benefit of thinking about whether your visitors are having to sift through a lot of material that could be in relevant chunks.

Making Use of Headings

The most important thing to remember when you're laying out a post with a large amount of text is to break up subtopics using headings. Not only is this helpful to your readers by breaking things up for them visually, but it's also useful for search engines that use headings to understand the relative importance of chunks of data. That's why you need to use the headings in the Format menu of the Text Editor in a logical way.

To a lot of people, the purpose of headings in the drop-down menu is about sizing — like they're choosing a font size. Though it's true that Heading 2 is typically sized larger than Heading 3 in style sheets, the reason for the size change is semantic. In other words, difference in size is meant to be a visual cue about relationships (importance, topic vs. subtopic, and so on) and even if you don't think about this a lot when reading a page, search engines do.

Just as the structure in Figure 8-5 would not make much sense to your visitors, it would baffle a search engine as well. That's because Heading 2 is being used in a subsection of a Heading 3 section.

Headings are a very important part of making your text more readable for your visitors. Check to see how the designer has set up headings on your pages (check the source code using your browser's View Source function). Very likely, the H1 tag is reserved for the site's title and then the page title is an H2. This means you would use H3 for the first level of headings within the text, and H4 for subheadings.

Do not use headings simply to size your text and certainly not for re-sizing a paragraph. If you want a sentence or possibly even a short paragraph to stand out, bold it. Make the sentence a separate paragraph to help it stand out. If you absolutely need the sentence larger, use the HTML mode of the editor and create your own styling using CSS, which I touch on in Lesson 28. However, in my experience, a lot of what people mean by "making things stand out" involves amateurish-looking typography. At that point, call in your designer to help you out.

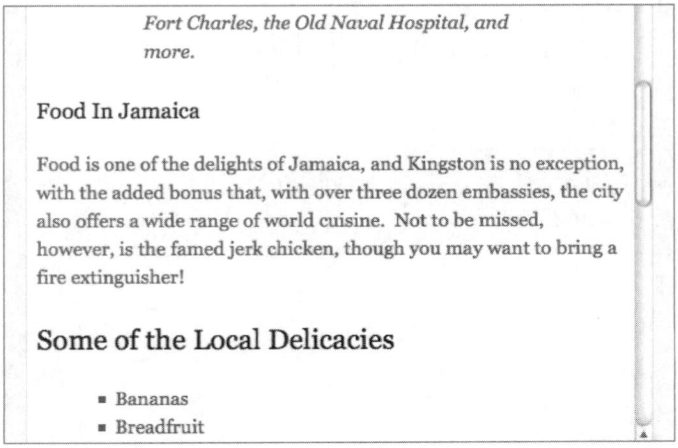
Fort Charles, the Old Naval Hospital, and
more.
Food In Jamaica
Food is one of the delights of Jamaica, and Kingston is no exception, with the added bonus that, with over three dozen embassies, the city also offers a wide range of world cuisine. Not to be missed, however, is the famed jerk chicken, though you may want to bring a fire extinguisher!
Some of the Local Delicacies
Bananas
Breadfruit

FIGURE 8-5

TRY IT

In this lesson, you create a list, remove an item, and then change it from ordered to unordered.

Lesson Requirements

A post with some existing text.

Step-by-Step

1. Make sure you're in the Visual mode of the Text Editor.
2. Go to the end of the paragraph after which you want the list to appear.
3. Hit Enter or Return and your cursor will move down as if to start a paragraph.
4. Click the ordered list button — the one with numbers next to small lines on the top row of the button bar. You should see a number 1 appear.
5. Enter the first item on your list.
6. When finished, hit Enter or Return.
7. You should now see the number 2. Enter the second item on the list.
8. Continue entering in this way until you have five items in the list. At the end of the line of the fifth item, hit Enter twice to end the list.
9. Place your cursor at the end of the third item.

10. Keep hitting the Delete key until the line disappears and all the other items in the list renumber themselves.
11. Highlight the entire list.
12. Click the unordered list button. You should see all the numbers disappear and be replaced with bullets.

> *To see some of the examples from this lesson, watch the video for Lesson 8 on the DVD with the print book, or watch online at* `www.wrox.com/go/wp24vids`.

9

Advanced Post Options

You've been looking at the most commonly used functions of the Add New Post or Edit Post screens; time now to look at the remaining functions.

The two functions from the default Post screen that I haven't covered yet are Format and Featured Image.

FORMAT

Beginning with WordPress 3.1, it's possible for theme creators to set up different formatting for different types of posts (not pages), and these are available to users through the Format meta box. If a theme does not support Post Formats, the meta box shown in Figure 9-1 won't be displayed.

FIGURE 9-1

The default WordPress theme has three Post Formats: Standard, Aside, and Gallery. By default, a new post is set to Standard, which really means there is no special post format. There are nine possible formats for theme writers to choose from — aside, chat, gallery, link, image, quote, status, video, audio — so the content of this box could vary widely from theme to theme. Figure 9-2 shows the same post in the Twenty Ten theme with no post format (top) and with a post format of aside (bottom):

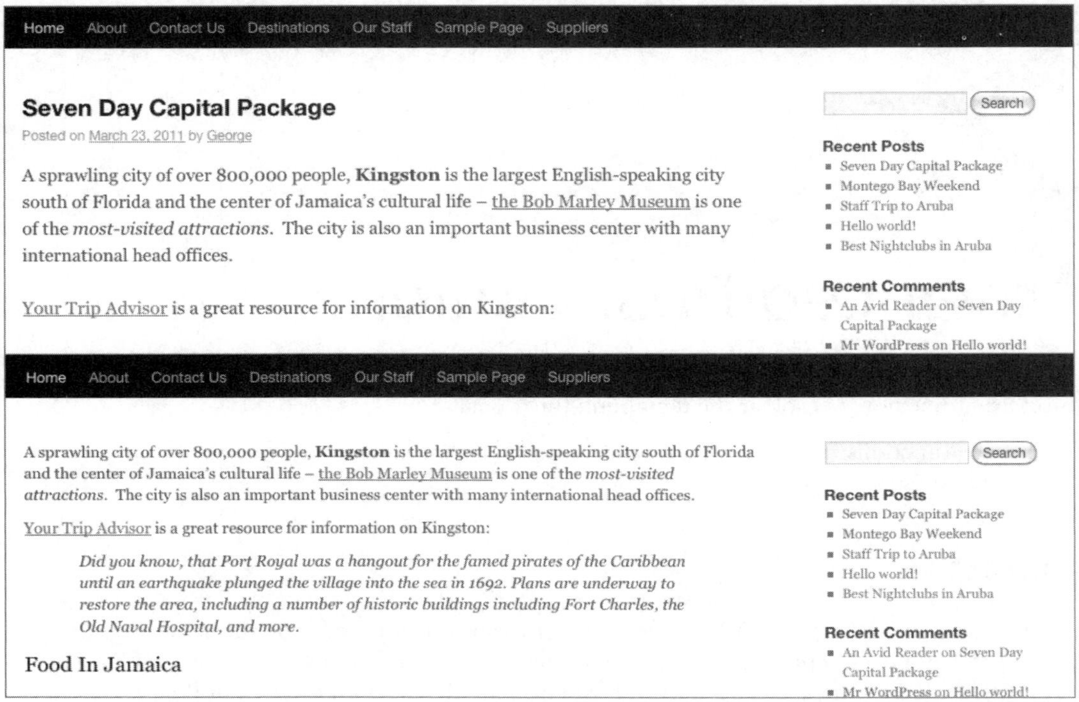
Home About Contact Us Destinations Our Staff Sample Page Suppliers
Seven Day Capital Package
Posted on March 23, 2011 by George
A sprawling city of over 800,000 people, Kingston is the largest English-speaking city south of Florida and the center of Jamaica's cultural life – the Bob Marley Museum is one of the most-visited attractions. The city is also an important business center with many international head offices.
Your Trip Advisor is a great resource for information on Kingston:
Search
Recent Posts
Seven Day Capital Package
Montego Bay Weekend
Staff Trip to Aruba
Hello world!
Best Nightclubs in Aruba
Recent Comments
An Avid Reader on Seven Day Capital Package
Mr WordPress on Hello world!
Home About Contact Us Destinations Our Staff Sample Page Suppliers
A sprawling city of over 800,000 people, Kingston is the largest English-speaking city south of Florida and the center of Jamaica's cultural life – the Bob Marley Museum is one of the most-visited attractions. The city is also an important business center with many international head offices.
Your Trip Advisor is a great resource for information on Kingston:
Did you know, that Port Royal was a hangout for the famed pirates of the Caribbean until an earthquake plunged the village into the sea in 1692. Plans are underway to restore the area, including a number of historic buildings including Fort Charles, the Old Naval Hospital, and more.
Food In Jamaica
Search
Recent Posts
Seven Day Capital Package
Montego Bay Weekend
Staff Trip to Aruba
Hello world!
Best Nightclubs in Aruba
Recent Comments
An Avid Reader on Seven Day Capital Package
Mr WordPress on Hello world!

FIGURE 9-2

The idea behind Post Formats is to try to standardize types of content that sites and blogs typically use, and make it easy for users to designate a post with that format. For example, if you set the format of a post to Aside, that designation remains no matter what theme you're using. If a theme supports that format, it will be displayed differently from other posts; if not, it displays like the rest. The next theme you choose might support Asides, so it will know to display the post differently from the others.

FEATURED IMAGE

Many themes will use this function, for example, to automatically display a thumbnail beside each post on a category page. Another use of featured images is to replace the header image with an image specific to the page. Through this meta box, users can easily change the image used by the theme.

> *It's possible you may not see a Featured Image meta box on your screen. This is not a default function in WordPress — themes have to explicitly support it.*

Clicking the Featured Image link brings up the Upload/Insert window (which I cover in detail beginning in Lesson 11), where you can choose any image in the WordPress Media Library. Simply click the Use as Featured Image link and the image appears in the Featured Image meta box, so you can quickly see what you've currently designated as the featured image, as shown in Figure 9-3.

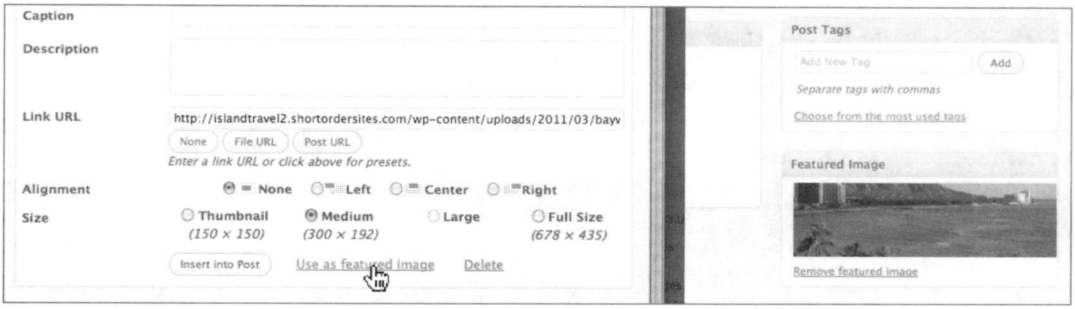

FIGURE 9-3

Keep in mind that a featured image might need to be a specific size; for example, if it's going to be used to replace a header image. Your web designer or the theme writer should make this clear to you so you'll know what you need to upload a new image.

ADDITIONAL POST BOXES

By default, WordPress shows less than half of the available meta boxes in the Add New Post screen. They can be revealed by using Screen Options and checking off the ones you want. For demonstration purposes, I've made all of them visible, and they're displayed below the Text Editor. The first set of boxes is shown in Figure 9-4.

I'll look at these meta boxes in turn, except for Send Trackbacks, which I cover in Lesson 25.

The Excerpt Box and the More Button

When you're displaying lists of posts, it's helpful to have a short summary of each, and WordPress has what I think is a very elegant system for handling short summaries of posts:

- There's the Excerpt feature, which functions automatically on all posts if a particular theme template has been configured that way. For example, the WordPress default theme's category listing pages use the Excerpt function. In such cases, if you don't put anything in the Excerpt meta box, by default, the system uses the first 55 words of the post. That figure can be changed by theme authors, so, for example, the Twenty Ten theme only uses 40 words.
- There's the More button, which allows you to control each post individually and decide whether the full text is displayed or only a portion of it along with a text link to the full text (the default text link is "More..." but this can be changed by theme authors — in the case of Twenty Ten, it says "Continue Reading"). This works only if the Excerpt function is not being used by the theme for a particular page: for example, the default homepage in the default WordPress theme.

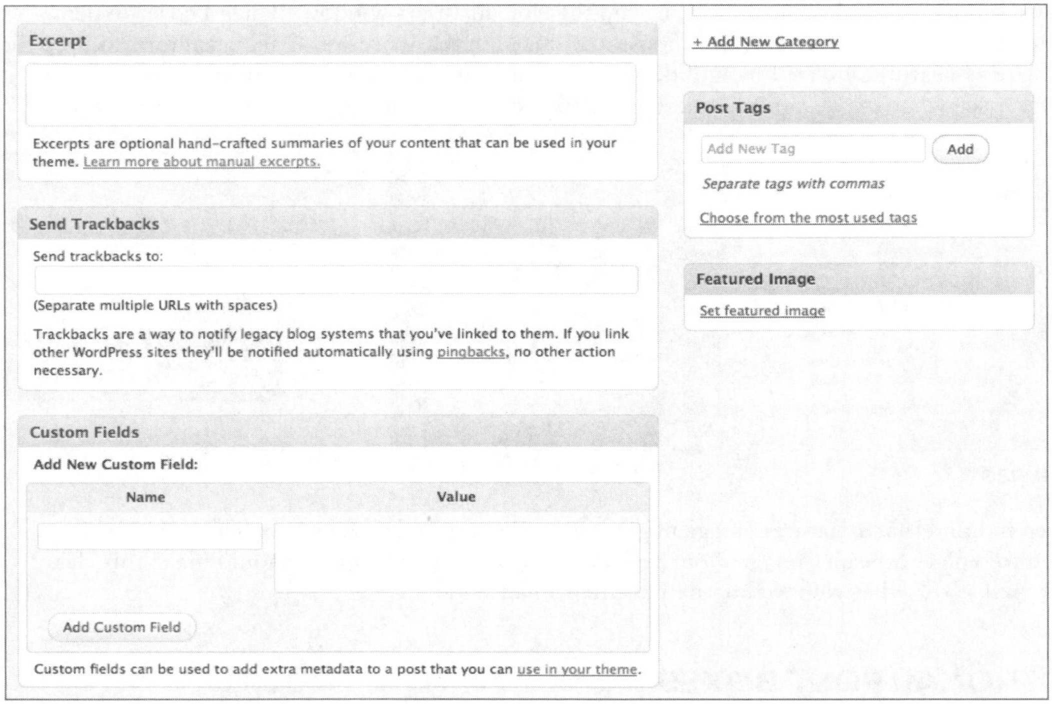
Excerpt
Excerpts are optional hand-crafted summaries of your content that can be used in your theme. Learn more about manual excerpts.
Send Trackbacks
Send trackbacks to:
(Separate multiple URLs with spaces)
Trackbacks are a way to notify legacy blog systems that you've linked to them. If you link other WordPress sites they'll be notified automatically using pingbacks, no other action necessary.
Custom Fields
Add New Custom Field:
Name
Value
Add Custom Field
Custom fields can be used to add extra metadata to a post that you can use in your theme.
+ Add New Category
Post Tags
Add New Tag
Add
Separate tags with commas
Choose from the most used tags
Featured Image
Set featured image

FIGURE 9-4

I like to use the Excerpt box because often, I find that the opening lines of a post don't always effectively summarize the post or the 55-word limit cuts things off too soon. Even if your theme doesn't currently use the Excerpt function, you might change your mind in the future or you might switch to one that does. If you've entered excerpts for posts, you won't need to go back through everything and add them in later.

Many people use the More button to create their summary because you set the length for each individual post. Simply place your cursor at the point in the text where you want WordPress to display a Continue Reading link, then click the More button. Your Text Editor changes to look like Figure 9-5.

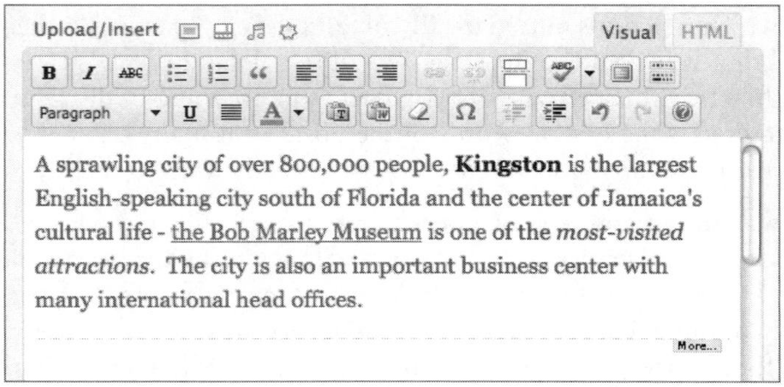
Upload/Insert
Visual
HTML
Paragraph
A sprawling city of over 800,000 people, Kingston is the largest English-speaking city south of Florida and the center of Jamaica's cultural life - the Bob Marley Museum is one of the most-visited attractions. The city is also an important business center with many international head offices.
More...

FIGURE 9-5

That line does not show up in the full text of the post — it's only there as a marker so you know where you've set it. The easiest way to get rid of the More line is to click it so that you see drag points around its edges, and then hit Delete on your keyboard. Don't click the More button or you'll just get another More line.

> *Another important difference between excerpts and the More button is that excerpts show only text, whereas the More button displays the section of the post exactly as it would normally display, with images and any HTML coding, such as bolding.*

Custom Fields

Custom Fields is a feature that allows users to create fields in the WordPress database for storing additional information. You would only be creating new fields yourself if you learned how to incorporate them into your Theme files, and though I touch on that in Lesson 39, the details of it are beyond the scope of this book.

However, you may well need to use the Custom Fields box depending on what plugins you install. Some of them will use Custom Fields, either to display information about a post or to ask you to enter information. Sometimes, a theme author will use Custom Fields and provide you with instructions on using the fields he's set.

Typically, though, you won't need to deal with the Custom Fields box at all, so it's a good candidate for leaving hidden.

The remaining set of post meta boxes is shown in Figure 9-6.

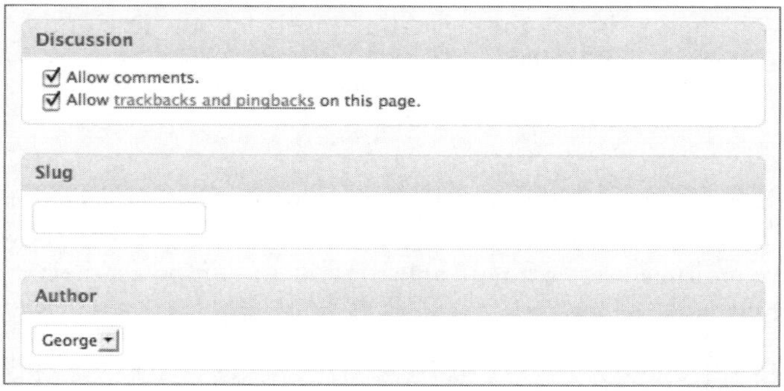

FIGURE 9-6

Discussion

The Discussion box is the place where you can override two of the site-wide parameters set under Settings ➪ Discussion: comments and trackbacks/pingbacks. By default, WordPress allows both for all posts or pages, so unless you've changed anything in Settings, both boxes will be checked.

This is a box that I tend to keep open using Screen Options because it reminds me to check whether comments are on or off for the particular post I'm working on.

> *You've probably seen blogs where it says that comments are now closed. Depending on how your theme is set up, that's the message you'll get if you uncheck the comments in the Discussion box for the post. Any comments made up to that point will continue to be displayed, but no new ones can be entered. You can also have WordPress automatically close comments after a fixed period of time — see under Settings ⇨ Discussion.*

Comments

If a post has any comments, you'll see the Comments box in Screen Options. When activated, it displays the full text of the comments for that post, and when you mouse over each, you'll see a menu allowing you to approve, reply, edit, mark as spam, or trash. This is very handy because you don't have to go to the Comments admin panel and sort through all comments to find the ones for that post.

Keep in mind that this box can get very large if you have lots of comments or long comments — another good candidate for turning off when you're not using it.

Slug

When you reveal the Slug box, you'll see the title of your post in lowercase, with dashes in place of any spaces. If you have your permalinks set to include titles in the URL, you can control that title from this box, which can be important for SEO purposes (I cover permalinks in Lesson 31).

Mostly, this is for making very long titles shorter for the post's URL. You can also make changes like that through the Edit button, which appears beside the permalink just below the title of the post, depending on how you've structured your permalinks.

Author

When beginning a new post, the Author meta box should show whatever name you've selected in your personal profile as your display name. If you haven't made any choice, the default is to show your WordPress username. If you have multiple users who are able to write or edit posts, their names will appear on this drop-down list.

In the case of the Island Travel site, for example, you might create a post for a press release and then change the author to a different staff member so they have permission to go in and edit the release. There may also be instances when you're ghostwriting an item for another user, so you change the Author drop-down to give them the credit for the post.

REVISIONS

Has this ever happened to you? You rewrite something on a web page, save it, and then discover a week later that the new information is wrong and you don't have a copy of the original. That's where WordPress's revision feature comes in handy.

You may remember that WordPress has an autosave feature that regularly saves what you're working on, but once you've published, saved, or updated a post, WordPress also starts keeping a copy of earlier versions of the post. At that point, your Screen Options menu will show a Revisions box that you can select. This displays a list of revisions at the bottom of your post, as shown in Figure 9-7.

FIGURE 9-7

The process of changing a page back to an earlier state is called *restoring* and the way to do that is to click the revision you want. If you're not sure which revision it is, don't worry, clicking here does not restore anything yet. What you get is the HTML for the earlier version of the post, as shown in Figure 9-8.

If this isn't the right version, you can look at others until you find the right one. I've trimmed the height of the screen so you can also see the bottom menu, where all the revisions are listed again. You'll see that the revision you chose has one of the radio buttons highlighted, and at the top of the list is the current version of the post, and it too has a highlighted radio button. Those highlighted buttons mean you can compare those two versions by clicking Compare Revisions. If you want to compare two different revisions, click their respective radio buttons, one in the left column and one in the right.

When you do a comparison between two revisions, you get the HTML of each one side by side with different colored backgrounds for paragraphs with differences, and the text that's different in each is highlighted in a darker color, as demonstrated in Figure 9-9.

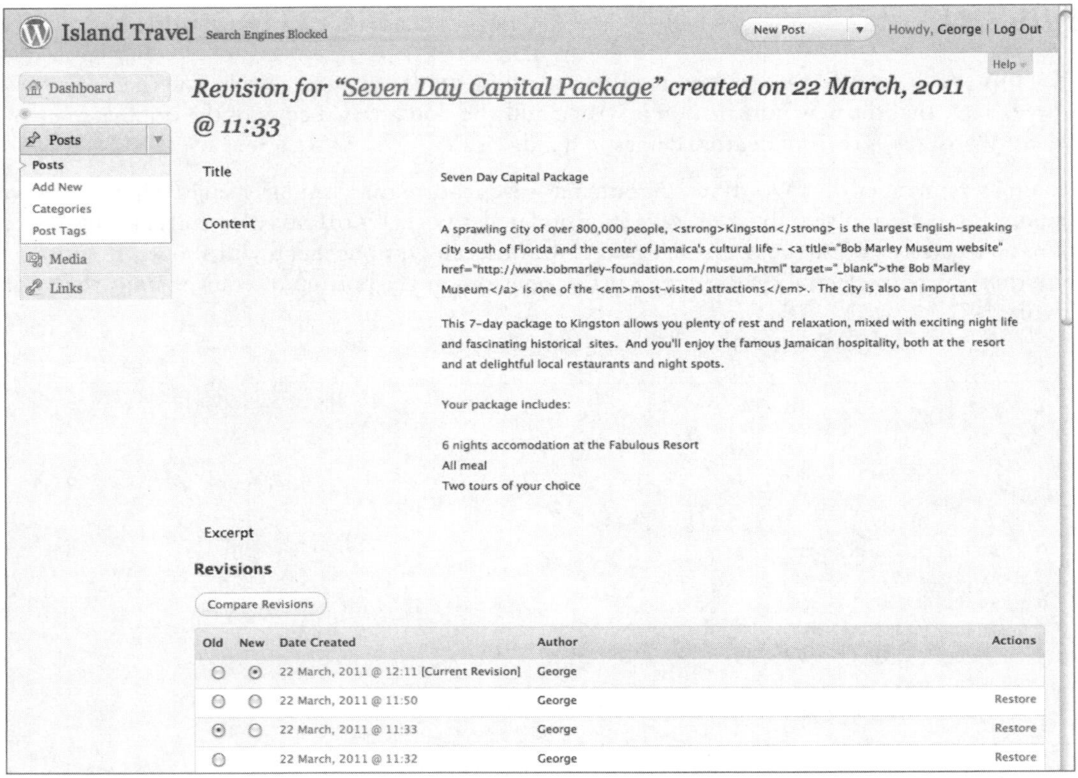

FIGURE 9-8

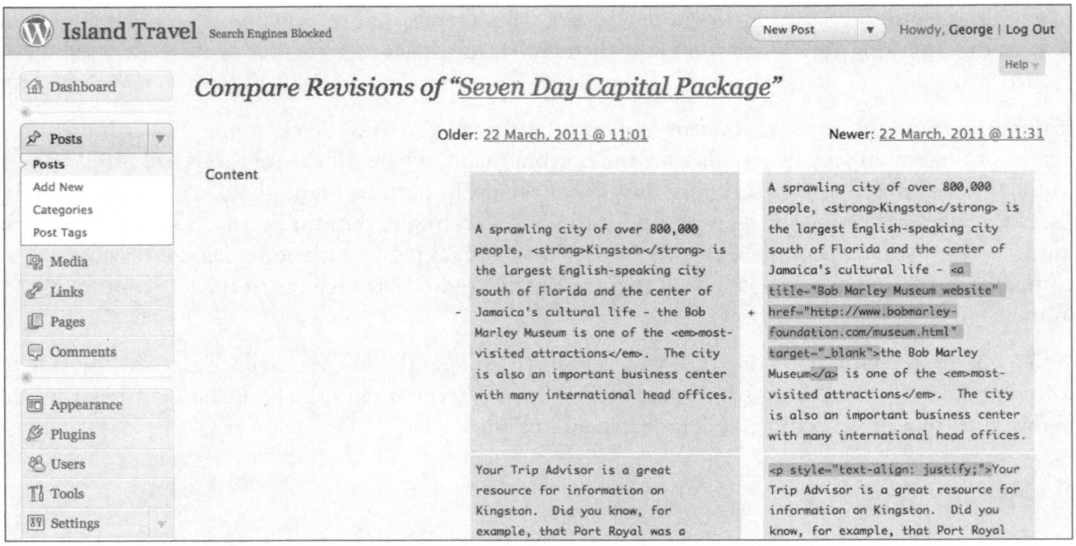

FIGURE 9-9

If you want to use a revision, simply click the Restore link to the right of the revision date. If you decide you want the current post to stay as it is, just click the date of the current post (always at the top and labeled "current") and you'll return to the Edit Post screen.

TRY IT

In this lesson, you create a "More…" breakpoint in the text of a post.

Lesson Requirements

A post with at least three or four paragraphs of text.

Step-by-Step

1. Make sure you're in the Visual mode of the Text Editor.
2. Place your cursor where you'd like the summary to end, but at least five sentences into the post.
3. Click the More button on the top row of the button bar.
4. A line with the word "More" should appear where your cursor is.
5. Click Update Post.
6. Navigate to the homepage of your site if it displays your posts, or if you've set a specific page to display blog posts, go there.
7. Find the post you worked on. You should see a link with the words Continue Reading at the point where you put your More tag. You should also see any images or links that you may have within that text.
8. Click Continue Reading to test that you're taken to the full version of the post.

> *To see some of the examples from this lesson, watch the video for Lesson 9 on the DVD with the print book, or watch online at* `www.wrox.com/go/wp24vids`.

10

Adding a New Page

Virtually everything covered so far about writing content applies to both posts and pages in WordPress. I've also covered the key functions unique to posts, such as categories and tags. Now, in this lesson, it's time to cover the functions unique to WordPress pages.

PAGES VS. POSTS

A detailed discussion of when to use posts and when to use pages was covered in Lesson 1, but it's worth reviewing the key points.

Posts tend to be numerous short pieces of information that could be grouped in many different ways. In the case of Island Travel, people's testimonials are short and can be about several different topics at one time, and there are (hopefully) lots of them. Countries in the Caribbean are limited in number, have a lot of relatively static information, and, for our purposes at least, require only one designation — countries or destinations. That makes them good candidates for WordPress pages.

You know already that categories, tags, and formats apply only to posts, so let's look at what's unique to pages.

THE ADD NEW PAGE OPTIONS

The default Add New Page screen does not look much different from Add New Post, as you can see from Figure 10-1.

As with Add New Post, the default screen doesn't show all of the meta boxes available, but for pages, there are fewer choices: Custom Fields, Discussion, Comments, Slug, Author, and Revisions. These all work exactly the same way as for posts, so I'll just cover the Page Attributes box, which has three functions.

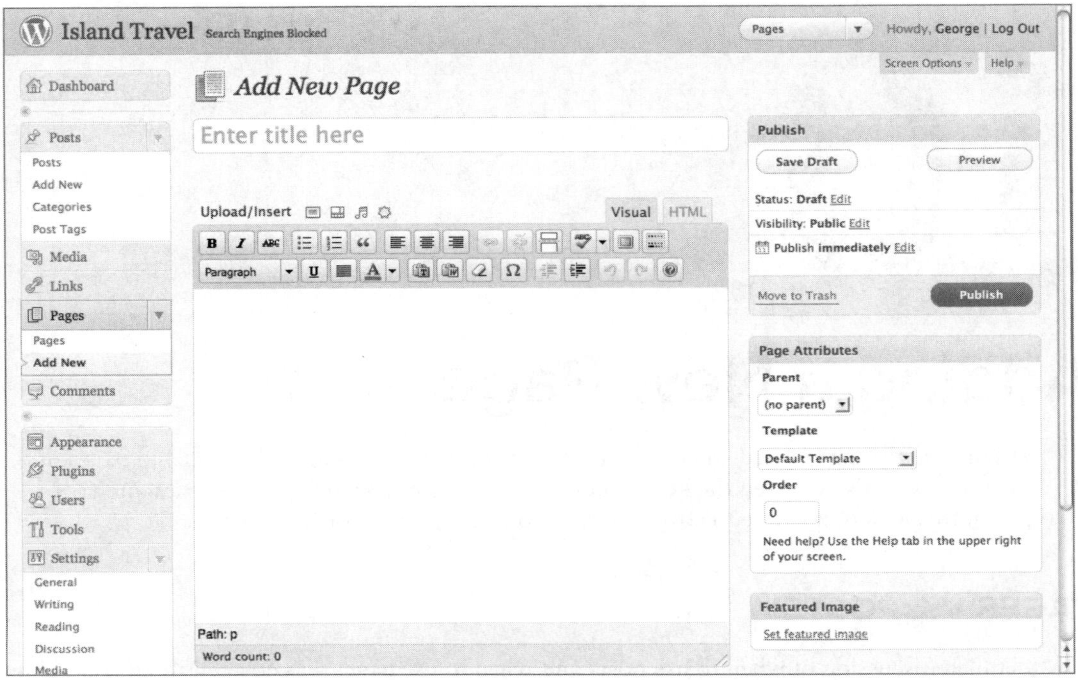

FIGURE 10-1

PARENT

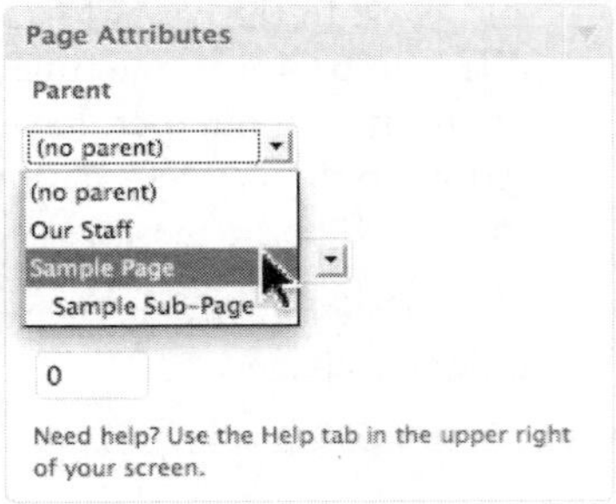

FIGURE 10-2

The first option in the Page Attributes meta box is the Parent drop-down menu, shown in Figure 10-2. It displays a list of all published pages on your site (drafts are not included), allowing you to make this new page a child of any one of them. A child is just another way of saying a sub-page. By default, any new page is a top-level parent: that is, it isn't the child of any other page.

As you can see from this, some of the pages on the drop-down are shown with an indent. That means they're sub-pages of the first flush-left page above them. In a very complex Web setup, you could have sub-pages of sub-pages, as deeply nested as you need.

You can change the relationship of a page to other pages at any time by using this same drop-down menu while editing the page.

Creating sub-page relationships is useful in a number of ways, even if it's just to keep the relationships clear in your own mind. But remember that you're not tied to that relationship when it comes to WordPress's menu system. You can create sub-pages on a menu independently of the relationship you designate in the Parent box. In fact, you can make anything a submenu item of anything else. I cover that in detail in Lesson 21.

TEMPLATE

The next option is the Template menu. This displays all the page templates available for the theme you're currently using (which could be none or dozens). For the default theme, the drop-down looks like Figure 10-3.

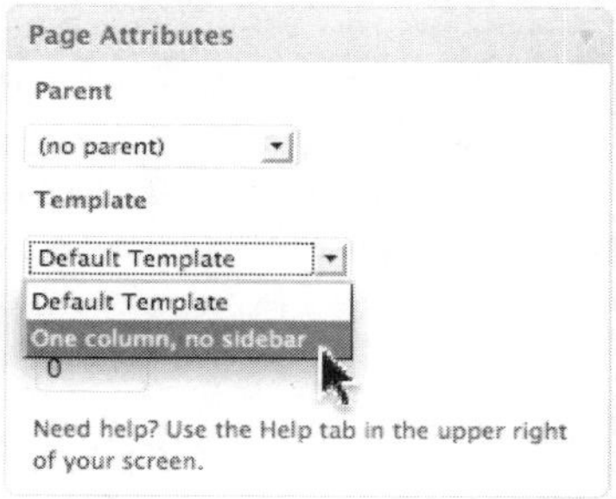

FIGURE 10-3

Page templates have layouts that differ from the default page layout as much as the theme developer likes. In the case of the default theme, for example, the One Column, No Sidebar template removes the right sidebar and displays content across the full width of the page. Templates are extremely powerful tools. For example, you could have different templates for different areas of your site or have templates that pull in content from another site (Island Travel could show a reservations system run by a third party).

ORDER

Below the Template menu is the Order input box. This can be used to control the order of pages if you use the default menu. WordPress normally orders pages alphabetically according to their titles, but this Order box will override that. However, if your theme uses the WordPress menu system, this Order won't have any effect.

TRY IT

In this lesson, you practice making a new page a child of an existing page.

Lesson Requirements

At least one page already in the system.

Step-by-Step

1. Click Add New on the Page area of the Admin menu.
2. Enter a title and then some text.
3. In the Attributes box, drop down the Parent menu.
4. Choose a page to be the parent of your new page.
5. Click Publish.
6. Refresh the homepage on your live site and see how the page menu looks — you should see your new sub-page.

> *To see some of the examples from this lesson, watch the video for Lesson 10 on the DVD with the print book, or watch online at* `www.wrox.com/go/wp24vids`.

SECTION IV
Working with Media Content

11

The Basics of Handling Media Files

Up to now, you've learned about entering, editing, styling, and laying out text content. In this lesson, you begin the same process for media files, which primarily means images, but also includes video, audio, and documents. I start with the basics of uploading and inserting an image into a post and then take a brief look at how WordPress stores it along with other media files.

THE UPLOAD/INSERT MENU

There are several points within the WordPress admin screen where you can upload images and other media files, as shown in Figure 11-1.

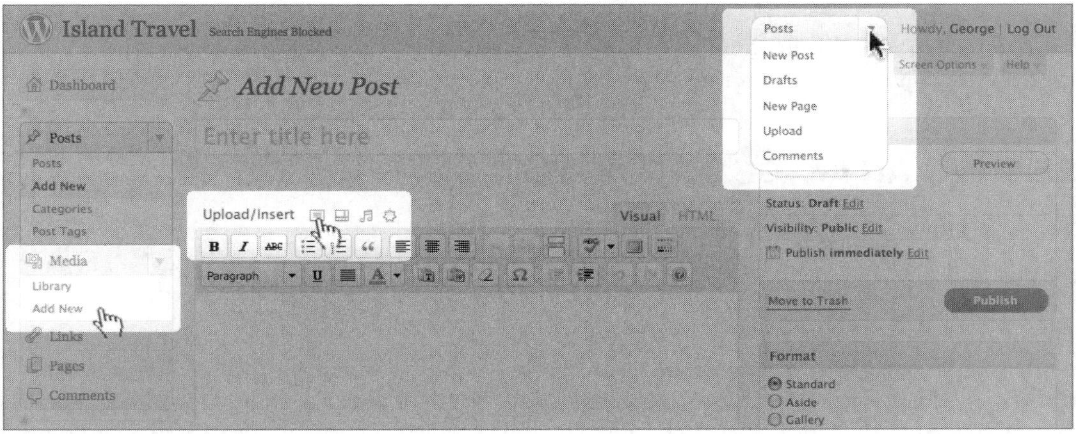

FIGURE 11-1

- The Add New link in the Media section of the side menu
- The Upload link on the Shortcut menu at the top right
- The Upload/Insert menu at the top left of the Text Editor

Typically, you'll be using the Upload/Insert menu when creating posts and pages, so I'll use it to illustrate the basics of uploading an image.

The title of this menu is important because it's a reminder that it fulfills two functions, both of which are completely separate:

- Uploading media files
- Inserting media files into posts

You can upload media files and not insert them into the post, and you can insert media files that were previously uploaded.

Figure 11-2 shows a close-up of the menu.

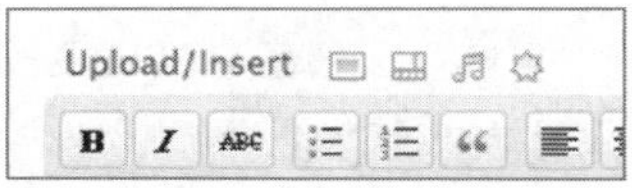

FIGURE 11-2

The four icons represent four types of media files. From left to right (with examples of file types), they are:

- Images (photos, graphics — jpg, gif, png)
- Video (swf, mp4, wmv, avi, mov, and so on)
- Audio (mp3, ram, and so on)
- Media (doc, ppt, xls, zip, and so on)

If you forget which is which, just mouse over one and you'll see the name of it.

Click any of these icons and you get a popup screen where you perform the upload or insert functions. I go into all the details of that screen in Lessons 12 and 13. For the moment, I want to show you the basic steps for getting an image into a post.

INSERTING AN IMAGE INTO A POST

The most common way you'll add images is when you're working on a post, so here's how you upload a photo as part of a post about a vacation package on the Island Travel site. You begin by locating the Add an Image icon of the Upload/Insert menu. Clicking that icon produces the popup window in Figure 11-3.

Notice the menu at the very top of the screen. It has the various locations from which you can obtain your image: From Computer, From URL, and Media Library. If at least one item had already been uploaded to this post, a fourth option would be visible: Gallery. In this case, the photo is on the computer, so you can use the default From Computer tab.

Click the Select Files button and up pops a browse window showing the hard drive. Locate the image you want, highlight it, and click the Open button (or whatever your system displays), as shown in Figure 11-4.

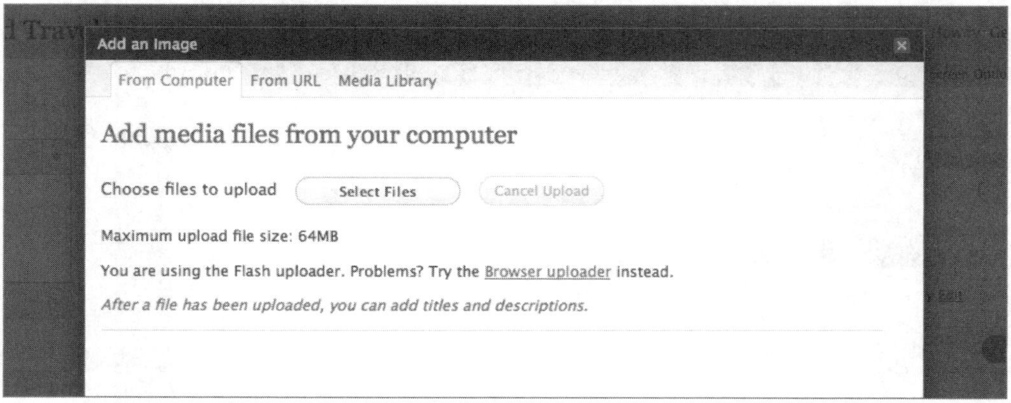

FIGURE 11-3

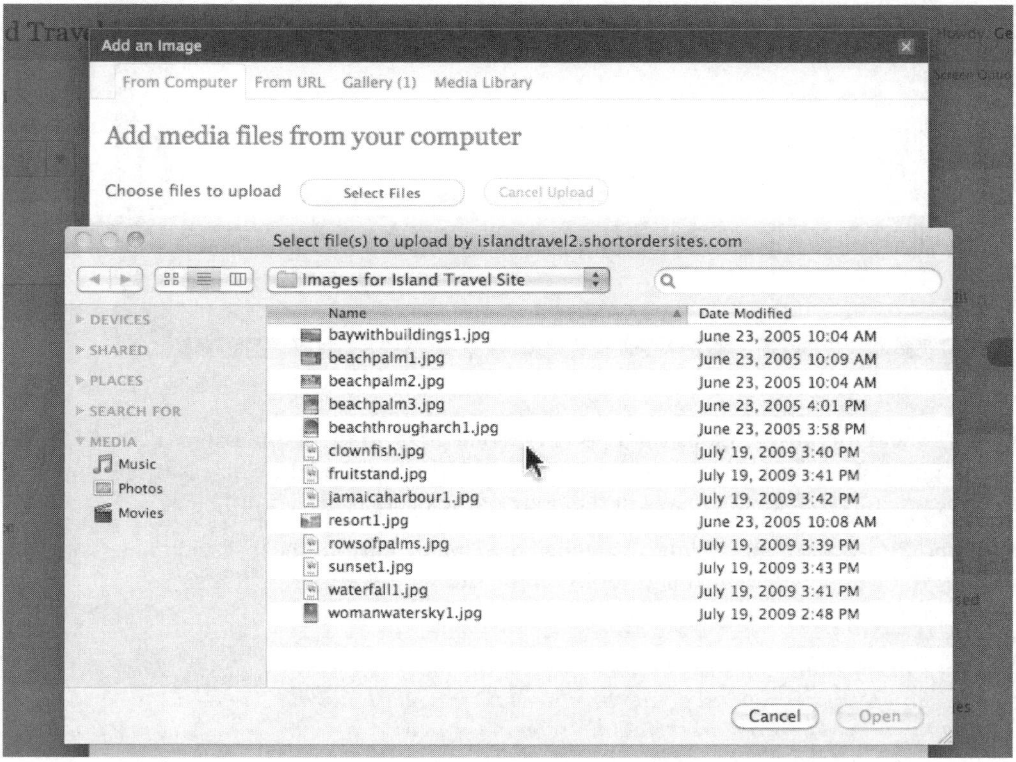

FIGURE 11-4

At that point, the browse window disappears and WordPress displays a progress bar for the uploading of the image. Depending on the size of the image, it could take a little while. When it's finished, you see a thumbnail of the image with a whole lot of options, as shown in Figure 11-5 (you'll probably need to scroll to see all this, depending on the size of your screen).

FIGURE 11-5

Don't worry about all those options right now (I'll come back to them in Lessons 12 and 13). What you're looking for is the Insert Into Post button down at the bottom left. Click that, the popup window disappears, and you see the image in the body of the post, as in Figure 11-6.

You're still not finished, though. Unless you click the Update button, the inserted image won't be saved. Now, you can see how the image looks on the site.

You can, of course, use the Preview button to view changes on your site, but I much prefer to keep a separate browser tab open with my live site — it saves having to load and reload the admin screen. Of course, if your post is still just a draft, you'll need to use the Preview button.

Seven Day Capital Package
Permalink: http://islandtravel2.shortordersites.com/?p=17
Change Permalinks
Upload/Insert
Visual
HTML
Paragraph
A sprawling city of over 800,000 people, Kingston is the largest English-speaking city south of Florida and the center of Jamaica's cultural life - the Bob Marley Museum is one of the most-visited attractions. The city is also an important business center with many international head offices.

FIGURE 11-6

THE MEDIA LIBRARY VS. GALLERIES

As I mentioned, once you upload at least one media file to a post or page, you'll see a tab on the Upload/Insert menu called Gallery. The relationship between these Galleries and the Media Library takes a little getting used to, but once you understand it, you'll see what a powerful system they form. The key to it all is where and when you upload a media file into WordPress.

Let's start with the Media Library. Essentially, it's a list of every single media file you upload to WordPress. You can use these files over and over again by accessing the library at any time. You can upload files directly into the Media Library, but more often than not, they're uploaded while working on a specific post (and that includes pages). When that happens, the media file becomes "attached" to the Gallery of that post. You can still access the file through the Media Library and use it as much as you want in other places, but there's a special relationship to that initial post. Another way to think of this is that *all media files are part of the Media Library, but a media file isn't necessarily attached to a Gallery.*

You have several ways to attach a media file to a post's Gallery:

- By uploading it into WordPress through the Upload/Insert menu for that post.
- By having its first insertion from the Media Library made into that post.
- By selecting the post using the Attach function in the Media Library (see Lesson 19).

So, what exactly does "attached" mean? It's a status used by WordPress as well as plugins and themes to automatically use images in a certain way.

The most common of these — and where the name Gallery comes from — is the built-in gallery function of WordPress. I cover this in detail in Lesson 15, but the idea is that you can instantly create an image gallery for a post by clicking a button. WordPress then uses whatever images are listed in the Gallery for that post. What's really handy is that once you've inserted the image gallery, it continues to automatically pick up any new images you attach to the post (through any of those three methods listed previously).

Attached images could also be used by a plugin or theme writer to create a revolving slide show, for example. Just like WordPress's built-in Galleries, the slideshow script would look for whatever images are attached to the post and insert them as needed. All you have to do as a user is upload images to the post or attach them from the Media Library.

Understanding the relationship between the Media Library and Galleries will not only help you think of ways to use media files in WordPress, but it will help avoid two common confusions:

> *I inserted a photo into a post but it doesn't show up in that post's Gallery.*
>
> That's because you "borrowed" an image from the Media Library that had already been inserted into at least one other post, so it's permanently attached to some other post.
>
> *I uploaded an image to a post for a particular use and now it's also showing up in the image gallery I created for that post.*
>
> Any image you upload to a post becomes part of any image gallery in the body of the post. If you don't want this new image in the image gallery, you will need to upload it to the Media Library instead, attach it to some other post first, and then insert it into the post you're dealing with. Or there is a special kind of coding you can use — called *shortcode* — and I cover that in Lesson 15.

TRY IT

Rather than doing exactly what I did in this lesson, try uploading an image to the Media Library first, and then inserting it into a post.

Lesson Requirements

A post with text.

Step-by-Step

1. Find the Add New link under the Media section of the admin menu and click it.
2. Click Select Files.
3. In the popup window, choose the file to upload and click Select. You should see a progress bar for the upload. When the upload is complete, you'll see a series of options.
4. Fill in any of the fields you choose.

5. Click Save All Changes.
6. Navigate to the post where you want to insert the image.
7. Click the Image icon of the Upload/Insert menu.
8. Click Media Library.
9. Locate the image you just uploaded and click Show.
10. Click Insert Into Post. You should see your image in the body of the post.

> *To see some of the examples from this lesson, watch the video for Lesson 11 on the DVD with the print book, or watch online at* `www.wrox.com/go/wp24vids`.

12

The Upload/Insert Window Tabs

When you click any of the four icons on the Upload/Insert menu and the window pops up, you see tabs at the top of the window, and in this lesson, you learn the details of using each. Briefly, here's what they do in order, from left to right:

- **From Computer:** This is for uploading media files from your computer.
- **From URL:** This is for creating links to media files elsewhere on the Web.
- **Gallery:** This displays a list of every media file (not just images) that is attached to this post. That is, they were either uploaded through this post, or attached to it through the Media Library. This Gallery tab is also used to insert a thumbnail list of all images (what I'm calling an "image gallery") into the post.
- **Media Library:** This is for inserting any files listed in your Media Library.

The following sections cover each of these tabs in some detail.

THE FROM COMPUTER TAB

Because the From Computer tab is the one you'll use the most, and it's the default tab when the window opens, let's start with it, as shown in Figure 12-1.

You're told to Choose Files to Upload and the good news is that it really does mean files, so you can process many files at one time instead of having to choose them one by one.

After locating your file and clicking the Upload button, you'll see a progress bar telling you that WordPress is "crunching" the file. I'll explain later what that means. If you're uploading several files at once, each will have its own progress bar running simultaneously. And if you're uploading really large files, the process can, of course, take quite a while.

> *There's a warning message stating that the WordPress uploader, which uses Flash, may not work with some browsers, and a link is provided to an alternative Browser Uploader. So, if you don't see a Choose button, just click the browser link and you'll get a regular upload function — only you'll have to do it one file at a time.*

What you see after uploading is finished depends on whether you're uploading multiple files or just one. If it's several files, you'll see a thumbnail for each file with a Show link, as illustrated in Figure 12-2.

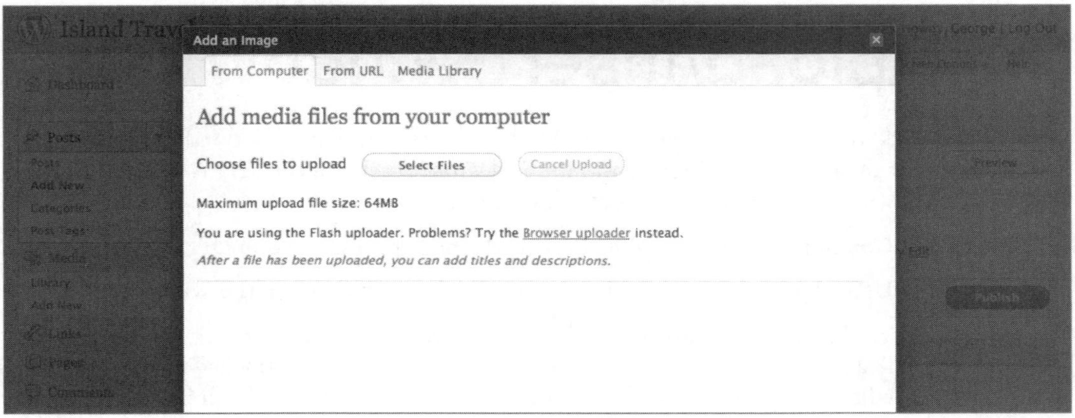

FIGURE 12-1

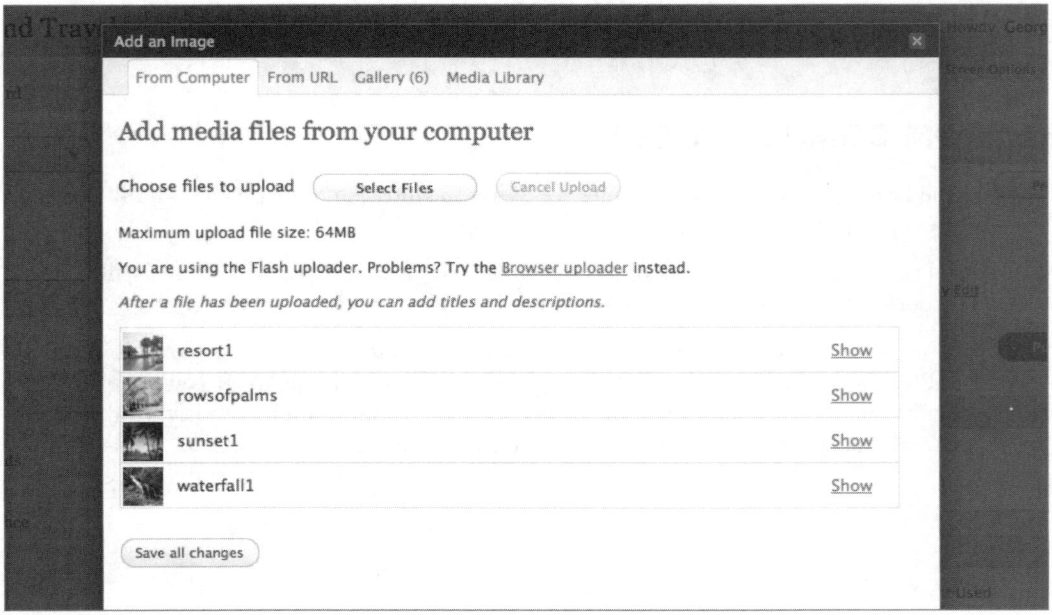

FIGURE 12-2

If you're uploading just one file, you'll get a larger thumbnail and a whole series of options (the ones you would see if you clicked the Show link for multiple files). These options will vary depending on the type of media file you're uploading. I cover the options for images in Lesson 13, and the others I cover when I'm talking about that particular file type.

The one option shared by all screens is the ability to either insert the file into your post or save it for future use.

THE FROM URL TAB

This is the place to insert media files that are located somewhere else on the Internet. You may want to use this option in cases where you run multiple websites and have an image or document common to all, so you simply use the URL on all the sites. Another example is when a company whose product you're selling provides you with a URL to an image of the product — this is where you'd insert that URL.

As you can see in Figure 12-3, unlike the From Computer tab, you're presented with all the options right up front.

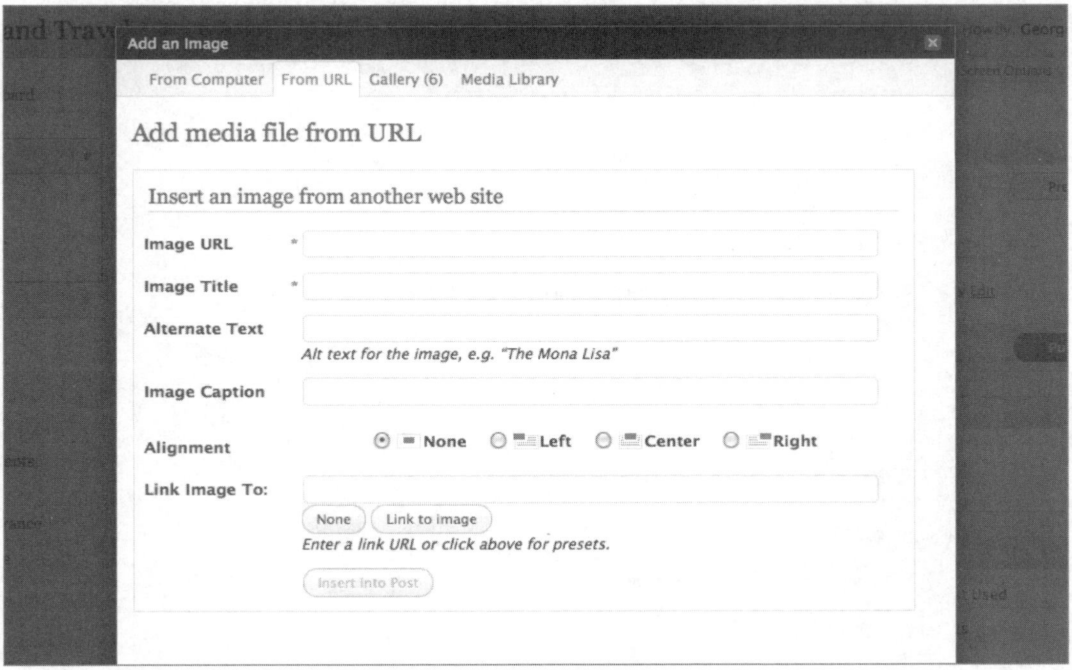

FIGURE 12-3

> *You can't just start grabbing images from anywhere — you need to have permission to use the image, not just for copyright reasons, but because you'll be using their server's bandwidth to load the image every time someone views that page.*

Notice that the title says Add Media File from URL and the options say Image. The reason for that is you'll have different options in the From URL tab depending on which icon you chose from the Upload/Insert menu. In this case, I had chosen the image icon.

I cover the details of each type of option in the lesson for that particular media type, but there is one option that's the same on all From URL tabs, and that's the URL box — in fact, it's a required field.

You'll need the full URL for the media file in a form like this: `http://www.somedomain.com/folder/filename.extension`. (The extension is the .jpg, .avi, .pdf, and so on.)

Type or paste that URL into the URL box. As soon as you move your cursor off that box, you'll see a tiny spinning graphic to the left of the URL box. If WordPress successfully locates the file, you'll see a green check mark — if not, you'll see a red X after a certain amount of trying. An example of each is shown in Figure 12-4.

If you get the red X, you'll need to make sure you typed in the URL correctly (that's why I prefer to copy and paste) or that you've actually copied the right URL.

> *You can usually get the URL by right-clicking an image, .pdf, video, or other media file and selecting Copy Image Location (Firefox), or Properties and then highlighting the URL and copying it (Internet Explorer).*

Add media file from URL

Insert an image from another web site

Image URL	✖	ndtravel.shortordersites.com/wp-content/uploads/2011/03/thebuilding.jpg
Image Title	*	
Alternate Text		
		Alt text for the image, e.g. "The Mona Lisa"

Add media file from URL

Insert an image from another web site

Image URL	✔	el.shortordersites.com/wp-content/uploads/2009/07/baywithbuildings1.jpg
Image Title	*	View from Port Royal
Alternate Text		
		Alt text for the image, e.g. "The Mona Lisa"

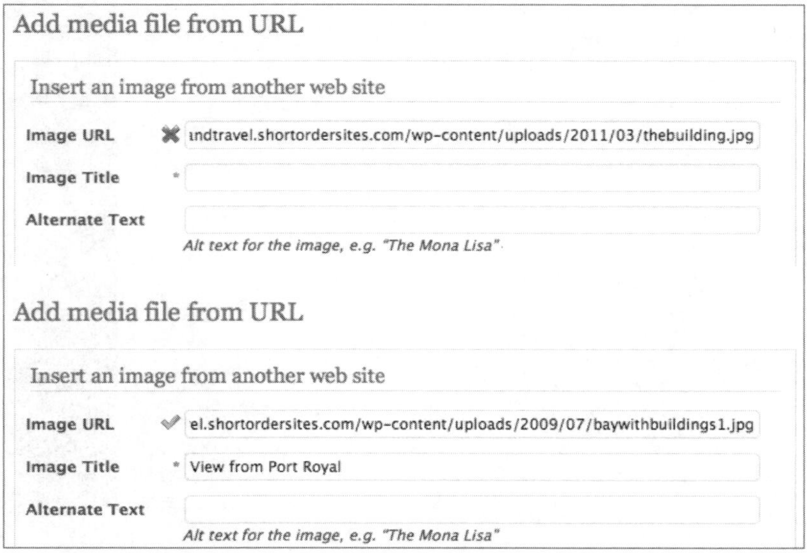

FIGURE 12-4

The other option that all From URL tabs share is the Insert Into Post button. It will remain grayed out until WordPress has confirmed the existence of the file and given you the green check mark. At that point, you can do the insert. There's no Save function because you can't put these files into the Gallery or the Media Library.

> *Keep in mind that if you don't have control over the URL where the file is located, it could disappear in the future without warning, so you'll need to keep an eye on such files so your visitors aren't left with broken images/links.*

THE GALLERY TAB

You will not always see a Gallery tab when you click a button on the Upload/Insert menu — only if there is at least one item already in the Gallery. The number in the bracket on the tab title is the total number of media files in the post's Gallery — that's all media files, not just images.

Figure 12-5 shows an example of the screen you get when you click the Gallery tab.

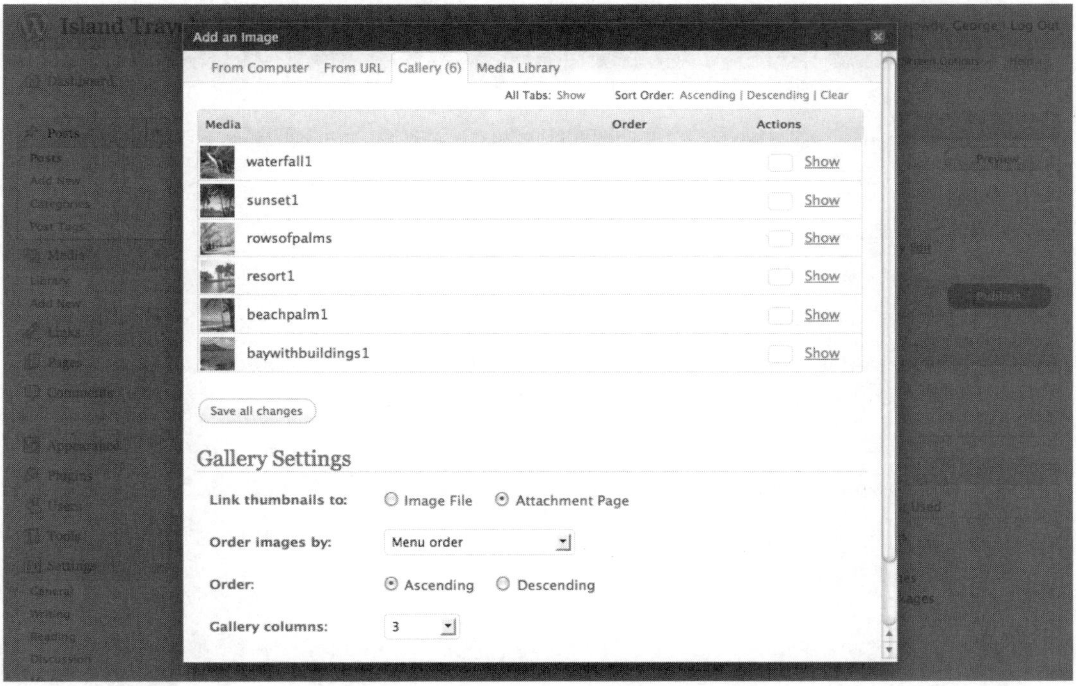

FIGURE 12-5

If you have more than one image, a Gallery Settings area will display at the bottom. That's where you create image galleries for your posts, and I deal with them in Lesson 15. Right now, I'm focused on the top area, which, as I said, displays all media, not just images.

On the left-hand side, you'll see image thumbnails or icons representing other types of media files. On the right of each file is a Show link. Clicking that reveals all the options for the particular type of file, including the option to insert the file into the post. While the options are displayed, this link will say Hide — click it to hide the options.

There's also the option at the top of the screen called All Tabs: Show, and by clicking that, you'll open the options for all files at one time. Just click Hide to close them all again.

Next to All Tabs is a small menu called Sort Order and this is part of how you control the order of images when you've inserted an image gallery into a post, so you don't need to worry about it at this point.

THE MEDIA LIBRARY TAB

What you get in this tab is a quickie version of what you would see under Media ➪ Library in the main admin menu. It allows you to see every media file that's been uploaded to your site and use any of them in the post you're working on. An example is shown in Figure 12-6.

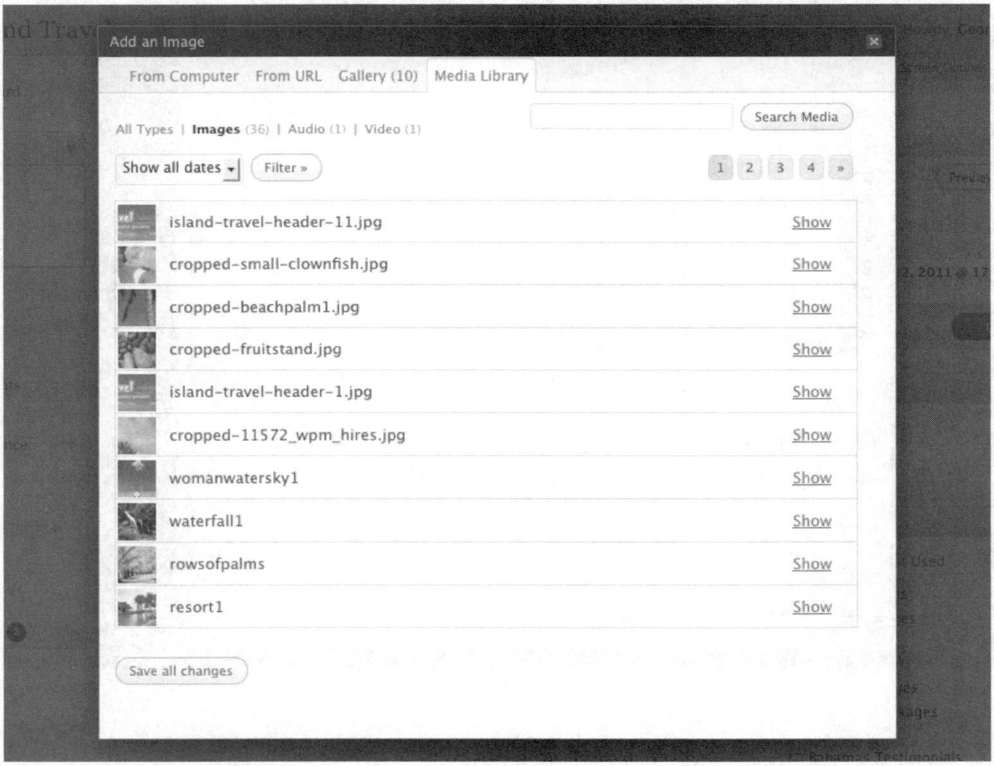

FIGURE 12-6

As you can see, it's very similar to the Gallery tab, with the thumbnails on the left and the Show link on the right. If there are more than 10 items in the library, you'll see pagination at the top right, allowing you to navigate through numerous screens of file listings.

Most of the time, you'll be working with images and, if you click the Media Library tab, you might wonder where all your PDFs or other media files have gone. That's because by default, WordPress shows you only the file type you're working on. You need to click All Types at the top right of the Media Library tab to see every file in the library.

From this tab, you can not only insert a media file into your post, but also change the options on those files whether or not you're inserting them. Whether you change the options on one or more files, be sure to click Save Changes at the bottom left. It may or may not be visible depending on the height of your screen, so you may need to scroll down to see it.

I've been talking here about the Media Library tab, but in Lesson 19, I cover the Media Library itself, which you access from the admin menu.

TRY IT

In this lesson, you practice inserting an image into a post using the From URL tab.

Lesson Requirements

An existing post and an image that's live on your website (if you have permission to use an image from another site, great). The goal is to use a URL for the image, so the simplest thing is to use one from your own site.

Step-by-Step

1. Open a post for editing.
2. Click the image icon of the Upload/Insert menu.
3. Click From URL.
4. In a separate tab of your browser, find the page with the image you want to insert.
5. Right-click the image and choose View Image or Show Picture — if neither is available, choose Properties and highlight the URL in the popup window.

6. If View Image or Show Picture works, you'll see the image by itself in your browser — copy the URL in the address bar.
7. Paste the address for the image into the Image URL field.
8. Click the Image Title or any other field. A small, spinning circle displays beside Image URL, indicating it's checking that your image is where you say it is.
9. If the image is found, you'll see a green check mark.
10. If the image is not found, you'll see a red X.
11. Assuming you get a check mark, you can finish entering information, like the Alternate Text — this is what people see if there is no image and is used by search engines.
12. Enter a Caption if you want one to appear in the post.
13. Alignment is the position of the image relative to the text around it — you can choose from None, Left, Center, and Right.
14. If you want the image to link somewhere, enter that URL in the Link Image To field.
15. Click Insert Into Post.
16. Click Preview to see the image in your post.

> *To see some of the examples from this lesson, watch the video for Lesson 12 on the DVD with the print book, or watch online at* `www.wrox.com/go/wp24vids`.

13

Image Options in Detail

When I showed you the procedure for uploading and inserting an image into a post, you briefly saw the options screen for the image, and I talked about some of the choices you could make. This lesson examines those options in detail.

TEXT THAT ACCOMPANIES IMAGES

WordPress makes it easy to add various types of text to your image — shown in Figure 13-1 — each of which serves a particular function.

Title

WordPress automatically gives images a title, using the name of the file minus its extension (.jpg, .gif, and so on). If this default title does not look exactly like the name of the file you uploaded, that's because WordPress cleans up names by stripping them of spaces, changing upper- to lowercase, and adding numbers if there's a file of that name already in the system.

You don't have to change this default title, but it makes a lot of sense because it's the wording that will show up when people mouse over the image. Also, some image gallery plugins will use this as a title. Besides, six months later when you're looking through the Media Library, you'll appreciate "Sailboat off Cape Cod" much more than "img000534."

> *If it's able, WordPress automatically extracts some of the data embedded in digital images (aperture, shutter speed, and so on) and stores it in its database. If your image has an embedded title and caption, they'll be displayed in their respective fields onscreen, shown in Figure 13-1. The other data may be used by plugins or you could make use of it through customized theme files.*

FIGURE 13-1

Alternate Text

This is what's known as ALT text and it's very important for telling visually impaired visitors what's in an image. Search engines also use this ALT text as one of the factors for determining what a page is about. For both these reasons, it's important not only to give your image some ALT text, but also to make sure its description of the image is accurate and uses keywords relating to the page's content — if appropriate (don't try stacking your ALT tags with keywords). I cover this search engine angle further in Lesson 30.

Caption

As the name suggests, any text entered here automatically displays as a caption when you insert an image into a post, or beneath the thumbnail when you insert an image gallery. Figure 13-2 shows the actual placement of the caption in a published post and a common way of styling it (this will vary depending on your theme's style sheet).

Captions function very differently depending on whether you're inserting an image into a post or using it in a post image gallery. Inserted images have the caption inserted into the HTML as well — in other words, even if you erased the Caption field in the image's listing in the Gallery tab of the Upload/Insert window, it would still display with the inserted image. But if you were to now insert that same image into another post, it wouldn't have the caption because you erased it from the Caption field.

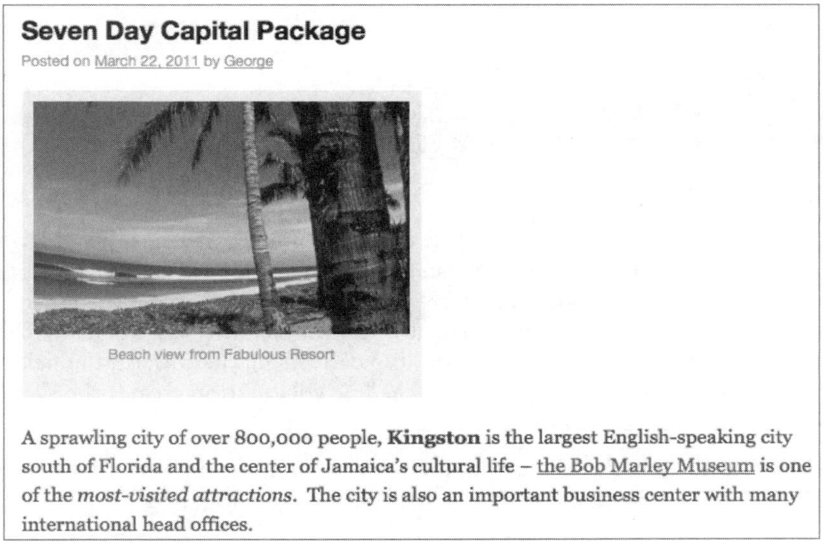

Seven Day Capital Package
Posted on March 22, 2011 by George
Beach view from Fabulous Resort
A sprawling city of over 800,000 people, Kingston is the largest English-speaking city south of Florida and the center of Jamaica's cultural life – the Bob Marley Museum is one of the most-visited attractions. The city is also an important business center with many international head offices.

FIGURE 13-2

If you insert an image gallery into a post, however, any captions are taken directly from the Caption field, not embedded into the HTML. So, if you clear an image's Caption field in the Gallery window, it will disappear from the image gallery that's inserted in the post.

Description

This setting allows you to provide a lot more detail about the file. Whether or not the description gets used will depend on your theme. Even if your theme doesn't currently make use of descriptions, you might want them later if you customize WordPress, so if you have time, enter a description when you upload/insert the image.

OTHER IMAGE OPTIONS

The rest of the options on this screen deal with parameters, other than describing the content of the image.

Link URL

By default, the Link URL field, shown in Figure 13-3, contains a link to the full-size version of the image.

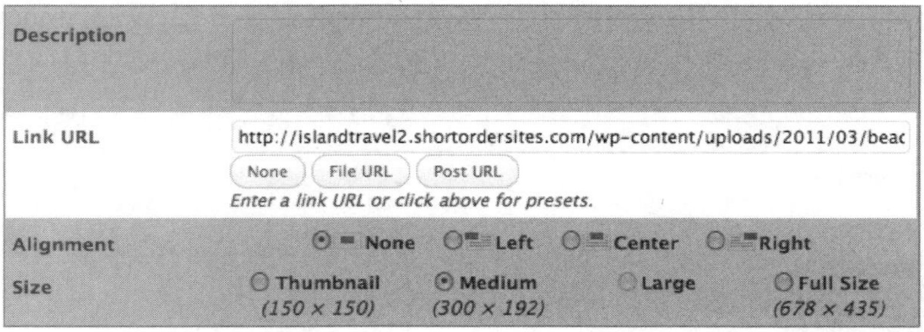

FIGURE 13-3

You can change this default either by using one of the three preset buttons provided, or by entering any URL you choose. The first of the preset buttons, None, gets rid of any URL whatsoever. The Post URL button creates a link to a separate web page displaying the image (complete with your header and footer, as opposed to simply showing the image by itself in the browser). Some themes have distinct template files for creating these separate pages (typically using the Description field from above) or you could have one created for your theme. The File URL button creates the same link as the default — a link to the full-size version of the image.

However, you're not limited to these presets. You could, for example, put in a link to a related page on your site or some other site, or you could put in a link that takes visitors to a PDF.

> *WordPress remembers how you configured the last image, and if you chose a link option, it does the same again for the new image, so it may not always show the default link to the original image.*

Alignment

I briefly mentioned choosing an alignment option for an image in the Step-by-Step section of Lesson 12, but Figure 13-4 provides a quick reminder of what those options look like.

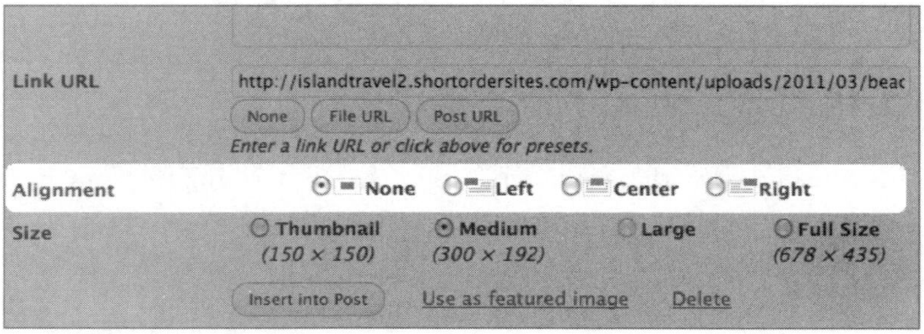

FIGURE 13-4

The Alignment setting tells WordPress how to place your image relative to the text and other images on the page. The Left and Right options place the image to one side of the text and the text flows around the image. The Center option places the image in the center of the screen with text above and below it. Selecting None also breaks up text above and below the image, but the image sits over on the left (the default position in HTML).

As with Link URL, WordPress remembers the last way you aligned an image and repeats that setting. So always check this option and don't take for granted that it will default to None.

> *Choosing an alignment option does not do the actual aligning — it assigns a class to the image. Your theme's style sheet must have those classes set up or else the alignment won't occur in the published version of the post. Most themes do have these CSS styles, but it's something to be aware of, especially when modifying or creating a theme.*

Size

You're given a choice of one or more sizes for the image you're going to insert, with the pixel size in brackets, as shown in Figure 13-5.

When you upload an image, WordPress automatically creates smaller versions of it (that's what the word "crunching" refers to in the progress bar during the upload process). Depending on how large the original is and depending on what values are in Settings ➪ Media (I look at those settings in Lesson 19), the system will create more or fewer versions. By default, WordPress creates Thumbnails of 150 pixels, Medium images of 300 pixels, and Large images of 1,024 pixels (these refer to the longest side of the image).

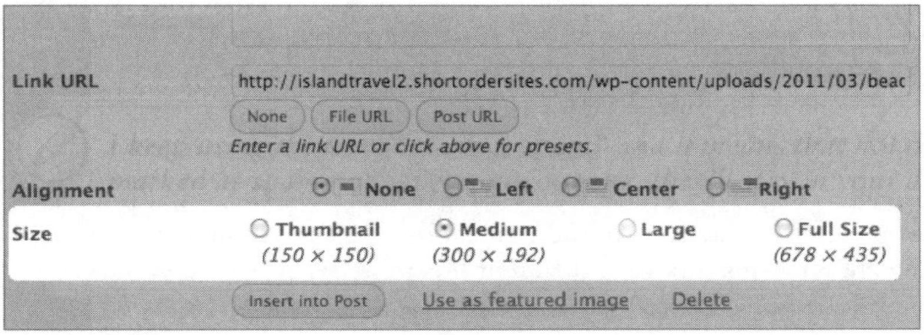

FIGURE 13-5

Based on those settings, if your image is 800 pixels wide, you'll have a choice of Thumbnail, Medium, and Full-Size. If you upload an image of 125 pixels, you will only have the choice of Full-Size. If a sizing option is not available, it won't have any dimensions listed below it and you won't be able to choose it, as in the case of Figure 13-5 where there is no choice for Large.

HOW LARGE DO IMAGES NEED TO BE?

Before leaving this discussion of sizing, it's important to say something about the size of images you upload to your site. As the average digital camera offers increasingly larger pixel sizes, I see clients uploading image files from which you could print a poster!

Unless you intend visitors to be able to download print-quality photos (for example, on a media page where magazines and newspapers would download material for print), you should be keeping the files you upload as small as possible. That does not mean you can't display huge photos on the Web; you just need to understand that even a small file will produce gigantic Web images — an image of just 100K could fill your entire screen.

How do you make images smaller? This is not the place to discuss the details of resizing and file compression for the Web, but the simplest answer is to think in terms of pixels. In your image-editing program, check the longest side of the image — if it's more than 1,200 pixels, reduce it to, at most, 1,200 before uploading. Even 800 pixels is probably more than enough for most situations.

Currently, the average screen is 1,024 pixels wide, so 800 would fill the majority of the screen. It's true that WordPress creates small versions for you to use in your posts, but you don't want people waiting for long downloads when they click to view the full-size image, and you also don't want to be using up valuable storage space on your server.

Use as Featured Image

Clicking this link, which is located beside the Insert Into Post button, designates this image as the one to be used in various ways depending on your theme. For example, a page of post summaries may display a small version of the featured image beside the text, or the featured image of a page might automatically be inserted into the header of the site.

Once chosen, the featured image is displayed on the Edit Post screen at the lower right in the Featured Image meta box (you can also use the link there to choose a featured image). You can change the featured image by clicking this link on a different image.

INSERTING VS. SAVING

The two buttons shown in Figure 13-6, Insert Into Post and Save All Changes, can sometimes cause confusion.

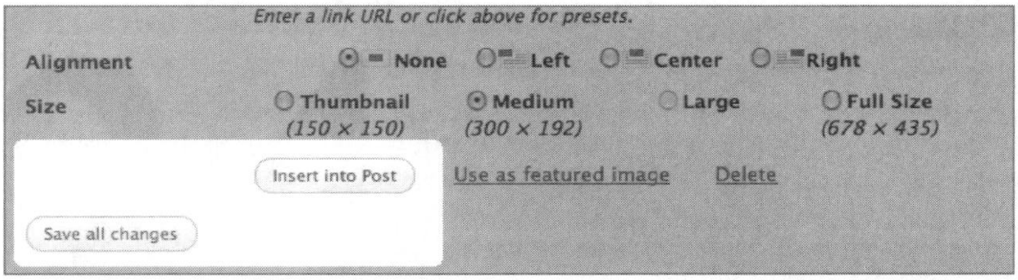

FIGURE 13-6

Insert Into Post

Clicking this button places the image into the text at whatever point the cursor currently sits. Don't worry if the image doesn't end up in the right place; as you'll see in Lesson 14, it's easy to move. In addition to inserting the image, this button simultaneously saves all the text you entered about the image and the options you chose.

Sometimes, people look at the Save All Changes button at the very bottom of the popup window and see the word Save, but clicking that does not put the image into the text of the post. You must click Insert Into Post.

Save All Changes

The word *Changes* might be a bit confusing if this is the first time you're uploading this image; you're not changing existing information. More to the point, though, if Save All Changes doesn't insert the image into the post, why use it? Why else would you be uploading an image if not to insert it?

Suppose you've already inserted an image gallery in the post — like the one for the Jamaican travel package. You want the thumbnail of this new picture to appear with the others, but nowhere else in the post. If you use Insert Into Post, the image will show up in the body of the text as well as in the image gallery. Using the Save All Changes feature, it will show up only in the image gallery.

Delete

If it turns out you want to get rid of the image — erase it from WordPress completely — there is a Delete function. A new line will appear warning you that you're about to delete the image, with a Continue link and a Cancel link. As a further warning, the Continue button turns red as you're about to click it. Don't say you weren't warned.

TRY IT

In this lesson, you practice uploading and inserting an image with a number of options.

Lesson Requirements

A post with text and an image to use for uploading.

Step-by-Step

1. Find the post you'll upload to and click Edit.
2. Make sure you're in the Visual mode of the Text Editor.
3. Click the image icon of the Upload/Insert menu.
4. Using the From Computer option, upload your image.
5. Change the Title from the filename to something else.
6. Enter a short Caption for the image.
7. Enter a Description for the image.
8. If there is a URL in Link URL, click None to clear the field.
9. Choose Alignment Right.
10. Choose the Medium size if it's not already selected.
11. Click Insert Into Post.
12. View the image in the Text Editor — the caption should be displayed.

> *To see some of the examples from this lesson, including a quick demonstration of how different-sized images display on the Web, see Lesson 13 on the DVD with the print book, or watch online at* `www.wrox.com/go/wp24vids`.

14

Editing and Laying Out Images

Once an image has been uploaded into WordPress, you have a lot of options for editing it and laying it out in your content. In this lesson, I show you ways to physically change the image and virtually change it from within the Text Editor, and the tools to lay out images for great-looking posts and pages.

THE WORDPRESS IMAGE EDITOR

Sometimes, after uploading an image into WordPress, you may decide that it isn't looking exactly the way you'd like it. Or you've just uploaded it raw from your camera, and it needs some fixing up (I don't recommend loading images that way because they'll be way too big for the Web, but sometimes it happens). In other cases, the image is fine, but the default way that WordPress creates thumbnails — taking the center area of the image — may not make for an effective thumbnail and you'd like to change it.

That's where the image-editing function comes in so handy. You can access it during the Upload/Insert process or later from the Gallery or the Media Library. It's a part of the image-editing popup window, though the button can sometimes get overlooked — it's highlighted in Figure 14-1.

Clicking this button reveals a set of tools that allow you to:

- Crop
- Rotate
- Flip
- Scale

The image-editing area is shown in Figure 14-2.

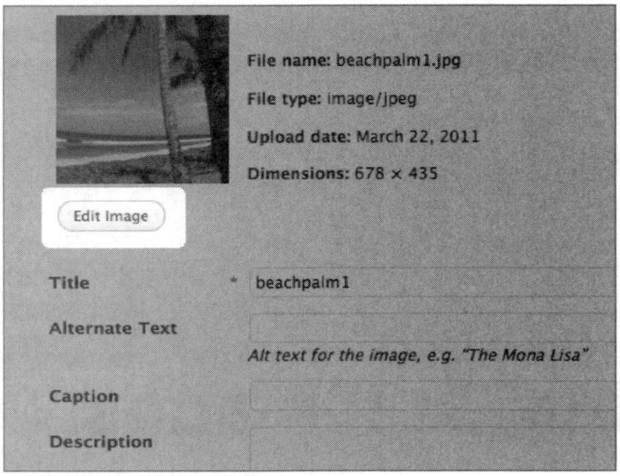

FIGURE 14-1

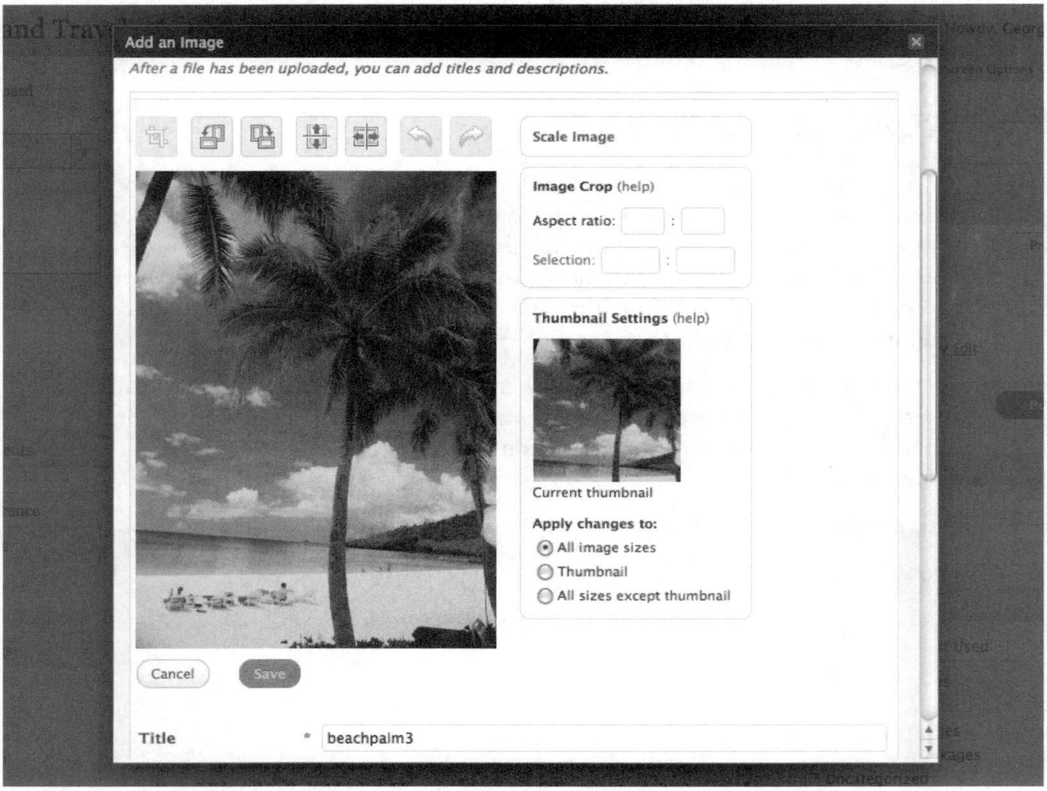

FIGURE 14-2

I'm going to leave the details of how the image editor works for one of the videos accompanying this lesson, because it's very difficult to show in print. What I do want to give you here are some tips that will save a lot of time and energy, and possibly some panic:

- Before you start doing anything, look at the radio button menu at the lower right, which says Apply Changes To, and make sure you've selected the right option. By default, this is set to All Image Sizes. More often than not, I find, people are in here to change the thumbnail image only. They make all the changes, click Save, only to discover that they've altered the actual image itself, not just the thumbnail. A quick check of this menu will save a lot of confusion.
- If you do make a mistake and have saved changes to all the images, you're in luck. If you go back into Edit Image, you'll see your changes, but at the top right, below the Scale Image link, you'll see a new link called Restore Original Image. Whew!
- The Crop button (the left-hand one of the icons at the top of the image) is grayed out at first. To activate it, you simply click anywhere within the image and a select box will appear. You adjust it to the way you want, *then* click the now-lit Crop icon.
- WordPress thumbnails are squares, but it's not immediately obvious in the image editor how to make your selection square. You can try to manually move the cursor around until you see the two numbers in the Selection box are the same — but it's much easier to enter a number in one box that matches the other. That will make your selection frame square, and then you can drag on a corner, thus keeping your square proportions automatically.

These are some quick tips to help make your image-editing experience easier from the start. Again, watch the video for this lesson to see it in action and get a sense of what each of the tools can do.

Remember, what you're doing in this image-editing area is physically changing the image itself.

AN EXAMPLE OF ALIGNING AND RESIZING

Two of the most common tasks you'll do when inserting images into posts are aligning and resizing, so let's take a quick look at them. I've started a page for biographies of the Island Travel staff, including their photos. As you can see in Figure 14-3, the image doesn't look all that great in relationship to the text.

An easy way to improve this layout would be to move the image over to the right-hand side of the page and let the text flow around it. In other words, change the alignment of the image relative to the text. Here's how.

Just click the image and you'll see several things — a set of two buttons at the top left and a number of squares around the edges of the image, called drag points, as shown in Figure 14-4.

Our Staff
We're proud of our dedicated vacation specialists. With a total of over 50 years of experience in the travel industry, we can offer you the detailed knowledge to help make your Caribbean vacation the holiday of a lifetime. Get to know our staff a little bit better:
Diana Smith
Diana's background includes a BA from Overton College majoring in Hotel, Restaurant & Institutional Management with a focus on Travel & Tourism. After graduating, she worked in corporate travel and meeting planning for Donnair Travel in Houston. She came to Island Travel in 1998 and

FIGURE 14-3

FIGURE 14-4

Click the left-hand button — the one that looks like a little picture — and up pops the editing options window as shown in Figure 14-5.

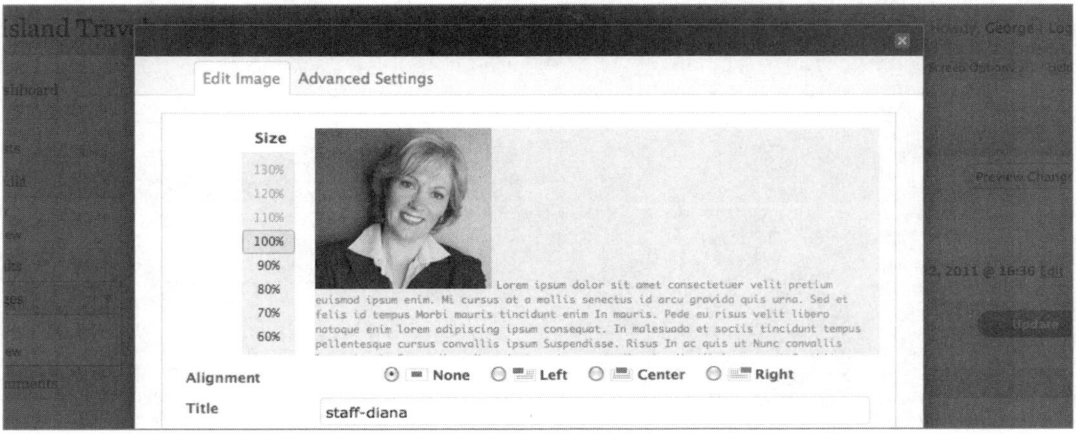

FIGURE 14-5

I'll go over the details of this window shortly, but for now, find the Alignment options. Choose Right, and then click Update at the bottom left. As you can see in Figure 14-6, the photo is now over at the right side of the editor and the text flows around it.

FIGURE 14-6

With the photo aligned the way you want, it's obviously a bit big for that spot, so let's resize it. If your image isn't showing the drag points, just click it again. Place your cursor over any of the corner squares, then click and drag inward.

Drag the corner until you get the size you want and let the cursor go. *Remember to update your post.* The finished version, shown in Figure 14-7, looks much better.

Unfortunately, Safari and Chrome users will not see any drag points. As of this date, the engine controlling these two browsers does not support image resizing in any visual editor, not just the TinyMCE editor used in WordPress.

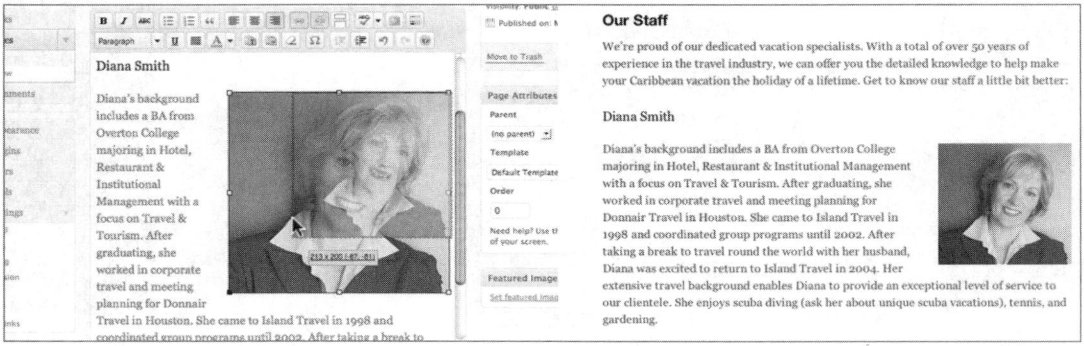
Diana Smith
Diana's background includes a BA from Overton College majoring in Hotel, Restaurant & Institutional Management with a focus on Travel & Tourism. After graduating, she worked in corporate travel and meeting planning for Donnair Travel in Houston. She came to Island Travel in 1998 and
Page Attributes
Parent
Template
Default Template
Order
Featured Image
Our Staff
We're proud of our dedicated vacation specialists. With a total of over 50 years of experience in the travel industry, we can offer you the detailed knowledge to help make your Caribbean vacation the holiday of a lifetime. Get to know our staff a little bit better:
Diana Smith
Diana's background includes a BA from Overton College majoring in Hotel, Restaurant & Institutional Management with a focus on Travel & Tourism. After graduating, she worked in corporate travel and meeting planning for Donnair Travel in Houston. She came to Island Travel in 1998 and coordinated group programs until 2002. After taking a break to travel round the world with her husband, Diana was excited to return to Island Travel in 2004. Her extensive travel background enables Diana to provide an exceptional level of service to our clientele. She enjoys scuba diving (ask her about unique scuba vacations), tennis, and gardening.

FIGURE 14-7

That's a quick overview of the basic tools needed for aligning and resizing an image in a post. Let's go back now and look at all the possibilities in some detail.

THE INSERTED IMAGE WINDOW

When you've inserted an image into a post, you can then edit the settings relating to its place within the text. As you saw in the example in Figure 14-2, you open this window by clicking the left-hand button that displays when you highlight an inserted image. The red circle icon beside it is for deleting only this instance of the image — it does not delete the image from the post's Gallery or the Media Library.

Getting back to the edit icon — the one that looks like a picture — clicking it pops up an edit window. It's important to note that the settings in the window affect only this instance of the image. They don't control the actual image in the Gallery/Media Library, which is why there is no image-editing button in the sample window displayed in Figure 14-8.

I'll run through the items on the screen, though you'll be familiar with most from your work with the Upload/Insert image screens.

The first item in the window, however, is noticeably different from the Upload/Insert screen. There's an image icon with some filler text, and the idea is that you can see relative positioning of the image, as well as relative size. First-time users may try to use their mouse to move the image icon around the screen, but you can't — it's only controlled by the settings.

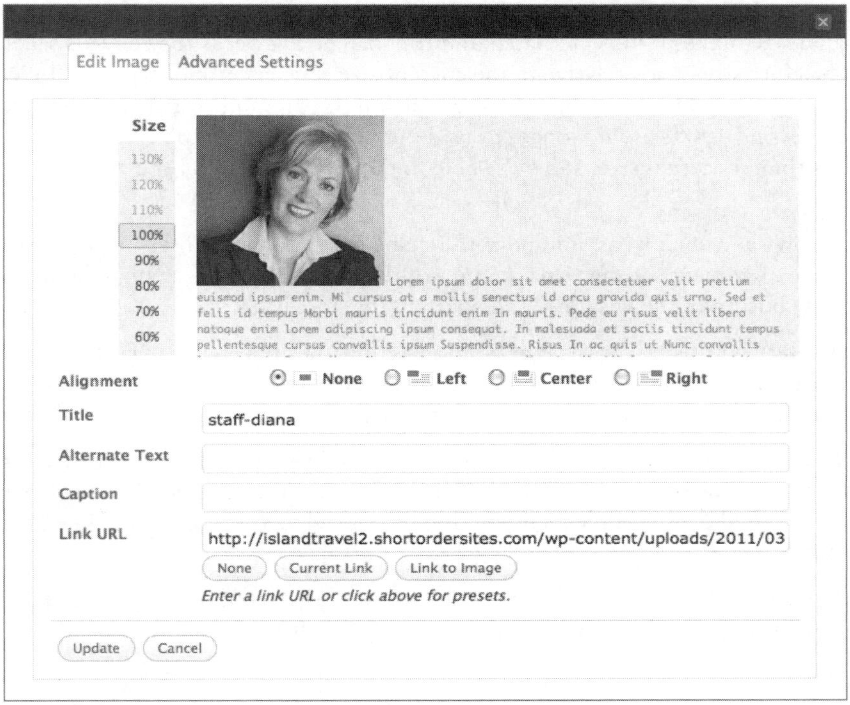

FIGURE 14-8

On the left-hand side of the filler text, you'll see a column of percentages; this is where you can alter the size of the image (though not physically, as you can in the image editor I showed you earlier). Remember how WordPress makes different-sized copies of an image when you upload it? The sizing we're talking about here is not about choosing one of those copies; this is resizing the version you chose to insert. In other words, if you chose the medium-sized image at, say, 300 pixels, the sizing function in this window allows you to shrink that image to less than 300 pixels.

The sizing scale works by moving your cursor up and down the numbers, and as you mouse over a value, the image adjusts to that sizing. *However, you need to actually click the number in order for the image to stay resized.* If you're sure that's the size you want, you then must click Update at the bottom to apply the sizing change.

> *This is another example of something appearing to have been changed, but the change doesn't really take effect until you hit Update or Save. That's why it's so important to get in the habit of clicking Save or Update before you leave a window or a screen.*

You might wonder why the sliding scale includes values larger than 100%. After all, increasing an image beyond its original size makes it look pixilated and rough. The answer is that on this scale, 100% does not mean original size — it's relative to the current size settings. You'll see what I mean if you click, say, 70% and then update the image. Now go back into edit mode for that image and you'll see that numbers beyond 100% are no longer grayed out. That's because the current size setting for the image is less than its actual size, so you're able to go beyond 100% of the current size setting.

Just as the image icon grows and shrinks as you move the sizing scale, it will change position based on what you choose in the alignment setting. And again, nothing will happen to change the setting until you click the Update button in the window, and again in the post itself.

The remainder of parameters on this tab of the edit window will be familiar to you: Title, Alternate Text, Caption, and Link URL. Remember, these do not change the comparable settings of the image in the Media Library — they affect only this instance of the image.

At the top of this window, you'll notice another tab called Advanced Settings. The average user is not going to need anything on this screen. More importantly, it's best to leave this tab alone because some things on this screen could cause problems if you don't know what you're doing — like altering the source information.

On the other hand, if you're comfortable with CSS, some powerful styling tools are available on this screen, such as adding your own classes or IDs, again, just for this instance of the image.

REPOSITIONING IMAGES IN THE TEXT EDITOR

The WordPress Text Editor allows you to move an image around the screen in real time — you can see it changing position relative to the text as you move. This greatly speeds up the process of achieving the layout you want on the page. It's also helpful because you don't always know exactly where you want an image to appear when you're doing the upload and insert process.

When you're working on image layout in the Text Editor, I would recommend giving yourself roughly the same width in the Text Editor that you have in the content area of your website. That way, your layout decisions will be fairly close to the real deal.

To re-create the width of your site's content area, use the Full Screen button that you learned about in Lesson 7. The difference now is that once the editor takes up the entire screen, you should shrink your browser window to a width that closely matches your website content area.

To move the image in the body of the post, simply click and drag it around. As you drag, the text cursor moves with the mouse, showing you where the image will be dropped into the text if you let go of the mouse button. On some browsers on some systems, a semi-transparent copy of the image moves with the cursor. While you can see the text underneath, spotting that cursor through the image and among all the text isn't easy. The trick is to watch the tip of your cursor arrow, as highlighted in Figure 14-9.

Even if you can't see it clearly, there's a bar moving around the text and it's located right at the tip of the cursor arrow. That's how you can precisely place your image.

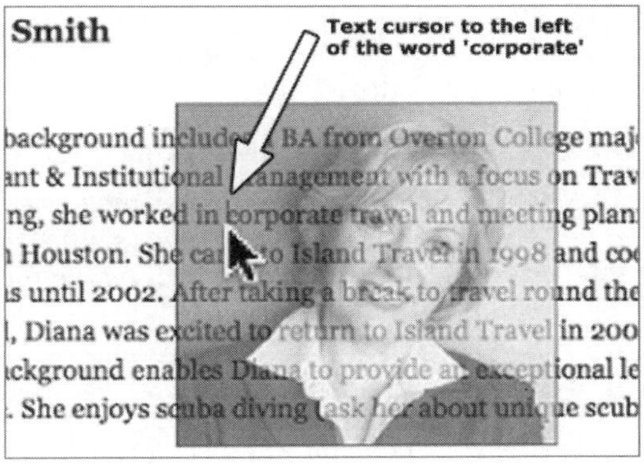

FIGURE 14-9

As you move the image around, it aligns itself to the text according to whatever alignment setting you chose. If you don't like the alignment, just click the image, click the picture icon, and edit the alignment in the popup window. Click Update to save your changes and exit the popup.

Once you've placed your image exactly where you want it, remember to save or update your post.

RESIZING IMAGES IN THE TEXT EDITOR

I showed you how to alter the size of an image in its popup edit window using a percentage scale, but that may involve a bit of trial and error, and opening the edit window several times. As you saw at the start of this lesson, it's much easier to resize while working in the body of the post, and WordPress makes that simple.

Click the image again so that you can see the drag points. Mouse over one of the corner drag points until you see that special arrow I showed you earlier. It's important to use the corner drag points because they will adjust the height and the width of the image proportionately. Using the side drag points means you'll be changing just the height or just the width.

> *Users with Internet Explorer 7 or 8 will find that the corner drag points do not produce proportionate sizing. If you're careful and drag a corner at a 45-degree angle, you'll get close to a proportionate sizing. If it doesn't work, see the following note about image sizing in the Advanced Settings window.*

Aside from the fact that you have continuous sizing available with this method (compared with the percentage change in the popup edit window), some browsers, like Firefox, also display a small gray popup box showing the actual dimensions of the image in real time, as shown in Figure 14-10.

FIGURE 14-10

So, as you drag the corner to make the image smaller, you see the dimensions changing in the box. This allows you to be very precise if you want to make several images the same size or you have particular size restrictions in your layout.

If you need that precision and don't see the popup dimensions, you can click Edit on the image, go into Advanced Settings on the popup window, and enter a specific height and width.

> *If you need to get your image back to its original size, all you need to do is click the image edit icon, choose the Advanced Settings, and you'll see a button called Original Size. That will return the image to its full size — that is, the size of the image you inserted.*

As always, when you've finished resizing, be sure to click Update Post.

WHICH KIND OF RESIZING TO USE?

Although the click-and-drag resizing feature in the WordPress Text Editor is very convenient, there's an argument against using it. The method relies on HTML coding to tell a visitor's browser to reduce the size of the image. In other words, the 300-pixel image that you "resize" in the post to display at, say, 230 pixels, is actually still 300 pixels — the HTML instructions cause it to be resized when the browser loads the page.

First, this will only work well with JPG or PNG file types. Images in GIF format break up very badly with this kind of forced resizing. However, even a JPG will degrade to a certain extent. Here, there's some debate about how badly.

Partly, it will depend on the initial quality of the image, partly on the visitor's screen quality, and partly on the visitor's ability to see signs of reduced quality. I must say that I've rarely noticed anything poorer in the quality of a reduced image, but then, I'm pretty careful to start with a good original image and then not over-compress it when saving for display on the Web.

In the past, I tended to say to use the Text Editor's virtual resizing unless you notice poor quality in the reduced image. In part, that was due to the extra work required to erase the image from WordPress, go back to your image-editing program, resize and resave the image, then upload it again to WordPress. I know some would say it's worth it, but for practical purposes, when you're creating an image for one blog post — as opposed to a graphic that's part of the site design — it's often not worth the time.

Now, however, with the built-in image editor in WordPress, it's much simpler to go back and resize the physical image, then reinsert into the post. In fact, I often use the Text Editor resizing tool to get my dimensions first — after all, you can instantly see whether the change is going to work in the post's layout — then, I take those new dimensions to the image editor and physically resize the image.

The one point to be aware of in all this: yes, perhaps the physical change in size is good for the particular post you're working with, but maybe you'll want the larger version later, in which case, it's now too small. But how many images do you actually reuse, and if you did need to, it's simple enough to upload the original large version and use that instead.

These are some considerations when it comes to how to resize, but at least now, you have more choice right inside WordPress.

MORE COMPLEX IMAGE LAYOUTS

The example of a staff photo aligned to the right of the person's bio was a nice, straightforward layout. But what if you're doing a post about the latest travel convention you attended, with several paragraphs of text and six images to be placed throughout? What are your layout options then?

You could do it in a number of ways — especially when you start working with templates in the advanced section of the book — but the best advice at any level is to not worry about getting fancy. One straightforward layout technique is to alternate image alignment left and right, as I've done in Figure 14-11.

Remember that, although HTML defaults to aligning images to the left, it's not the type of alignment that will let text flow around it. You must choose Alignment Left in the image's edit window.

One of the problems you can run into with this technique is that if two images are too large or not vertically separated enough, their left and right alignments will cause some strange consequences, as you can see in Figure 14-12. Other problems include having a column of single-word text between the images, or if the images are really wide, one forces the other to drop below it with large white gaps in between.

Staff Trip to Aruba
Posted on March 22, 2011 by George
Lorem ipsum dolor sit amet, consectetur adipiscing elit. Ut lorem neque, tincidunt at dictum vitae, facilisis ac magna. Donec eget suscipit libero. Fusce in diam nulla, non facilisis metus. Phasellus suscipit urna commodo enim consectetur convallis ornare ligula accumsan. Morbi lectus augue, fringilla quis porttitor in, imperdiet consectetur nibh.
Aenean scelerisque, erat eget aliquet cursus, purus urna dapibus turpis, in tempor nulla lectus quis tellus. Ut tincidunt, eros id pulvinar elementum, justo libero faucibus justo, quis tincidunt arcu velit quis leo. Praesent posuere, dui laoreet rutrum auctor, urna risus accumsan tortor in diam nulla facilisis ac magna. Praesent posuere, dui laoreet rutrum auctor, urna risus accumsan tortor, eget posuere risus mauris hendrerit massa. Integer hendrerit, arcu porttitor semper pretium, erat odio sodales justo, quis accumsan nulla justo eget lacus. Fusce at risus dui, ut consequat eros. Integer imperdiet, lacus a pharetra accumsan, enim nibh faucibus mauris, a vestibulum purus nibh nec tellus.
Duis ornare neque eget odio luctus lacinia. Mauris sit amet ultricies lorem. Vivamus blandit, odio eu laoreet pulvinar, justo risus vestibulum odio, sit amet suscipit ante eros feugiat nunc. Morbi lectus augue, fringilla quis porttitor in, imperdiet consectetur nibh. Donec a nisi faucibus augue rhoncus auctor. Nullam commodo, sapien vel mattis convallis, sem elit bibendum mauris, vitae faucibus

FIGURE 14-11

This is where the ability to resize images right on the screen comes in handy. You can reduce the size and see what effect it's having on all the other elements on the page. Remember to make your Text Editor about the same width as your live content area or you won't get an accurate picture of how the images are interacting with the text and one another.

If you don't want to make one or more of the images smaller, you can drag the lower image farther down the text — well below the bottom of the higher image — to give a more readable result. You always have a number of ways to lay out your content. You just need to try different combinations and see what works best.

Staff Trip to Aruba
Posted on March 22, 2011 by George
Lorem ipsum dolor sit amet, consectetur adipiscing elit. Ut lorem neque, tincidunt at dictum vitae, facilisis ac magna. Donec eget suscipit libero. Fusce in diam nulla, non facilisis metus. Phasellus suscipit urna commodo enim consectetur convallis ornare ligula accumsan. Morbi lectus augue, fringilla quis porttitor in, imperdiet consectetur nibh.
Aenean scelerisque, erat eget aliquet cursus, purus urna dapibus turpis, in tempor nulla lectus quis tellus. Ut tincidunt, eros id pulvinar elementum, justo libero faucibus justo, quis tincidunt arcu velit quis leo. Praesent posuere, dui laoreet rutrum auctor, urna risus accumsan tortor in diam nulla facilisis ac magna. Praesent posuere, dui laoreet rutrum auctor, urna risus accumsan tortor, eget posuere risus mauris hendrerit massa. Integer hendrerit, arcu porttitor semper pretium, erat odio sodales justo, quis accumsan nulla justo eget lacus. Fusce at risus dui, ut consequat eros. Integer imperdiet, lacus a pharetra accumsan, enim nibh faucibus mauris, a vestibulum purus nibh nec tellus.

FIGURE 14-12

When you think you have everything placed the way you want it, be sure to click Preview Changes to see what your layout will look like live. If everything's good, remember to save or update the post.

UPDATING AN IMAGE

You might be used to — in a non-WordPress environment — replacing an existing image by uploading a new one of the same name, using an FTP program. As long as you're placing it in the right location, the URL will continue to be the same, so you wouldn't have to change anything in the HTML and visitors would simply see the newest version.

Although it's possible to do this with WordPress, you should keep in mind that multiple versions of an image are created when it's first uploaded to WordPress. As you've seen, depending on the size of the original, there could be as many as three extra versions of the image. Unless you replace all of them — with the appropriate dimensions for each — there's going to be one new image and several older versions.

WordPress makes no provision for uploading and overwriting images (the system will simply add a number to the filename if there's another already with that name). The safest method, then, is to erase the old image and upload the new one to WordPress.

However, depending on how you've got WordPress set to organize folders in the uploads directory, the URL for the new image may likely be different from the original. The default folder organization is by month, so an image uploaded in March would have a URL ending in this: `/wp-content/uploads/2011/03/montego-nightlife.jpg`, while if you uploaded a new version in April, it would be: `/wp-content/uploads/2011/04/montego-nightlife.jpg`.

That may not be a problem — people tend to link to posts rather than to individual images — but if you yourself have been reusing the image in even one or two other places on your site, then erasing the original will cause broken images. You'll need to go into those other posts, erase the inserted image, and reinsert the new version.

TRY IT

In this lesson, you practice two things: moving and resizing an image, and replacing an image by uploading a new version.

Lesson Requirements

A post with text and at least one image in its Gallery.

Step-by-Step

The following steps explain how to move and resize an existing image:

1. Find a post with an image in it and click Edit.
2. Make sure you're in the Visual mode of the Text Editor.
3. Click the image so that you see the two buttons at the top left and the drag points around the edges.
4. While continuing to click, drag the image to a new paragraph or somewhere else in the existing paragraph.
5. Release the mouse and the image appears in its new location.
6. Click the image again to get the drag points showing.
7. Click any of the corner drag points and drag inward.
8. If you can see a box showing dimensions, keep dragging until you get the width to 200 pixels, then let go.
9. If you don't see a box of dimensions, keep dragging until you have made the image significantly smaller, then let go.
10. Click Preview Changes at the top left to see what your post will look like.
11. If the changes look good, click Update.

The following steps explain how to replace an existing image by uploading a new one:

1. Make sure you're in the Visual mode of the Text Editor.
2. Click the image you want to replace, so you can see the red delete icon at the top right.
3. Click the delete icon. The image will disappear from the Text Editor.
4. Click the image icon of the Upload/Insert menu above the Text Editor.

    If you don't need the old image for any other purposes:

    1. Click the Gallery tab.
    2. Find the thumbnail for the old image.
    3. Click the Show link.
    4. Click the Delete link.
    5. Click Continue when prompted.

5. Click the From Computer tab if you're not already there.
6. Click Choose Files.
7. Upload the image.
8. Make any necessary changes, such as to the Title, Caption, or Alignment.
9. Choose the appropriate size.
10. Click Insert Into Post.

    In the Text Editor window:

    1. Adjust the position of the image if necessary.
    2. Adjust the size of the image if necessary.

11. Click Preview Changes.
12. If need be, make more position and size changes.
13. If okay, click Update.

> *To see some of the examples from this lesson, watch the video for Lesson 14 on the DVD with the print book, or watch online at* `www.wrox.com/go/wp24vids`.

15

Working with Image Galleries

You've seen how WordPress makes it easy to upload and insert images into your posts, but what if you have a lot of images for a single post, say, the pictures for that Jamaican travel package? It would be nice to just show thumbnails of each picture and then have people click them to see the larger version. WordPress lets you insert an image gallery into your posts with only the click of a button.

The term *gallery* can be a little confusing. In WordPress, it could mean:

- The complete set of media files attached to a post (not just images)
- The set of image files for a post that can be inserted into the post using WordPress's built-in Gallery button
- The output of one of many plugins available for WordPress to display images

Still with me? In this lesson, I'm talking about the galleries you insert into posts using WordPress's own Gallery button, but to avoid confusion, I'll call these image galleries, and I'll use Gallery to refer to the list of files in the Gallery tab.

CREATING AN IMAGE GALLERY IN A POST

Start by going to the Upload/Insert menu and clicking the image icon. If you're inserting an image gallery, I'm assuming you have more than one image uploaded, so you'll see a Gallery tab with the number of files in the Gallery listed in brackets (that total, remember, is all media, not just images).

Click the Gallery tab and, as in Figure 15-1, you'll see all your images with thumbnails and the Show link.

Below the list of media files, you'll see the Gallery Settings title.

If you have other types of media files in the Gallery, don't worry. WordPress automatically uses only the image files when inserting an image gallery.

FIGURE 15-1

If you have a lot of files, you'll need to scroll down to see all of the Gallery Settings options.

Let's go through each of those options in the order you see them.

Galleries of images look best if each one is roughly the same size. In other words, if most are 800 pixels on the longest side, try not to have the others be any more than, say, 100 pixels longer or shorter.

Link Thumbnails To

You can choose where visitors are taken when they click an image gallery's thumbnails. Choosing Image File will display the full-size version of the image in a plain browser window. If you choose

Attachment Page, the image links to a page determined by your theme — often, this will be the default single post template. What gets displayed will depend on the theme template, but typically, this includes the image Title and Description fields.

Several plugins for WordPress bypass either of these options and automatically create the nice popup slideshows that have become so popular. I'll talk about some of these in Lesson 37 when I'm covering photo gallery plugins.

Order Images By

The four choices are Menu Order, Title, Date/Time, and Random. The Title is the image title option I talked about in Lesson 13 — remember that unless you give the image a title, WordPress automatically uses the filename of the image. Date/Time is the date and time you uploaded the file. Even if you did a multifile upload, the time stamp would be different on each by a few milliseconds, so they would be in the order you uploaded them.

The default choice is Menu Order, which means the order of the images as you see them in the Gallery tab. I come back to the methods for changing the menu order in a later section of this lesson.

Order

Based on the Order By method you just chose, you make that order either Ascending or Descending. Ascending is the default.

> *If you're using Menu Order for the Order By option, the choice of Order has no effect.*

Gallery Columns

This sets the number of columns across the page — the default is 3. That's pretty safe for most sites based on the default thumbnail size of 150 pixels. However, it will all depend on thumbnail size and the width of your theme's content area — it's just a matter of experimenting.

For this Jamaica image gallery, I'm going to choose the following options:

- Link Image to Image File
- Order By Date
- Descending Order (ordering by the Date and using Descending order means that any new images I add later will automatically show at the beginning of the group)
- Gallery Columns — 3

Once these are set, I click the Insert Gallery button at the bottom of the screen and the image gallery placeholder appears in the post wherever I placed my cursor, as shown in Figure 15-2.

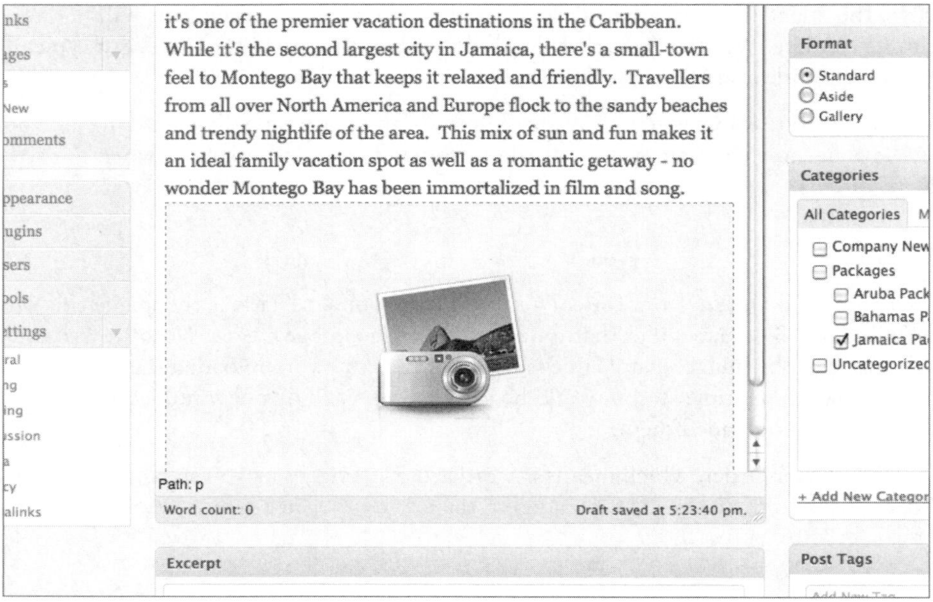

it's one of the premier vacation destinations in the Caribbean. While it's the second largest city in Jamaica, there's a small-town feel to Montego Bay that keeps it relaxed and friendly. Travellers from all over North America and Europe flock to the sandy beaches and trendy nightlife of the area. This mix of sun and fun makes it an ideal family vacation spot as well as a romantic getaway - no wonder Montego Bay has been immortalized in film and song.
Path: p
Word count: 0
Draft saved at 5:23:40 pm.
Excerpt
Format
Standard
Aside
Gallery
Categories
All Categories
Packages
Uncategorized
+ Add New Categor
Post Tags

FIGURE 15-2

That large box with the camera in the center is the placeholder for the image gallery. Don't worry, you'll see the images on the live page, as in Figure 15-3, but only after clicking the Update button!

If I had written a caption for one or more of the images, these captions would appear below their respective thumbnails. There's no further control over captions appearing in a particular image gallery — if you enter a caption, it will appear.

from all over North America and Europe flock to the sandy beaches and trendy nightlife of the area. This mix of sun and fun makes it an ideal family vacation spot as well as a romantic getaway – no wonder Montego Bay has been immortalized in film and song.
This entry was posted in Jamaica Packages. Bookmark the permalink. Edit

FIGURE 15-3

ADDING AND REMOVING IMAGES FROM A GALLERY

Once you've inserted an image gallery into your post, you can easily add or remove images and it will automatically update itself. But you should be aware of a few things.

Any image you upload to a post in the future will automatically appear as part of its image gallery. I've talked before about the fact that uploading a media file to a post does not mean it will appear in the post — you must actually insert it. This is an exception to that rule. An image gallery will display any image that's been uploaded to the post, regardless of whether it was individually inserted into the post.

Removing an image from an image gallery but still leaving it attached to the post requires a bit of coding. If an image appears both in the post and as part of the image gallery, deleting it from the body of the post will not remove it from the image gallery (that follows from the preceding point). If you've created a particular order for the images in the Gallery by numbering them (see the next section), simply deleting the image's number from that order will not remove it from the image gallery.

Of course, you could delete the image from WordPress entirely, but what if you still wanted to use the image in the post, just not in the image gallery? For that, you can use what's called *shortcode*. It sounds complicated, but it's not, as you'll see in the section "More Options with Gallery Shortcodes," later in the lesson.

CHANGING THE ORDER OF GALLERY IMAGES

The default order of images in an image gallery is the order in which they appear in the Gallery tab, but you have a number of ways to change that order.

The easiest, I find, is to drag and drop the thumbnails into the order you want. Place your cursor over the thumbnail you want to move, then click and drag. Onscreen, you see the thumbnail move with your cursor, as shown in the middle frame of Figure 15-4.

Once the thumbnail is in place, let go of your mouse button. The list has been reordered, as you can see in the final frame of Figure 15-4.

Remember to click Save All Changes or else this reordering will not take effect.

> *Clicking Update Gallery Settings does not save any reordering of the menu — you must click Save All Changes.*

You'll notice in the last frame of Figure 15-4 that under the Order column, numbers are now listed in each box. This is another way you can rearrange the order of items: changing the numbers in the order boxes.

> *Even though all file types will have a number beside them, and you can move them around in all the ways described here, only images will appear in the image gallery.*

Media	Order	Actions
waterfall1		☐ Show
rowsofpalms		☐ Show
resort1		☐ Show
clownfish		☐ Show
beachthrougharch1		☐ Show

Media	Order	Actions
waterfall1		☐ Show
rowsofpalms clownfish		Show Show
resort1		☐ Show
beachthrougharch1		☐ Show

Media	Order	Actions
waterfall1	1	Show
clownfish	2	Show
rowsofpalms	3	Show
resort1	4	Show
beachthrougharch1	5	Show

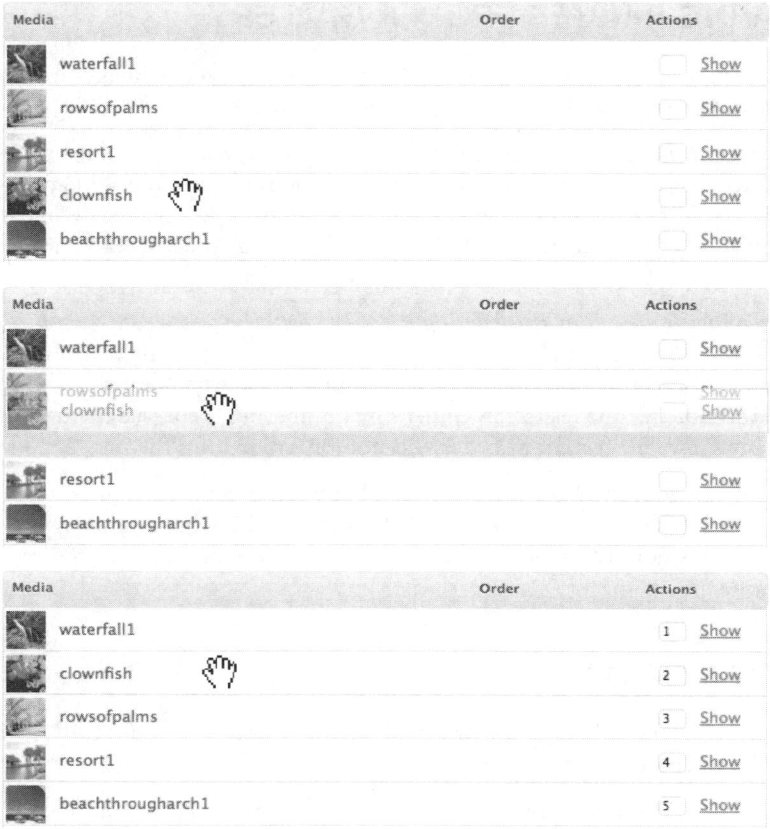

FIGURE 15-4

If you change item 4 to item 2, and then click Save All Changes, item 4 will move into the second spot.

> The change may not happen exactly this way in all browsers. You may end up with two number 2's, for example. Simply click Ascending or Descending to correct the numbering.
>
> It's also worth noting that changing the order in the Gallery tab will not change the order of an image gallery you've inserted into the post, unless the Order By setting for the inserted image gallery uses Menu Order.

MORE OPTIONS WITH GALLERY SHORTCODES

In Visual mode, as you've seen, an image gallery appears as a big box, but in HTML mode, it's really just a bit of code — what's called shortcode — as you can see on the right side of Figure 15-5.

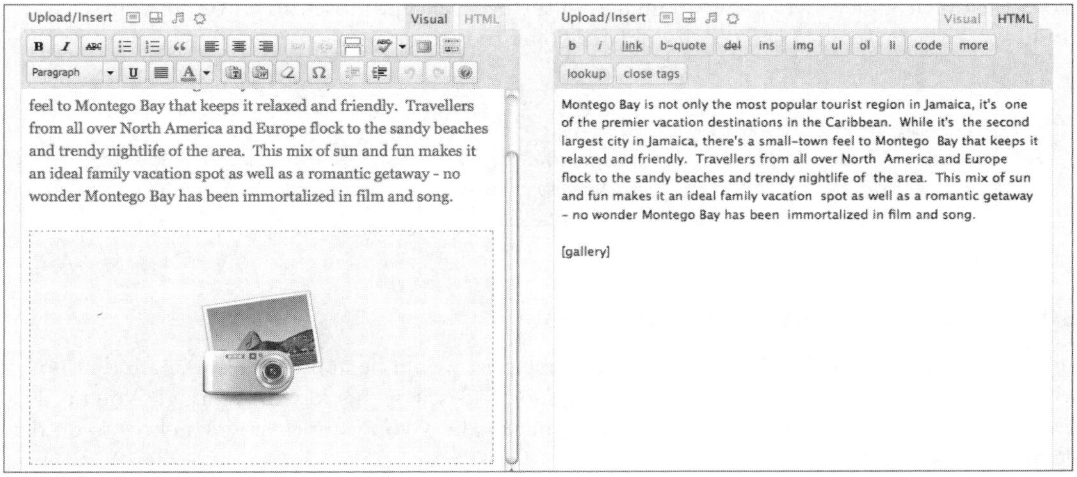
Upload/Insert
Visual
HTML
Paragraph
feel to Montego Bay that keeps it relaxed and friendly. Travellers from all over North America and Europe flock to the sandy beaches and trendy nightlife of the area. This mix of sun and fun makes it an ideal family vacation spot as well as a romantic getaway - no wonder Montego Bay has been immortalized in film and song.
Upload/Insert
Visual
HTML
b
i
link
b-quote
del
ins
img
ul
ol
li
code
more
lookup
close tags
Montego Bay is not only the most popular tourist region in Jamaica, it's one of the premier vacation destinations in the Caribbean. While it's the second largest city in Jamaica, there's a small-town feel to Montego Bay that keeps it relaxed and friendly. Travellers from all over North America and Europe flock to the sandy beaches and trendy nightlife of the area. This mix of sun and fun makes it an ideal family vacation spot as well as a romantic getaway - no wonder Montego Bay has been immortalized in film and song.
[gallery]

FIGURE 15-5

Using this shortcode, you can do most of the functions I've described — how images link, how many columns, what order — but it can do more.

Image Size

By default, image galleries display the thumbnail, but with a shortcode, you can tell WordPress to use a different size:

```
[gallery size="medium"]
```

The other choices are "large" and "full," but it's unlikely you'd ever want to use those.

Excluding or Including Images

Shortcode can be used to decide which images are displayed. By default, WordPress grabs all images in the post's Gallery, but as I mentioned earlier, there may be times you only want some of them listed. For that, you would use the "include" or "exclude" options.

To do that, you'll need the ID number for each image, which you can find by, for example, viewing the post in Preview and then mousing over the image in question. Look at the status bar of your browser and you'll see a big long URL, which will include "attachment_id=68." Put that number in your shortcode like this (comma between each ID if there are multiples):

```
[gallery size="medium" exclude="68,139,160"]
```

Now, the image gallery will show all images in the post, except those three. And of course, you could work the other way and specify only the ones to include.

> *You can enter gallery shortcodes in Visual mode, but you won't be able to edit them, because the Text Editor will immediately display the big placeholder box. Just go into HTML mode if you want to change settings.*

Displaying Other Image Galleries

Sometimes, an image gallery you've created in one post would be handy to have in another post as well. WordPress makes it easy to do that using shortcodes. For this to work, though, you need to know the ID number for the post that has the image gallery you want (I show you how to do that in detail in Lesson 18).

Once you have that ID, find the place where you want to insert the gallery and enter the code this way:

```
[gallery id="32"]
```

Of course, you'd replace the ID number with the one you want, and you could have other options as well, such as sizing, order, and so on.

If you want to add more image galleries to the post, you can't simply add more IDs separated by commas, the way you do with exclude and include. You'll need a separate shortcode for each image gallery, but you can have as many in a post as you'd like.

> *You can read all the details about gallery shortcodes in the WordPress Codex at* `http://codex.wordpress.org/Using_the_gallery_shortcode`.

TRY IT

In this lesson, you practice inserting an image gallery into a post.

Lesson Requirements

A post with text and at least five images in its Gallery.

Step-by-Step

1. Find a post with at least five images and click Edit.
2. Make sure you're in the Visual mode of the Text Editor.
3. Click the Image icon of the Upload/Insert menu.
4. Choose the Gallery tab.
5. Locate Gallery Settings below the list of media files.
6. Choose Image File for linking thumbnails.
7. Choose Title for ordering images.
8. Choose Ascending for the order.
9. Choose two gallery columns.
10. Click Insert Gallery. You should see the big Gallery box with the dashed border in the body of the post.
11. Click Preview to see what the post will look like.

> *To see some of the examples from this lesson, including how to reorder the images listed in the Gallery, see Lesson 15 on the DVD with the print book, or watch online at* `www.wrox.com/go/wp24vids`.

16

Adding Video and Audio

Video on your website is one of the most popular types of content for visitors these days, and WordPress offers a number of built-in options for including video. In this lesson, I help you sort through them, as well as the options for audio files.

For the greatest flexibility and ease of handling video files, particularly if you're going to have a lot of video on your site, I would recommend using one of the many WordPress plugins for video, and you can read about those in Lesson 37. If you're just going to have the occasional video, the choices offered in this lesson should be adequate.

UPLOADING/INSERTING VIDEO

Although there is an Add Video icon on the Upload/Insert menu of posts and pages, it's rare that you'll want to use it. That's because it simply creates a text link to the video file (whether it's uploaded to your site or is from a video-sharing site like YouTube), and that's just not very useful to your visitors.

However, let me quickly cover this method of putting video in your posts, just in case you ever need it. Video is the second icon from the left on the Upload/Insert menu. Clicking it brings up a window that looks exactly like the one for images. The From Computer tab is always the default so I'll begin with that.

Click the Select Files button and, in the popup window, locate your video file on your computer. When you're done, click Select and the file begins to upload, with the regular progress bar. Video files can be quite large, so the upload could take a while.

> *Servers vary on the file size limit for uploading and although WordPress attempts to set that limit at 64MB, it does not always work, so depending on your server, you might get an uploading error. You could try getting your host to raise the limit or you can try resaving the video at a smaller size or different compression to reduce its size. Or make the video shorter.*

When the upload is complete, the popup window changes, as shown in Figure 16-1.

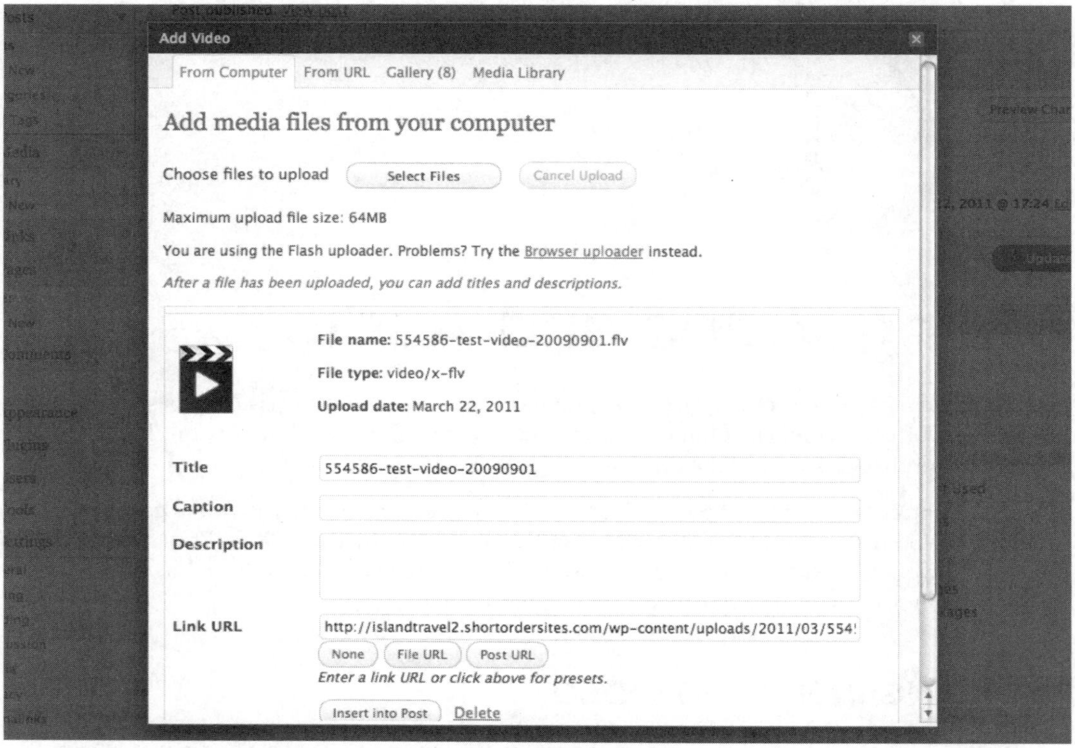

FIGURE 16-1

It looks similar to the images window, but without options like alignment or sizing (WordPress doesn't make different-sized copies of videos). You can enter a title, caption, and description; at the very least, you need to enter a title because that's the text for the link that appears in your post.

You also need to click File URL or else there won't be any link to the video, just the words of the title, and the whole point of this is to allow visitors to click and see the video.

So what happens when visitors click the link? That all depends on the type of video file you uploaded and how their browser is set to deal with that type, but in the case of a Flash file, for example, the link should open a new browser window and start playing the video at the size of the browser screen.

This is the first difficulty with the Upload/Insert method when dealing with video files: because many different video standards exist and a plain link puts everything in the hands of your visitors' browser/computer, you're really leaving it to chance whether or not they can view your video.

You'll run into the same difficulty using the From URL tab and pointing to a video file somewhere else on the Web, unless you're pointing to a video contained in a stand-alone player that will work in virtually anyone's browser (such as on sharing sites like YouTube). Though this may solve the first difficulty, it raises the second difficulty of the Upload/Insert method, which is that you're taking visitors away from your page in order to view a video.

Fortunately, the answer to all these questions is easily solved through the Text Editor.

THE AUTO-EMBED FUNCTION

WordPress has made it incredibly easy for you to have video display right on your site. All you have to do is enter or paste the URL of a video from major sharing sites like YouTube, Vimeo, and more. You can do this in Visual mode or HTML mode. Through its Auto-Embed feature, WordPress lets your visitors watch the video right there on your site. Figure 16-2 shows the link on the left and the resulting video on the live site:

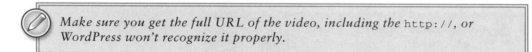

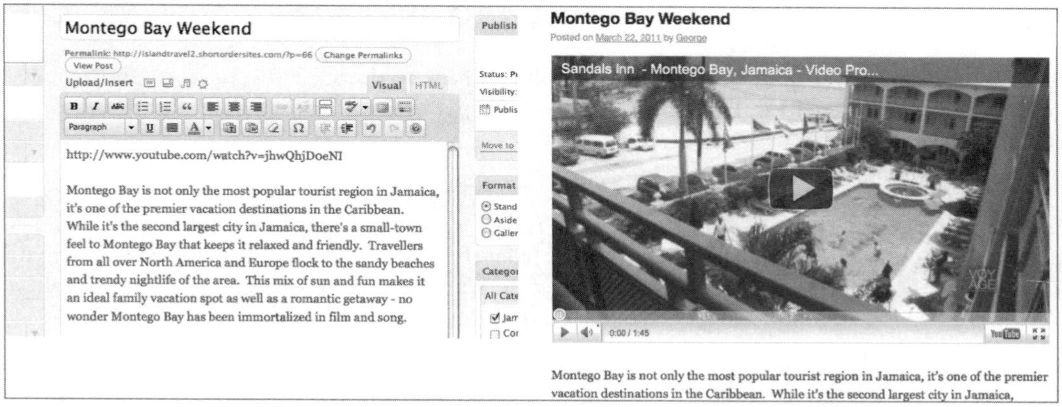
Montego Bay Weekend
Upload/Insert
Visual
HTML
http://www.youtube.com/watch?v=jhwQhjDoeNI
Montego Bay is not only the most popular tourist region in Jamaica, it's one of the premier vacation destinations in the Caribbean. While it's the second largest city in Jamaica, there's a small-town feel to Montego Bay that keeps it relaxed and friendly. Travellers from all over North America and Europe flock to the sandy beaches and trendy nightlife of the area. This mix of sun and fun makes it an ideal family vacation spot as well as a romantic getaway - no wonder Montego Bay has been immortalized in film and song.
Publish
Format
Montego Bay Weekend
Posted on March 22, 2011 by George
Sandals Inn - Montego Bay, Jamaica - Video Pro...
0:00 / 1:45
Montego Bay is not only the most popular tourist region in Jamaica, it's one of the premier vacation destinations in the Caribbean. While it's the second largest city in Jamaica,

FIGURE 16-2

That's all there is to it. You just have to **make sure the URL is on its own line**, and don't use the Link button to enter it — type it in or copy and paste it from an address bar or wherever.

> *Make sure you get the full URL of the video, including the* `http://`*, or WordPress won't recognize it properly.*

If no video shows up, it could be that WordPress doesn't support the sharing site whose URL you used, or it could be that Auto-Embed has been turned off. Go to Settings ➪ Media and make sure the Auto-Embeds box is checked off; it is by default, but something may have been changed in the meantime.

What about sizing the video? There isn't a great deal of choice there. By default, WordPress will let the video be as wide as the width of your theme's content area (or less, if the video isn't that wide). However, in that same Settings ➪ Media window, there is a place to set the maximum width of embedded videos.

> *Unless you have only one video file and you don't want many people to see it (why are you putting it on your website?), I would recommend getting an account on a video-sharing site and uploading your video files there, then paste their URLs into WordPress.*
>
> *For one thing, video-sharing sites do the automatic conversion to Flash of whatever kind of file you have. Then, there's the question of server space and bandwidth — they have lots and you not so much. Finally, your video has a chance of being seen by even more people and you can link back to your own website for more exposure. Is there any other way to video?*
>
> *One thing, though: make sure your video has clear identification on it — you want to share with it others, but you also want them to know where it came from and what your website address is!*

If you need control over individual video sizes, all you have to do is use the `[embed]` shortcode around the URL of the video. In that code, you would put the width and height you want, so it looks like this:

```
[embed width="123" height="456"]put URL here[/embed]
```

It's very important that you include that closing tag [`/embed`], and put the complete URL. Don't use your link button to create the URL, just paste it from the address bar or video-sharing information. You can do this in Visual or HTML mode, and it does not need to be on a separate line. Again, if Auto-Embed fails, a plain link to the video is automatically created.

Because the Auto-Embed feature only supports some video-sharing sites at the moment — albeit key ones like YouTube, Vimeo, Viddler, DailyMotion, Hulu, and others — a video plugin will often be your best bet when using lots of different types of video.

If you have a video from a site that isn't supported by Auto-Embed or any plugins, you can, as a last resort, use the HTML embed code that most sharing sites provide. Just copy and paste it into your post — *but you must be in HTML mode to do this* — as shown in Figure 16-3.

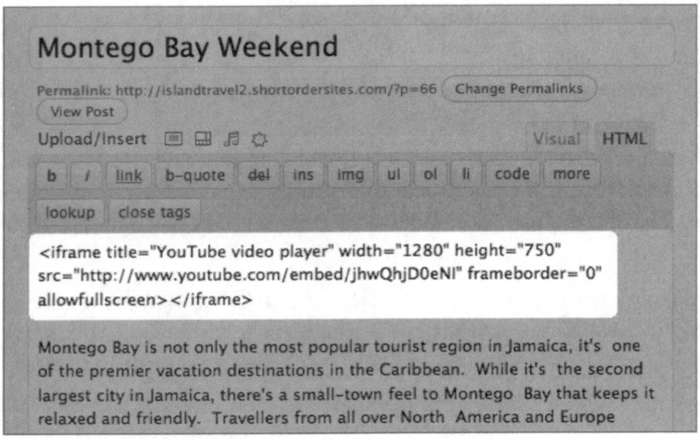

FIGURE 16-3

> *If a third-party URL is not from a video-sharing site, which usually makes it clear whether or not you have permission to embed a video, you need to get permission.*

ADDING AUDIO

The bad news about audio is that the Auto-Embed feature doesn't work with it very much at this point, though the plan is for supporting many more media types in future. The good news is that most people's browsers will play audio straight from a link, provided it's in MP3 format, and that's the standard these days, anyway.

So, the fact that the Upload/Insert functions — From Computer and From URL — just create links to files that either you've uploaded to WordPress or which reside somewhere on the Web is not so much an issue for audio, though people are still being taken off your site to be shown the audio player in the browser window. Granted, it's not like being taken to another site, but still.

The Add Audio icon on the Upload/Insert menu produces the usual popup window. On the left of Figure 16-4, you see the screen after uploading an audio file from your computer, and on the right is the screen if you're going to link to a file somewhere on the Net.

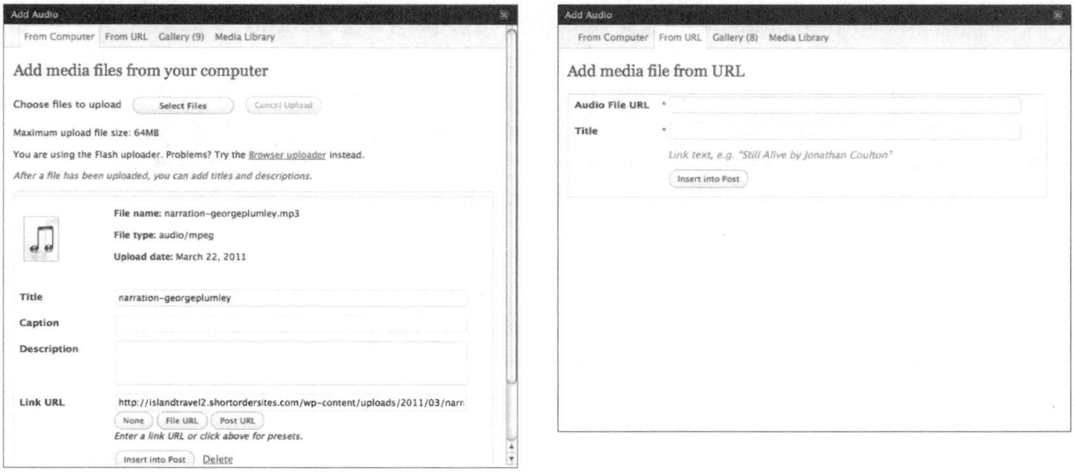

FIGURE 16-4

In both cases, the thing to remember is that the "title" is really the text that will appear in your post, linked to the audio file.

Still, it's nice to have the audio player right on your site, rather than having the browser replace the window with its own player. That's where plugins are useful. Some video plugins provide a player for both audio and video, while others specialize in not only providing a player, but also creating special podcasting feeds and other ways to help spread the word about your audio. I talk about some of those in Lesson 37.

TRY IT

In this lesson, you practice embedding a video from YouTube.

Lesson Requirements

A post with text and a video from YouTube that you would like to embed.

Step-by-Step

1. Find the post you want and click Edit.
2. Make sure you're in the Visual mode of the Text Editor.
3. Position your cursor where you want the video to appear and make sure you're on a new line. Hit Enter if you're not sure.
4. Go to YouTube.com and find a video you'd like to embed.
5. When you're on the page for that video, look for the Share button under the video.
6. Click Share and you'll see a field with a URL in it. It may be highlighted already, but if not, highlight the entire URL using Ctl+A, and then copy it (Ctl+C).
7. Back in your Text Editor, paste the URL, making sure there's nothing on the same line as it.
8. Update your post and you'll see a video player displayed on your live site.

> *To see some of the examples from this lesson, choose Lesson 16 on the DVD with the print book, or watch online at* `www.wrox.com/go/wp24vids`.

17

Adding Documents

It's often easier to make information available to visitors in the form of documents rather than trying to re-create the information on a web page. Plus, they have something to "take away" with all your contact information on it as well. So being able to upload and link to documents easily is important, and WordPress has that covered.

> *In this lesson, I'm talking about the Add Media button of the Upload/Insert menu. Though it can be used to upload any allowed media type other than images, video, and audio, it is most commonly used for documents.*

UPLOADING AND INSERTING A DOCUMENT

Unlike the cases of video and audio, the Upload/Insert function is well suited to documents because having a simple link is exactly what you want. When someone clicks the link, it causes the file to be downloaded, or in the case of PDFs, it will automatically appear in most people's browsers.

I've created a Press Releases category in WordPress and I've created a post for a press release, so now I'm going to add the PDF of the press release. I begin by placing my cursor where I want the link to appear in my text. Then I click the document icon of the Upload/Insert menu (the last of the four) and get the usual popup window tabs: From Computer, From URL, Gallery, and Media Library.

In this case, I'm adding the PDF from my computer, so I go through the steps of selecting the file and clicking Upload, and when the upload is complete, I get the options screen shown in Figure 17-1.

Remember, the Title is really what will show as the link text in the body of the post. You can, of course, change the link text later in the Text Editor, but it's always a bit faster to do it from here.

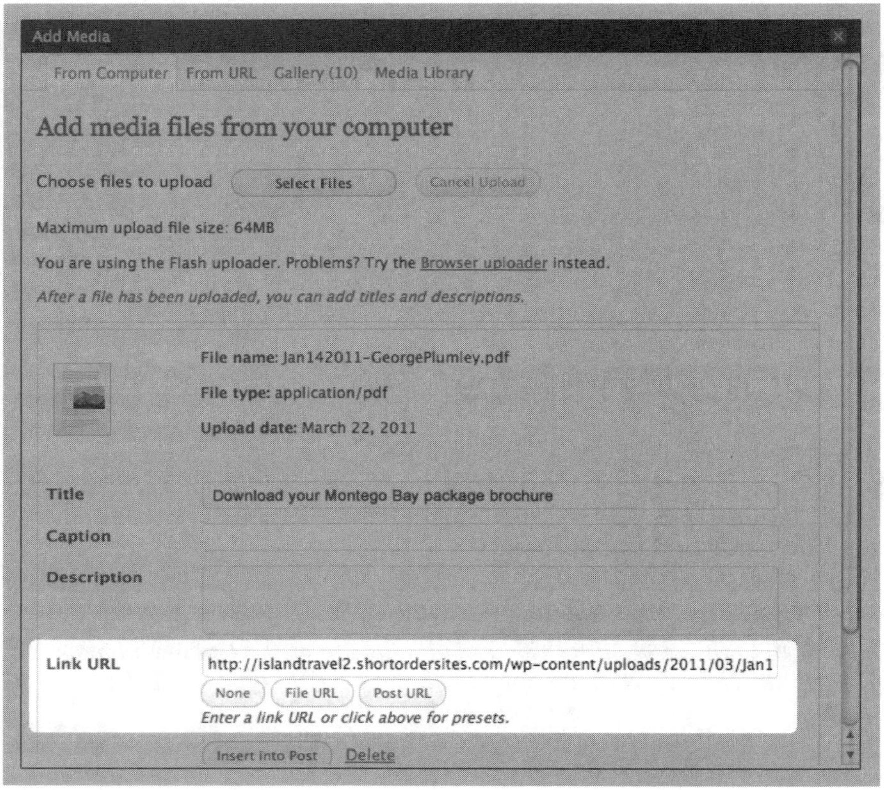

FIGURE 17-1

The only other thing to watch for when adding a document from your computer is to be sure the file's URL is showing properly in the Link area, as highlighted in Figure 17-1.

If not, just click File URL to insert it. Without that URL, your visitors won't be able to view or download the document.

Then I click the Insert Into Post button and the link shows up in the post, as illustrated in Figure 17-2.

> *If you see the Title text in your post but no link, don't worry, it just means you forgot to make sure that the Link URL box was filled in. Without that, WordPress won't create a link.*
>
> *To fix things, just erase the text that was inserted and go back to the document link of the Upload/Insert menu. Go to the Gallery tab in the popup window, find your document, click Show, and under Link URL, click File URL, click Insert, and the link should now appear in your post.*

Montego Bay Weekend
Permalink: http://islandtravel2.shortordersites.com/?p=66
Change Permalinks
View Post
Upload/Insert
Visual
HTML
Paragraph
Download your Montego Bay package brochure
Montego Bay is not only the most popular tourist region in Jamaica, it's one of the premier vacation destinations in the Caribbean. While it's the second largest city in Jamaica, there's a small-town feel to Montego Bay that keeps it relaxed and friendly. Travellers from all over North America and Europe flock to the sandy beaches

FIGURE 17-2

Once you've inserted a document link in your post, you can move it around by cutting and pasting it, but it's always easiest to have positioned your cursor in the exact spot where you want the link before doing the upload and insert.

Finally, remember to update your post and the link is ready for your visitors to use.

TYPES OF DOCUMENTS

You can upload all sorts of document files into WordPress, such as PDFs, PowerPoint presentations, Word documents, spreadsheets, and so on, but you should always be guided by the needs of your visitors. They want material to be accessible and safe.

Do visitors have the program to open the file and is their version capable of reading the document? My preference is to always post documents as PDFs where possible. Virtually everyone can open them and most importantly, they don't contain some of the hidden surprises that can be in other documents, such as names of other authors or collaborators, erased text, or pieces of other documents, not to mention viruses.

UPDATING A DOCUMENT

In many cases, you'll want to update an existing document that you've inserted into a post. How you do that depends on whether you need the existing URL of the document to remain the same.

If it isn't important to maintain the same URL as when you first uploaded the document, the process of updating is very simple: erase the old link in the post, then upload and insert the new document and link. If you don't need to keep a copy of the old document, you can simply erase it through the Media Library or the post's Gallery.

If you had linked to the old document elsewhere on your site, here's how to update those:

1. Place your cursor on the new link you just created.
2. Click the link button on the top button bar of the Text Editor (it should be highlighted).
3. Copy the URL from the popup box.
4. Wherever there's a link to that document on your site, you can go into the post, edit the link, and paste in this new URL. Then all the links will reference the new document you uploaded.

On the other hand, if you did a lot of linking to the old document, and perhaps others did too, then you'll need to upload the new document without changing the link. There may also be SEO reasons to have an updated version of the document remain at the same address as the old one. In that case, things get a little more complicated:

1. Make a note of the file's name and location by checking the link in the body of your post. The exact location depends on what pathways you've set up, but by default, WordPress puts all uploaded files into `wp-content/uploads` and typically organizes them by month and year, though you may have customized that as well.
2. Name the new version of the file exactly the same as the old.
3. Open your FTP program and log in to your server. Navigate to the location of the new file on your computer (usually the left side of the screen) and to the old file on the server.
4. Highlight the new file and click the upload button. The new file will overwrite the old version. To verify, you can check the date of the file on the server and it should now say "today" or today's date.

Fortunately, unlike images, WordPress doesn't make different copies of documents, so you only have the one to replace through this FTP method.

TRY IT

In this lesson, you practice uploading a PDF into a post.

Lesson Requirements

A post with text and a PDF file for uploading.

Step-by-Step

1. Find the post you want and click Edit.
2. Make sure you're in the Visual mode of the Text Editor.
3. Place your cursor where you want the document link to appear.
4. Click the Document icon of the Upload/Insert menu (fourth one).

5. In the From Computer tab, click Select Files.
6. Locate your PDF and click Select.
7. When the file is finished uploading, you should see all your options.
8. In the Title field, enter the name of the document (this will be the text in the link that WordPress creates in your post).
9. You can fill in Caption and Description if you'd like.
10. Make sure there is a URL displayed under Link URL and if not, click File URL.
11. Click Insert Into Post. You should see a link in the body of the post.
12. If you want to change the wording of the link, you can do so.
13. Click Update Post.

> *To see some of the examples from this lesson, including a demonstration of how to update a document using an FTP program, watch the video for Lesson 17 on the DVD with the print book, or watch online at* `www.wrox.com/go/wp24vids`.

SECTION V
Managing Your Content

18

Managing Posts and Pages

Up until now, I've talked about entering individual items of content, but what about managing content on a site-wide basis: finding materials, making large-scale changes, importing content, and so on? That's what this lesson is all about.

On the Island Travel site, for example, I might want to add a tag to every single post that mentions a particular airline. If I have dozens and dozens of posts that meet that criterion, and given the tools you've seen so far, that sounds like a long process. But in this lesson, you learn how to find posts and pages quickly, and then edit elements of all of them just as fast.

FINDING POSTS AND PAGES

If your site is new or relatively small, finding posts isn't too much of a problem. But as you add more material, more blog posts, and so on, it can be a hassle to find items, especially two years later.

By default, WordPress displays lists of content in reverse chronological order — the newest items first — and it shows you only 20 items at a time. Though you can increase the number of posts it displays using your Screen Options button at the top right, more efficient strategies exist for finding material than simply scanning long lists of posts.

Finding Posts

The starting point for finding posts is the Posts link on the admin menu. You already know that this brings up a list of all your posts, but look closely now at the top area of the screen, shown in Figure 18-1.

At the very top, you see a menu that contains all or some of the following: All, Published, Drafts, Pending, and Trash. The menu is contextual, so if there are no drafts, for example, you won't see it on the menu. These filters can be very helpful when you want to see only your Drafts, or if you have multiple users and you're the editor, you can quickly find all the items Pending Review before being published. The numbers in brackets, of course, refer to the number of posts.

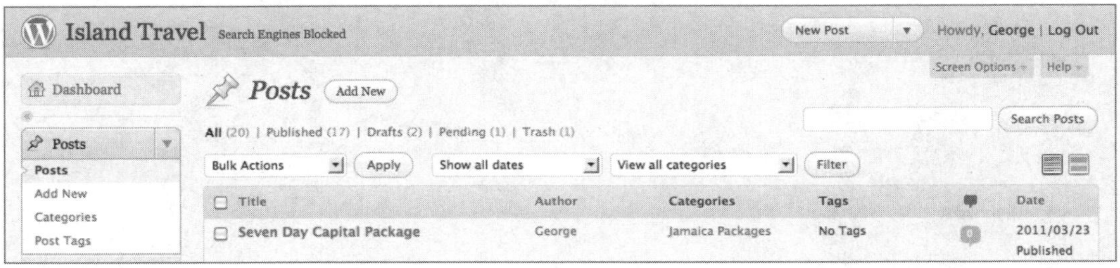

FIGURE 18-1

Over on the top far right is the Search box, which looks through the title and body of posts to find the word or phrase you enter. This search does not include categories or tags. Also, the search is performed on only the posts you have included through any filtering. So, if you're viewing posts in a particular category, the search is performed only on those posts.

> *If you want to return to your search results after editing one of the posts you found, use your Back button until you get back to that screen. If you click Posts on the side menu, you'll get all posts and not your search results.*

Just below the Search box are two icons. The one on the left produces the List View that you see by default. The one on the right is Excerpt View and it displays a short excerpt from each post, which is helpful if you can't remember what a post was about.

On the second row of the Posts search area, over on the left, is a series of drop-down menus. I'll leave the Bulk Actions to a later section of this lesson and focus here on the Filter function. You can use two parameters for filtering through posts: date and category.

- **Show All Dates:** This is handy when you remember posting a testimonial last April even though you can't remember anything else about it. By choosing April 2010, for example, you'll see every post from that month.
- **View All Categories:** This menu allows you to filter the display results by category, which is great when you want, for example, to view all Jamaican Packages or make bulk changes to all posts in the Sunstar category. (I cover bulk editing later in this lesson.)

Using both these filters at once allows even more fine-grained sorting.

Finally, you can also find posts by using the sort feature at the top of each column. By clicking Title, Author, or Date, you can re-sort the list of posts you're currently looking at.

Finding Pages

The listing functions under Pages are more limited than for posts, as you can see in Figure 18-2.

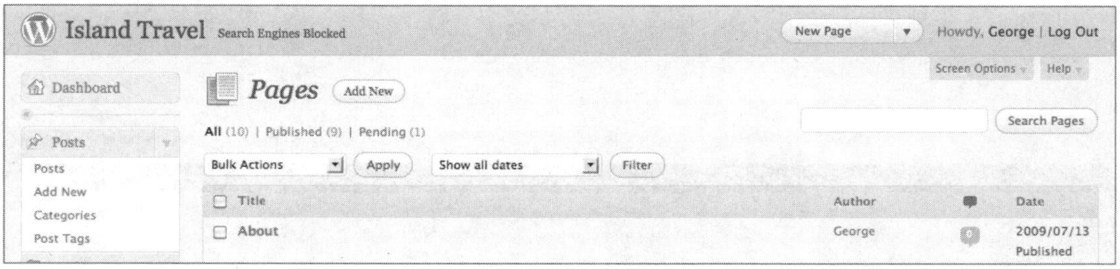

FIGURE 18-2

There are no categories for pages, so the Filter function is not available. You also don't have the Excerpt View option. There is a drop-down date filter, and you can filter pages by their status — Published, Draft, and so on. You can sort the results on the page by title, author, and date, and you can perform a search for words or phrases.

Linking to Your Own Content

One of the ways people used the Posts and Pages screens in the past was for finding related content they could link to. Since WordPress 3.1, you can now search for posts and pages through the Insert Link button when you're writing a post or page. When you've found what you're looking for, it creates the link for you. This is a huge time-saver and I think it encourages people to do more internal linking because it's so easy, and more internal linking creates a better visitor experience and can help improve your search engine rankings (more about that in Lesson 30).

RENAMING, RESCHEDULING, AND MORE WITH QUICK EDIT

There will be plenty of times when you'll want to change a parameter of a post or page — title, author, status, allowing comments, and so on — without needing to change anything in the body. With WordPress's Quick Edit feature, you can do that without having to open the entire post.

On the Posts or Pages screen, simply mouse over the name of the item and you'll see the menu shown in Figure 18-3A. Click Quick Edit and, in the case of posts, you'll see the options in Figure 18-3B, and for pages, you'll see what's in Figure 18-3C.

You simply change the parameter(s) and click Update, at which point the list returns to normal.

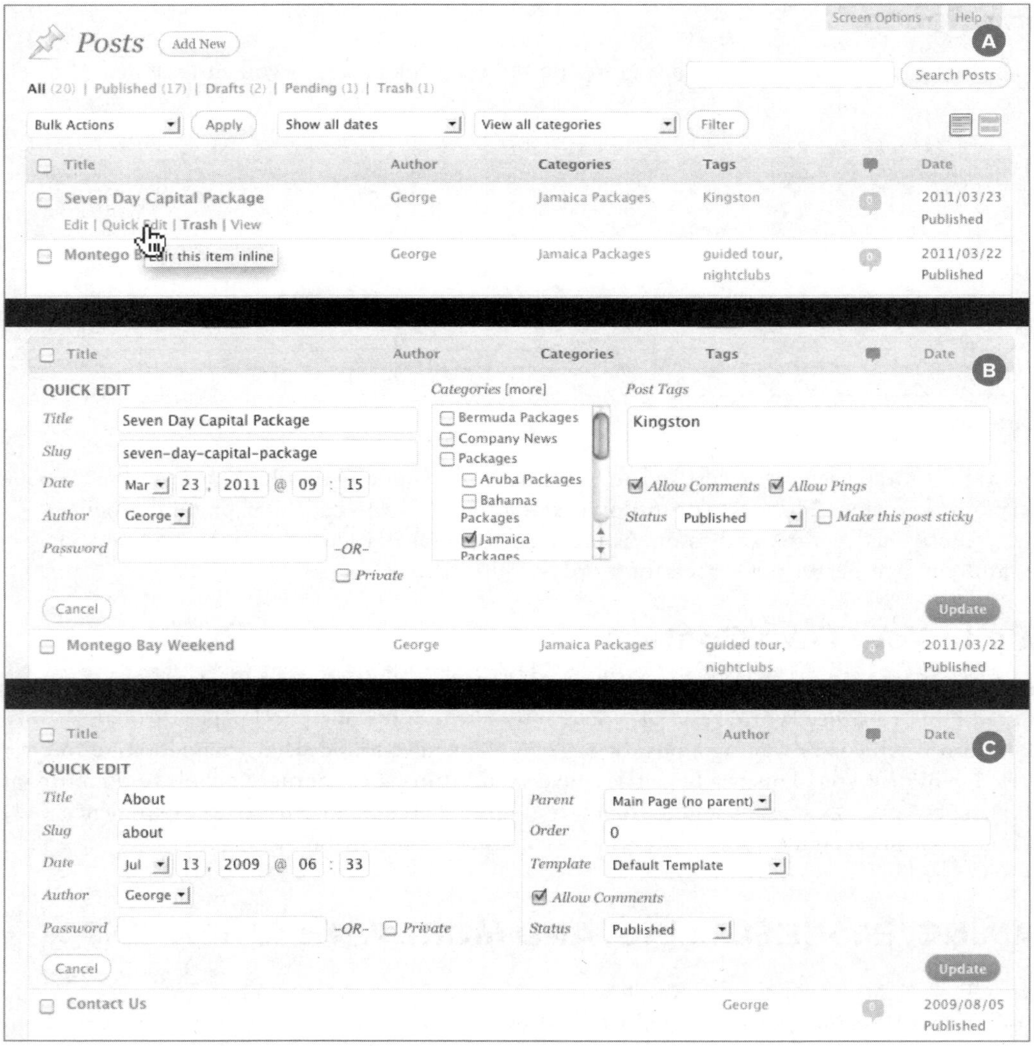

FIGURE 18-3

USING BULK EDIT

The advantages of the Quick Edit feature are also available in a more limited form when dealing with large numbers of entries under Posts or Pages. Using the Edit function on the Bulk Actions drop-down menu at the top of either screen, you can change most of the parameters you saw with Quick Edit.

> *If you want to get rid of large numbers of posts, Delete is the other option you see on the Bulk Actions menu. Simply check off the items you want (or use the Select All check box), choose Delete, and click Apply.*

Bulk-Editing Posts

These are the Edit functions you can perform on any number of posts at one time:

- Assign to one or more categories
- Add one or more tags
- Change the author (if there's more than one available)
- Allow or disallow comments
- Change the publishing status
- Allow or disallow pings
- Stick or unstick to the homepage

Suppose you want to include all Sunstar Testimonials in the TravelWhiz Testimonials category. Start by filtering out all the Sunstar Testimonials. If there were dozens and dozens of posts for Sunstar Testimonials, you could speed up the process even further by having the page display, say, 100 posts at a time, using the Posts Per Page setting under the Screen Options menu at the top right of the screen. When the relevant testimonials are displayed, click the check box at the left of the header bar, which automatically selects all the posts. Then, from the Bulk Actions drop-down, select Edit and click Apply, producing the screen in Figure 18-4.

On the left side of the highlighted area is a list of all the posts selected. Beside each is a circle with an X — clicking that removes the post from the edit, so there's still time to make changes in the list of posts affected by the edit.

Then, you locate the TravelWhiz Testimonials category from the list and check off the box. While you're here, it might be a good idea to add in any possible tags. Because Sunstar does only resort packages and they're now part of the TravelWhiz group of companies, you can add the tag "TravelWhiz resort packages." Because this tag already exists in the system, as soon as you start to type "Trav" you get a popup window — just select the one you want.

When you're finished making all your Bulk Edit changes, click Update Posts and you're done. If you decide not to make any changes, Cancel is over on the left of the highlighted area.

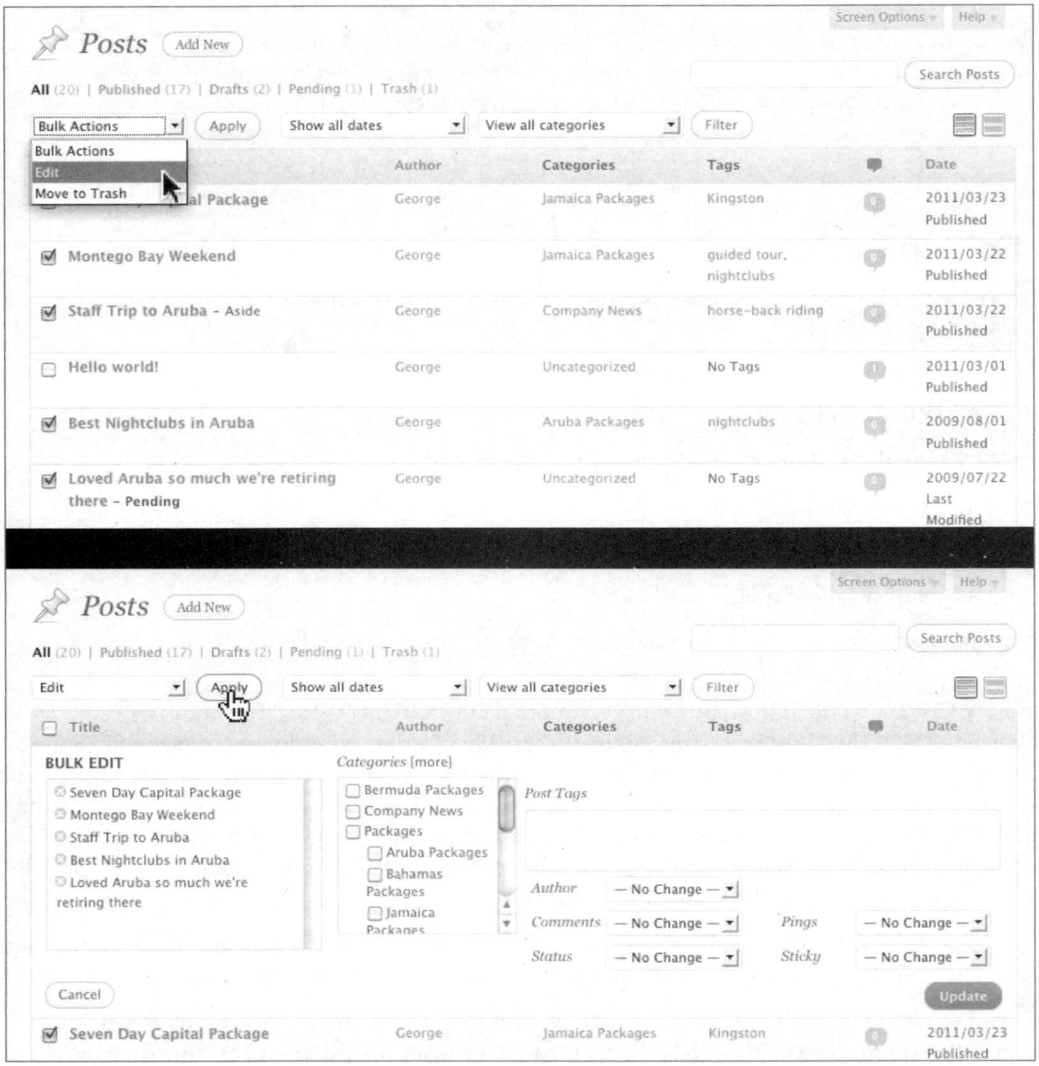

FIGURE 18-4

Bulk-Editing Pages

Because there are no categories or tags for pages, the Bulk Edit feature on the Pages screen looks a bit different, as you can see in Figure 18-5.

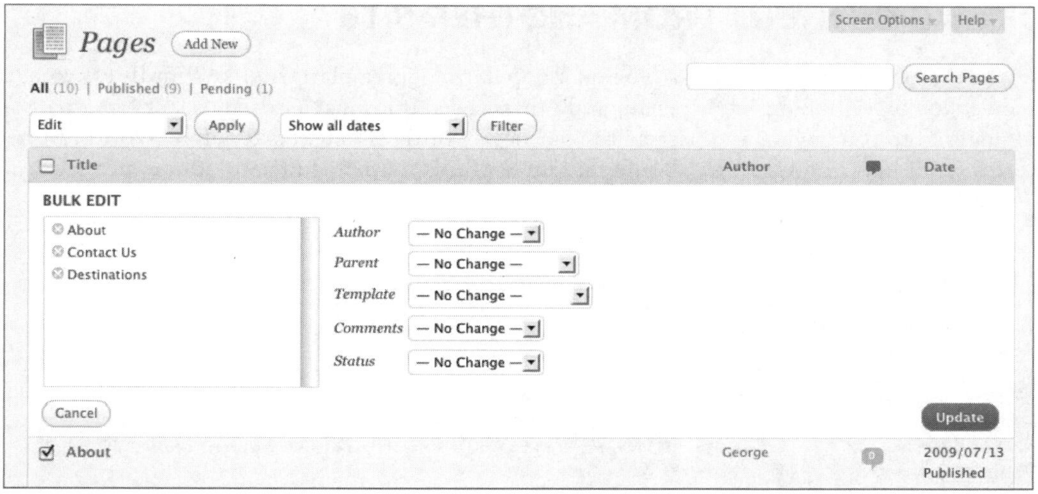

FIGURE 18-5

In the case of pages, you can:

- Assign a parent page
- Assign a page template
- Change the author (if there's more than one available)
- Allow or disallow comments
- Change the publishing status
- Change the publish date
- Change the slug
- Password protect the page or make it private
- Change the menu order (if the theme is using the WordPress template tag `wp_list_pages`)

The parent page would allow you, for example, to move a group of pages under a new parent page to create a new section of the website.

If you wanted that new section of the site to have a different look, you could also assign them to a specific page template you'd created. Remember when I spoke in Lesson 1 of having thousands of pages use a different header? Bulk Edit, along with a customized page template, is the means for making such a large change as simple as possible.

IMPORTING CONTENT FROM ANOTHER SITE

It may be that you've been running a blog on a popular blogging platform like WordPress.com (the hosted version of WP), Blogger, Typepad, and others. Even if it's just a dozen or so posts, that's a lot of material to be copying and pasting to your new WordPress site. Fortunately, WordPress has a powerful set of import tools, which you'll find under Tools ➪ Import in your admin menu, as shown in Figure 18-6.

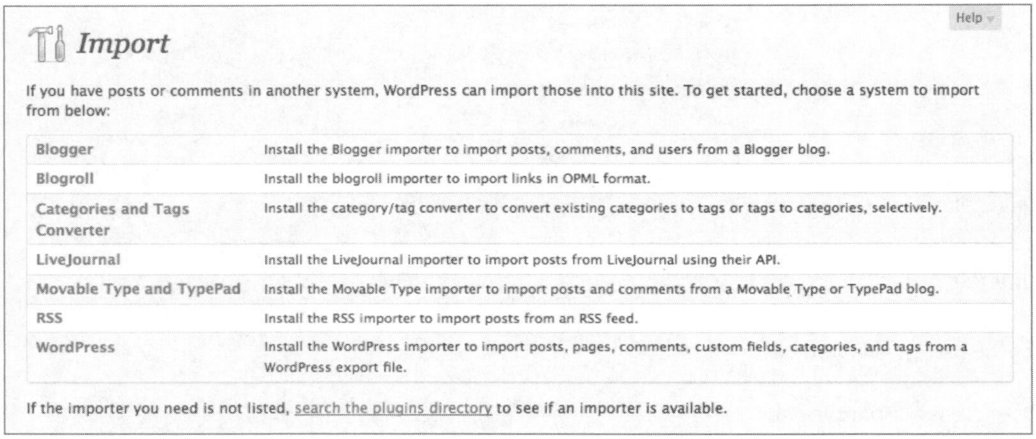

Help
Import
If you have posts or comments in another system, WordPress can import those into this site. To get started, choose a system to import from below:
Blogger
Install the Blogger importer to import posts, comments, and users from a Blogger blog.
Blogroll
Install the blogroll importer to import links in OPML format.
Categories and Tags Converter
Install the category/tag converter to convert existing categories to tags or tags to categories, selectively.
LiveJournal
Install the LiveJournal importer to import posts from LiveJournal using their API.
Movable Type and TypePad
Install the Movable Type importer to import posts and comments from a Movable Type or TypePad blog.
RSS
Install the RSS importer to import posts from an RSS feed.
WordPress
Install the WordPress importer to import posts, pages, comments, custom fields, categories, and tags from a WordPress export file.
If the importer you need is not listed, search the plugins directory to see if an importer is available.

FIGURE 18-6

This list of tools includes:

- Blogger
- Blogrolls (sets of links from other sites)
- Categories and Tags Converter (for within your own site — I discuss these in Lesson 20)
- LiveJournal
- Movable Type and TypePad
- RSS
- WordPress (other installations of WordPress or from WordPress.com)

When you click any of these, you're asked to install a plugin, which is very easy — just click the Install button.

At that point, you'll have a set of instructions, which includes details of how to prepare your content on the old site or blog for importing. For example, on WordPress.com blogs, there's an Export button that produces a text file that you save to your computer.

The Import function on your new WordPress site will prompt you to find whatever file was created by the export process on the old site and upload it. At that point, you'll be asked some questions about how you want to import the data; for example, do you want the authors created if they don't exist already or do you want to map an author to an existing author?

I won't go into the details of each of these import functions — they all run roughly the same way as I just described, except for the Categories and Tags Converter, which, as I said, I cover in Lesson 20. The point is that you have a fair number of options for bringing in materials from other sources. You can also search the WordPress plugins directory for other plugins that will handle the import process for sources not covered in this admin screen.

ADMIN SETTINGS AFFECTING POSTS AND PAGES

Although there is not a lot you can control from the administration panel for all posts and pages, a few items are worth looking at.

Allowing or Disallowing Comments

I've mentioned this setting before, but it's worth repeating here because it directly affects posts and pages. By default, WordPress allows comments on both posts and pages. If you look under Settings ➪ Discussion near the top, you'll see a check box that says "Allow people to post comments on new articles" ("articles" is just another way of saying both posts and pages). This check box is active by default, but you can turn it off any time.

> *Be aware that a change to the site-wide comments setting takes effect only from the moment you do it. If it's three months into your site and you disallow comments, it will apply only to posts or pages from that time forward.*

There's a reminder with this setting telling you that, no matter what you do here, comments can be controlled on an individual basis for each post or page. In other words, if they're turned off for the site as a whole, you can turn them on for individual posts or pages, and vice versa.

My rule of thumb for this setting is: if your primary form of content is blog-like (meant to generate response), then keep comments turned on. If your primary form of content is more informational, like a traditional site where you don't want people commenting on the 15 types of tax service you provide, turn off comments globally and turn them on individually only when you need them.

> *Whether comments appear on a post or a page can also be controlled through your theme's template files — by including or not including the coding for displaying comments. Some themes by default do not include comments in their templates for WordPress pages (but do for posts). Other themes, like the default Twenty Ten theme, do show comments on pages, and still other themes provide you the choice by offering a template that removes comments from pages.*

Assigning Your Home and Blog Pages

By default, the homepage or front page in WordPress consists of the 10 most recent posts from all categories. However, you can change that setting in a number of ways under the Settings ➪ Reading screen, which is shown in Figure 18-7.

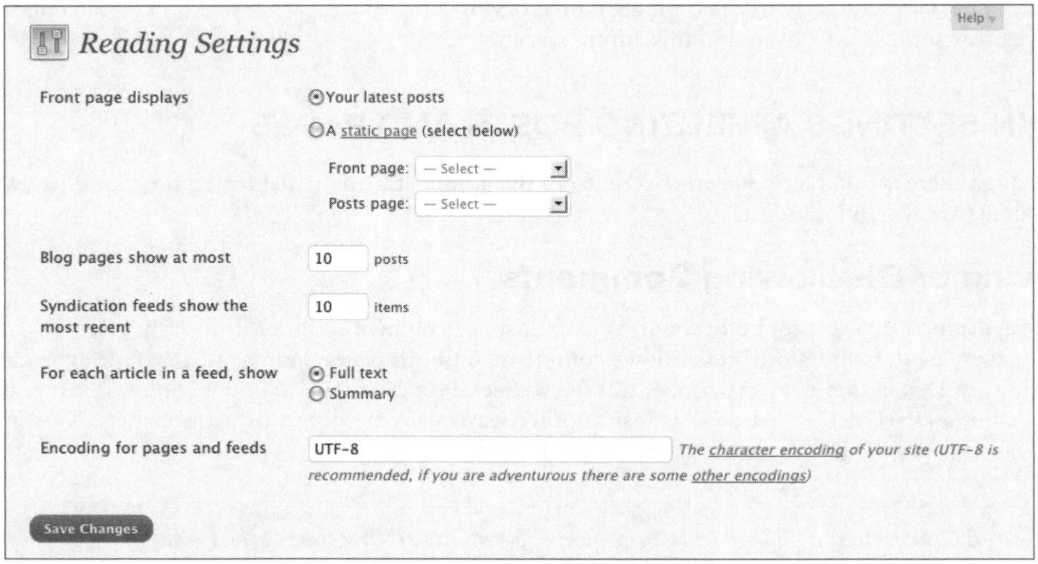

FIGURE 18-7

You can see the default setting of Your Latest Posts. The other choice is to make one of your WordPress pages the site's homepage, by choosing from the drop-down menu next to Front Page.

Keep in mind that the title of whatever page you choose does not change in the menu. If you decide you want the About page to be your homepage, the menu will still say About (though if your theme is using the WordPress menu system, this can easily be changed). Typically, you'll create a page called Home and then choose that from the drop-down menu.

> *On some older WordPress themes — created before WordPress introduced its powerful menu system — a link to "Home" is hard-coded into the theme files. If you change the Front Page setting, using a page you've named Home, your menu will end up with two Home pages listed. Removing that hard-coded Home page — probably from the header.php template — solves the problem. Or the theme might have an options page where you can disable that hard-coding.*

Though it's clear enough what choice you're making for Front Page, it may not be obvious what the second drop-down — Posts Page — is for. If you think about it, when you choose one of your static pages to replace the default homepage, there's no longer a place for people to find all your latest blog posts in one location. True, they can look at individual categories, but there isn't a "blog" page like the default homepage. That's what the Posts Page drop-down is for. It takes the page you choose from the menu and replaces it with your most current blog entries.

> *If you have existing content on the static page you choose as your Posts Page, be aware that WordPress will no longer display that content — it will only show blog posts. What you need to do is create a new page with whatever title suits it best — Our Blog, Blog Posts, Company News, or whatever — and leave the Text Editor blank, then publish the page. Now, when you choose that page from the Posts Page drop-down menu, no content is going to be hidden.*

Other Admin Settings for Posts and Pages

On the Settings ➪ Writing screen, you can change:

- Size of the Post Box (the Text Editor). Default is 10.
- Default Post Category. Default is Uncategorized.

On the Settings ➪ Reading screen, you can change:

- Blog Pages Show at Most. Default is 10 posts.

TRY IT

In this lesson, you practice changing the homepage for your site.

Lesson Requirements

At least four or five posts, plus at least one additional page besides About that has some existing content on it.

Step-by-Step

Change the homepage and add a Posts Page.

1. Go to Settings ➪ Reading.
2. Click the radio button for A Static Page.
3. Select a page from the drop-down menu to become your new homepage.
4. Click Save Changes.
5. On the live site, try clicking the header title or simply enter the domain name in your address bar — your new homepage should be shown.
6. Back in Settings ➪ Read, choose a page for Posts Page.

7. Click Save Changes.
8. On the live site, click the menu item for the page you just chose and instead of its content, you should see your blog posts.

> *To see some of the examples from this lesson, watch the video for Lesson 18 on the DVD with the print book, or watch online at* www.wrox.com/go/wp24vids.

19

Managing Media Files

You learned earlier that all media files you upload to WordPress are listed in the Media Library. In this lesson, I show you how to work with the library, both sorting and finding media files, as well as editing and deleting them. I also show you some administrative settings for media files.

FINDING FILES IN THE MEDIA LIBRARY

You've already seen how the Media Library works on the tabs of the Upload/Insert popup window. The Media Library screen accessed from the Media ⇨ Library link of the admin menu, shown in Figure 19-1, is very similar.

One important difference with this screen is that you can see whether a media file is attached to a post, and if so, the name of the post with a direct link. To be attached to a post means that the file is listed in that post's Gallery.

Why is it useful to know if a media file is attached? If a file's not attached, you know it's available to be used in a Gallery, because media files can be attached to only one post.

If a media file is already attached and you want to use it in a different post's Gallery, you cannot simply unattach and reattach. But you do have a couple of options:

- Delete the file, which removes it from the first post's Gallery, then upload the file into the new post.
- If the image has to stay in the first post's Gallery, upload a second copy of the file (WordPress automatically renames it by adding a number so there's no conflict with the existing copy) into the new post where you want it to appear.

Of course, if you don't need a file to be part of a post's Gallery — you only want to insert it into the body of the post — you're free to insert media files in as many posts as you'd like, whether or not the file is attached.

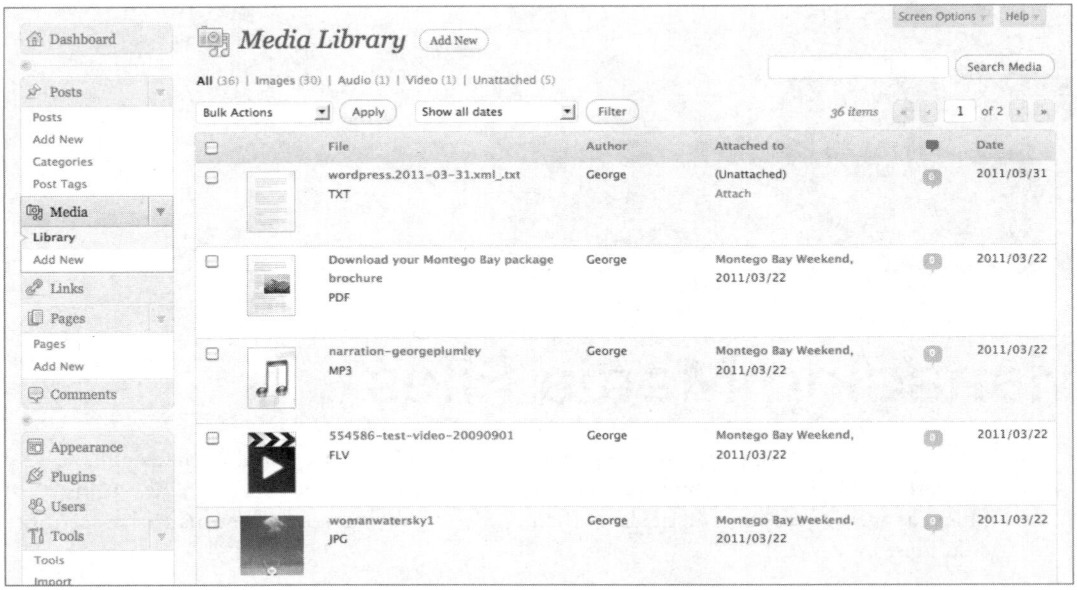

FIGURE 19-1

If you're looking for unattached files, an easy way of finding them is to use the menu at the top of the page just below Media Library. The links in this menu will vary depending on the types of files in your library. There will always be an All link, but there can also be Images, Video, Audio, and Unattached. Clicking Unattached displays all media files that are not in a post Gallery.

This little menu is important because it tells you what type or types of files you're looking at in the library. If you don't notice that the Images link is selected, for example, you're left wondering why your PDFs, videos, and audios aren't listed. Just click All to display every type of media file. The currently selected choice will always be in bold black.

You can also find items in the Media Library by the date they were uploaded into WordPress. The Show All Dates menu at the top of the page drops down a list of available months.

The Media Library displays files in descending chronological order (newest first) and there is no option for changing this. However, you do have some display choices in the Screen Options tab (at the top right of the screen), such as which columns to show and how many files to display per page.

The last method for finding media files is the Search field at the top right. Keep in mind that it looks for words and phrases only in the Title and Description fields of media files. If you don't have descriptions for your files and your titles all say things like img829384.jpg, this search isn't going to be very useful. Yet another reason to give your files good descriptive titles!

Also, keep in mind that the search is conducted on all media files, regardless of which type or types are currently displayed.

EDITING AND DELETING MEDIA FILES

To edit a file in the Media Library, just click its name. Or, when you mouse over the row for that media file, a text menu appears allowing you to Edit, Delete, or View the file.

Clicking the name or the Edit link takes you to a new page — the page for images is shown in Figure 19-2 — where you see the file and the options to edit.

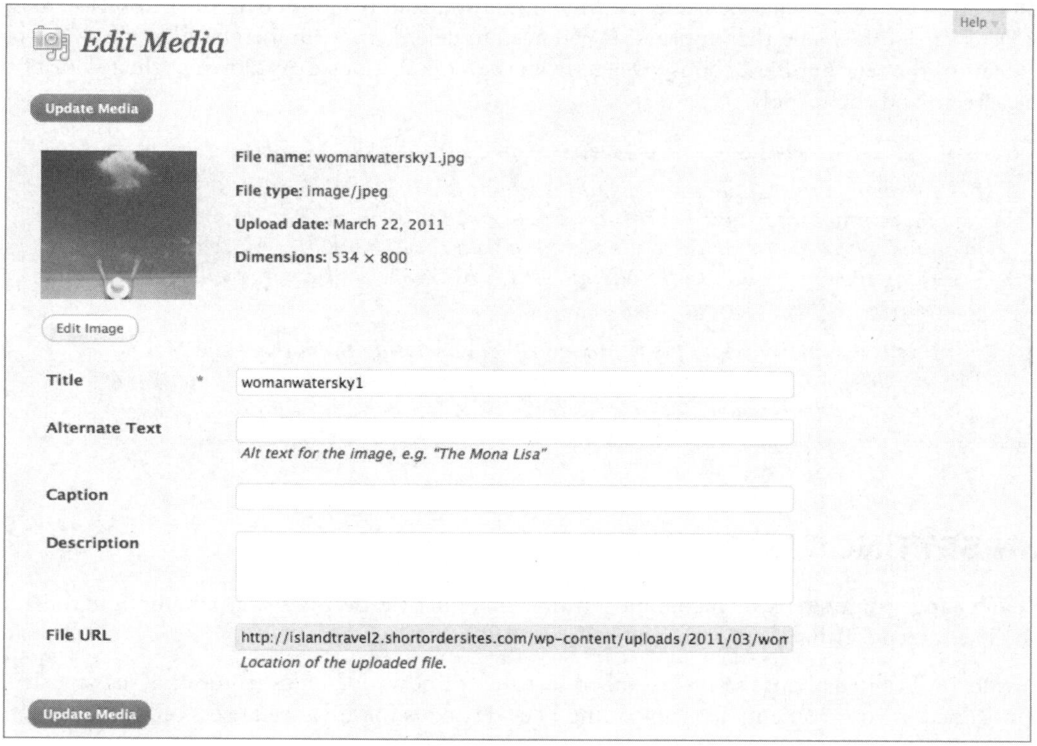

FIGURE 19-2

You have fewer options for this image than you saw in the Upload/Insert window, because these relate only to the file itself, not to parameters for inserting into a post. Even with files that are attached to posts, you cannot edit parameters like alignment or size from this screen because you're not editing the post, just the media file. If you do need to change those other options, WordPress makes it easy by having the link to the post right there in the Media Library.

If a media file is attached to a post, changes made in the Media Library are reflected in the file's listing in the Gallery. However, inserted copies of the file will not be affected — their titles, captions, and so on are independent on a per-post basis.

Clicking the Edit Image button brings up the image editor window you looked at in detail in Lesson 14. Here, you can crop, rotate, and resize the actual image or just its thumbnail. I won't go into the details here, but I will remind you again that once you've clicked the Save button and you see your changes on the screen, *you must also click the Update Media button* or those changes won't actually be processed.

Other file types have a similar edit screen, but without the image editing button or the alternative text field.

If you need to delete a media file using the Media Library, simply mouse over the title of the file and click Delete from the menu that appears. If you need to delete large numbers of files, check the box on the left of the relevant files, choose Delete from the Bulk Actions drop-down at the top or bottom of the screen, and click Apply.

> *If you delete a media file that's been inserted into a post(s), the link(s) will remain in place and show on the website as broken. You need to go into each post and get rid of the code that's trying to find the deleted file. All that means is finding the empty box in the Visual Text Editor and clicking it; you'll get the familiar red X for deleting.*
>
> *For images displaying in a post's image gallery, deleting them from the Media Library does not leave a broken link; the image simply won't display next time the visitor loads the page.*

ADMIN SETTINGS FOR MEDIA

You can change some site-wide media file parameters under the Settings ⇨ Media link on the admin menu. The screen for that page is shown in Figure 19-3.

In Lesson 16, I talked about the Auto-Embeds setting for how video files from some sharing sites get embedded in your content. The Uploading Files setting is for advanced users only. Leave it at its default settings.

That leaves the Image Sizes settings. These are the dimensions that WordPress uses when it creates as many as three different versions of images you're uploading: Thumbnail, Medium, and Large. These additional versions are created only if the longest side of the uploaded file is larger than the maximum dimensions set here on this page.

For example, if the maximum width or height for Medium is 300 pixels (the default WordPress setting) and the image being uploaded is 400 pixels wide by 270 pixels high, a Medium version will be created with dimensions of 300 pixels by 203 pixels. WordPress keeps the proportions of the original and makes the longest side whatever you've set as the maximum width or height. Had the image been 270 pixels wide by 400 pixels high, the Medium version created would have been 203 pixels by 300 pixels.

The one exception to this is the Thumbnail setting. By default, WordPress checks the box that says Crop Thumbnail to Exact Dimensions. This means the Thumbnail version will be exactly what's in the two fields for height and width (150 pixels by default). If you want Thumbnails to be proportional, you'll need to uncheck that box.

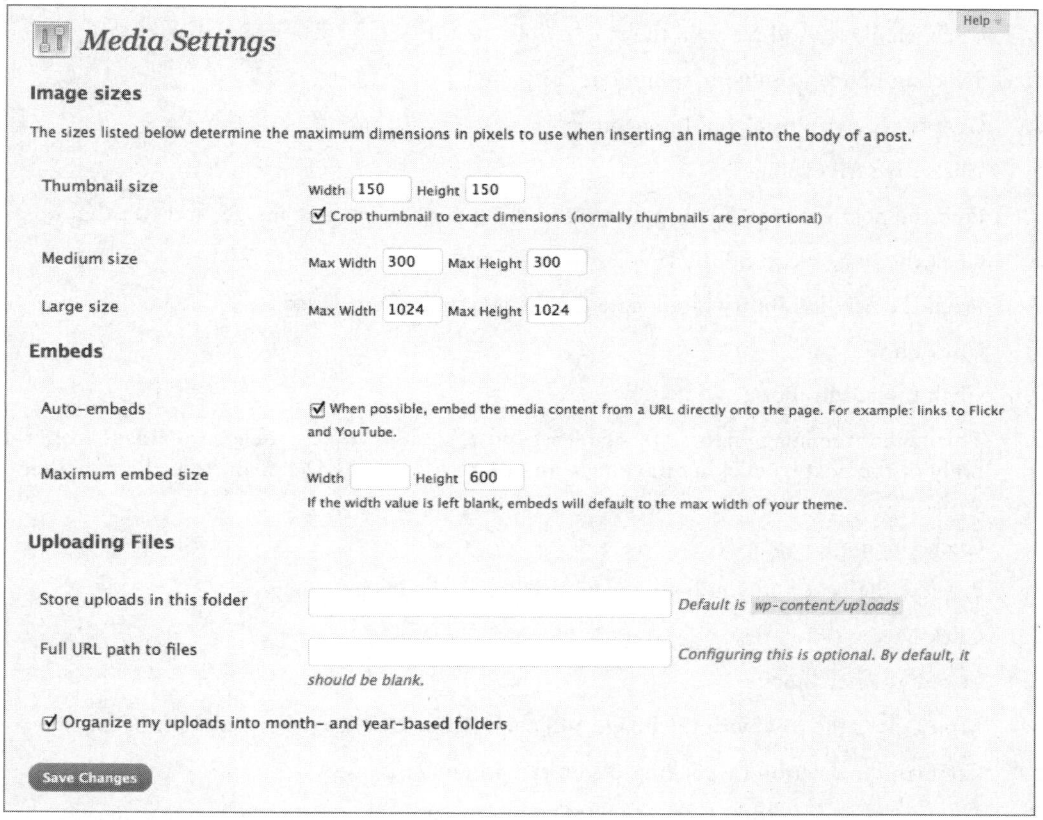

FIGURE 19-3

For most people, these settings are fine, though with larger and larger screens, and wider content areas, you may be able to afford to bump up the Medium setting (the one most typically used when inserting images into posts). Of course, it all depends on how much space your theme gives to the main content area.

TRY IT

In this lesson, you practice uploading an image to the Media Library, placing it in an image gallery, and then deleting it from the Media Library.

Lesson Requirements

An image you don't need and an existing image gallery in a post.

Step-by-Step

How to upload a media file, insert it in an image gallery, and then delete it.

1. Click Media ➪ Add New on the main admin menu.
2. Select an image from your computer.
3. Give the image a title you'll remember.
4. Click Save All Changes.
5. Find the post with the image gallery where you'll place the new image, and edit that post.
6. Click the Image icon on the Upload/Insert menu.
7. From the Media Library tab, locate the image you just uploaded.
8. Click Show.
9. Click Insert Into Post.
10. This makes the image part of this gallery's post, so now you can delete the image from the body of the post by clicking the image and then clicking the Delete button (the red circle with an X).
11. Click Update Post.
12. Preview the post and you'll see the new image in the image gallery.
13. Click Media ➪ Library.
14. Locate the new image.
15. Mouse over the row with the image and click Delete on the text menu that appears.
16. Confirm the deletion by clicking OK in the popup window.
17. On the live site, refresh the post and the image will be gone from the image gallery.

> *To see some of the examples from this lesson, including deleting an image that was inserted into a post, watch the video for Lesson 19 on the DVD with the print book, or watch online at* `www.wrox.com/go/wp24vids`.

20

Managing Post Categories and Tags

As your website grows and evolves, you may need to change the names of tags or the relationships between categories, for example. In this lesson, I show you how to manage all aspects of your categories and tags.

MANAGING CATEGORIES

I showed you in Lesson 6 how to add new categories from the Add New Post Screen (or the Edit Post screen). You also saw in Lesson 18 how to add and remove categories for a post through Quick Edit or how to add categories to multiple posts at one time with Bulk Edit. Now it's time to look at managing the categories themselves.

You can manage categories through the Posts ➪ Categories link on the main menu, which produces the screen in Figure 20-1.

The left side of the screen is for adding categories and the right is for editing, moving, or deleting existing categories.

Adding Categories

When you add a category in the Add/Edit Post screens, you only have the option of choosing a category parent. Here, you can also enter a description for the category and what's called the *category slug*.

The description is helpful when you have several people working on a site and you need to make clear what belongs in a particular category. Sometimes, the description might be used by a theme at the beginning of a category page, for example, or you could customize your theme to make use of it.

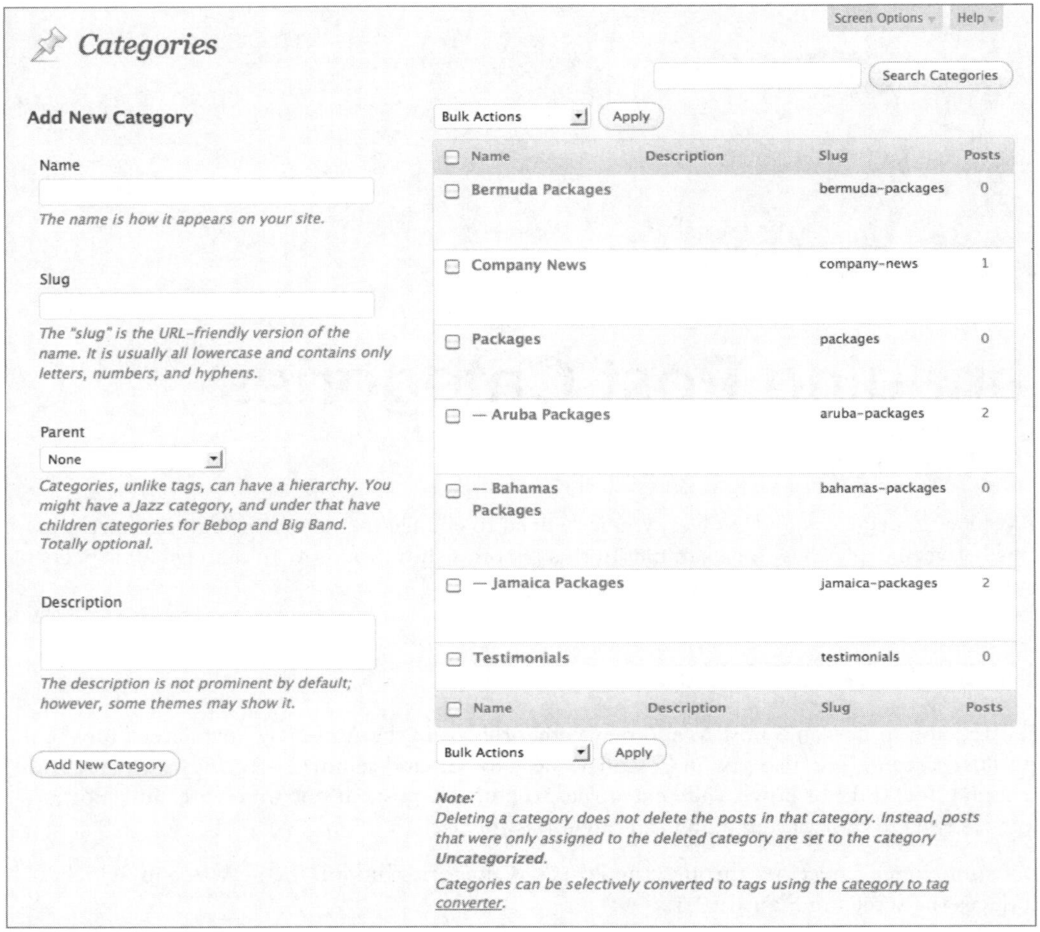

FIGURE 20-1

The category slug is used by WordPress to create friendly or nice versions of URLs. Normally, a WordPress URL for a category would be something like `http://www.yourdomain.com/?cat=4`, but if you have friendly URLs turned on using the Permalinks settings (see Lesson 25), it might look like `http://www.yourdomain.com/category/jamaica-packages`. The `jamaica-packages` part is the category slug.

By default, WordPress takes whatever name you enter for the category and creates a slug by making it all lowercase and replacing spaces with dashes. However, you can enter your own slug if you'd prefer. You can also change the slug at any time using the edit function for categories.

> *If you've had your site public for even a short time, it's not good to mess with existing slugs. If someone has linked to your category with a friendly URL, and you change the slug, the URL link will be broken.*

When you've finished entering information for your new category, remember to click Add New Category down at the bottom left of the screen.

Editing, Moving, or Deleting Categories

On the right side of the Categories screen, you see a list of all your categories in alphabetical order. If you have a lot of categories, remember that under Screen Options at the top, you can change how many are displayed at one time. If you have subcategories, they're displayed with a dash beside them and in alphabetical order underneath their parent category. If you have sub-subcategories, each level is represented with an additional dash.

Finding categories is also aided by a search function up at the top right, and the ability to sort on any of the columns: Name, Description, Slug, and Posts.

> *Sometimes, a theme may ask you for the ID of a category (or page or post). That information is not displayed in the categories listing (though there are plugins to do this), but you can still find it by mousing over the title of the category and looking in the status bar of your browser. You'll see something like this:* `http://www.yourdomain.com/wp-admin/categories.php?action=edit&cat_ID=5`.
>
> *That number at the end is the ID. You can find the ID for posts and pages the same way.*

Like other listings, you can see an options menu appear below the title of a category by mousing over its row: Edit, Quick Edit, and Delete.

The Quick Edit feature allows you to change the name and the slug right there in the list. If you click Edit or the title of the category, you're taken to a new screen, as shown in Figure 20-2.

This is where you can change not only the name and the slug, but the description and, most importantly, the parent. I like to think of changing the parent as a kind of moving process, whether it's to a new subcategory of a parent, or to a new parent, or to the top-level categories. Depending on how you have your site set up, moving a category in this way may change where it appears on your website or if it will appear at all. You may need to make some additional adjustments after the move.

For example, if you made Sunstar Packages a subcategory of TravelWhiz Packages, they would now show up under the packages link on the TravelWhiz page. However, because the name and the category ID number remain the same, the link on the Sunstar page would still work as well. Notice that you could have bulk-edited the Sunstar Package posts to be assigned to the TravelWhiz Packages category, but because Sunstar is now part of TravelWhiz, you don't want to have to remember to put future Sunstar entries under both categories.

> *Posts can be in two subcategories of the same parent, but if you display a list of all posts in the parent category, those posts will show up only once.*

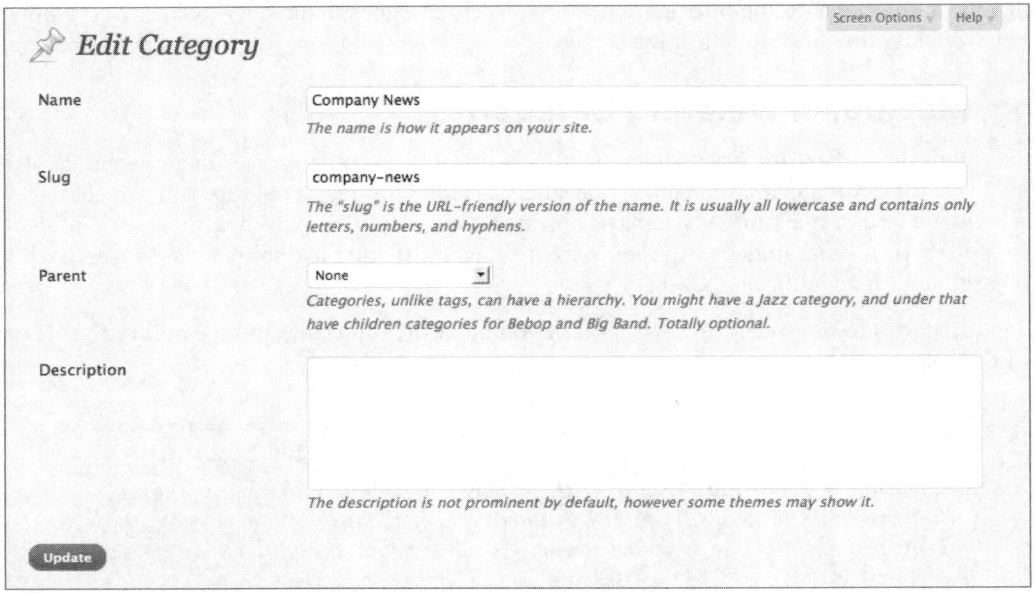

FIGURE 20-2

The final option for managing categories is to delete them. Don't worry about the posts, however. You're deleting only the category and not the posts that belong to it. However, in the case of posts that belong only to that category, WordPress automatically assigns them to the default category. Your best bet before deleting a category is to find all posts in that category. For those that don't appear in any other category, assign them to some appropriate category, and then proceed with the deletion.

Managing the Default Category

I mentioned in Lesson 6 that posts must be in at least one category and that WordPress comes with one category that can never be erased — if you forget to assign a category to a post, WordPress automatically assigns it to this default category. Though you can never get rid of this category, you can change its name from the default Uncategorized to whatever you like.

Once you've added at least one additional category, you can also change the category used by WordPress as the default. You do this under Settings ⇨ Writing, where you'll see a drop-down menu for Default Post Category.

MANAGING TAGS

Tags are managed in almost exactly the same way as categories via the Posts ⇨ Post Tags link on the side menu, as you can see from the screen in Figure 20-3.

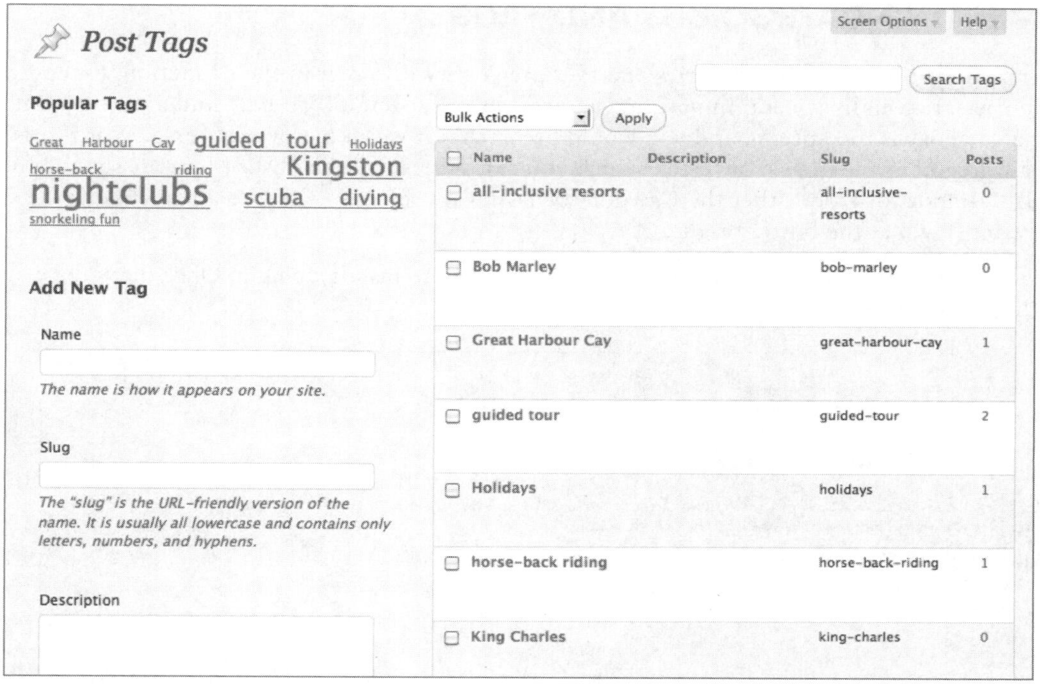

FIGURE 20-3

The only difference between the two is that tags can't be hierarchical — no parent-child structure.

You also see what's called a *tag cloud* up at the top left. It shows the most popular tags on your site, using size to represent the level of popularity. You can display this same tag cloud on your site using what are called *widgets*, which are covered in Lesson 21.

Another important difference between tags and categories is what happens when you delete tags. Posts do not have to have at least one tag, so when you delete a tag from the Post Tags screen, it simply disappears from any posts that used it; posts that used only that tag will not be assigned some default tag.

> *If you delete a tag from a particular post, and that was the only post to which the tag had been assigned, the tag remains in the system. You'll be able to see it in Post Tags and it would come up if you started to enter the first few letters in the Add Tag window of a post.*

CONVERTING CATEGORIES AND TAGS

I've mentioned before that categories and tags aren't very different in their function, except that categories are usually general in nature whereas tags are specific. You may find at some point that a category is too specific and you would prefer that it was a tag or vice versa. WordPress has a Categories and Tags Converter, which you can access from the list of options shown under Tools ➪ Import or from either the Category or Post Tags screens — there's a text link to the converter down at the bottom right.

The first time you try to use the converter, you'll be asked to install a plugin. Once that's done, you'll get the screen shown in Figure 20-4.

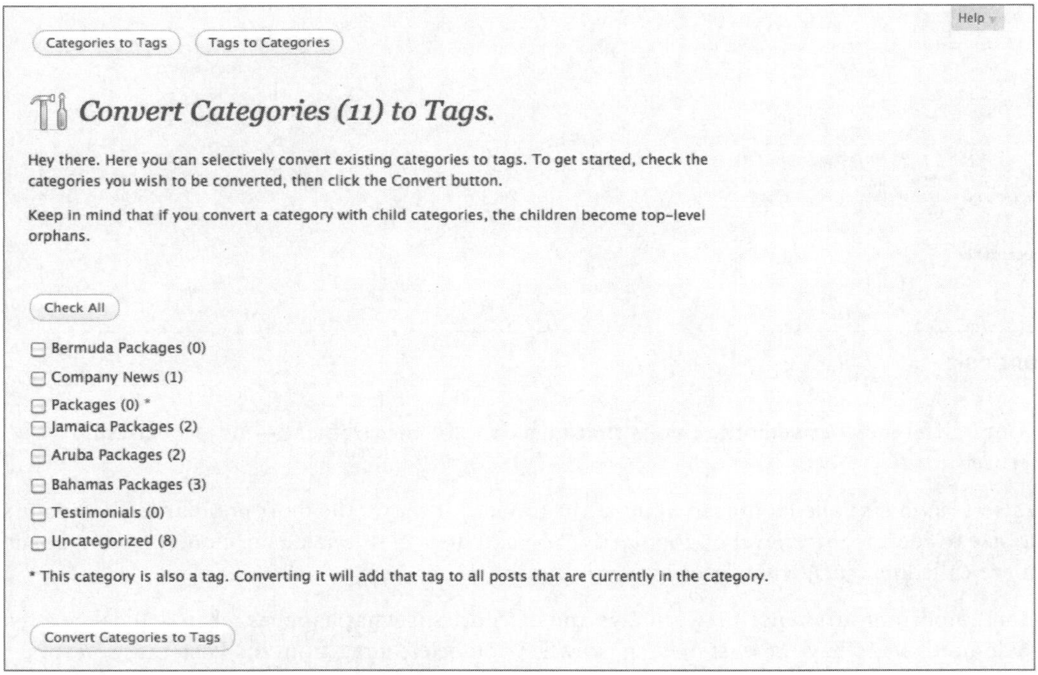

FIGURE 20-4

You simply select the category(s) that you want to convert and click Convert Categories to Tags.

> *Sometimes, people think converting categories to tags is a way of just creating tags with the same names as the categories you select. No, you're actually changing the categories into tags and the categories no longer exist.*

WordPress reminds you that if you convert a category that has children, those subcategories will become individual top-level categories. So, if you were relying on category hierarchy to include a post under several categories, you'll need to rethink your category structure or assign the relevant posts to the additional category(s) you need.

To change tags into categories, you need to click Tags to Categories at the top of the screen. This displays a list of all existing tags and again, you can either use the Check All button or select only the tags you want to convert.

TRY IT

In this lesson, you practice changing an existing category by giving it a different name and assigning it to a parent category.

Lesson Requirements

At least four or five existing categories.

Step-by-Step

Changing the name and relationship of a category.

1. Click Posts ➪ Categories on the main admin menu.
2. Locate the category you want to modify.
3. Click the title or the Edit link of the mouseover menu.
4. Change the name of the category.
5. From the drop-down menu, choose a parent category.
6. Click Update Category.
7. You should be returned to the Categories page.
8. Check that your renamed category is showing below the parent category.
9. You can verify that all your posts in the modified category are displaying under the new name and parent by going to your site and refreshing the category display, then clicking the category. Or you can go to Posts ➪ Posts and search for the posts under the renamed category.
10. Change things back if you were just experimenting.

> *To see some of the examples from this lesson, watch the video for Lesson 20 on the DVD with the print book, or watch online at* `www.wrox.com/go/wp24vids`.

21

Managing Widgets and Menus

Up to now, you've worked with content that appears in the main body of your website, but WordPress makes it easy to control the content in the sidebar and other areas of the layout, without having to know HTML or other coding. That's the purpose of what are called *widgets*. In this lesson, I show you how they work and how they can work for you.

WordPress recently added a menu system which makes creating and managing navigation areas as simple as using widgets and widget areas. In this lesson, I'll show you how to create new menus and then manage the items on those menus.

WHAT ARE WIDGETS?

Widgets can be described as elements on a web page that users can easily add, delete, and move around. A widget might produce a list of all your blog categories, another might be a text box where you can update all your contact information, and yet another could contain the coding your mailing list manager provides for inserting a sign-up form.

The great thing about widgets is that although they can perform some pretty complex functions, they appear in your administration screen as a simple box that you just drag and drop. You drop them into what are called *widget areas* that are coded into your theme files.

Widget areas began life in the sidebar of WordPress themes, but these days, you'll find them anywhere — in the header, the footer, the content area. If you customize your theme, you can place widget areas wherever you'd like.

Some basic widgets come with WordPress, some are created by theme writers, and still others appear when you install a plugin. In fact, a widget is really just a kind of plugin.

What can be a little confusing for people is that if you remove all widgets from the sidebar area, you'll still see some functions on your site. Why isn't the sidebar empty?

Theme writers build in a safety element by hard-coding some functions into the sidebar, which show up only if no widgets are present (the Twenty Ten theme has three, for example). That way, in case you accidently delete all your widgets, the sidebar won't be completely empty. As soon as you add one or more widgets back, these default elements will disappear.

THE WIDGETS SCREEN

Widgets are controlled through the Appearance ➪ Widgets link on the side admin menu. You're presented with the screen shown in Figure 21-1.

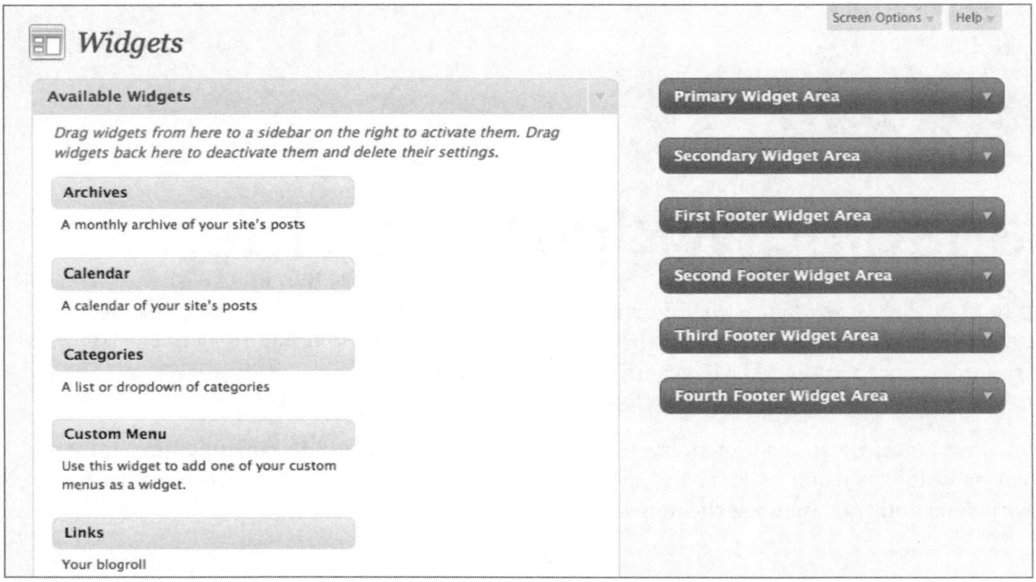

FIGURE 21-1

The left side of the screen shows the available widgets and the right shows the widget areas that your particular theme has created anywhere on the website. As you can see from Figure 21-1, the Twenty Ten default theme comes with a number of widget areas: two in the sidebar and four in the footer portion of the site.

Unlike the sidebar, there is no default coding to display something in the footer widget areas if there are no widgets present. So, don't worry that you're not seeing anything down there.

The widgets you see on the left of Figure 21-1 are some of the default ones that come with WordPress (they extend below the visible screen), but the list on your site will vary depending on your theme and what plugins you have installed. Plugins add new functionality to WordPress and some of them use widgets to allow you to customize that functionality as well as control where it appears on the site.

There are actually two lists of widgets on the left, Available and Inactive (which is not visible in Figure 21-1), and the difference between them is covered in the final section of this lesson.

ACTIVATING AND EDITING WIDGETS

Activating a widget is as simple as dragging it from the left side of the Widgets screen to an area on the right side of the screen. Figure 21-2A shows you what it looks like as you drag a widget across.

FIGURE 21-2

In Figure 21-2B, you can see how the widget automatically opens to show you whatever options it has available. If you try this yourself, you may wonder why there's still a Categories widget over on the left. That's because you can use the same widget several times (perhaps in different areas on the site if your theme is so enabled).

With the widget open, you can make the customizations you want, such as giving it a title or setting options such as how many posts to display. Always be sure to click Save when you're finished or else any changes you do make will not take effect.

When you're finished editing, you can click Close or click the down arrow at the right of the widget header bar (that same arrow will open the widget, too). You can also close or open the entire Primary Widget Area using the down arrow on its header (and do the same for each if you have multiple areas in your theme).

> *Widgets automatically activate when you drop them into a widget area — you don't have to click a Save button. The difference is that for some widgets, you need to do something before anything becomes visible on the site. The Text widget, for example, needs something typed in and then saved before it shows on the site. The Categories widget, however, will display categories on the live site the moment you drag it over to a widget area.*

MOVING OR REMOVING WIDGETS

Aside from the convenience of adding more functionality and content to your sidebar (I'll just speak of sidebars because that's how most people will be using widgets), widgets also allow you to easily change the look of your sidebar by reordering them. If you have Categories and then Pages, you can switch them around by moving Pages above Categories. The change is instantly reflected on your website. If you want to change the actual design of the sidebar or the way that widgets are displayed, you will need to change your style sheet.

Removing or deactivating widgets is as easy as dragging them from the right side back over to the left — they instantly disappear from the sidebar. Instead of dragging, you can also click Remove if the widget is open.

> *Every once and a while, your browser may not allow you to move widgets by dragging and dropping. If this ever happens, there's a backup method, which you'll find under Screen Options at the top right. There's a single link that says Enable Accessibility Mode and clicking it disables the drag-and-drop feature, replacing it with text links on all widgets — either Add if it's not in a widget area, or Edit if it is.*

However, you need to think carefully about where you put a widget when removing it from a widget area:

- If you drag a widget to the Available box, you lose all your settings and text for that widget.
- If you drag a widget to the Inactive box, you keep all your settings. This is handy, particularly if there are complicated settings such as URLs or specific wording that you might forget later.

It's easy to forget about the Inactive box because it's often very far down the screen. It's also very difficult to drag widgets back and forth from that box, again because it's so far down the screen and your browser doesn't always want to move nicely with your mouse. An easy answer is to collapse the Available widgets box, so that it brings Inactive closer to the top of the page.

THE WORDPRESS MENU SYSTEM

As of WordPress 3.0, a powerful menu system was introduced which makes it simple for a user to create menus, add almost any type of content to those menus, order the menu with drag-and-drop functionality, and assign menus to various locations on the site. In this lesson, I'll show you how to create and manage menus using this system.

One of the key features that makes the system so powerful is that you create menus and then assign them to areas within your site's layout. By default, you can assign menus to any widget area using a special widget. However, it's up to theme writers to include specially-coded navigation areas in their templates in order for users to be able to assign menus to traditional navigation points such as in the header or the footer. In other words, depending on your theme, you may not be able to use these menus anywhere except in widget areas.

If your theme does not support navigation areas, you'll see the warning message at the top of the screen in Figure 21-3, which is accessed via Appearance ➪ Menus.

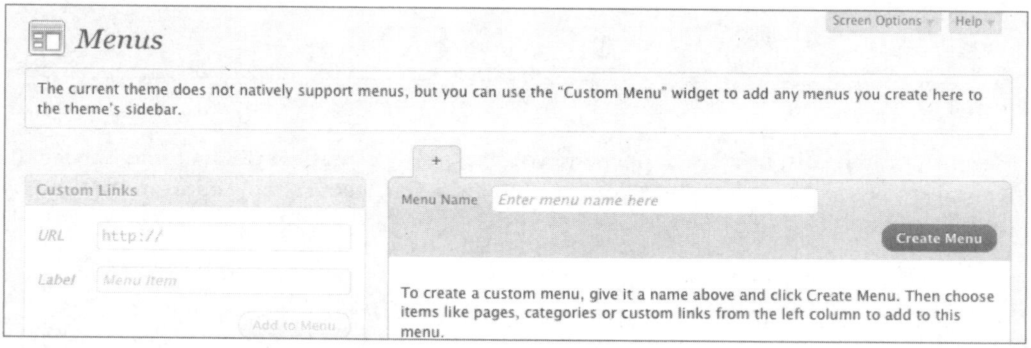

FIGURE 21-3

In that situation, you'll still be able to create menus and assign them to widget areas, and that's all explained in that warning message in Figure 21-3.

CREATING A MENU

Menus are all located in the right-hand column of the Menus screen. When you first install WordPress, there are no menus set up, and you'll see a text box on the right side labelled Menu Name. By giving the menu a name and clicking Create Menu, not only do you get a success message and a new tab for the menu, but all the boxes on the left become active instead of grayed out, as shown in Figure 21-4.

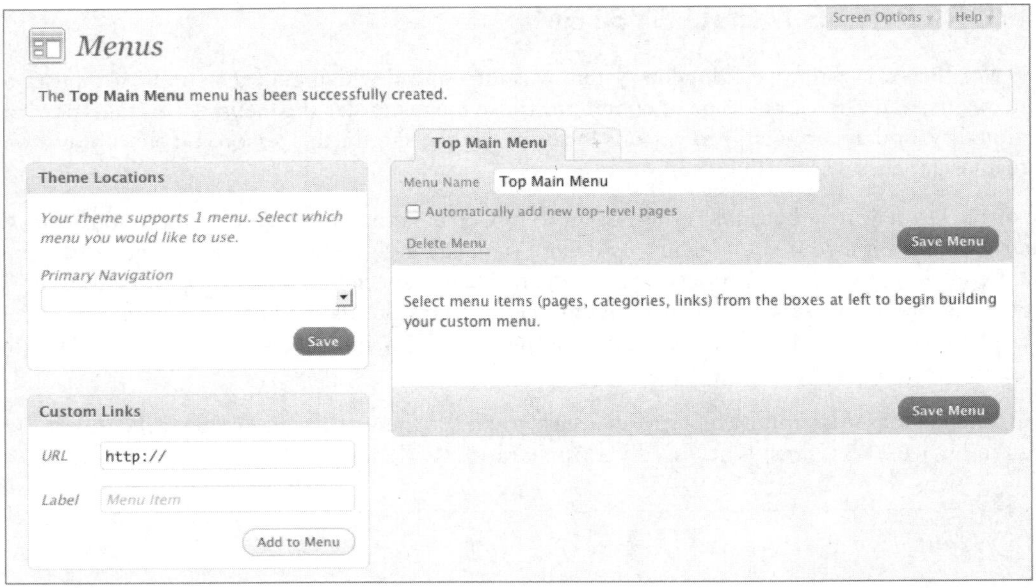

FIGURE 21-4

Only one menu can be displayed at a time, and you access any others via the set of tabs at the top of the Menus meta box. That's also where you go to create a new menu: simply click on the little tab with the plus symbol.

> *Make sure you name menus clearly so anyone can understand their purpose, particularly if you're going to have other menus. For example, if I made special pages that only Island Travel staff could see, I could easily customize my theme header to show one menu for staff and one for the public. In that case, it would be crucial to name the menus so it's clear which is which when it comes time to assign them.*

Once you've named your menu and saved it, you can start adding items to the menu. In this case, I've created a menu called Top Main Menu and it's going to be my primary navigation for the site, so I want all my key content pages up there.

Menu items are found in the left-hand column of the Menus screen. By default, the first two meta boxes of content items you can see are Custom Links and Pages. If you keep scrolling down, you'll also see Categories. Posts and Post Tags are also available, but you'll need to activate them using Screen Options at the top right. If you have any custom post types or custom taxonomies, they can be made available, too. In other words, virtually any type of content can be a menu item!

But how do you get these menu items onto a menu? Simply check the box beside one or more menu items, then click the Add to Menu button. Make sure, of course, that the menu you want to add to is displayed over on the right. A rounded rectangle that looks like a widget will then show up in the Menu area for each of the menu items, as illustrated in Figure 21-5.

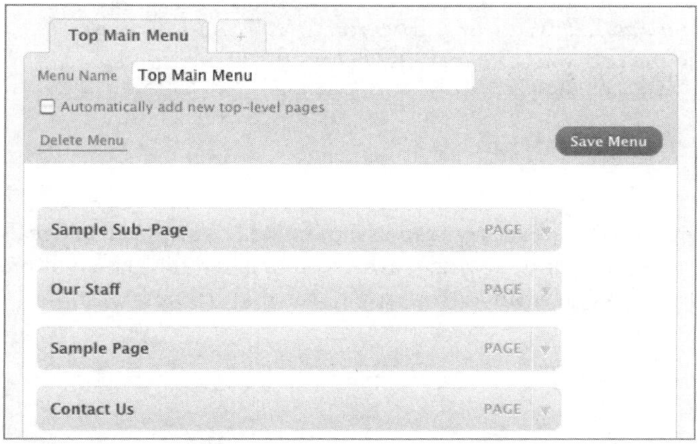

FIGURE 21-5

One thing that can be a little confusing is that the meta boxes displaying Pages, Categories, Posts, and so on all default to Most Recent. That's good in one sense because usually, when you're adding something to a menu, it's an item you've just recently added to WordPress. However, if you're trying to add something not so recent, it looks as if the item isn't available. All you have to do, though, is click the View All tab, and you'll see every item of that type. Figure 21-6 shows the difference between Most Recent (left) and View All (right).

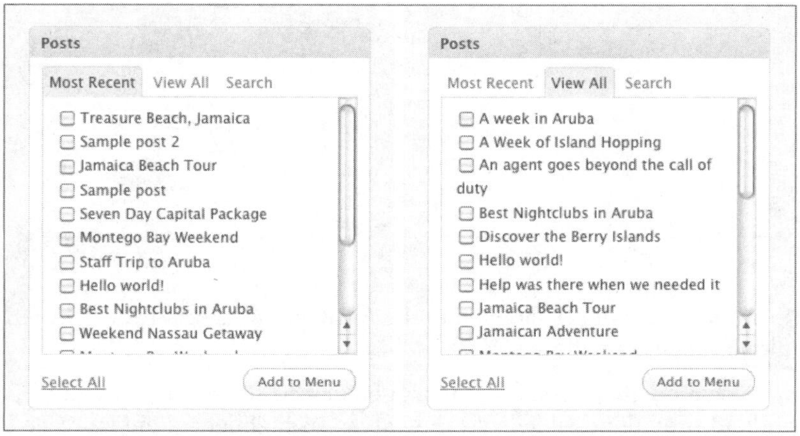

FIGURE 21-6

Once you have a menu set up on your site and you add a new page to the site, you might be wondering why the page doesn't show up on your menu. That's because you have to manually add new content items to menus.

However, in the case of top-level WordPress pages (ones that aren't children or sub-pages of another page), you can tell WordPress to automatically add them to a particular menu by checking the box that appears just below the menu name.

ASSIGNING A MENU

Whether or not your theme supports navigation areas, you can assign menus to any widget area using the Custom Menu widget. When you drag it to a widget area, you're given the choice of naming the menu and choosing which menu to assign from a drop-down list of all menus, as shown in Figure 21-7.

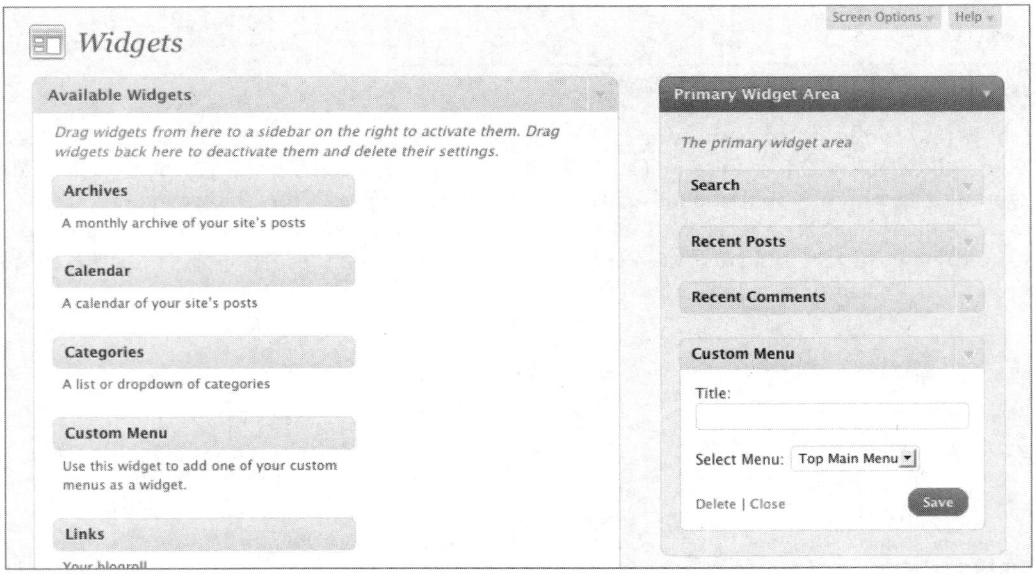

FIGURE 21-7

Notice that there's still a Custom Menu widget showing in the Available Widgets area on the left. You can create and use multiple menus in widget areas.

If your theme does support navigation areas, you'll see a meta box at the top of the left-hand column called Theme Locations, with a list of all possible navigation areas, as highlighted in Figure 21-8.

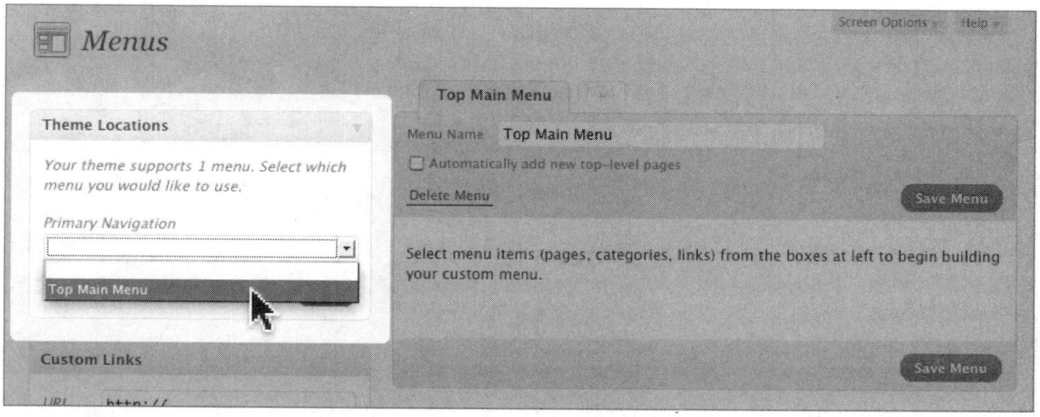

FIGURE 21-8

For each navigation area, there's a drop-down menu showing all possible menus that could be assigned to that area. You simply choose a menu and click Save.

The default theme in WordPress supports additional navigation areas and you'll notice that even though no menu has been created, let alone assigned to that navigation area, the site still displays a navigation menu. That's because the theme author coded in a default menu that kicks in if no menu has been assigned. Typically, these default menus simply show a list of all published WordPress pages, the order of which can be altered using the Order field on each page's admin screen (or via plugins which are available). However, you'll want to use the WordPress menu system, trust me.

MANAGING MENUS

Once you have items added to a menu, you have a lot of options. One of the most important is the ability to rename the item, which you can do by clicking the down arrow on the right side of the menu item box, as shown in Figure 21-9.

This is particularly important if something has a long name that needs to be shortened for use on a menu. Even when you change the name, you're reminded what the original name of the menu item was. This is also where you go to delete a menu item.

If you want to change the order of menu items, it works exactly like widgets, using the drag-and-drop method. Unlike widgets, though, *you must click Save Menu every time you make any changes.* If not, the changes won't appear on the site and will be lost if you leave the screen.

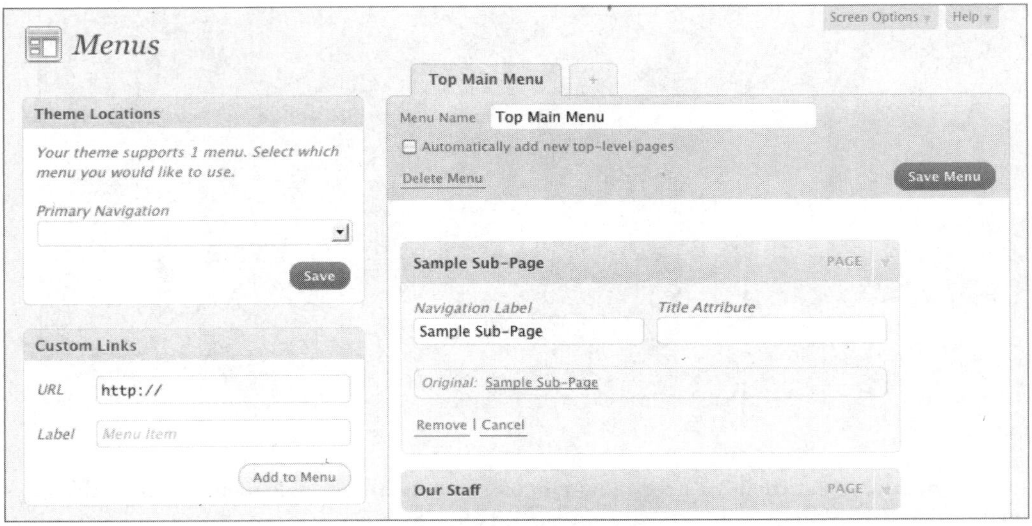

FIGURE 21-9

Creating submenu items (assuming your theme supports them, and most do) is as easy as changing the order. The only difference is that you need to drag a submenu item to the right and below its parent item, as shown in Figure 21-10.

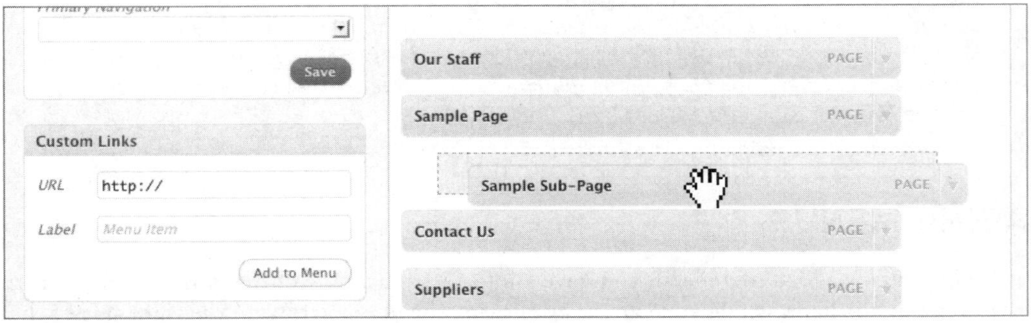

FIGURE 21-10

You can have sub-submenu items and so on, provided that the theme supports more than one level of submenu items.

> *If you create a sub-page in WordPress and then add it to a menu, it does not automatically show up as a submenu item. You need to manually make it a sub-item, if that's how you want it to appear on the menu.*

TRY IT

In this lesson, you practice moving a widget to the sidebar.

Lesson Requirements

A widget-enabled theme. If you're using the default theme, you're okay.

Step-by-Step

Get sidebar widgets functioning and activate a Categories widget.

1. Take a look at the sidebar of your site and note what's there.
2. Click Appearance ➪ Widgets on the main admin menu.
3. Locate the Categories widget on the left-hand side.
4. Drag the Categories widget over to the area on the right called Primary Widget Area (this might have a slightly different name depending on your theme). The Categories widget should now be open.
5. Give the widget a title.
6. Check Show Post Counts.
7. Click Save.
8. Take a look at your live site and see how the sidebar has changed.
9. Back in the Widgets screen, drag Categories from the right side over to the Inactive box at the bottom left. You should see Categories with the title you gave it.
10. Open the widget. You should see your settings preserved.
11. Take a look at your live site again and the old sidebar should be visible once more.

> *To see some of the examples from this lesson, watch the video for Lesson 21 on the DVD with the print book, or watch online at* `www.wrox.com/go/wp24vids`.

SECTION VI
Making Your Site Social

22

The Links Manager

Back in Lesson 7, I covered the creation of links in the body of a post or page. However, these kinds of links have nothing to do with the Links area of the admin menu. That leads to a links management system within WordPress, sometimes referred to as a blogroll or bookmarking system. In this lesson, we look at how to add, edit, and categorize these links, and how they can be used on your website.

MANAGING LINKS

The WordPress Links Manager operates in a very similar way to how posts are managed. From the Links area of the admin menu, you have Links, Add New, and Link Categories. The Links screen shown in Figure 22-1 is similar to Posts but with some slightly different information.

The navigation should be familiar from earlier lessons — filtering by category, searching, sorting by clicking a column title, and so on. To edit a particular link, click the name or click Edit in the text menu that appears when you mouse over a row. For the key elements of a link listing, look at the top region of the Links ➪ Add New Link screen in Figure 22-2.

Here's an overview of all your options:

- **Name:** This is entirely up to you — it's the title for the link that'll appear on your Links page or in the sidebar.
- **Web Address:** This is the URL of the website. WordPress reminds you to include the `http://` at the beginning. The simplest thing, of course, is to highlight and copy the address out of your browser's address bar, or in the case of a text link, just right-click and choose Copy Link Location.
- **Description:** This is a short summary of or comment on the site. Not all themes make use of this if they have a Links page template, but it's available to use if you're customizing a theme. The description does, however, automatically appear as a little popup window when you mouse over the link and is one of the options in the Links widget.
- **Categories:** This works in the same way as categories for posts — you can assign a link to multiple categories and you can add new categories on the fly. However, you can't have subcategories for links — in other words, their categories are not hierarchical.

- **Save (top right):** There's a check box here to make the link Private, which means the link will be visible only from the administration area.

The lower half of the link options screen is shown in Figure 22-3.

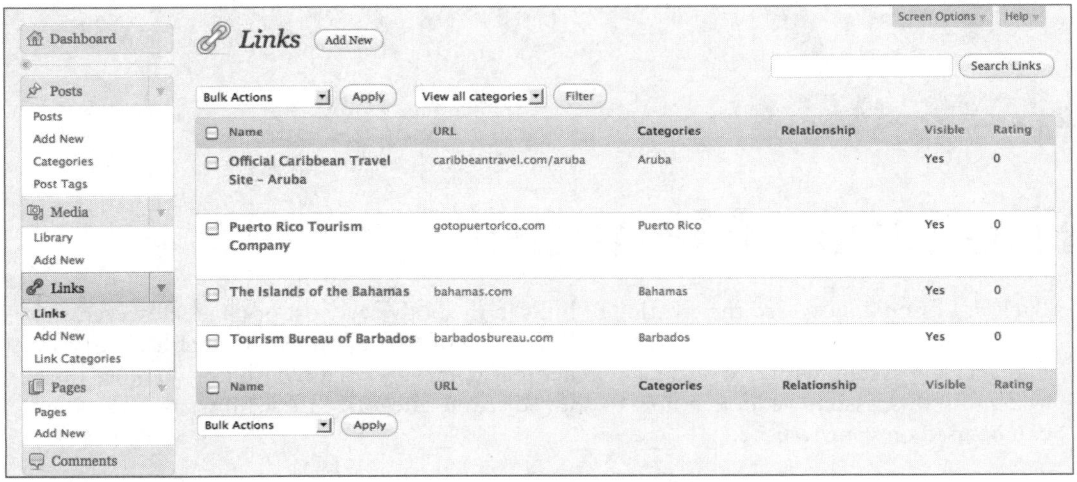

FIGURE 22-1

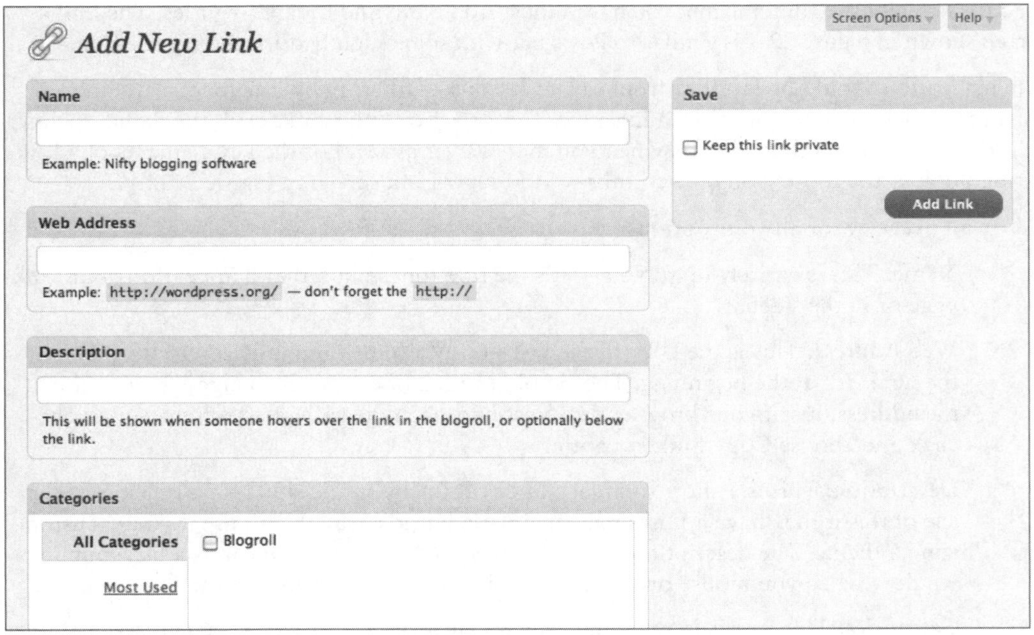

FIGURE 22-2

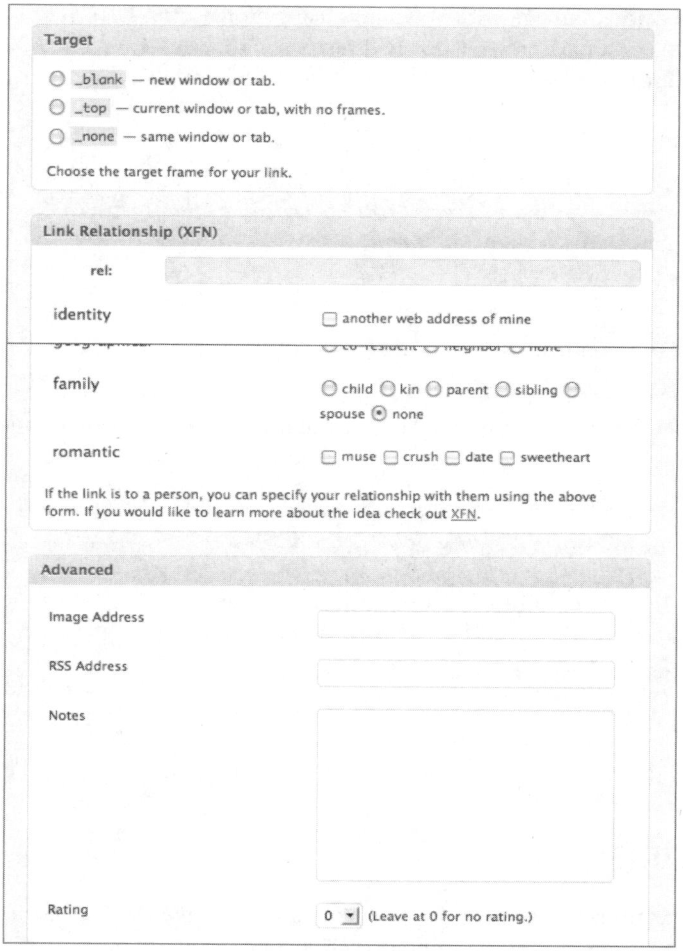

FIGURE 22-3

- **Target:** This tells your browser where to open up the website when the link is clicked: either in a new window/tab or in the current window/tab. If you choose nothing, WordPress defaults to the current window/tab.
- **Link Relationship (XFN):** (To fit everything onto the screen, I've cropped out part of this box where you see the line.) The Xhtml Friends Network is a standard to show the social relationships between you and the people behind the sites you're linking to, such as family, business, or romantic relationships. For that purpose, clicking a relationship creates a special attribute in the HTML code for your link, which you can then use to designate unique styles using CSS (for example, you could give your "crushes" a different color than your "date" links or display an image to indicate a family member).
- **Advanced:** One of the features you're most likely to use in this box is the Rating menu. You can sort links by their rating or display a link's rating. The other feature I want to mention is

the Image field. You can associate an image with your link, using either a full URL (perhaps from the site you're linking to) or a path to your image directory (`/images/mylink.jpg`). You'll want the image to be fairly small, say, 16 x 16 pixels, so it fits nicely next to your link.

> *Remember, if you find you rarely use sections like Link Relationship or Advanced, you can hide them altogether by going to the Screen Options button at the top right of the Add New Link screen and de-selecting them.*

Once you've entered all the information, you just click the Add Link button at the top.

The screen where you edit a link looks exactly the same as the Add New Link screen, except you'll see a Visit Link button up at the top right. That lets you test the link and make sure it's still working.

> *If you need to check a number of links to see if they're still functional, it's easiest to do this from the Links screen. The URL for each link is displayed there and you can click right through to the site. Better still, install one of several plugins that will do this for you, such as Broken Link Checker (this checks all links on your site, not just in the Links Manager).*

Always remember to click Update Link when you've finished making any changes.

MANAGING LINK CATEGORIES

From Links ⇨ Link Categories on the admin menu, you get to a screen which, like the Categories for Posts screen, is divided into two sections, as shown in Figure 22-4.

On the left, you add link categories, and on the right, you manage existing ones. Categories are displayed in alphabetical order by name, though you can click any column title to sort a different way.

To edit a link category, you simply click its name or click Edit in the text menu that appears when you mouse over. You can also choose Quick Edit to change just the name or the slug.

This screen displays 20 links at a time and there is no option to change that, so if you have a lot of link categories, you'll need to page through them using the page links at the top and bottom of the list or you can do a search for a particular category.

You can delete link categories individually or in bulk, using the Bulk Actions menu. As with posts, if you delete a link category and links are assigned to it, they will be reassigned automatically to the default category — the links are not deleted.

Just like posts, WordPress also has a permanent category for links that you cannot delete. That category is called Blogroll (you can edit the name) and it's set as the default category — if you forget to assign a link to at least one category, it automatically goes in the default category. You can choose a different default link category under Settings ➪ Writing.

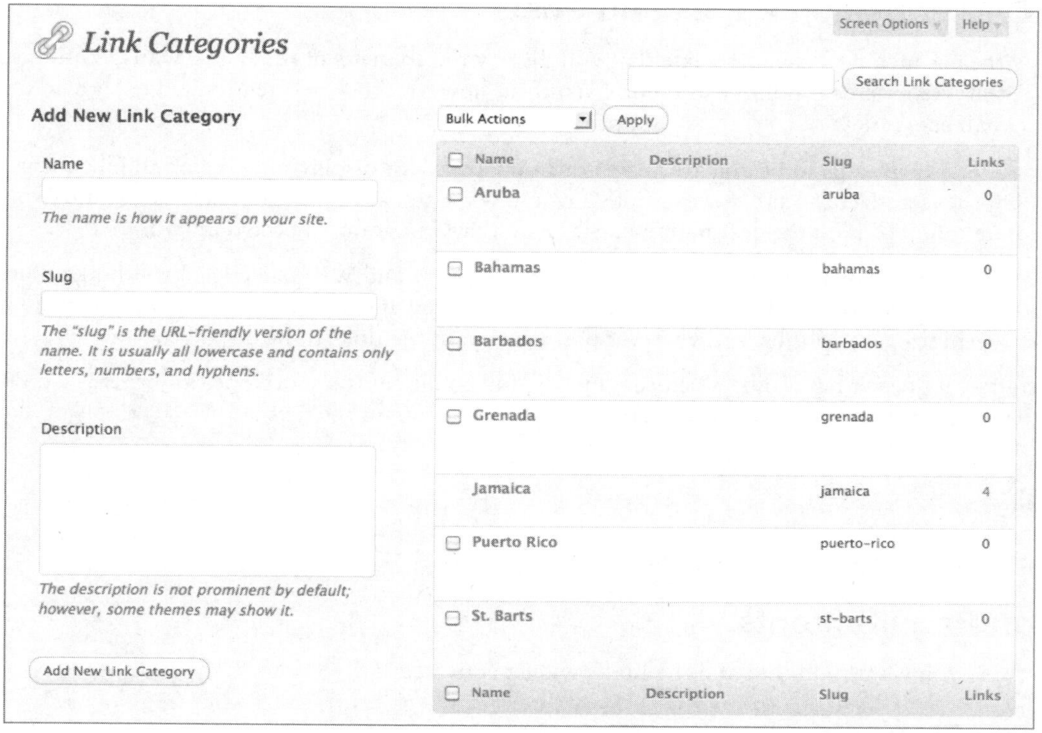

FIGURE 22-4

DISPLAYING LINKS

Despite a handy interface for creating and managing what amounts to a link directory, WordPress does not have a lot of default options for displaying those links. Much of what I talk about in this section relies on installing plugins.

Links Widget

There is one built-in option for displaying links, and that's the Links widget. As you can see from Figure 22-5, it's got some flexibility, but you can only choose between all categories or just one category to display.

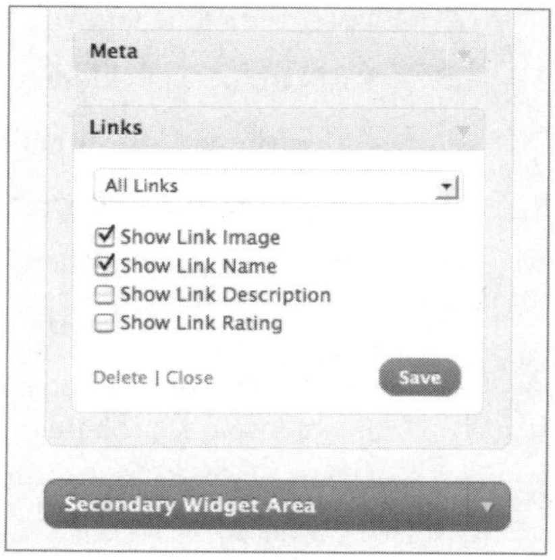

FIGURE 22-5

Plus you're limited to displaying lists of links in widget areas, and if you have a list of any size, that's not going to look great in the places where widget areas tend to be placed (like in the sidebar).

Link Categories on Pages and Posts

Many themes include a page template that will display the contents of the Links Manager, though the Twenty Ten theme is not one of them. Even then, however, they're often limited to showing all links in all categories.

What would be ideal is to be able to create your own pages for displaying some or all link categories. On the Island Travel site, for example, I would want a page of links for each destination so I could put a link to it on the destination page. To do that, I'm going to need a plugin.

Two very good plugins for displaying links are Link Library and WP Render Blogroll Links. Both create shortcodes (you saw those in Lesson 15 when I talked about Gallery shortcodes), which you then insert into pages or posts at whatever point you want the links to be displayed.

Of course, it doesn't have to be a dedicated page. You could put the shortcodes anywhere — on my Aruba page, I might want my list of links down at the bottom of the text.

TRY IT

In this lesson, you practice adding a link.

Lesson Requirements

A website you want to link to and the Links widget activated.

Step-by-Step

Add a link to the WordPress Links Manager.

1. Go to Links ➪ Add New.
2. Enter the name you want to give this link.
3. Paste in the web address from your browser's address bar.
4. A description is optional, but if entered, will display when you mouse over the link.
5. Assign the link to one or more categories.
6. Choose the target where the browser will show the link's website.
7. When finished, click the Add Link button.
8. On the live site, check your Links widget in the sidebar to make sure the new link is displayed (you'll probably need to refresh the page).

> *To see some of the examples from this lesson, watch the video for Lesson 22 on the DVD with the print book, or watch online at* `www.wrox.com/go/wp24vids`.

23

Managing Comments

One of the best ways to interact with your visitors is to allow them to leave comments on your site, and because WordPress was developed as blogging software, it has an extensive comments system. In this lesson, I show you how WordPress handles comments and the ways you can manage them.

ALLOW COMMENTS OR NOT?

WordPress offers two ways of deciding whether visitors will be able to leave comments: on a site-wide basis and on a per-item basis. I've mentioned both of these in earlier lessons on site administration and on creating posts and pages, but it's worth repeating here.

How you control your settings will depend on the kind of content you have on your site. If it's the kind that cries out for comments, such as a blog or a newspaper/magazine style site, then it makes sense to turn on comments so that they're activated by default each time you create new content. Then, you simply turn them off in those situations that don't call for comments (like your Privacy Policy page).

If your site is more informational — not talking about issues, controversies, opinions, and so on — you'll probably want comments off by default, turning them on only when you need them.

The important point is that you need to consider the purposes of your website and how the WordPress comment function might fit in with those purposes. Every site will be different and every area on your site needs to be considered separately as well.

ADMIN SETTINGS FOR COMMENTING

You can find the site-wide settings for commenting in the admin menu under Settings ➪ Discussion. By default, WordPress sets up the following parameters:

- The comment form and existing comments will appear on any post or page.
- To post a comment, visitors must fill out their name and e-mail address.

➤ The ability to comment is always open — there's no time limit on the comments for a particular post or page.

➤ All comments are held for approval unless the commenter has been approved before.

➤ The e-mail address listed in WordPress administration will be notified if any comments are posted or if any comments are held for moderation.

➤ Any comment is held for moderation if it contains more than two links.

➤ No words or web addresses are blacklisted.

➤ Avatars (small graphics or photos) are displayed with each comment and a default avatar is selected if the visitor doesn't provide one.

When comments are active, these are pretty standard settings, so in most cases, you won't need to make any changes. The key setting you need to decide on is the ability to comment on every post and page, shown in Figure 23-1, under Default Article Settings.

Discussion Settings

Default article settings	☐ Attempt to notify any blogs linked to from the article.
	☑ Allow link notifications from other blogs (pingbacks and trackbacks.)
	☑ Allow people to post comments on new articles
	(These settings may be overridden for individual articles.)
Other comment settings	☑ Comment author must fill out name and e-mail
	☐ Users must be registered and logged in to comment
	☐ Automatically close comments on articles older than 14 days
	☑ Enable threaded (nested) comments 5 ▾ levels deep
	☐ Break comments into pages with 50 top level comments per page and the last ▾ page displayed by default
	Comments should be displayed with the older ▾ comments at the top of each page

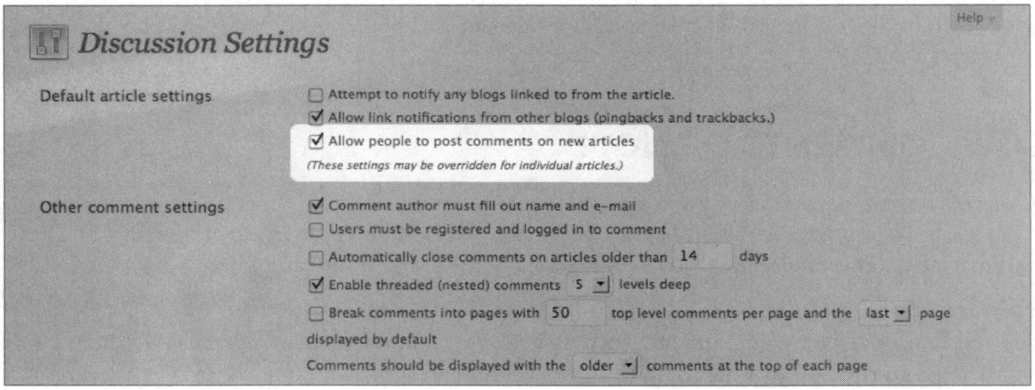

FIGURE 23-1

 Don't be confused by the use of the term "article" in the Discussion Settings. Article just means posts or pages.

If you turn off commenting for every post and page, you still have the ability to allow commenting on any particular post or page. WordPress reminds you of that when it says, "These settings may be overridden for individual articles".

In the past, WordPress showed the Discussion settings for individual content at the bottom of each screen, so it was there to refresh your memory and check the status for that item. Now, however, the Discussion box is hidden by default and you need to choose it under Screen Options if you want to make any changes.

> *If you've had site-wide commenting turned on and then turn it off, all posts up to that time will continue to allow comments unless you manually turn them off. For new posts, commenting will not be available unless you manually turn it on for a specific post.*

One other useful option under Settings ➪ Discussion is the ability to automatically have comments close after a specified period of time, say, 60 days. Existing comments will continue to show; there just can't be any new comments. Some people use this feature if they're having trouble blocking spam comments, but they want to allow a bit of time for legitimate comments to be made. Others don't want to deal even with legitimate comments on old topics. With this feature, you don't have to remember to manually turn off commenting after a post has been up for a while.

> *If you have commenting turned on, and you're seeing the comment box on posts but not pages, it's probably because the page template for your theme does not have the code for displaying comments. Some theme writers leave it off on the assumption that no one wants comments on pages. Other theme writers provide two page templates, one with comments showing and the other without. The WordPress default theme does show comments on pages, and does not have an alternative template.*

Display Order of Comments

Traditionally, blogs have shown the oldest comments first. Part of the reason is that comments can often flow in the form of a discussion — you need to know what's been said earlier to follow what a later commenter is reacting to.

However, some people prefer to show the most recent comments first, one theory being that visitors who keep returning will want to first see what's new in the comments area, without having to scroll (sometimes a very long way) to the bottom.

WordPress makes it possible to choose between the two. The default is still oldest comments first, but under Settings ➪ Discussion in the Other Comment Settings area, you'll see a drop-down menu allowing you to select Older or Newer comments first.

Threaded Comments

No matter what order comments are displayed in, comments often don't flow in an orderly manner. If someone is commenting on a point made 15 comments earlier, it can get difficult to keep track of the conversation. That's why WordPress has threaded or nested comments enabled by default. This creates a Reply link with each comment in addition to the general comment box at the bottom of the post. If visitors use the Reply link, the comment shows up inside the comment they're replying to.

You can turn off this feature under Settings ➪ Discussion Settings. Look for Enable Threaded (Nested) Comments and you can also allow the nesting to go up to 10 comments deep (default is 5).

> *Be aware, though, that not all themes will properly display threaded comments. Even if yours doesn't, plugins are available to help you manage them or you can have your style sheet modified to do so.*

FINDING COMMENTS

When I was showing you the WordPress Dashboard in Lesson 4, you saw the Comments area, which displays several of the most recent comments. From there, you can link directly to the comments admin area.

Another way to find comments is the Comments link on the admin menu (there are no submenu items for this), which takes you to the Comments screen, shown in Figure 23-2.

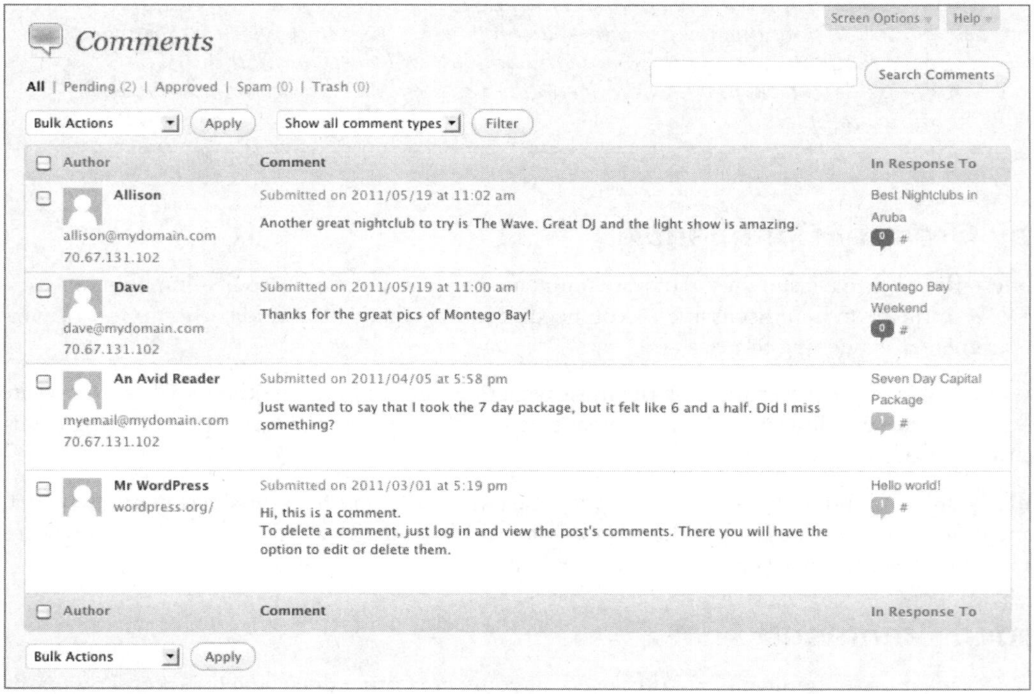

FIGURE 23-2

For each comment, you're shown the author's name and a URL if the author entered one. Then you'll see the comment itself, along with the date and time it was submitted. Underneath the comment, if you mouse over the row, you'll see a menu with the following options:

- **Approve:** You can approve the comment (or unapprove it, depending on context).

- **Spam:** This marks the comment as spam so the information can be used by anti-spam plugins to learn what to block.
- **Trash:** This removes the comment to the Trash area. From there, you can restore it later or permanently delete it.
- **Edit:** Use this to edit the parameters of the comment, including the body, so you can remove bad language and so on.
- **Quick Edit:** This allows you to perform virtually all Edit tasks without going to a new screen.
- **Reply:** This lets you reply directly to the comment in the way described earlier when I talked about threaded comments. If your theme is set up to do so, your reply is shown with the comment it's in response to.

On the far right of the comments listing, you see the title of the post that the comment was responding to, with a link to the post's edit screen. The tiny speech bubble icon shows how many comments that post or page has, and the hash symbol (#) provides a link to the post as it appears on your site.

You can filter the comments by Comments or Pings. I explain pings or pingbacks in more detail in Lesson 25, but basically, these are links to your post as opposed to someone making a comment through your site.

You can also filter comments based on whether they're Pending (awaiting approval), Approved, Spam, or sitting in the Trash. You can also sort by Author and by the item the comment is in response to.

Finally, you can search through the text of the comments by using the Search Comments box at the top right of the screen.

A further way of finding comments is to enable the Comments box under Screen Options for posts and pages. That way, you could go to the edit screen for any of them and easily locate the comment you need.

APPROVING, EDITING, OR DELETING COMMENTS

Assuming you've retained the default settings that require comments to be approved (at least the first time someone comments) and for the administrator to be e-mailed about it, you'll know there are comments waiting because you'll get an e-mail. There are several other ways to know about comments within the admin screens:

- There'll be a tiny icon beside Comments on the side menu, telling you how many are awaiting approval.
- The Posts list shows a highlighted comment icon for any posts that have comments awaiting moderation.
- The Dashboard shows the most recent comments, and those needing moderation are highlighted with a different-colored background.
- If you have the Comments box turned on for display, you'll see any new comments for individual posts or pages when you open their edit screen.

You can approve a comment by clicking Approve on the text menu that displays when you mouse over a comment on the Comments screen. If you have a lot of comments to approve, just check the box for each, choose Approve from the Bulk Actions drop-down menu at the top or bottom, and click Apply.

Before or after you've approved a comment, you can edit the contents by clicking Edit on that text menu. You'll see a screen like the one in Figure 23-3.

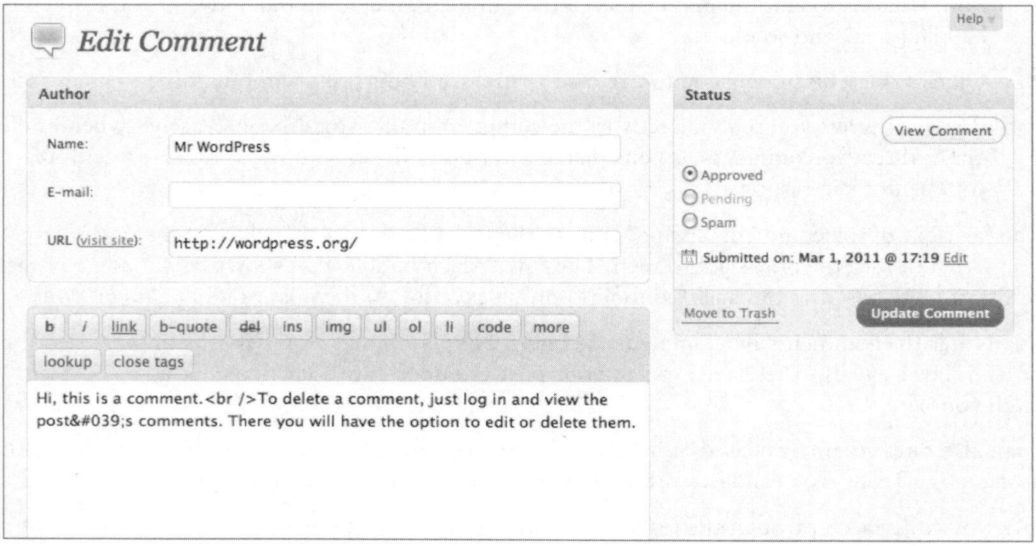

FIGURE 23-3

From this screen, you can edit all the parameters, including the date and time it was submitted (see the Status box).

Notice that the comment Text Editor is available only in HTML mode and the buttons are the same as the ones whose functions are described in detail in Lesson 7. Visitors do not get any formatting buttons when entering comments, but plugins are available that offer all sorts of options in that regard.

As always, remember to click Update Comment when you're finished editing.

To delete a comment or comments, you again have the choice to delete individually or in bulk when you're in the Comments listing screen. When you're editing an individual comment, you can delete it from the link in the Status box.

> *If you set WordPress to e-mail you whenever a comment is being held for moderation, the e-mail will contain direct links for approving or deleting the link, or marking it as spam.*

DEALING WITH SPAM COMMENTS

Although spam comments are dealt with from the same menus as approving or deleting, I've left them for a separate section. WordPress comes with a number of methods for dealing with spam comments and dozens of plugins. I talk about the plugins in Lesson 37; here, I want to mention some of the built-in tools.

The first line of defense with spam comments is to make sure you require all comments to be moderated (not counting those visitors you've approved once already — if you keep that setting in place). That way, you don't have just anything appearing on your site without knowing about it.

On the Settings ➪ Discussion screen, you'll find several settings under Comment Moderation that can help deal with spam comments. The first checks how many links are contained in a comment and holds it for moderation if the threshold is exceeded. The default setting is 2, the idea being that spam comments will often contain multiple links. This option functions no matter what other moderation settings you have.

> *Never set this number to 0 or make the field blank. That would send every single comment to moderation, no matter what other settings you have in place.*

The next option allows you to specify words, names, URLs, e-mail addresses, or even IP addresses against which WordPress will check each comment — be sure to have only one item per line. If anything on this list appears in a comment, it will automatically be held for moderation, again, no matter what your other comments settings are.

The final moderation option allows you to create a blacklist. You specify words, names, and so on, but in this case, if a comment contains anything on the list, it's automatically marked as spam, not simply put into moderation. You're still able to approve a comment if it wrongly gets caught by this blacklist.

> *I keep using the term "mark as spam" and it means that not only will comments marked as spam not appear on your site, they'll stay in your database and can be used by anti-spam plugins (see Lesson 37) to compare with future comments and help determine if they're spam too.*

TRY IT

In this lesson, you practice approving a comment.

Lesson Requirements

Have someone comment on one of your posts, or you can do it yourself as long as you log out of WordPress before doing so (if you're still logged in, you'll be commenting as an administrator and automatically be approved).

Step-by-Step

How to approve a comment.

1. Log in to WordPress.
2. On the Dashboard, you should see the new comment in the Comments box, and on the left side menu, there should be an icon beside Comments with the number one in it (or if you had existing pending comments, the number should have increased by one).
3. You could approve the comment right from the Dashboard if you mouse over the comment and use the Approve link on the menu that appears.
4. If you want to read the entire comment first, click Edit and, when you're satisfied, mark it as Approved in the Status box. Finally, click Update Comment.
5. From the Dashboard, you can also click Pending in the Right Now box and you'll see a list of comments requiring approval.

> *To see some of the examples from this lesson, watch the video for Lesson 23 on the DVD with the print book, or watch online at* `www.wrox.com/go/wp24vids`.

24

Bringing in Content from Other Sites

It's important to say at the outset that when I talk about bringing in content from other sites, I do not mean:

- Stealing content from others (using it without their permission)
- Duplicating content that's on other sites (even using it with permission)

Both of these actions have very bad consequences, so just don't go there. The first is wrong morally and legally; the second can cause, at worst, blacklisting of your page/site by search engines, and at the very least, if you're duplicating content from your own site(s), a potential dilution of your search engine ranking (when some people link to one page or site and some to another).

The kind of content I'm talking about can be divided into three primary groups:

- Social media feeds (Twitter, Facebook, and so on)
- Content you own, pay for, or have permission to use, that comes from a third party (real estate listings, shopping cart systems such as Amazon stores, or weather, stock, or other updated information)
- RSS and other headline-type feeds

In this lesson, I talk about how to integrate them into WordPress and a bit about how to find them.

SOCIAL MEDIA FEEDS

If you have social media accounts, such as Twitter or Facebook, the content you're generating on those sites could be useful on your WordPress site. If you don't have any social media accounts related to the topic of your site, you should get some! In this lesson, I deal with very simple ways to display social media feeds on your site using WordPress right out of the box. In Lesson 37, I show you some plugins that allow you to actually interact with your social media accounts.

I'm going to show you how to get your Twitter account feed onto your site, but the process is very similar for most social media tools.

On the Twitter site, there's a link to Resources (others might say Widgets or Promote) and there you'll find all kinds of tools for integrating with your website. The one I'll show you here is a Profile widget (not to be confused with a WordPress widget), which displays your live Twitter feed of all your tweets.

Many sites make it easy, as Twitter does in Figure 24-1A, to customize how the feed will look on your site, how many items it will display, and so on. When you're through customizing, you'll click something like Finish & Grab Code or Generate Code, and you're presented with the HTML you'll need to paste into WordPress, as shown in Figure 24-1B.

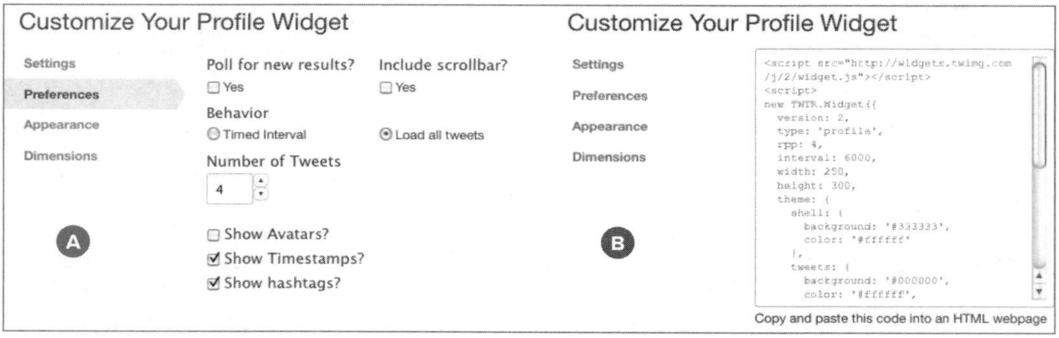

FIGURE 24-1

Sometimes, there will be a button to automatically copy the code for you, but in many cases, you'll need to do it yourself, as is the case with Twitter. Place your cursor in the text box and press Ctrl+A to select it all, then Ctrl+C to copy it. Now you're ready to paste the code into a widget on your site.

In WordPress, go to Appearance ➪ Widgets and find the Text widget on the left-hand side. When you drag it over to the Primary Widget Area on the right, it opens up and you can paste in your coding, as shown in on the left half of Figure 24-2.

When you save the widget, you'll see your Twitter stream displayed on your site — see the right half of Figure 24-2 — just as it was in the preview when you set it up.

Keep in mind that you're not limited to displaying your own Twitter feed. You can bring in the feed of someone else on Twitter (provided it's not a private feed) or you could have the feeds for various authors on your site.

You could also choose the Search widget, which allows you to do a search in Twitter, and then continuously display anybody's tweets that match the search criteria.

Be aware that you're opening yourself up for all sorts of content with a search feed: possibly from competitors or possibly offensive. The more likely scenario for this kind of feed is when your organization or business is using a hash tag, such as #ourconference. The feed would pull in any tweets that use that tag.

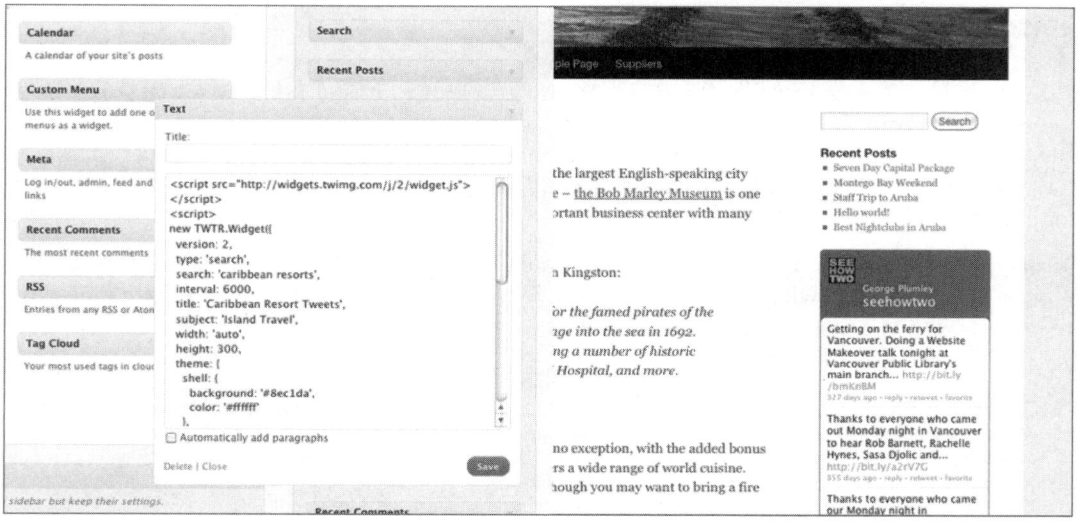

FIGURE 24-2

ADDING CONTENT FROM THIRD-PARTY SITES

Sometimes, you'll have content that's hosted by a third party and you need to integrate it with your site. Amazon.com stores, for example, are full-blown shopping cart programs that are hosted by Amazon, but are made to appear as if they're on your site, using what's called an iframe. Realtors will quite often have their properties listed on a third-party site that offers them a more powerful database system than they could afford to produce themselves. The listings are then displayed on the realtor's site using iframes.

An iframe — inline frame — is an HTML tag that creates a kind of window in the middle of a regular web page and inserts content, usually from a different site. All modern browsers support the iframe, unlike a few years ago, so they're safe to use these days. Very often, you don't even know there's content being pulled in from another site.

You can use iframes in WordPress, *but you must use HTML mode on the Text Editor.* If you try to use Visual mode or if you switch to Visual mode after inserting the code, it will get damaged and no longer function.

To avoid this problem altogether, it's better to use a plugin that keeps the Visual mode from hurting your code. A couple of these include Embed Iframe or Easy iFrame Loader.

Iframes aren't the only way of bringing in third-party content.

When you see a weather forecast on a website, that's often handled using JavaScript. In any case, it's simply a matter of copying the code from the third-party site (double- and triple-checking that you've got permission) and pasting it into a text widget or in the body of a post/page (and have taken the precautions noted previously).

RSS FEEDS

RSS stands for, at least according to some, "really simple syndication." TV shows, newspaper columns, and radio shows are examples of content that gets syndicated — the producers send out their shows to companies that pay to show or publish the content. The beauty of RSS is that it makes the distribution process extremely simple. Literally, paste in a URL and you've got a live feed coming into your site.

Displaying RSS feeds from other sites is pretty straightforward in WordPress. Go to Appearance ⇨ Widgets and look for a widget called RSS. Drag it over to the Sidebar area on the right, and it opens up to display the window shown in Figure 24-3.

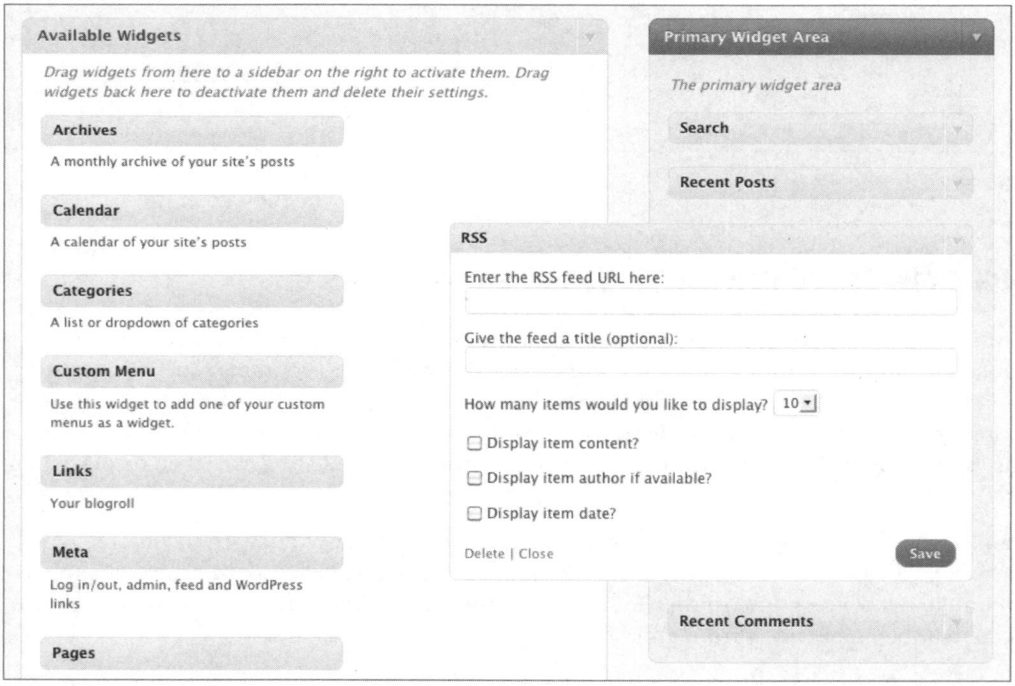

FIGURE 24-3

The first thing you're asked for is the URL for the RSS feed. This is the information you copy from the website providing the feed.

You can find RSS feeds in two simple ways, as shown in Figure 24-4.

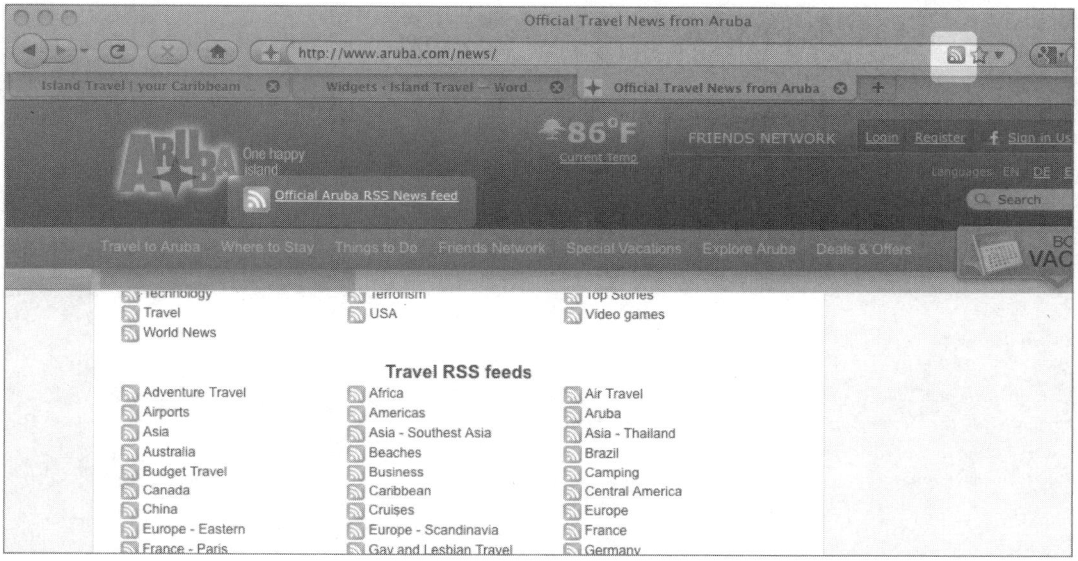

FIGURE 24-4

The first way is by checking websites that have content you think would be useful to your visitors on an ongoing basis. The top half of Figure 24-4 shows two highlighted locations on a website about Aruba where you can find the RSS feed URL and copy it.

The second way is by checking directories of RSS feeds. In the bottom half of Figure 24-4, you'll see an example of a feeds directory: `www.feedzilla.com`. You simply right-click the link of whichever feed you want and copy the URL.

You then take your copied address and paste it into the WordPress widget where it says "Enter the RSS Feed URL Here."

You can then give a title to what will appear in your sidebar, after which you have a choice of how many items to display from the feed (default is 5) along with which parts of the feed you would like to display: Content, Author, and Date.

Click Save and close the widget. When you refresh your live site, you'll see the RSS feed in your sidebar, like my Caribbean Travel feed on the Island Travel site in Figure 24-5.

> *Ok, I know I keep saying this, but always make sure you have permission to use a feed of any type. Generally, sites are happy to have people using their feeds, but even then, there may be some registration process required or even a small fee.*

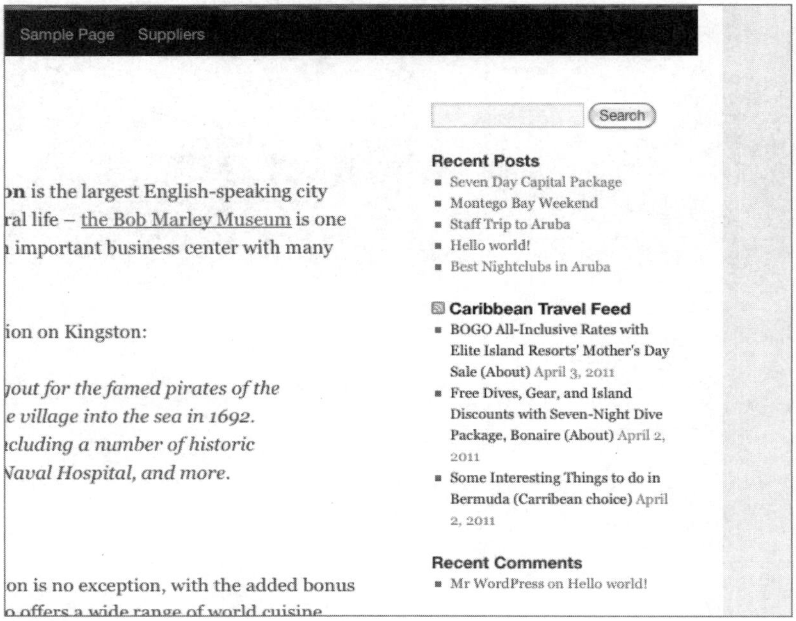

FIGURE 24-5

TRY IT

In this lesson, you practice putting an RSS feed in your sidebar.

Lesson Requirements

Have the URL of a content feed that you would like to put in your sidebar. One simple way is to go to a friend's blog and get the URL for his or her feed.

Step-by-Step

Add an RSS feed to the sidebar.

1. Have the URL of the RSS feed available on your clipboard or in a text file somewhere.
2. Go to Appearance ➪ Widgets.
3. Locate the RSS feed widget in the Available box on the left side.
4. Drag the RSS feed over to the Primary Widget Area on the right.
5. Paste the URL into the field marked "Enter the RSS Feed URL Here."
6. Give the feed a title if you like.
7. Check Display Item Content if you want more than just the title of each item.

8. Do the same for Author if you want that to display.
9. Do the same for Date.
10. Click Save.
11. Refresh your website and view the feed live.
12. If you're seeing nothing or you have an error, double-check the URL of the feed once more and try again.

> *To see some of the examples from this lesson, watch the video for Lesson 24 on the DVD with the print book, or watch online at* www.wrox.com/go/wp24vids.

25

Helping Others Connect to Your Site

In the preceding lesson, I showed you how to bring in content from other sites; now, it's time to look at ways WordPress can help others make use of your content. Using social media ("liking" your site, bookmarking it, and so on), publishing an RSS (really simple syndication) feed of your site, subscribing to your site through their RSS reader, or simply linking to your site: these are examples of how others can use your content. Making it easy for people to take these actions should be an important part of your promotional plans for developing online relationships.

CONNECTING VIA SOCIAL MEDIA

Although the options I talk about here aren't about others directly connecting to your site, the connections made indirectly through social media are too powerful to go unmentioned.

I talk about social media plugins in Lesson 37, and they'll offer a whole host of new options, but for the moment, let's look at how you can quickly get some social media connections going even without the use of plugins.

I showed you in Lesson 24 how easy it is to insert code on your site that displays various social media feeds, such as your Twitter account activity. It's just as easy to allow others to connect your site to social media.

In the case of Twitter, you simply choose the Twitter Buttons option and you're given some HTML to paste into a WordPress text widget, creating a nice button on your sidebar (or wherever the widget area is) that lets people follow your Twitter feed. As I said, this isn't directly connecting to your website, but for most people, their Twitter feed is, in part, a kind of headline service leading people to their website.

Lots of social bookmarking sites exist, where you could encourage people to bookmark your content. Delicious is one of the most popular of the bookmarking sites and it provides an easy-to-use button, the coding for which is shown in Figure 25-1.

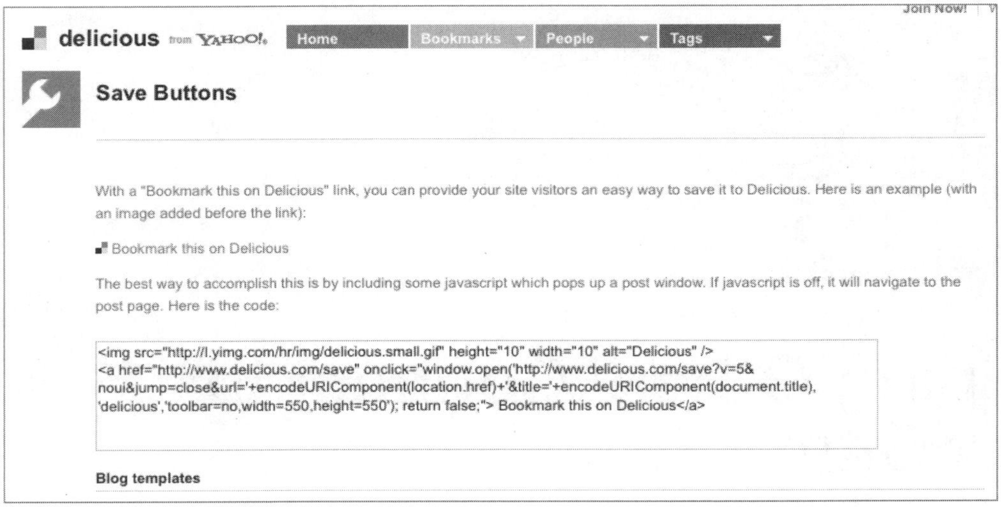

FIGURE 25-1

I simply copy the code and paste it into a text widget on the sidebar, and you can see the results in Figure 25-2.

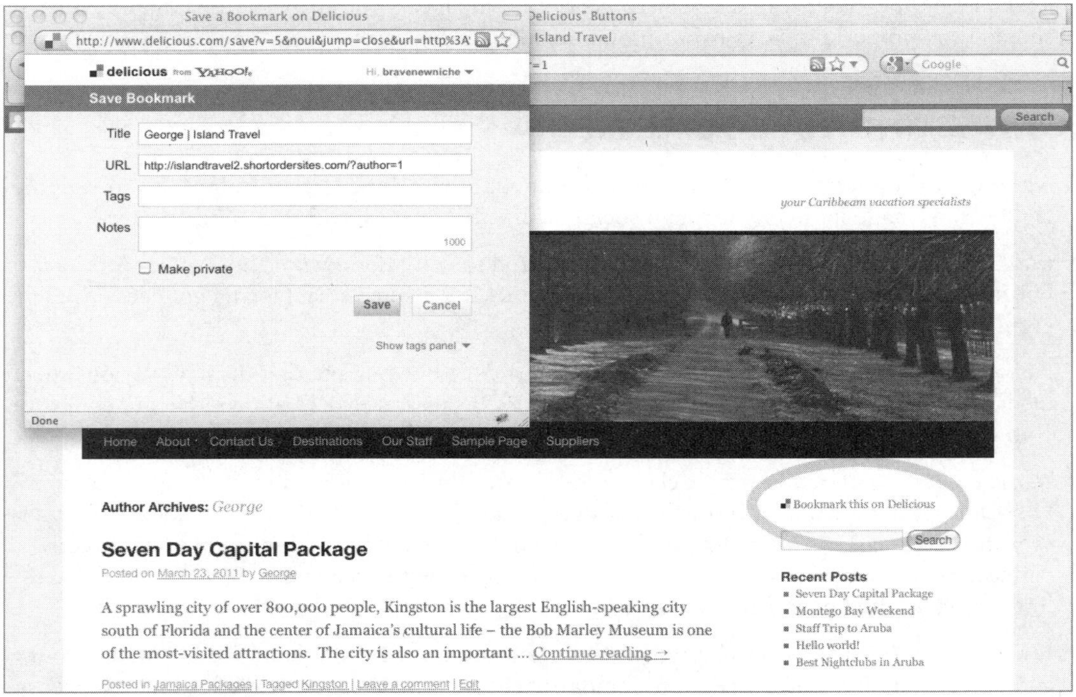

FIGURE 25-2

The Delicious button is highlighted over on the right, and the popup window on the left is the result of clicking that button (visitors are given the chance to log in to their Delicious accounts if they're not already logged in). Notice that the exact URL of the page I'm on has been inserted automatically into the Delicious form — so people will be bookmarking the exact page they're on.

As I said, lots of plugins for WordPress make this whole process even easier and can deal with dozens of social media sites all at one time, and I talk about those in Lesson 37. But you can certainly do a lot just with simple cutting and pasting into a widget.

RSS FEEDS OF YOUR CONTENT

In the previous lesson, I showed you how to bring in the RSS feed of another site, to provide your visitors with some relevant headlines. But why would anyone want to do the same with your site?

It could be that other people value your opinion and want to share that stream of thought with their visitors. Or you might have a very good roundup of news posts about your industry, and other sites want to tap into and save themselves the trouble of gathering all that information. In the case of Island Travel, people might want to display our latest travel deals on their blog about a particular destination. These are all great candidates for a publishable feed. But how do you create that feed and make it available to people?

WordPress makes good on the "really simple" in really simple syndication (RSS) feeds because on their own, they aren't so simple. First of all, there are many syndication formats, of which RSS is only one. Add to that the fact that several versions of RSS exist, let alone the question of how to output your content in each format, and you get a sense of how complex the world of web feeds can be. Thankfully, WordPress takes care of all of it for you, generating four separate feeds for a post's content: RSS 0.92, RSS 2.0, Atom, and RDF/RSS 1.0.

> *Although WordPress automatically generates these different feeds, themes typically include only one or two (RSS2 is the most common). If you want help customizing your theme to include more feeds, go to* `http://codex.wordpress.org/WordPress_Feeds`.

WordPress also makes it easy for your visitors to get the URL for these RSS feeds by making it simple for theme writers to include site, post, and comment RSS links automatically. You can tell if your site is generating the RSS feeds by looking at the source code of your page (right-click and choose View Source). You should see lines like the ones in the top half of Figure 25-3 or, alternatively, look for the RSS symbol in your browser address bar while viewing one of your pages, as shown in the lower half of Figure 25-3.

To get the RSS feed URL, someone just has to click the RSS symbol in their browser and then copy the resulting address. However, you might want to make things even more obvious by creating a link in your sidebar containing the RSS feed address and the RSS symbol and a short description, such as "Show Our Travel Industry News Feed on Your Site." You can get that address by clicking the RSS symbol in your browser on the appropriate page of your site. RSS symbols are easy to find at free icon sites around the Web.

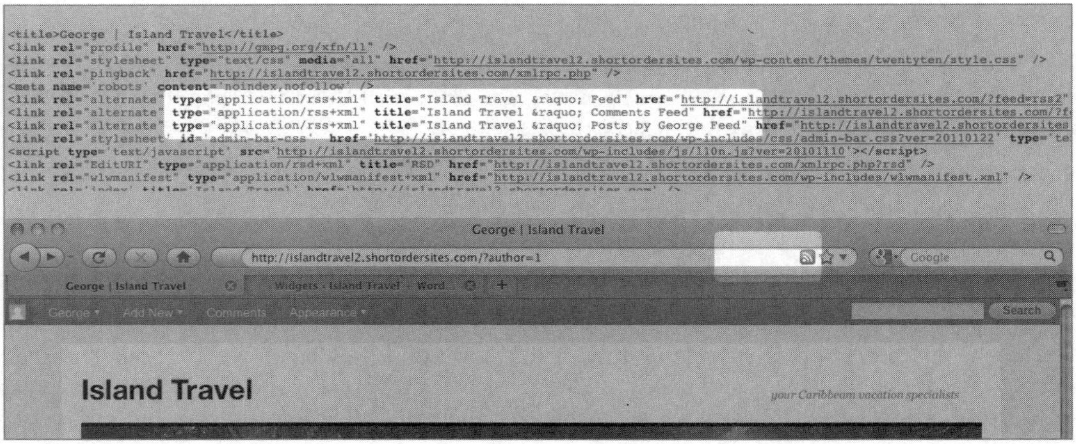

FIGURE 25-3

Although WordPress automatically generates RSS feeds, you do have a couple of parameters you can set for how your feeds will be displayed, and you'll find them under Settings ➪ Reading, as shown in Figure 25-4.

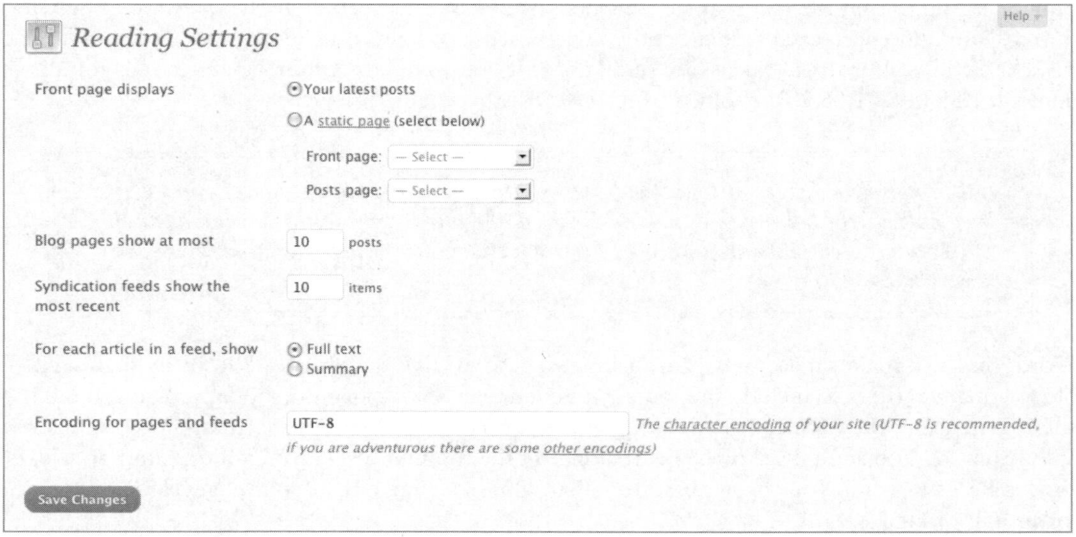

FIGURE 25-4

You can set the number of items to be shown in any syndication feed (the default is 10). The other option is whether to allow the full text to be shown in the feed or just a summary — the default is full text, but the choice is not cut and dried.

The theory behind allowing the full text is that subscribers might be more likely to read it because they don't have to click through to get the complete story. If your goal is primarily to get the content read, this option makes sense. If your goal is to drive traffic to your site, providing only a summary is a way of getting readers to click through to view the rest of the material. I leave you to ponder the pros and cons.

> *You can extend your RSS feed capabilities by using a third-party service, such as Feedburner, to manage your feeds (these services provide ways of tracking how many people are subscribing to you, what they're doing when on your site, and so on). A number of plugins for WordPress make it simple to integrate your site with these services, such as FD Feedburner.*

SETTING PINGBACKS AND TRACKBACKS

Pingbacks and trackbacks are types of notifications that someone has linked to your site, and these notifications show up in the comments on your posts. Pingbacks are the more important of the two, because trackbacks are really only used for linking to older blogging systems.

Creating a pingback to another site is easy — just link to that site in the body of your post. In order for the other site owner to be notified, they have to have pingbacks enabled on their site. Trackbacks to another site also require that site's owner to have them turned on; the difference is that you need to paste a special URL into the trackback notification box on your Add/Edit Post screen, and you have to do that even if you linked to the site in the body of the post.

This means that to receive pingbacks to your own site, you simply have to have pingbacks and trackbacks turned on (you'll see how to do that in a moment). You can test that pingbacks are working by creating a link in one of your posts to another of your posts, and then watch for the pingback to show up in the comments.

If you want people to be able to trackback to your site, you'll have to provide them with the trackback URL that they need to paste into their trackback box. Check if your theme displays the trackback URL — the default theme doesn't, for example. If not, you can add it by modifying the necessary template(s) in your theme.

So, how do you make sure pingbacks and trackbacks are enabled on your WordPress site? Go to Settings ➪ Discussion and you'll see this under Default Article Settings (Figure 25-5).

By default, WordPress allows trackbacks and pingbacks for all posts and pages. You could turn this off and you would still be able to activate them for individual posts or pages in the Discussion section of the Add or Edit screens, but it's simplest to leave this activated for everything. If you have WordPress set to allow comments to appear only after they've been approved, the same will be true for trackbacks and pingbacks. You can moderate the ones that appear in the Dashboard or click through to the Edit Comments area if you have more waiting.

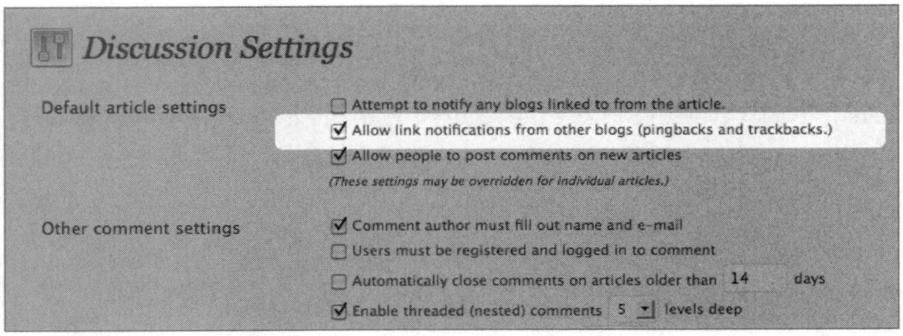
Discussion Settings
Default article settings
Attempt to notify any blogs linked to from the article.
Allow link notifications from other blogs (pingbacks and trackbacks.)
Allow people to post comments on new articles
(These settings may be overridden for individual articles.)
Other comment settings
Comment author must fill out name and e-mail
Users must be registered and logged in to comment
Automatically close comments on articles older than 14 days
Enable threaded (nested) comments 5 levels deep

FIGURE 25-5

> *Because trackbacks to your site can be created without the other site owner actually linking to you in the body of a post, some people don't feel they're reliable indicators that someone has linked to you. Others find they get a lot of spam through trackbacks. WordPress enables/disables pingbacks and trackbacks together, so they're either both on or both off. Some plugins allow you to deal with them separately.*

SETTING PERMALINKS

You want other sites to link to your content — it's one of the most important ways to build traffic to your site — but you want to make sure that the link will continue to work over time and not produce a 404 error or take visitors to the wrong place.

On a blog page, for example, posts display only until they're replaced with newer posts, or the title of a post or page may get changed even slightly over time, or a post might be moved from one category to another. That's good for flexibility, but not so good for people linking to your content. It would be like moving to another city and not letting your friends and family know where you are. One way to solve the problem is to have a permanent address for each post on your site, and WordPress does that through what are called *permalinks*.

Every post, page, and category in WordPress has a fixed permalink. That's because they all have unique and permanent IDs — even if you delete something, its ID cannot be used again. An example of a permalink would be `http://www.yourdomain.com/?p=45`. As long as someone knows that URL, they can always get to item #45.

You can see the permalink for a post or a page just below the Title area (it won't show until you've entered something for the title), as illustrated in Figure 25-6.

However, WordPress's default permalinks are not very memorable URLs and they don't give search engines much of a hint as to what the content is for a particular item (I talk more about permalinks and search engines in Lesson 31). That's why you can tell WordPress to show the world what are sometimes called "pretty permalinks."

FIGURE 25-6

Under Settings ➪ Permalinks, you can customize the look of these links as much as you'd like — the screen is shown in Figure 25-7.

The default setting is shown at the top, and then you see several suggested presets (I generally use the third one down — Month and Name). You can even create your own custom permalinks using the set of tags at the WordPress.org website — a link is provided at the top of the Permalinks page.

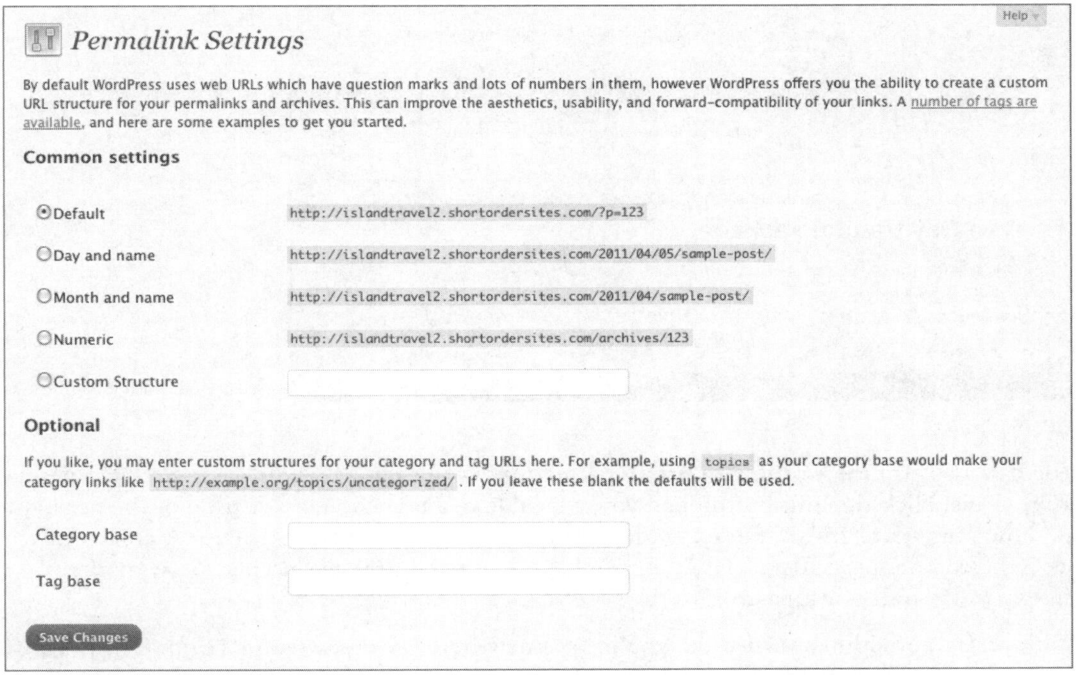

FIGURE 25-7

If you switch to one of these custom settings, you'll find that the permalinks option also changes below the titles of posts and pages, as shown in Figure 25-8A.

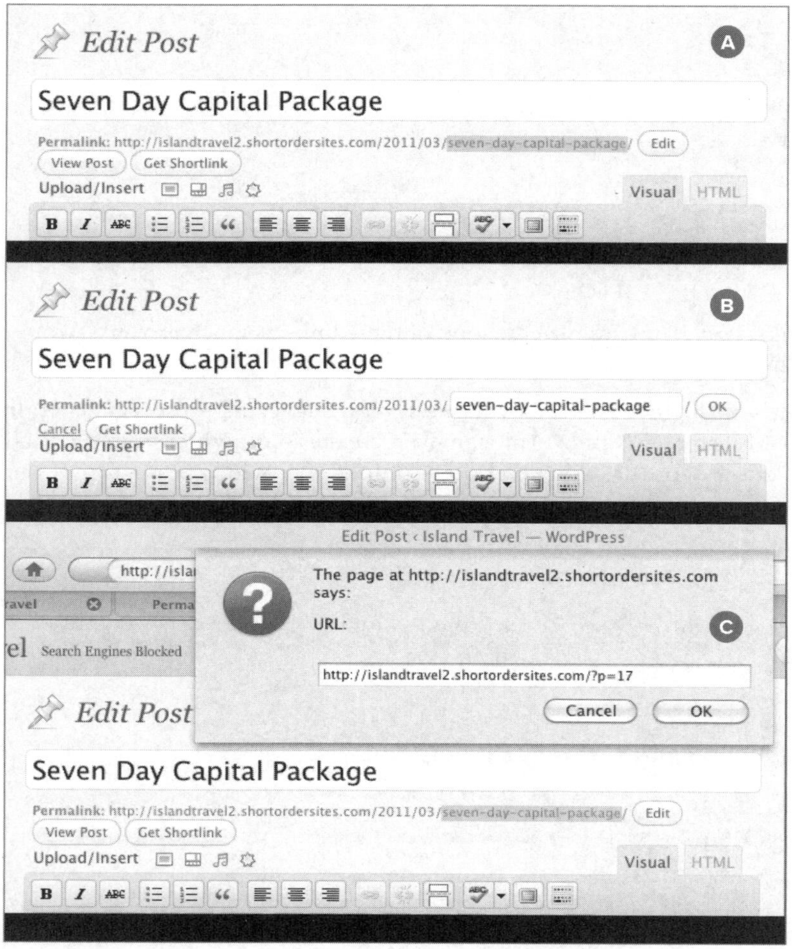

FIGURE 25-8

You can also edit the wording of pretty permalinks (you can never edit the underlying permalink) — just click the Edit button and you'll be able to change the last section of the permalink, as shown in Figure 25-8B. For example, if you have a very long title such as "A great way to see Kingston on just $30 per day," you could go in and edit the permalink to say, perhaps, "inexpensive-tours-of-kingston."

With pretty permalinks turned on, you'll see a new button called Get Shortlink (as shown in Figure 25-8C). By default, this button will give you the original permalink, which, of course, will always be shorter than any pretty permalink. However, the real purpose of the button is to allow the authors of URL-shortening plugins to hook into it and display the shortened URL when someone clicks Get Shortlink.

> *It's all well and good to say that you can edit pretty permalinks, but you need to be careful. If you've just created the post or page, changing the pretty permalink even a day or two later could be a problem. Anyone who's linked to that pretty permalink before you made the change is going to get an error — their link won't work. If you need to change a pretty permalink, try to do it before you publish the piece, or as soon after you publish as possible.*

TRY IT

In this lesson, you practice setting up your RSS feed parameters.

Lesson Requirements

No special requirements.

Step-by-Step

How to set up an RSS feed.

1. Go to Settings ➪ Readings.
2. Set *Syndication feeds show the most recent* to 5 (default is 10).
3. Set *For each article in a feed, show* to Summary (default is full text).
4. Click Save Changes.
5. In your browser, navigate to any page of your live site and in most browser address bars or on one of the toolbars, you should see the RSS feed icon (a small square, usually orange or blue, with three curved lines).
6. Click the RSS icon and you'll see a page listing all the current items in your feed or, if there are multiple feeds on the page, a list of those feeds (clicking on an individual feed will display the current feeds items).
7. If you have an RSS reader, such as Google News Reader or Bloglines, try subscribing to your site. Simply go to your live site and click the Subscribe button on your reader — it should pick up your RSS feed.

> *To see some of the examples from this lesson, watch the video for Lesson 25 on the DVD with the print book, or watch online at* `www.wrox.com/go/wp24vids`.

26

Having Multiple Site Users

One of the ways people are making their sites more social these days is to create membership sites. These can range from multiple levels of paid membership to something as simple as a multiauthor blog. All of these structures depend on WordPress's built-in user roles. Even in a small company or organization, you may need more than one person working on your website. At the same time, you may not want each of those people to have the same access to the site, such as the ability to change the theme or delete pages. WordPress makes the management of these various levels of access quite easy through what are called *roles*.

I discuss membership plugins in Lesson 37, which you'll need to help manage more complicated membership structures, but there's a lot you can do with the basic user function that comes with WordPress and that's what I cover here.

> *Don't confuse multiple users with WordPress's multisite capability. However many sites you may be running with a single WordPress installation, any one site can have multiple users. The multisite function is covered in Lesson 38.*

USER ROLES AND THEIR CAPABILITIES

There are five user roles in WordPress and, in order of decreasing capabilities, they are:

- Administrator
- Editor
- Author
- Contributor
- Subscriber

In the case of Island Travel, with its two offices, I could have a single Administrator to take care of technical aspects of the site, and a single Editor who oversees all site content. Each travel agent could be an Author managing their own posts, with a few non-agency people who act as Contributors. Customers and potential customers could be Subscribers, who are able to view website content that the public can't see.

With these examples in mind, let's go through each of the five user roles in a bit more detail:

- **Administrator:** As the name suggests, an Administrator has access to every single administrative function in WordPress, including editing theme files, changing themes, adding plugins, user details, and so on. It's probably not a good idea to have more than a couple of Administrators or they could wind up overriding each other's work — the "too many cooks" syndrome.
- **Editor:** The Editor role allows the maximum amount of control over all the content of the website, without being able to change settings that control the site itself, such as themes or plugins. Editors can add or delete any content-related items in WordPress, including categories, posts, pages, and links. They have full access to the Media Library and full control over publishing content. Editors can also add and delete users, but they cannot edit user information.
- **Author:** Authors within WordPress are meant to be like columnists in a newspaper or magazine. They have full control over their own content — adding, editing, publishing, and deleting — but no one else's. Authors cannot add or delete post or link categories and they cannot use unfiltered HTML in their posts — code such as JavaScript or certain HTML tags or attributes pasted from a program like Dreamweaver.
- **Contributor:** Contributors can create, edit, or delete their own posts, but they cannot publish those posts (they can save drafts or submit them for review). They can't edit or delete even their own posts once those have been published by an Editor or Administrator. Contributors do, however, appear on the Post Author drop-down menu.
- **Subscriber:** The name of this user role shouldn't be confused with subscribing to a website or blog through an RSS feed. In this case, Subscriber is meant in the sense of a registered visitor — someone who can see content or take actions on a site that unregistered visitors can't. Basically, the only permission subscribers have in the admin section is the ability to change their profile (name, e-mail, interests, avatar, and so on).

For complete details on each role's capabilities, check out the WordPress site at `http://codex.wordpress.org/Roles_and_Capabilities`

> *Keep in mind that users only see or have access to the WordPress capabilities for their role. If you're an Administrator talking to an Editor about some issue, keep in mind that they can't see a lot of what you can see on the menu.*

ADDING A USER

There are two ways to become a user on a WordPress site: being added manually by an Administrator or registering through a registration form. The automated form is meant for easily signing up subscribers so they can view special content on your site, and you would use the manual process for adding any of the other roles.

By default, the automated sign-up form is disabled. You can activate it on the Settings ➪ General screen by checking the Membership box. However, the best advice is to leave the automatic sign-up disabled. If you're dealing with a lot of membership sign-ups, you'll probably want to use a plugin anyway, and these plugins handle the sign-up process in a different manner. Stick to manual user creation for anything else.

The word "membership" is a bit confusing because what you're setting here is the ability for people to register themselves as new users on the system. There is no user role called "member" and you may or may not think of the users who sign up as members. The wording on the drop-down menu just below is clearer: New User Default Role. This sets the role that users will be assigned if they're able to register themselves, but it's also the default role in the drop-down menu when manually creating new users. By default, that role is Subscriber.

> *Don't change the Default User Role unless you've really thought things through. Even allowing just anyone to become a Contributor opens up your system to people posting content (even if they can't publish) and being listed on the drop-down author menu for posts. And you certainly wouldn't want to allow just anyone to be an Editor, Author, or Administrator.*

To manually add a new user to the system, click Users ➪ Add New on the main admin menu and you'll be greeted with the screen shown in Figure 26-1.

Only three items are required to create a new user:

- Username
- E-mail address
- Password

Users can fill in the other details as they choose once they've logged in for the first time.

Always double-check which role you're assigning to the user (the default is Subscriber). If you'd like the login details sent to the user by e-mail, be sure to check the Send Password box. Once users have their login information, they can change or fill in any of the fields on the Profile screen I showed you in Lesson 5 (except the username).

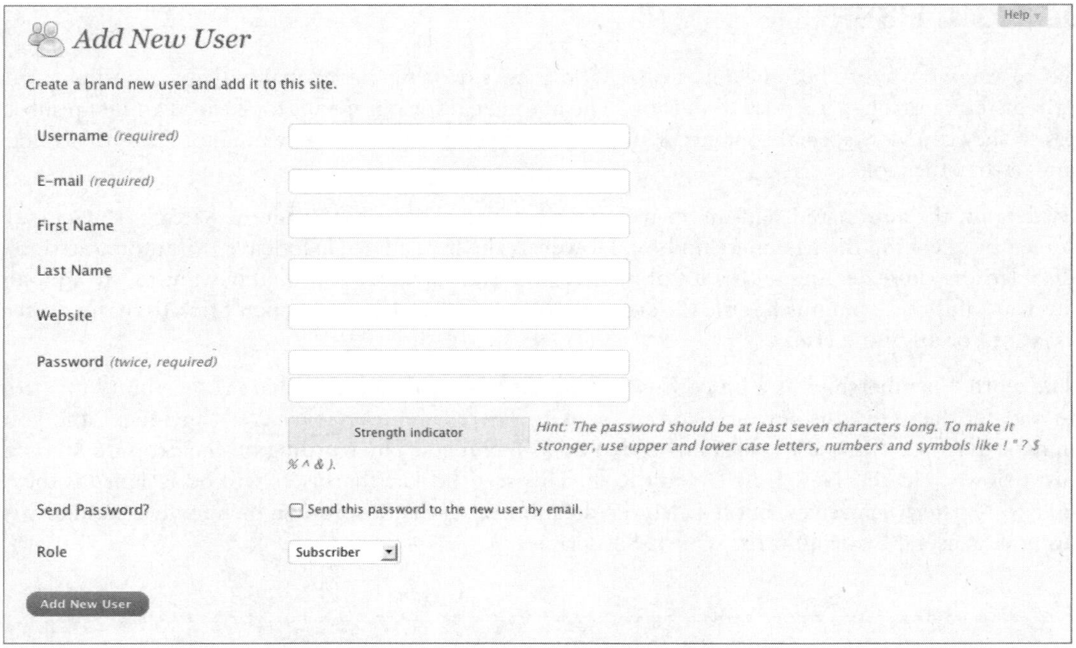

FIGURE 26-1

> *Usernames and e-mail addresses must be unique. WordPress warns you if either already exists in the system.*

CHANGING A USER'S CAPABILITIES

Need to promote a Contributor to Author status? Tired of one of the Administrators always switching themes and you want to bump them down to Subscriber? An Administrator can change a user's role by going to Users ➪ Users, finding the user on the list, and going into their personal profile by clicking Edit, which appears when your mouse moves over a listing. Figure 26-2A shows the top portion of the resulting personal profile screen.

Just below the username is the drop-down menu for their role. Select a role and click Update User.

You can also change any user's role from the Users screen, as shown in Figure 26-2B. Check the box beside their name, choose a new role from the drop-down menu, and click Change.

If you need to change large numbers of users at once, simply check all the users you want to change. Then, from the Change Role To drop-down menu at the top of the page, select the new role and click Change, as shown in Figure 26-2B.

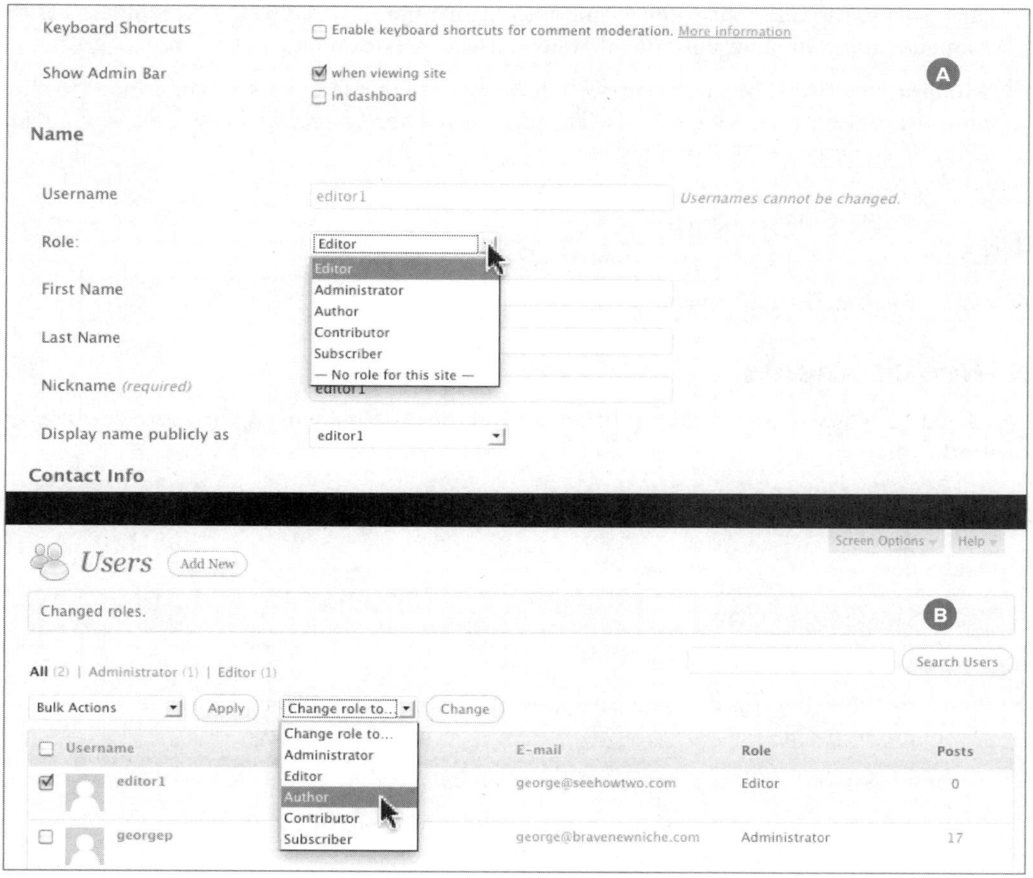

FIGURE 26-2

If you have a lot of users on the site, you can change the number of users displayed using the Screen Options menu at the top right, and further, you can filter and show only one particular role at a time rather than having to sort through them all.

USERS AND SECURITY

Following are three key points concerning users and security:

1. **Choose the lowest possible role:** Don't make someone an Editor when they really just need to be an Author. The higher the role, the more power you're entrusting to the user. And if you turn on the self-registration feature, don't allow users to sign up for anything more than Subscriber.
2. **Emphasize the importance of tough passwords:** You may give new users a diabolical password, but they can go in and change that later. Impress on them the need to not use natural

language words, and to use upper- and lowercase, numbers, and so on. (WordPress has this reminder and a strength indicator that gives users an extra nudge.)

3. **Monitor your users:** In particular if you have more than a few users, it's important to check your list of users on a regular basis. The unexpected appearance of a new user with a high-end role could be the sign of a hacker.

TRY IT

In this lesson, you practice adding a new user.

Lesson Requirements

An e-mail address you can access that is different from the one you're using for your WordPress administrator role.

Step-by-Step

How to add a new user.

1. Go to Users ➪ Add New.
2. Enter a username.
3. Enter an e-mail address that you can access (must be different from the e-mail you use in your current profile).
4. Enter a password (follow the suggestions given by WordPress).
5. As you enter the password the first time, the Strength meter will tell you how good it is — at the very least, make it Strong or Very Strong.
6. Enter the password a second time.
7. Make sure the Send Password box is checked.
8. Select a role for this user (other than Administrator).
9. Click Add User.
10. Log out of WordPress as an Administrator.
11. Check your e-mail for your user information.
12. Try logging in with your username and password.
13. As long as the new user's role was not Administrator, you shouldn't see Settings on the side menu, and depending on the user level, you may not see other parts of the menu either.

> *To see some of the examples from this lesson, watch the video for Lesson 26 on the DVD with the print book, or watch online at* `www.wrox.com/go/wp24vids`.

SECTION VII
Choosing and Customizing Themes

27

Overview of WordPress Themes

WordPress is well known for the thousands of free and paid themes that are available for it, but a lot of misconceptions exist about what a theme is. In this lesson, I help you understand better why they're so important and also help you navigate through the constantly changing array of themes out there on the Web.

WHAT IS A WORDPRESS THEME?

A theme is a set of files, graphics, and scripts that, in simplest terms, controls the look of your site. You can add or remove themes from WordPress with the click of a button, giving you great flexibility when it comes to updating the look of your site. But themes do far more than provide the design for your site.

In fact, design is almost secondary as web developers take on greater and greater challenges in building sites that go way beyond the basics of a blog or business card website. The template files that make up a theme are taking on increasingly complex roles as WordPress gets used now as a full-fledged content management system. Figure 27-1 on the right shows all the files and folders that make up one of the most sophisticated free themes at the moment — Suffusion — and on the left, you see the files for Kubrick, the old default theme for WordPress.

I talked about some of this in the opening lessons, but it's worth making clear again here. WordPress themes have two distinct roles:

- Functionality
- Layout/Design

The functionality of a web page is all about how you gather and organize the content. WordPress plugins also add functionality — adding Facebook like buttons, showing random content on the sidebar, and so on — but most of the basic functionality of a site is controlled by the theme.

Name
Date Modified
404.php 08-09-27
archive.php 09-04-16
archives.php 08-10-17
comments-popup.php 09-05-05
comments.php 09-05-05
footer.php 09-04-16
functions.php 09-05-09
header.php 09-04-16
image.php 09-04-17
images 09-06-11
index.php 09-04-16
links.php 08-09-27
page.php 09-04-16
rtl.css 09-04-12
screenshot.png 05-08-07
search.php 09-04-16
sidebar.php 09-04-20
single.php 09-04-17
style.css 09-05-20
19 items
Name
Date Modified
1l-sidebar.php 11-02-24
1l1r-sidebar.php 11-02-24
1r-sidebar.php 11-02-24
2l-sidebars.php 11-02-24
2r-sidebars.php 11-02-24
404.php 11-02-24
admin 11-02-24
attachment-styles.css 11-02-24
attachment.php 11-02-24
author.php 11-02-24
authors.php 11-02-24
belatedpng.js 11-02-24
bookmarks.php 11-02-24
categories.php 11-02-24
category.php 11-02-24
ChangeLog.txt 11-02-24
comment.php 11-02-24
comments.php 11-02-24
custom-styles.php 11-02-24
dark-style.css 11-02-24
date.php 11-02-24
dbx.js 11-02-24
featured-posts.php 11-02-24
footer.php 11-02-24
functions 11-02-24
functions.php 11-02-24
gradient.php 11-02-24
header.php 11-02-24
ie-fix.css 11-02-24
image.php 11-02-24
images 11-02-24
index.php 11-02-24
layouts 11-02-24
login.php 11-02-24
magazine.php 11-02-24
no-sidebars.php 11-02-24
now-reading 11-02-24
page.php 11-02-24
posts.php 11-02-24
readme.txt 11-02-24
rounded-corners.css 11-02-24
rtl.css 11-02-24
screenshot.png 11-02-24
scripts 11-02-24
search.php 11-02-24
searchform.php 11-02-24
sidebar-2.php 11-02-24
sidebar-tabs.php 11-02-24
sidebar.php 11-02-24
single.php 11-02-24
skins 11-02-24
style.css 11-02-24
suffusion-classes.php 11-02-24
suffusion-widgets.php 11-02-24
suffusion.php 11-02-24
tag.php 11-02-24
template-sitemap.php 11-02-24
translation 11-02-24
widget-areas.php 11-02-24
widgets 11-02-24
60 items

FIGURE 27-1

Page templates are an excellent example of this. Yes, they can be used to vary the design of a page — no sidebar or a different header — but more often, they're used to provide new functionality: a page of links, a list of courses pulled from three different categories, or a meeting page that brings in data about a speaker, a topic, and the facilitator, for example.

You can customize a theme to make WordPress do virtually whatever you want, but more and more themes are building in this kind of functionality and making it easy for users to control such things as which category to display in each of three separate regions on the homepage or choosing the kind of slideshow to be used in a featured items box.

The same is true for design. The trend with themes is to build in a lot of user-friendly control over design elements: color-choosers, layout changes with the click of a button, and uploading your own imagery for backgrounds, headers, and more.

> *With so much functionality being performed by themes, it's important to understand that switching themes is no longer simply a matter of switching skins. You're actually changing how the site works, which means you may be losing some functionality. This doesn't mean you're stuck; there's a way to change the look and keep the functionality that I cover later in Lesson 28.*

One of the implications of this growth in the power and sophistication of themes is that it makes the experience of each WordPress user increasingly different. Just as some people use more or different plugins than other users, the theme used by one person can provide far different administrative options and site functionality than the theme used by someone else.

I notice more and more people asking me questions about using WordPress, which turn out to be questions about how their particular theme works. Unlike the elements of WordPress that we all share, these sophisticated add-ons put us in different places in terms of how we use the software. That's not a bad thing; it's just a noticeable change from the world of WordPress just a couple years ago.

CHOOSING A WORDPRESS THEME

It used to be that you looked for WordPress themes that matched the kind of design you wanted for your site. Things are more complicated these days and so it's harder to know what choices to make.

Here's my rule of thumb for picking a theme:

> *Quality, functionality, and flexibility first, design second.*

The reason? It's much easier (read, lower-cost) to make a site look exactly the way you want than it is to make the quality of coding better or create new functionality (especially easy-to-use functionality).

Most importantly, though, don't just grab the first theme that you really like the look of or that has lots of fancy functions (like slideshows and so on). Do some homework:

- Does the theme appear on a number of top-10 WordPress themes lists?
- Is it made by an author or a company who gets good reviews for other work?

- How many people are downloading it (if it's available at WordPress.org) and what are they saying about it in the forums?
- Put the question to the forums yourself — what are other people experiencing with this theme?
- Would it be worth paying a consultant for a half hour to pick out a good theme with you?

I know this sounds like a lot of work, but this theme is going to run your website (along with WordPress), hopefully for many years to come. It should be the backbone on which to hang all future design changes. You want to get this right. Is it well-built, does it offer a lot of functionality (not simply for controlling the design), and is it flexible? What do you need your site to do and will this theme help make that possible and easier?

One of the features that a lot of people are impressed by in a theme is the ability to quickly switch layouts and change colors, fonts, and all kinds of design elements through easy-to-use interfaces. Don't get me wrong, I think a lot of them are not only cool, but also extremely well-thought-out and brilliantly designed.

But think about design for a moment. How often do you need to change colors and layouts? And if you are doing it often, should you be? Does it help you get and retain visitors? The point is, these useful tools are great when you're first setting up a site and they allow you to change your mind a lot, but once you settle on something, how often do you need them again? And, not to be too blunt about it, maybe you should be hiring a designer to set up some of these things, anyway — they've got the eye for it.

I know, I'm back to the "functionality is a bit more important than design" rant, but that's because it's those functions that you're going to be using day in and day out. A theme that makes it easy to create and manage your own custom widget areas is more valuable, in my opinion, than one that focuses on cool color wheels for picking the shade of your H2 headers. If the theme can do both, more power to it.

There's also a part of me that worries about complexity in the back end. It takes a lot of programming to produce these amazing interfaces, and to me, that's just one more point at which something can go wrong. I would rather see simpler (but clear and usable) interfaces that produce good functionality on the site, than be wowed by cool effects and massive backends. OK, rant over.

So, here are some key features I would look for in a theme, aside from it being compatible with WordPress 3.0+, having good support, and so on:

- Lots of widget areas, especially ones that I can place myself anywhere on the page (I'm not talking about the widgets themselves, but the areas where you can place widgets).
- Lots of front page control options — easy to update and control slideshows, user-selectable content areas (allowing you to put either post or page, or custom post-type content, into these areas), and multiple layouts.
- Several areas (or even the ability to easily create areas) where you can have menus that use WordPress's built-in menu system. (Themes used to create their own versions of what is now a part of WordPress, and those were great when WordPress's menu system was clunky, but they're not needed anymore, so why have the extra coding and interfaces?)

- Lots of useful page templates.
- An interface to make the creation of custom post types and taxonomies easy.
- Well-written, secure coding — you'll need to do some extra research on that end.
- Lots of hook points within the template structure. These are special places where programmers could easily add code without having to take apart the structure (for example, allowing you to put something between the header and the content areas). You may not make use of these day to day, but such hooks can speed up customization you may want to do down the road.

And what's interesting is, when you find themes with these kinds of features, they're usually very good-looking themes too. So design and functionality *can* live harmoniously....

Finally, I tend not to worry about whether themes have features such as the following:

- SEO controls (they should still have SEO-friendly coding and structuring, but not additional elements like entering Title tags or controlling search engine indexing).
- Any social media functionality beyond possibly integrating your "follow me" buttons into the design.
- Contact or other forms.
- Mobile capability.

These are all functions I would rather leave to plugins so that I have more choice and don't become dependent on the theme. Lots of good plugins are available for these functions and I don't need to clutter the theme files with more than is necessary. Certainly, you can simply choose not to use these functions even if a theme offers them, so I'm not saying I'd reject a theme because it has these features, only that a great theme without them would be just fine for me.

One area I didn't talk about is theme frameworks, such as Hybrid, Gantry, Thematic, Genesis, Carrington, Thesis, and more. In essence, these are parent themes that aren't meant to be used themselves, but rather as a framework on which to build child themes. An advantage of this is that framework builders usually have a whole range of child themes to choose from, all based on the original parent. This is one way to reduce the problem I mentioned earlier of moving away from a design and losing functionality. The thing to watch for is that you commit yourself to a good framework. Time to hit the research again!

TRY IT

There is nothing specific to try in this lesson except getting to know what themes are out there. Start in the themes directory at WordPress.org, including the list of commercial vendors over on the left menu (it has grown by leaps and bounds over the past couple of years).

Some theme authors allow you to try out a theme on their site, but if you have a WordPress installation and you're just getting started, simply load up a theme and try it out yourself! If you have a working site, plugins are available, like Theme Switch and Preview, that allow administrators to see a theme without the rest of the world seeing it (not to be confused with allowing visitors to switch themes).

> *To see some of the examples from this lesson, watch the video for Lesson 27 on the DVD with the print book, or watch online at* `www.wrox.com/go/wp24vids`.

28

Creating a Child Theme

Unless you have a WordPress theme built specifically for you, it's unlikely you'll get exactly what you want in any theme you choose, and that means customizations. The problem is, no matter how small the customization, you run the risk of the theme getting updated sometime in the future, which may mean having your files automatically updated, which, in turn, means losing all the changes you made. The answer to this and other issues of customization is to create what's called a child theme. This is a theme that lives primarily off the files of the parent theme, but introduces files of its own whenever it needs to make changes to the parent.

In this lesson, you not only learn about the power of these types of themes, but you create your own child theme using the default WordPress Twenty Ten theme as its parent.

WHAT IS A CHILD THEME?

The concept of a child theme grew out of the realization that often, the changes people wanted to make to a theme were fairly minor. For example, they just wanted the header area to be smaller or the menu placed in a different spot, or they needed some extra widget areas. All of these changes can be made with a few adjustments to just a few files.

So the WordPress developers came up with a simple answer: a theme hierarchy.

If the necessary files don't exist in your theme, the system will look in another. As long as WordPress knows who the parent is, the child can use whatever files it needs to, and what it doesn't have, the system will get from the parent.

For example, if I want to modify the `header.php` file in the parent theme, I simply copy it, make my changes, and drop the new version (still named the same way, of course) in my child theme folder. Because my child theme is active, WordPress checks its folder first, so in this case, it would stop looking for `header.php`. If the file isn't present in the child theme folder, it looks in the parent.

> *There's one file that WordPress does not use in this "either/or" manner, and that's* `functions.php`*. If there's one in the parent and one in the child folder, the two get combined.*

But why not simply make a copy of the original theme, rename it, and then start making your own changes? That's certainly an option, but several reasons why you might as well use a child theme include:

- You'll be missing out on upgrades to the original theme (unless you had so much free time — not to mention patience — that you could go through and replicate all the changes in your new theme).
- It makes it easy to know what you've changed because you're dealing only with the files that are different from the parent.
- You always have the original set of files to fall back on — they're already installed in WordPress.
- It maintains credit where credit is due — the parent theme remains intact and your modifications are clearly separate (make sure you give credit in your child theme — parents always like that).

Plus, when you see how easy it is to make a child theme, you'll just say, "Why not?" Let's get started.

> *For this next section, you need to be using a plain text editor program, so put away any word processing program you have. For Windows, there's a plain text editor called Notepad in the Accessories folder of Programs, and Mac users have TextEdit, which comes with OSX.*
>
> *TextEdit does not work in plain text mode by default, so check your preferences before using it; set them to Plain Text, and turn off all spell checking and auto anything. (Better still, search the Web for "plain text editor mac" and download another program). If you don't use a plain text editor, you'll end up with all sorts of nasty hidden code that word processors use behind the scenes, and that will likely cause things not to work properly on your server.*

STARTING A CHILD THEME

Only one file is required to create a child theme: `style.css`. That's it.

As long as it's formatted correctly (which is easy) and placed in a uniquely named folder in the `/wp-content/themes` directory, WordPress will see it as a theme and display it in the Manage

Themes directory of the admin area. I'll go over that again shortly, but I want you to start building the `style.css` file. I've created an example of the minimal file you need in Figure 28-1.

```
/*
Theme Name: My Very First Theme
Template: twentyten
*/

@import url("../twentyten/style.css");
```

FIGURE 28-1

The first line must have the `/*` because that tells the system that it's a comment and not part of the style rules for the style sheet.

On the next line, type "Theme Name:" followed by the name of your theme. The actual name can be whatever you want. Best to make it something clear because this is the name that will appear in your Manage Themes directory and it should make it easy to know which one you're choosing; I'm going to use My Very First Theme.

The next line must start with Template: followed by the name of the folder where the parent theme resides. That's why the name is in lowercase — it's not the Theme Name like the one you just created. This is the folder name in the Themes directory of `wp-content`. This is how WordPress will know where to look for files that aren't in your child theme.

> *Just to be clear, you don't have to be making a child theme for Twenty Ten, so whatever the folder name is of the theme you want as a parent, that's the name you put after Template.*

Now you'll need the closing comment symbols `*/` (notice that it's reversed this time — asterisk first, then the forward slash). This means the comments are over and it's time for the CSS rules.

But there's one more thing you need to do. If things were left at this point, your style sheet would completely replace the parent style sheet — that's how the theme hierarchy works. What's more, because your style sheet has no rules yet, the site would have no styling! In fact, you want to use the parent style sheet (in the vast majority of cases), so you need to tell WordPress (or, more accurately, your browser) to pick up the parent style sheet along the way:

```
@import url("../twentyten/style.css");
```

You use the `@import` rule to do that and the URL you specify needs to be relative to your child theme. The `..` tells your browser to get out of the child theme and look for a folder called `twentyten` and then go in and grab `style.css`.

> *There can't be any CSS rules above* `@import` *and before the closing comment characters* `*/`*. If there are, the import function won't work. So, start any CSS* after *the line with the import rule.*

So, that's all you absolutely have to have in your child theme's `style.css` file. However, a couple more items would be useful in the comments area.

The first is a description of the theme. Theme developers use this to help pitch their work — it tells visitors and users what the theme is capable of and so on. That's not particularly useful in this case because it's your own theme, but here are two things I think are a must:

- **Make it clear which theme this is a child of:** That gives credit where it's due, but even more importantly, it could help prevent some well-meaning soul from deleting the parent theme a year down the road, thinking it serves no purpose.
- **Warn people about switching themes:** Whether you're putting a lot of customized functionality into your child theme or you're relying on the functionality of the parent, you should warn users about simply switching themes: they're not just changing the look, they're changing how the site works. Tell them that they can change the look and keep the functionality by making a copy of the child theme and renaming it.

You can see examples of these two points in an updated version of the `style.css` file shown in Figure 28-2.

```
/*
Theme Name: My Very First Theme
Description: NOTE: This is a CHILD THEME using the default WordPress Twenty-
Ten. WARNING: If you switch themes you may lose functionality. If you want to
change the look, make a copy of this theme, rename it, and install it in WordPress -
then start changing the design.
Author: George Plumley
Author URI: http:/www.bravenewniche.com
Template: twentyten
*/

@import url("../twentyten/style.css");
```

FIGURE 28-2

Other than the description, you can see I've added an Author line as well, and if you're doing this for someone else, you could put an Author URI and/or a Theme URI if you wanted to make sure others saw who created the child theme. If you anticipate modifying the theme down the road, it's also a good idea to include a version number so you can easily identify which is which.

With the basics of your style sheet done, save the file from your text editor by creating a new folder with a short name. This is the folder that's going to be put into `/wp-content/themes`, so it has to be lowercase, with no spaces (a dash is okay between words or numbers). I'm going to use the name `my-first-theme`.

Next, you'll need to compress the child theme folder, and how you do this will depend on your computer's system. Typically on a Windows machine, you would actually select all the files inside the folder (in this case, just one) and then right-click, at which point, you choose Send to Compressed Folder. You'll then need to rename the folder with the lowercase theme name you decided on earlier.

On a Mac, simply highlight the child theme folder, right-click, and choose Compress Folder. In both cases, you end up with `my-first-theme.zip` (or whatever you named it followed by the `.zip` extension). Make a note of where this file is, because you're going to need it in the next section.

INSTALLING A THEME

Because you've now created a theme, let's use it to demonstrate how to install any theme.

The entire installation process, from finding a theme to installing it, can be done from inside WordPress, using the Install Themes screen shown in Figure 28-3.

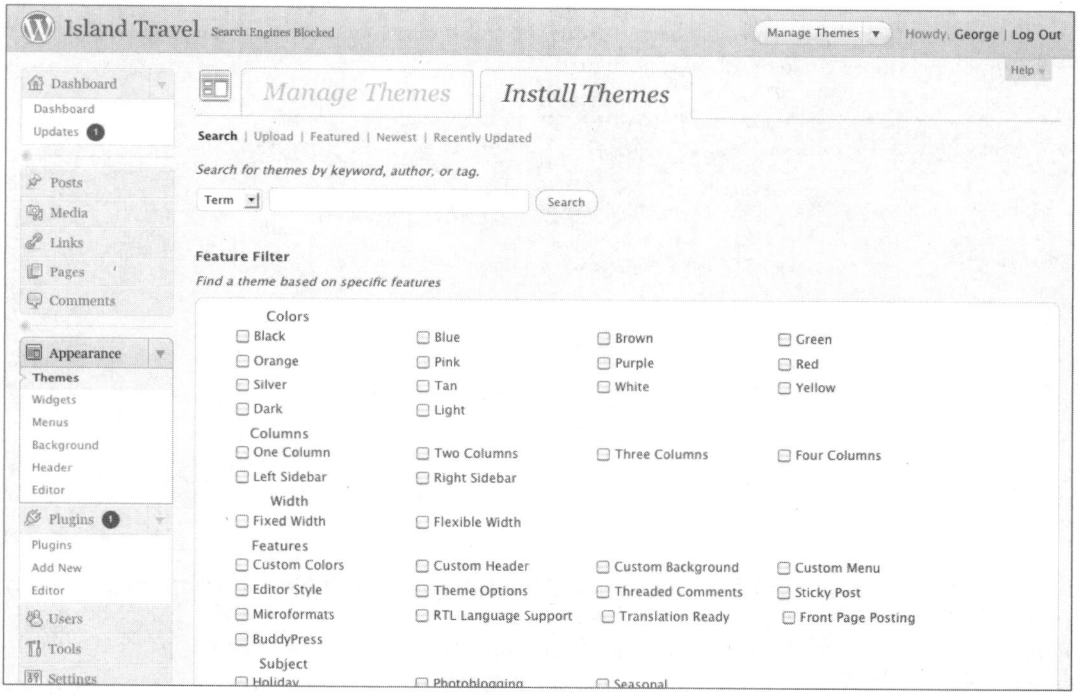

FIGURE 28-3

The search function, which is the default screen, is tied in to the Free Themes Directory at WordPress.org, so you can search that database and preview themes just as you would if you were on that site. There's a wide range of parameters to help narrow your search, as you can see from all the check boxes in Figure 28-3; search for colors, layouts, and functions.

> *Though there are lots of parameters, keep in mind that these are dependent on how accurately theme authors have described and tagged their creations. You may need to try several variations and be creative with your thinking sometimes.*

On the text menu at the very top are filters for Featured, Newest, and Recently Updated themes, again, all from the WordPress.org site.

When you find a theme you want, just click the Install button and WordPress automatically uploads and installs it. You can install any number of themes, by the way, and they'll all sit in the Manage Themes window, but only one can be active at any time.

Of course, you're not limited to using themes from the WordPress.org directory. Other free themes are available, along with a lot of paid themes. You access those by downloading a `.zip` file from the author or company website and saving it to your hard drive.

Then, you use the Upload screen, accessed from the small text menu at the top of the Install Themes page, which produces the page shown in Figure 28-4.

FIGURE 28-4

You simply browse your hard drive for the `.zip` file and click Install Now. If everything's successful, you'll be asked if you want to preview or activate the theme or return to the Themes page. I've uploaded the child theme I just created and when I return to the Manage Themes page, there it is, as shown in Figure 28-5.

Notice that WordPress reminds you at the bottom of the description that this is a child theme and where WordPress will look for files. I find that people often don't read that and it's good to say it in the description that appears right below the theme title. Plus, that WordPress message doesn't display when the theme is active, and that's when you need the warnings the most.

Don't worry that there's no screenshot above the title — you could always add one later (just name it `screenshot.png` — you can also use .gif or .jpg files — and use your FTP program to upload it into your theme).

Now, activate your child theme by clicking Activate (you can also preview, too, if you'd like). Once that's been activated, it will show at the top of the page as the Current Theme.

Take a look at your live site after refreshing your browser. No difference. You have nothing overriding the parent theme or adding to it, so everything is just as it was when Twenty Ten was the current theme. And that's a good thing. Now, you're ready to start making some customizations using your child theme in the next lesson.

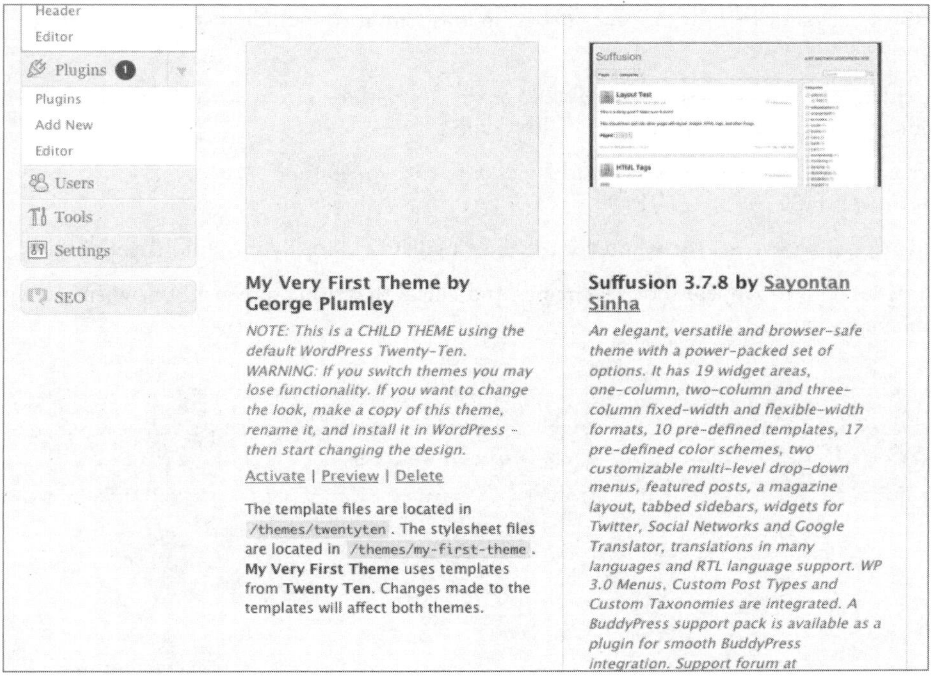

FIGURE 28-5

TRY IT

In this lesson, you practice accessing your child theme with an FTP (file transfer protocol) program, and upload a `screenshot.png` file at the same time.

Lesson Requirements

A graphics program, an FTP program, and access to your server files. Lesson 3 dealt with accessing your server via FTP.

Step-by-Step

Uploading the `screenshot.png` file to your child theme.

1. Open your website in your browser and make sure you're on the homepage. Don't worry if you haven't got much in there right now; you just need a small picture of it.
2. Take a screenshot of your browser window. On Windows, press Shift+Print Screen (near the top right on most keyboards) then open a graphics program and you should see Edit ➪ Paste highlighted. When you paste, you should see the image of the screen. On Mac, press Command+Shift+3 and the image will be saved to the desktop.

3. Open the screenshot in your graphics program and trim it to include just the browser window.
4. Resize the image to 300 pixels wide by 225 pixels high, then save it with the name `screenshot` — it can be a JPG, GIF, or PNG file.
5. In your FTP program, on the server side, navigate to `/wp-content/themes/your-child-theme`.
6. Upload `screenshot.png` (or whatever the file extension is) into your child theme folder.
7. In WordPress, go to Appearance ➪ Themes and check that your screenshot now shows up in your theme listing.

To see some of the examples from this lesson, watch the video for Lesson 28 on the DVD with the print book, or watch online at `www.wrox.com/go/wp24vids`.

29

Basic Customization of Your Design

For a long time, the default theme with WordPress didn't change much, until version 3.0 and the introduction of the Twenty Ten default theme. It's not only quite a nice theme for almost any type of personal or small-business website, but it was made to be customized fairly easily.

In this lesson, I show you how to use the built-in tools of Twenty Ten, as well as some simple changes you can make with style sheets to get the look you want. There isn't room here to go into a lot of detail or develop the skills necessary to make major changes, but there's a lot you can do with even a little bit of knowledge.

> *In this lesson, you'll be making use of the child theme I showed you how to make in Lesson 28. If you've skipped that lesson altogether or if you didn't actually make the child theme, you'll need to go back and do that now.*
>
> *Trust me, it's easy and it will save a lot of heartache because if you make any changes to the default Twenty Ten theme files, they'll get overwritten in the next update of WordPress and all your hard work will be lost.*

CUSTOMIZING THE HEADER IMAGE

One of the best things about the Twenty Ten theme is the flexibility of its header image area. The most obvious fact when you click Appearance ➪ Header is that you can easily upload your own header image any time you want, as you can see from Figure 29-1.

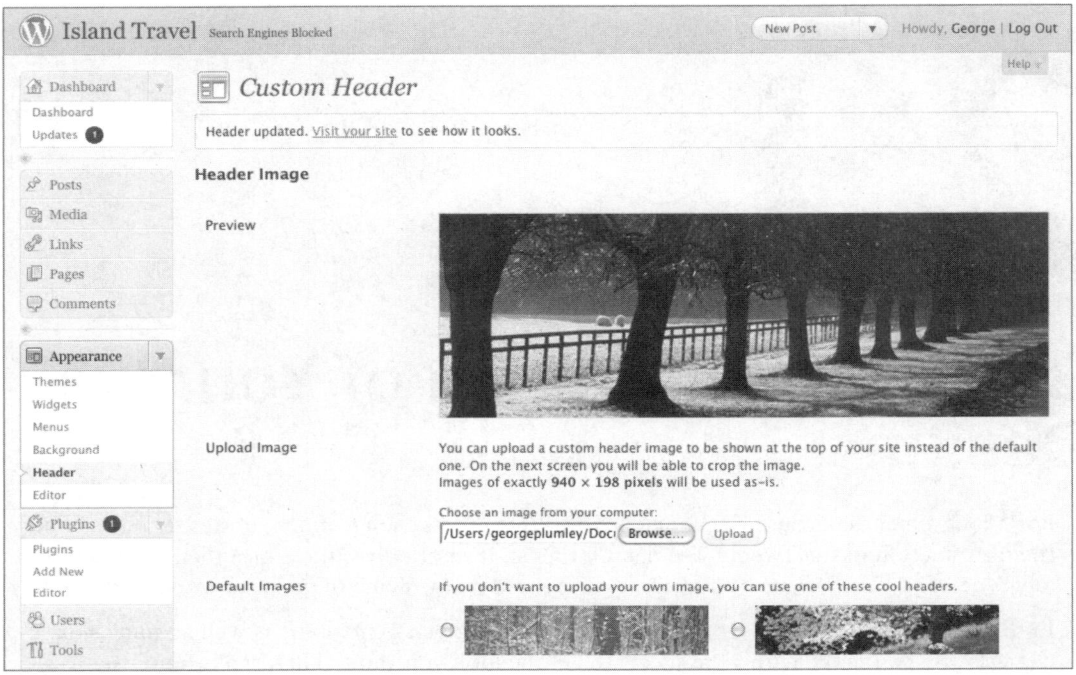

FIGURE 29-1

You can also use some very nice built-in alternative images, but most people are interested in uploading their own.

WordPress makes it very simple by giving you the dimensions of the header image. This is the minimum size the image must be. The note above the upload field explains that if the image is larger, you'll be given the chance to crop it, as shown in Figure 29-2.

The default size of the header image is 940 x 198 pixels, so in my graphics program, I build a header that matches those dimensions. Then I optimize it for the Web to reduce its size in terms of kilobytes, at which point I save it to my hard drive.

> *You can change the default header sizes using your child theme's* `functions.php` *file. It's possible to do it yourself, but it's a very simple change for a programmer to make if you're looking at hiring someone to do customizations.*

Back in WordPress on the Custom Header page, I'm ready now to choose my image and I click Browse. Once I've found my header, I click Upload and now, the default image of the trees is replaced with my graphic, as shown in the two frames of Figure 29-3.

FIGURE 29-2

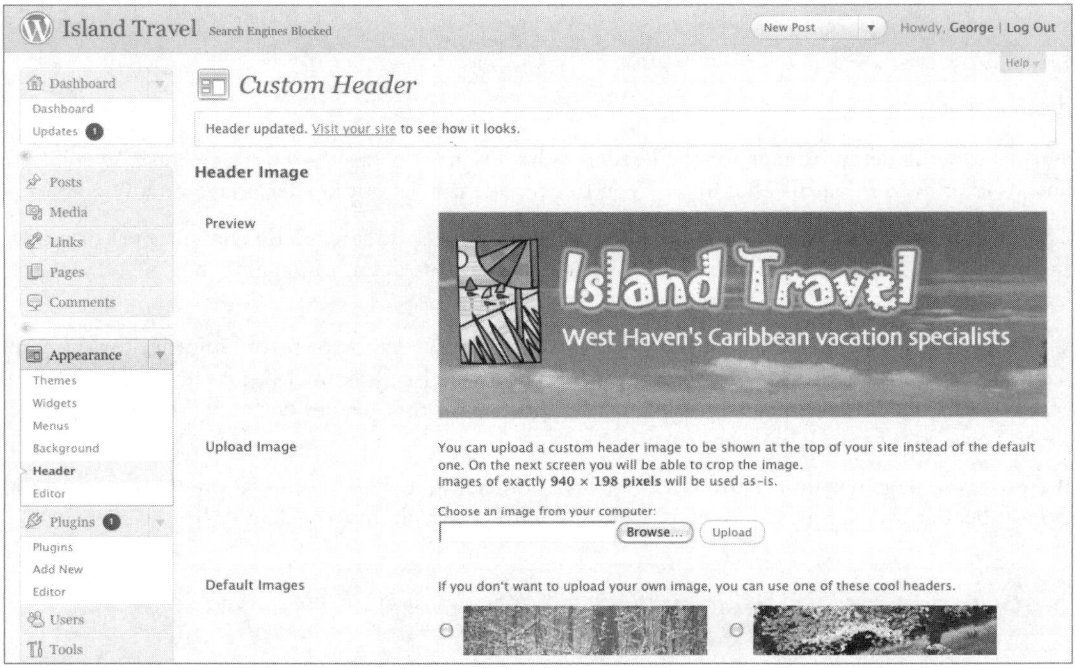

FIGURE 29-3

If your image is smaller than the dimensions given on the Custom Header screen, WordPress will present you with the crop screen and a highlighted area that's proportional to the dimensions, but when it crops that area, it then blows it up to fill those dimensions. You'll end with a pixelated, chopped-off version of the picture, so it's important that your image matches or is larger than the dimensions given.

My graphic is now visible on the website, as shown in Figure 29-4.

FIGURE 29-4

This is now the default image for the header. Why do I say "default"? That's because Twenty Ten has another header feature that allows you to override the default header image on any post or page.

There's coding in the theme's `header.php` file that looks for a featured image on a post or a page. If there is one, it compares the dimensions with those of the default image. If they're the same or larger, WordPress uses the featured image as the header.

This means that I could have a special header image for the Aruba page and another for the Jamaica page. And because it's so easy to change a featured image (see Lesson 13), I could even keep a general Jamaica header and replace the right-hand portion of that header with advertising for a weekly special or a contest, or whatever I want.

If a post or a page has no featured image or it's not the right size, the theme simply reverts to the default header image I just uploaded. And, of course, I can change the default header any time.

Keep in mind that this is a feature of Twenty Ten (and by inheritance, of my child theme) and not of WordPress. The theme is using features of WordPress to accomplish all this, but it's not something every theme will have.

CUSTOMIZING THE SITE BACKGROUND

I'm going to come back to the header area later when we start to mess with the CSS (style sheets), but I want to continue with Twenty Ten's built-in customizations. The background of the site has its own screen that you get to from Appearance ➪ Background as well; it's shown in Figure 29-5.

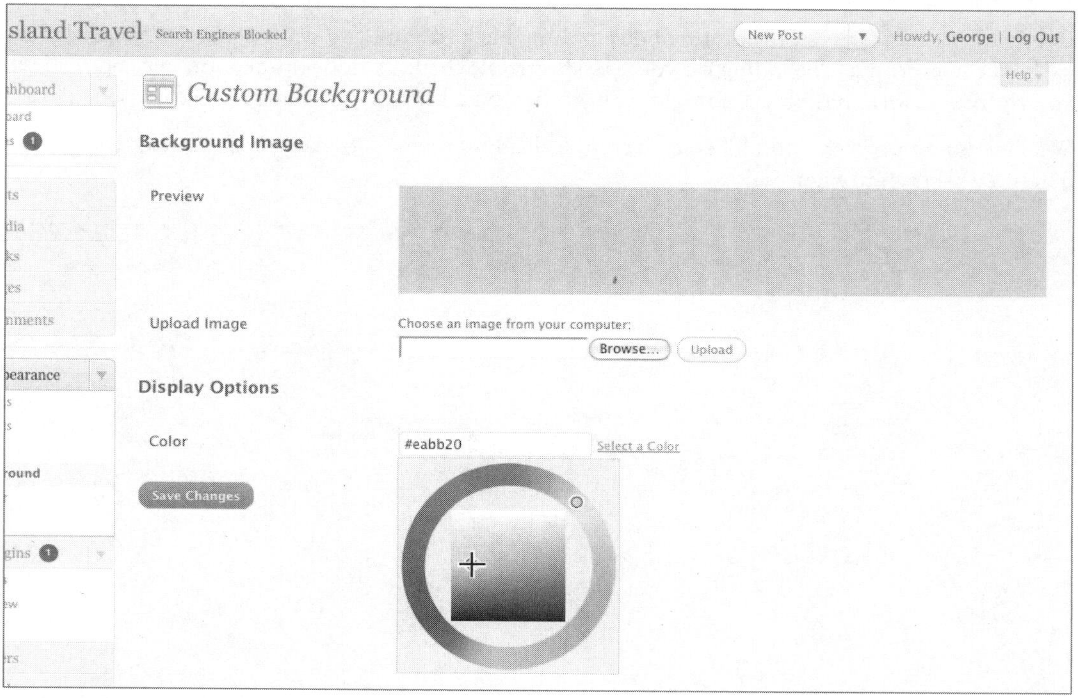

FIGURE 29-5

I'm using the built-in color wheel to select a new look for the background. The default gray isn't quite what I'm looking for. The color in the large area at the top changes as I move the wheel, so it's easy to get a feel for what the color will look like. For the Island Travel site, I'm thinking of going with a sandy-colored background, which is what I choose in the end. It's hard to see the difference in black and white, but I show it on the video that goes with this lesson.

I could also find an image to use for the background. The theme provides an upload interface for that purpose. When I say background image, I'm talking primarily about tiny images that get "tiled" to fill up the whole background. If you've never made one before, you should search for tutorials on the subject: "create a background image for a website."

Large background images that fill the entire browser window can be tricky. You don't want something that's eating up precious loading time for your site and you don't want something that works well in only certain screen sizes. Again, you'd need to research this online, but I'd stick with tiled images that don't have a set pattern — that's the simplest.

USING YOUR CSS FILE TO CUSTOMIZE

In this part of the lesson, you edit the CSS file that is currently the sole file in your child theme. The simplest way to do that is using the Appearance ➪ Editor screen, which gives you access to any theme files and allows you to edit them live. Notice I said "live," which means any changes will be visible to the public immediately, as will any mistakes. If that's too scary a thought, you might want to leave things to a web designer or developer who works with WordPress.

On the other hand, if you're careful about making backups and you do your work late at night (or early in the morning, depending on your perspective), when the odd slip-up won't get noticed while you restore the original file, you might want to try some of these customizations yourself.

When you first open the Edit Themes screen, it displays the `style.css` file of the current theme by default, as shown in Figure 29-6.

FIGURE 29-6

There's the style sheet you created and over on the right-hand side is a list of all files in a theme — right now, just one. But if you use the drop-down menu at the top right, you can see all the files for any installed theme. Choosing Twenty Ten and clicking Select takes you to the style sheet for that theme. What I recommend for the work you're about to do is keep this tab open at the Twenty Ten style sheet and then open a new tab in your browser.

In that new tab's address bar, enter your domain name followed by `/wp-admin`, which will take you to the admin screen (you won't have to log in because you're already logged in). Go to Appearance

➪ Editor and you'll see the child-theme CSS file again. The idea here is that you'll want to be going back and forth between the two style sheets if you need to copy and paste anything from the parent to the child.

Getting Rid of the Site Title and Description

Because I've uploaded a header image with my logo and tagline in it, I don't really want the default title text and description above the image header. I could make a copy of the `header.php` file, put it in my child theme, and then take out the code that creates those two text areas.

However, CSS allows me to simply make them disappear, and here's how: create a rule that says don't display those two items to regular browsers. If you check the source code of the web page, you'll discover that the two text areas have the attributes: `id="site-title"` and `id="side-description"`.

> *An even better way to study the CSS of any site is to use the F12 key on Internet Explorer, the Firebug add-on for Firefox, or in Chrome and Safari, right-click near the point on the page you're interested in and choose Inspect Element. In each case, you're presented with the CSS for the entire page, which you can also edit live, to see what the change will look like (you're not changing the actual site, just what your browser is displaying).*

Remember that my child theme style sheet will override anything in the parent file, so if I create a rule to hide the content using CSS selectors that match those attributes, my problem should be solved. WordPress has a rule to do this:

```
.screen-reader-text {
        position: absolute;
        left: -9000px;
}
```

This moves the text offscreen so it's not visible to regular browsers, but can be read by special screen readers and search engines. So, I'll just replicate this rule for these two cases. I'll go and put that in my CSS file and you'll see the exact formatting in Figure 29-7.

The top part of Figure 29-7 shows my header before the change, the middle section shows the CSS file as I saved it after making my additions, and the bottom portion shows the site afterward.

That's much better; I'm not repeating information and I'm not using up so much vertical space in my header area. Plus, if I need to bring back those two text items, it's one simple change in the CSS file.

Changing the Body Font

Some people aren't fond of the Georgia font used for the body text in the Twenty Ten theme. Personally, I like it, but what if I wanted to change it? The temptation is to use the Format drop-down in the WordPress Text Editor's Visual mode, because that seems to be the only way to change how text looks in your posts and pages.

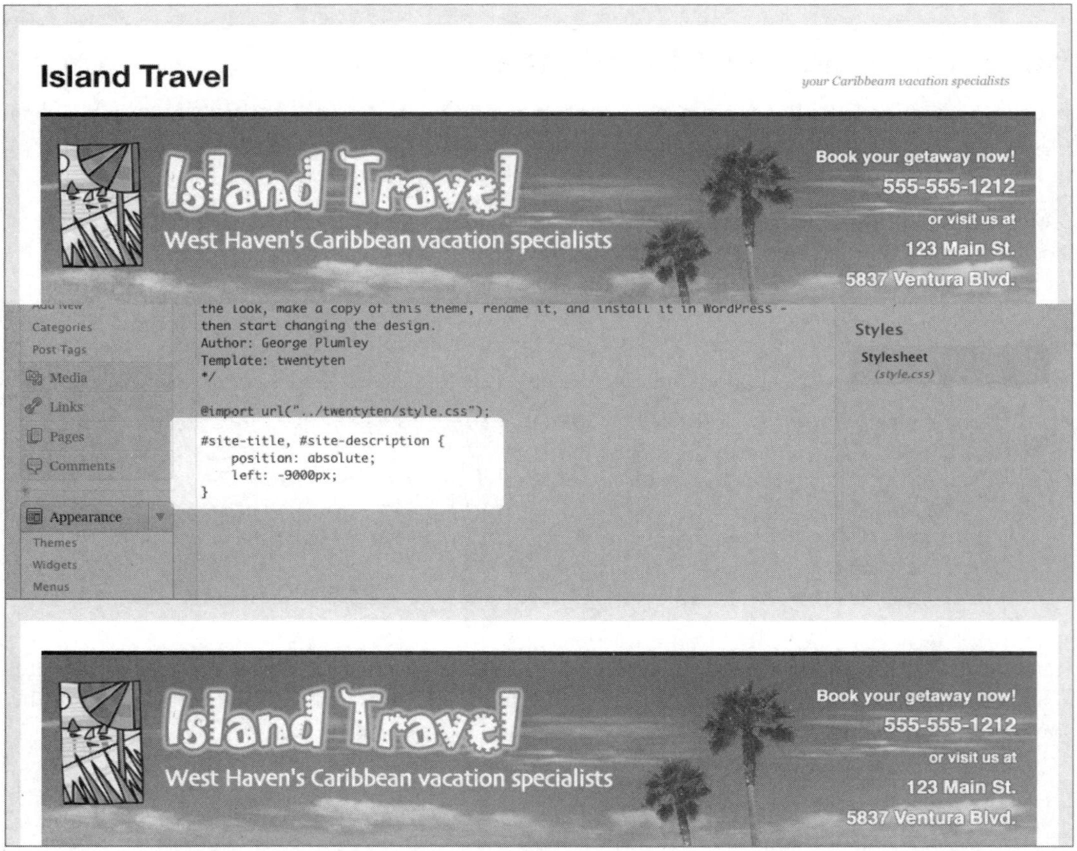

FIGURE 29-7

Not only are you actually using header tags when you use that drop-down menu, which is meant for headings and not body text, but you're manually changing each post/page and if you wanted to switch back later, you'd need to go in and change every single one by hand. Ouch!

What you really want to do is change your style sheet. You could use the browser method I spoke of earlier or you can look in the Twenty Ten style sheet to see how the body text is controlled. Figure 29-8 shows you the highlighted CSS rule.

The simplest method is to highlight and copy the relevant text, and then paste it into your child theme style sheet. At that point, you can edit your child theme file to change from Georgia to, say, Verdana, as in Figure 29-9.

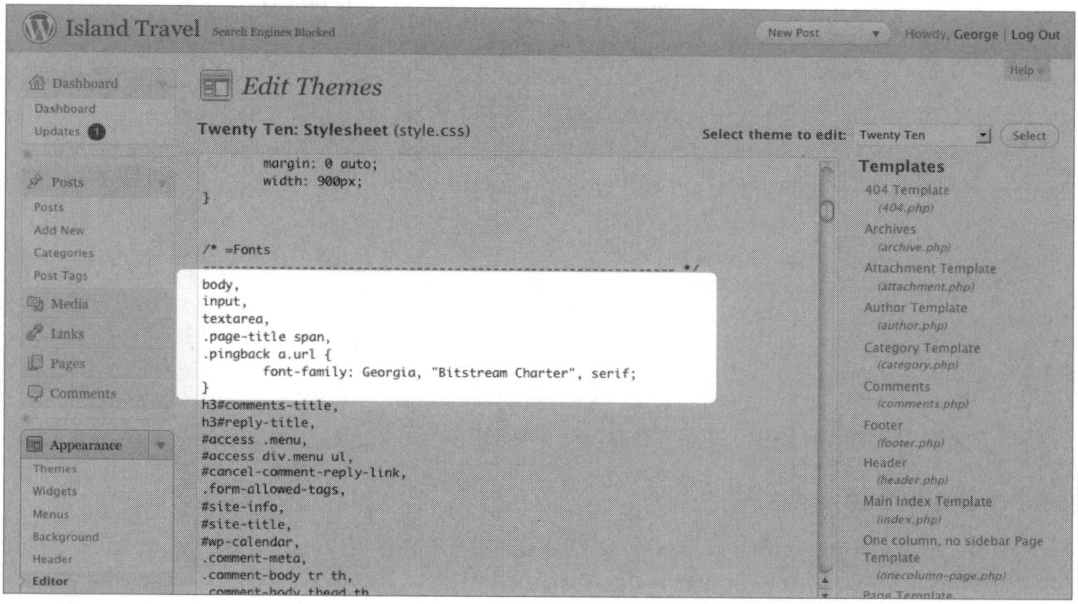

FIGURE 29-8

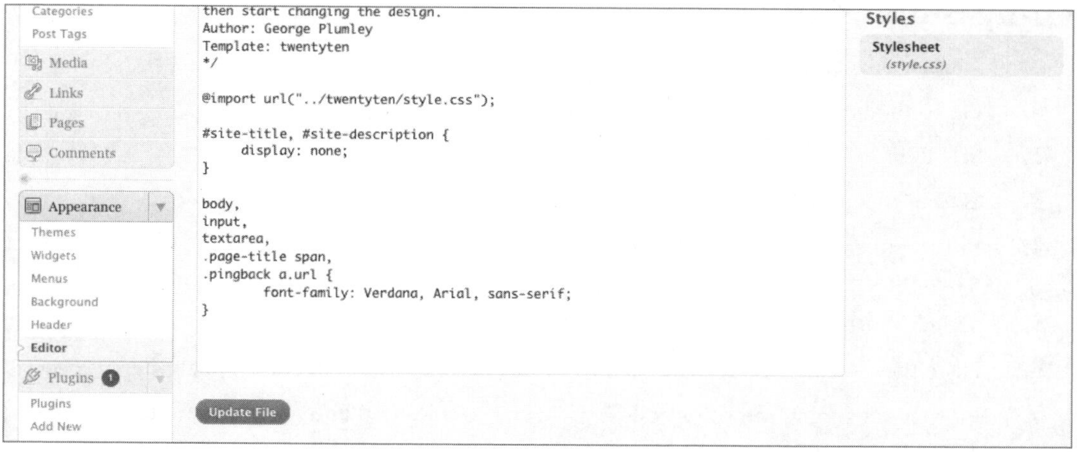

FIGURE 29-9

I've added Arial and the generic sans-serif in there as a safety net in case a browser doesn't have Verdana. Now, my body text will all be in Verdana.

It's often good to have body text and title text with opposite serif formatting, so I would probably want to grab the next CSS rule from Twenty Ten as well, because it set the font for titles and other related elements. Then I would switch it from a sans-serif to a serif font. You don't have to do that, of course, but visually, it can be more appealing.

And that's part of the problem that this freedom to edit your CSS or any other file brings with it — the responsibility of good design. Though anyone can get in and edit their style sheet for their site, not everyone should be doing that. There's a reason people are called designers and that's because not only do they usually have a better eye for all these little details, but they usually do it much, much faster.

Clearly, you could do a lot of customizing to any theme, but at some point, you need to ask whether it's time to bring in a professional.

TRY IT

In this lesson, you change the color of links on your site.

Lesson Requirements

Make sure you're set up with a child theme as described in this lesson and the Twenty Ten theme as the parent. Have two browser tabs open, each with the Appearance ➪ Editor open — one for your child theme's CSS file and one for the Twenty Ten theme CSS file.

Step-by-Step

How to change the color of links.

1. Go to the browser tab with the Twenty Ten theme CSS file.
2. Scroll down a little until you see a Text Elements section.
3. Within that section, look for `a:link`, `a:visited`, `a:active`, and `a:hover`.
4. Select and copy everything from `a:link` down to the final curly bracket after `color: #ff4b33`
5. Switch to the browser tab with your child-theme CSS.
6. Paste the code at the very end of the current file text and then click Update File.
7. Now try changing the color code for `a:link` to #dd0000 and click Update File.
8. Refresh your site and you'll see the unvisited links turn to red.
9. Go back to your child-theme CSS tab, change the color back to #0066CC again, and click Update File.
10. Check that the links have returned to their regular color. You can find color values in this format if you actually want to change link colors by searching for "hexadecimal color codes."

> *To see some of the examples from this lesson, watch the video for Lesson 29 on the DVD with the print book, or watch online at* `www.wrox.com/go/wp24vids`.

SECTION VIII
Becoming Search Engine–Friendly

30

Optimizing Your Content

The most common way for people to find what they want online is through search engines, but although searches return thousands, even millions of pages of results, few people go past even the second or third page. It's no surprise, then, that so much attention is paid to achieving high search-engine rankings.

Search engine optimization (SEO) is a complex and constantly changing topic, well beyond the scope of this book, but in this and the following lesson, I show you some things you can do in WordPress to better your chances of good rankings.

The healthiest way to think about SEO is to keep in mind the goal of search engines: to deliver the most useful, reliable, best-quality web pages that meet the search parameters. If you work hard to make your site useful to visitors, you have a better chance of being ranked well. In other words, think about your visitors' needs first.

Having said that, you also have to take into account the ways search engines read and interpret that content.

WRITING USEFUL TITLES

In this section, I cover the importance of relevant titles for posts (or pages). There is another kind of title used in HTML coding for links and images, but I'm leaving those for their respective sections later in this lesson.

Having good titles for posts is crucial because of the number of ways that WordPress uses them, all of which are related to search-engine ranking. Take a look at the highlighted coding in Figure 30-1.

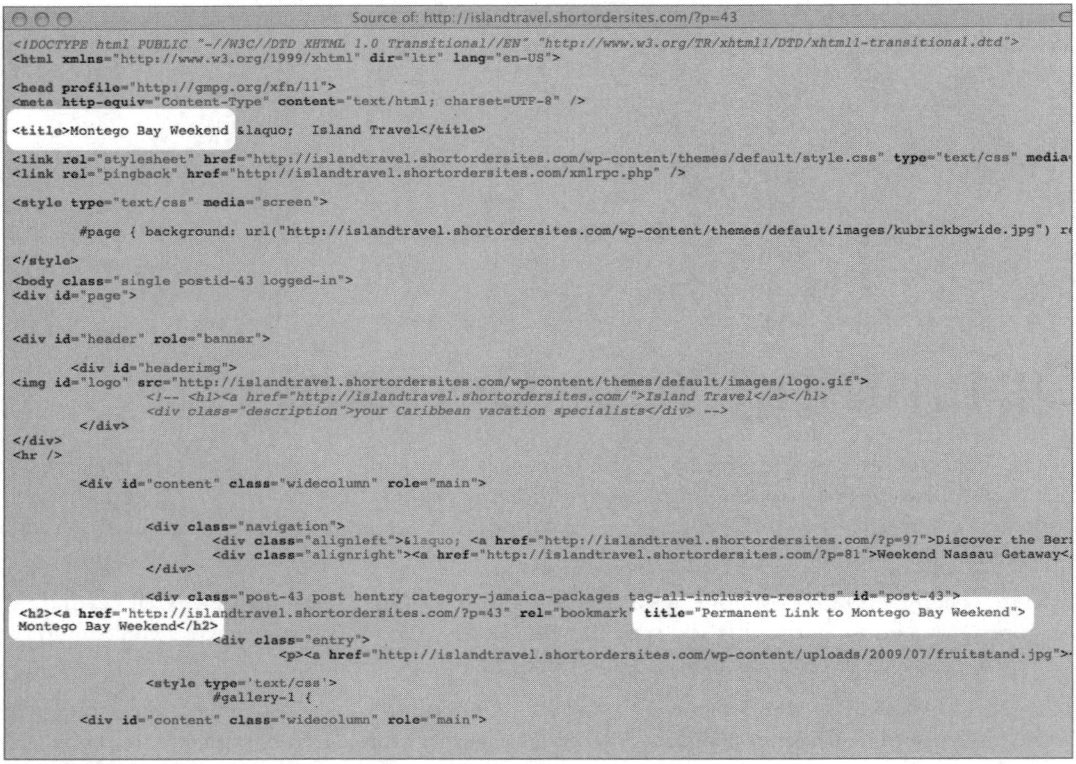

FIGURE 30-1

Here are some key ways in which a post's title gets used:

- In many themes, the `<title>` tag of the post's HTML page is created simply by combining the title of the post with the title of your website (set under Settings ➪ General).
- When the title is linked, WordPress themes typically create a title attribute for the link tag, which says something like, "Permanent link to [the title itself goes here]."
- As the first H1 or H2 element in the HTML, a post's title sits very high in the semantic (meaning) hierarchy.
- Also, if you have custom permalinks turned on, the title will likely be used to create the ending portion of the web page's URL: `yourdomain.com/aruba-beach-famous-for-sunsets` by replacing spaces with dashes and making everything lowercase.

> *When you're considering a WordPress theme, check the source code to see if it's creating HTML that uses titles in the ways described (and that it's SEO-friendly in general — not making page titles H3 and so on). Plugins are available that can make up for theme deficiencies and add further SEO features, and I talk about some of these in Lesson 31.*

These are all elements that search engines use in various ways when calculating the relevance of a web page — it's up to you to make sure the title itself is relevant.

By relevant, I don't just mean relevant to the content of the post. A title also needs to match the wording visitors are likely to use when searching. You need to think of not only what information your audience wants, but the terms in which they want to be spoken to. Very likely, those same terms are ones they'll use when searching.

Though the details of what makes a relevant or useful title will always depend on the particular post, a few guidelines can be helpful from a search standpoint:

- **Be succinct:** If you look at the titles of results in search engines, you'll notice that they're truncated if they're too long (around 60 characters is the typical stopping point). It would be nice for your entire title to show in the search results, but at the very least, have the most important words first.
- **Use key search terms:** Look at some search results and you'll see that search terms are highlighted everywhere, including in the result title, which is taken from your Title tag. If your Title tag has that search term, you'll benefit from the highlighting.
- **Be up front:** Put the key search terms as near the beginning of the title as you can. Search engines interpret what comes first as more important.
- **Don't try to be fancy:** If you can work a good turn of phrase into a title while keeping it clear and succinct, more power to you, but don't worry about being clever (unless that's important to your visitors).

Keep in mind that, while the title of a post may be used in custom permalinks and the Title tag, you can still control the wording of both: in the case of custom permalinks, that's done on the post edit screen, whereas for Title tags, it will depend on your theme or your SEO plugin. In other words, what shows as the title of the web page does not have to be exactly the same as the permalink or the Title tag. Of course, you would keep the keywords the same in each, but you could reduce the size of these two.

If you're having trouble boiling down the content into a succinct title, it may be that you're biting off more than your visitors can chew in a single post. Would the material be better handled in smaller units? Looking at it from a search engine's point of view, if too much of the content is not directly related to the title, it seems to the search engine that relevance is lost and the ranking could go down. Your visitors may see the relevance, but search-engine algorithms aren't as sophisticated.

In that case, you can help the search engines by breaking down a large amount of content into several linked web pages, each with its own information related to its own title. You need to balance this with not having so many extra pages that visitors have to do a lot of clicking to get all of the content. Also, search-engine experts disagree about the maximum length of content, so you should focus more on the needs of your visitors and the context. An academic paper is different from a product description — they each have a different criterion for length.

WRITING USEFUL CONTENT

What you say on your web page is the key to visitor satisfaction and therefore to search-engine ranking. If you have high-quality, relevant content, visitors will be happy and so will the search engines. But as I said earlier, search engines aren't as sophisticated, so you need to structure your content in certain ways to ensure that they get the relevance.

In the eyes of search engines, the primary factor for the relevance of content is keywords. They scan web page content to see how well it relates to the words entered by the searcher. The details of how search engines scan content for relevance vary between search engines and over time as well — their algorithms are constantly being tweaked to achieve better results. However, here are some basic tips concerning keywords, which, even if they somehow stopped being helpful with rankings, are still helpful to visitors:

- **Be consistent:** If your title says the post is about all-inclusive resorts, don't use the term "full-service resorts" in your content. Your visitor might understand that they're the same, but you can't take the chance that search engines will understand that.
- **Use keywords early on:** If the term "all-inclusive resorts" is in your title and yet doesn't appear until your second or third paragraph, your visitors and the search engines may be excused for wondering if they're reading the right page. Visitors may well continue on, but search engines are less forgiving.
- **Don't hit people over the head:** Visitors know from the title that the post is about all-inclusive resorts; it gets annoying to see the term in every single sentence. The search-engine equivalent is to assume that the repetition is meant to trick it into seeing the page as relevant, and apart from lowering your ranking, such behavior, taken to an extreme, could get your page (or even your site) marked as spam.

As the last point suggests, relevant content is not simply about keywords. Search-engine algorithms have become increasingly sophisticated over the years, and keyword density, as it's called, is one of only several factors for which content is analyzed.

As long as you're sticking to the topic, everything will be fine, though you should keep in mind the point I made earlier about breaking up huge pages into smaller ones, each with very focused content. This not only can be helpful to your visitors, but it also means that search engines can judge each of those pages on different criteria rather than trying to analyze vast amounts of text that range over several topics (no matter how relevant those topics may be).

Assuming all the content in a long post is focused and relevant (like the academic paper I mentioned before or a long investigative article), it's still helpful to visually and semantically group that content. To do this in a search engine–friendly way, you need to use HTML heading tags, which is easily done using WordPress's Text Editor in Visual mode (the Format drop-down on the second row of the button bars). Headings within content should take the next heading after the title. In other words, if your post title is an H1, all first-level headings should be H2 (if you have subheadings, then H3) and so on.

Write your headings with the same criteria you would for writing titles: succinct and keywords at the front, without repetition.

> *Never copy text from another site without quoting it and linking back to the site. Not only is it wrong, but it's usually illegal to take content from elsewhere and claim it as your own (you'd be amazed at the number of people to whom this comes as a surprise). Always check the fair use and copyright laws for your country.*
>
> *Keep in mind, too, that search engines are becoming more sophisticated at spotting duplicate content and this can affect the ranking of pages; if your site is nothing but duplicate content, it could even be blacklisted.*
>
> *Services are available that site owners can use to check for plagiarism on the Web.*

LINKING EFFECTIVELY

Search engines also determine the relevance of your site to someone's search by looking at links from two perspectives: inbound and outbound. Inbound links are ones on other sites that point to your site and though these are very important to search-engine rankings, getting other sites to link to you is far beyond the scope of this discussion. I'm concerned here with links in your posts that point to other sites. Search engines look at two aspects of outbound links in particular: relevance to the content of the post and the popularity of the site to which you're linking.

When you're creating links to other sites, always think of your visitors' needs and you're more likely to meet the standards of relevance. If the link promises to send me to a site with more information about great resorts in Jamaica and that site turns out to be a sales pitch for a time-share you're affiliated with, I will not be a happy visitor. What I read is what I want to get (if your link said I was going to find a great deal on a time-share, it would have been a relevant link).

> *In the popup link editor window of WordPress, there's a Title field. It's good practice to enter a very short description of what you're linking to, even if it's just the name of the site or the page. It's useful for your visitors and it's thought to have some role in search-engine ranking.*

Even when they're relevant, you can help improve the value of your outbound links — both to visitors and to search engines — by doing a bit of research. If there are two very good sites and one ranks higher in search results than the other, go with the higher-ranked site. Either site would be useful to your visitor, but the higher-ranked one may be given more weight by search engines. Of course, you would put both sites in a links list, but I'm talking here about making choices within the content of a post — you don't want to crowd the body with too many links or it gets a bit overwhelming.

And don't forget about linking to related material on your own site. This is not only beneficial to visitors, but can be helpful with search rankings. Remember the "link to existing content" feature of the Insert/Edit Link window I showed you in Lesson 7? This is another good reason to use it. I also talk about plugins in Lesson 37 that can automate the process of finding related content on your own site and linking to it.

TAGGING IMAGES

Search engines can't see images, so they rely on two attributes of the HTML image tag to tell them something about the image, as shown in this sample code:

```
<img src="http://yourdomain.com/images/image.jpg" title="My New Car"
alt="Photo of my new Toyota Prius sitting in the driveway">
```

It's important that all your images have this descriptive text and in Lesson 13, I showed you the screens in WordPress where you can enter information for these attributes. Now, let's look at these attributes with search engines in mind:

- **Title:** Titles should be very simple, leaving the details to the `ALT` attribute, and give the two or three keywords that describe the content of the image. Don't load up the title with keywords that aren't relevant to the immediate content. If the image is of a beach in Aruba, use "Beach in Aruba," not "Caribbean travel deals on beaches in Aruba." Your post may be about travel deals in the Caribbean, but that's not what the image is about. Stick to the facts. Also, keep in mind that WordPress automatically uses your image's filename for the `Title` attribute. Sometimes, people think you're stuck with that, but you can change it to a proper title. WordPress is just trying to make sure there's something for the `Title` attribute.

> *Speaking of filenames, search engines may give a bit of weight to names that contain keywords for what's in the image. So, save the file as* `aruba-beach.jpg` *instead of what comes out of your camera, like* `img39827.jpg`*. The dash is important — don't use an underscore because that can be misread by some search engines as no space at all:* `arubabeach`*.*

- **Alternative Text:** This is the name that WordPress gives to the content that's put in the `ALT` attribute. Though you can have a lot of detail in here, again, you need to stick to the facts. Avoid putting non-relevant material, and don't try to stuff the alternative text with keywords. For example, don't say, "Picture of a beach in Aruba. Beaches in Aruba tend to be less crowded especially this one located in Northern Aruba." Not only is it annoying to visitors, but you could get penalized by the search engines. However, do make sure you say, "Aruba" if that's a keyword for your post.

TRY IT

In this lesson, you optimize one of your important posts or pages.

Lesson Requirements

A post or page with three or four paragraphs of text, some links, and an image. If possible, make it one that's central to the theme of your website or blog.

Step-by-Step

How to optimize the content of a post.

1. Open your post in the Edit Post screen.
2. Read through the post and, in another program or on a piece of paper, write a short sentence describing what the post is about. Set aside this summary for the moment.
3. List two or three of the most important words or phrases in the post.
4. Ask yourself if these keywords are ones that people would use to search for the topic covered by your post.
5. Do some research by entering those keywords into a search engine and see what comes back — are these sites related to yours? Ask friends, coworkers, or customers to do a search related to your site and note what keywords they use. Check online keyword tools such as Google's (`http://adwords.google.com/select/KeywordToolExternal`) to get a sense of how people are using your keywords and what possible alternatives might be.
6. Revise your list of keywords as necessary.
7. Check the title of your post — does it use the most important of your keyword(s) and does it convey what that short sentence from step 2 conveyed?
8. Take the summary of your post that you wrote in step 2 and compare it with your opening paragraph. Does that paragraph clearly convey your summary? If not, rewrite it.
9. Check that your opening paragraph uses the keywords you've come up with. If not, rewrite it.
10. Check the rest of the post to make sure your keywords appear several times in the text in a natural way. Rewrite as necessary.
11. Check your links to make sure they're going to useful, high-ranking sites (check the search engines to make sure those sites are coming up on the first page for their keywords).
12. Check that any images in the post have clear and accurate titles and captions, and, where appropriate, they use the keywords chosen earlier.
13. Remember to update your post.

> *To see some of the examples from this lesson, watch the video for Lesson 30 on the DVD with the print book, or watch online at* `www.wrox.com/go/wp24vids`.

31

Optimizing Your Site as a Whole

In the previous lesson, I talked about optimizing your content in ways that help increase your rankings in the search engines. Now, it's time to look at site-wide factors that affect how search engines rank you, and how to control them using WordPress.

OPTIMIZING ADMIN SETTINGS

The first thing to check is whether WordPress is displaying the Search Engines Blocked message, as shown in Figure 31-1.

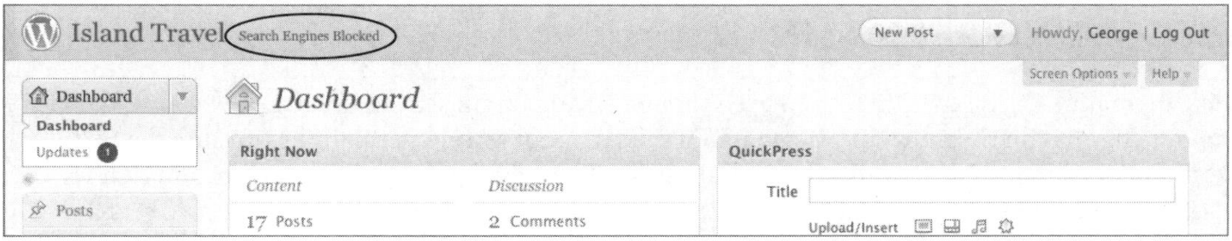

FIGURE 31-1

When you first installed WordPress, you had the option of making your site visible to search engines, and I said it was a good idea to keep it hidden until you were finished building it. Now, it's time to unblock your site and you do that under Settings ➪ Privacy, as shown in Figure 31-2.

If you don't unblock the site, WordPress continues to display the warning message next to your title, so there's no excuse for forgetting!

> *When it says "Search Engines Blocked," what's happening is that WordPress is adding a meta tag to your web pages that tells the search engines not to index the page or follow any links on the page.*

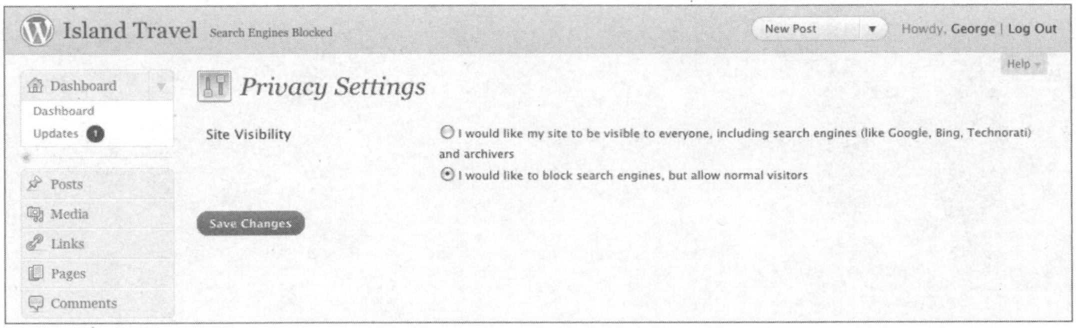

FIGURE 31-2

Another admin setting that's very important is your Site Title under Settings ➪ General. Even if you're using a graphic in your header instead of the default text title that many WordPress themes use, this Site Title setting remains important because, as I mentioned in Lesson 30, it's used by most WordPress themes when creating the HTML Title tag, which, in turn, displays at the top of your browser window. Make sure the site title is the one people would use if they were looking up your site's name.

One final admin setting that's important is for comments, under Settings ➪ Discussion. Where appropriate on your site, make sure you allow comments. You can either enable them for the whole site and turn them off for specific posts or pages, or you can leave them off and turn them on for specific posts or pages. Allowing comments is an important part of making your website part of a wider community and encourages linking back and forth between sites.

CUSTOMIZING PERMALINKS

I left permalinks as a separate section even though it's an admin setting because it warrants a completely separate discussion of its own. In Lesson 25, I talked about setting permalinks through the Settings ➪ Permalinks screen, as well as editing permalinks for individual posts. I was concerned in that lesson with how people link to your site, and now I want to discuss permalinks with respect to search engines.

Every web page generated by WordPress has a unique URL — a permanent link or permalink — which will never change, and it looks something like this: `http://www.mydomain.com/?p=45` (even if you delete a post, no other can have that number). The question mark indicates that what follows is a query string, which is used to query the database and find all the parts necessary to create the web page.

From an indexing standpoint, this permalink is perfectly fine for a search engine. Your page is not going to be left out of the indexing process because it has a query string in its URL.

From a ranking standpoint, will search engines rank a web page lower because it has a query string rather than useful keywords in its URL? There's a lot of debate about this in the SEO community, but from what I can tell, so many other important factors exist for ranking that even if this is a factor, it's a very small one.

The more important factor in all of this is the ease of use for visitors. I know I prefer a URL that says something about where I'm being taken — like `http://www.mydomain.com/destinations/aruba` — over one with just a number. So, from the perspective of user-friendliness, I'm in the custom permalink camp for WordPress.

The trouble with WordPress's custom permalinks is that they're anything but permanent. A user can change a custom permalink at any time, which not only ends up defeating the purpose of a permalink — any existing links to the page will no longer work — but is bad for search-engine ranking. Remember that search engines rank pages, and the URL is like an ID for a page. Changing a custom permalink is really like creating a new page in the eyes of a search engine; you're starting from scratch to establish a ranking.

Set it and forget it — that needs to be your motto when creating the custom permalink for a post. That means you should be very careful about the wording because it has to last forever.

> *If you have to change a pretty permalink in minor ways, all is not lost. If you're correcting a spelling error or you continue to use the date in the permalink and just change the wording, WordPress will often be able to redirect to the new permalink, and since that's done with a 301 redirect (which tells search engines to permanently use the new address), your page should be reindexed properly.*

First, remember what I talked about with respect to titles: keep custom permalinks clear and succinct. Avoid URLs such as `http://www.yourdomain.com/aruba-testimonials/our-favorite-spot-in-aruba-for-dining-and-dancing-all-night-long`. Even if you really want that as the title of the post, at least tidy up and shorten the custom permalink by editing it: for example, `http://www.yourdomain.com/aruba-testimonials/aruba-nightclub-24-karat`. You'll find the permalink edit button just below the post title, next to the permalink itself (but only if you have custom permalinks set; you won't see it with the default permalink setting).

NAMING CATEGORIES

Just as giving posts useful titles is important for search engines, so is proper naming of categories. The key here is to be as specific as you can: use Scuba Diving and not just Diving.

Remember how I named my Island Travel subcategories? Instead of Testimonials ➪ Aruba, I used Testimonials ➪ Aruba Testimonials so it wouldn't be confused with Destinations ➪ Aruba. Aruba Testimonials is more descriptive of my category, anyway, so it helps with visitors and search engines knowing where they are and what to expect from the content.

You can, of course, change the wording that permalinks use for categories, by going to Posts ➪ Categories and editing the category slug. Again, be careful not to change things once the category has started being used or you run the risk of breaking any links that had been created in the meantime.

> *Some SEO experts will argue that category names in URLs can hurt your rankings. As well, there can be performance issues with WordPress by having your custom permalinks start with a category name (or any text, for that matter). These are important issues that you'll need to research more based on your own circumstances. I'm concerned here with effective naming of categories.*

USING META TAGS

It used to be that everyone was worried about something called meta tag keywords. If you didn't have the right words in your keyword meta tags, the search engines wouldn't index you properly. Meta tags reside at the very top of the web page and though they're not visible, they're read by search engines. However, the meta tag for keywords has little if any role in search-engine ranking these days. The description meta tag, on the other hand, is extremely important.

Not only do search engines look for the search words in the description meta tag, but they compare what's said in the description to see if it tallies with the content of the page. On top of that, the description meta tag — if it meets these criteria — will often be used as the two lines shown below the page title in most search engine results. Clearly, it's important for your site's pages to have good description meta tags.

By default, however, WordPress does not include description meta tags in its coding. That's handled either by your theme or by a plugin.

More and more themes are including various ways of handling both description and keyword meta tags. Figure 31-3 shows a meta box created by the Suffusion theme for entering meta tag data on a per-post basis.

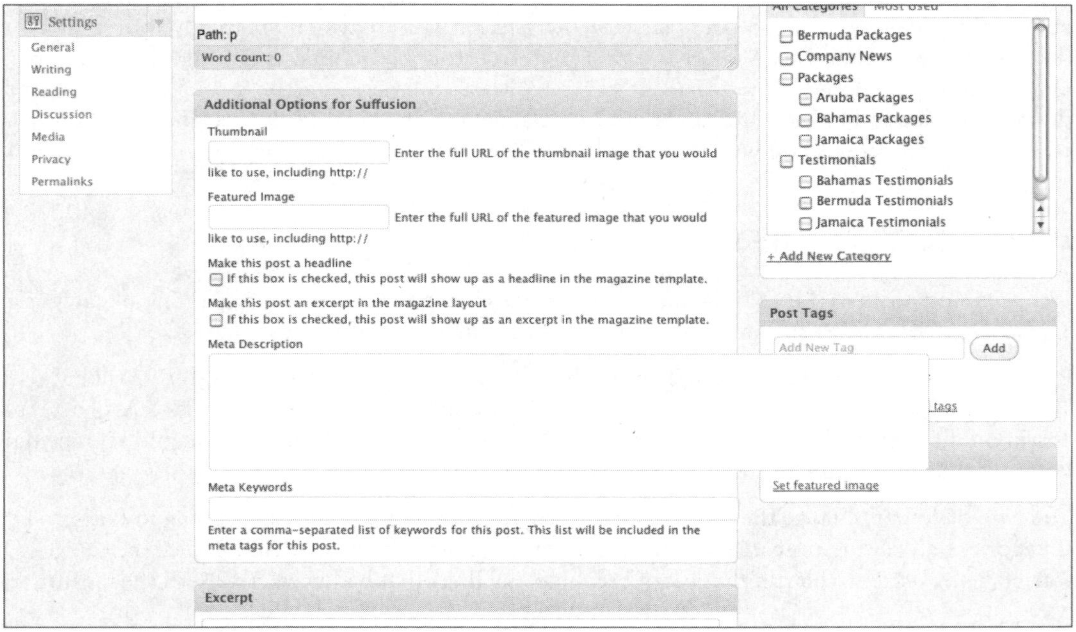

FIGURE 31-3

This is all very handy, but keep in mind that this data will be lost or at least be inaccessible if you switch themes. In the case of Suffusion, for example, the meta description data is saved as a Custom Field. If you change themes, the Custom Field and its data remain. However, the new theme likely doesn't have any coding that picks up that data and uses it. The problem is easily avoided, of course, by keeping the theme as the parent, and simply changing the look of the site by creating a child theme. Still, it's just as easy, a year later, to forget about using a child theme and to switch themes completely.

That's why I think SEO plugins are a better way to go, because the functionality is theme-independent, and I talk about some of them in a moment.

TITLE TAGS

Much of what I just said about meta tags applies to the Title tag as well, except virtually all themes will put some sort of Title tag in the head area of your HTML. How they do it and whether they give you any control over the content of the tag are other matters.

At the very least, make sure your theme puts the title of the post first and then the name of your site. If the site name is first, it can be confusing to search engines because the first item — the most important item — on every page title is exactly the same.

If you're absolutely set on a theme's look and it has poor Title tag structure, you can edit or have someone edit the `header.php` file quite easily. But in today's world, you should expect a theme to be better built *and* look great.

But you don't need to worry about any of this if you use an SEO plugin, so let me talk about a couple of them.

PLUGINS FOR SEO

The key function of all general-purpose SEO plugins is to give you complete control over meta tags and Title tags. Whatever else they do, the goal is to make it easy for users to customize these tags by providing an interface, similar to the one I showed you earlier for the Suffusion theme.

> *Be aware that SEO plugins also have some very powerful tools in them that, if used incorrectly, can actually hurt your rankings. Apart from the meta and Title tag functions, I would advise doing a lot of research before attempting anything more advanced, or let a professional come in and help. The plugin will save them time and they'll set things up or show you what you need to do on an ongoing basis.*

The most popular plugin listed at WordPress.org is an SEO plugin called All in One SEO Pack — it's been downloaded more than seven and a half million times as of the writing of this book. It's been around a long time and is constantly being updated. There's also a pro version available with even more functionality, but I'm talking here about the free version.

When you install All in One SEO Pack, it creates a meta box on your post and page screens, as shown in Figure 31-4.

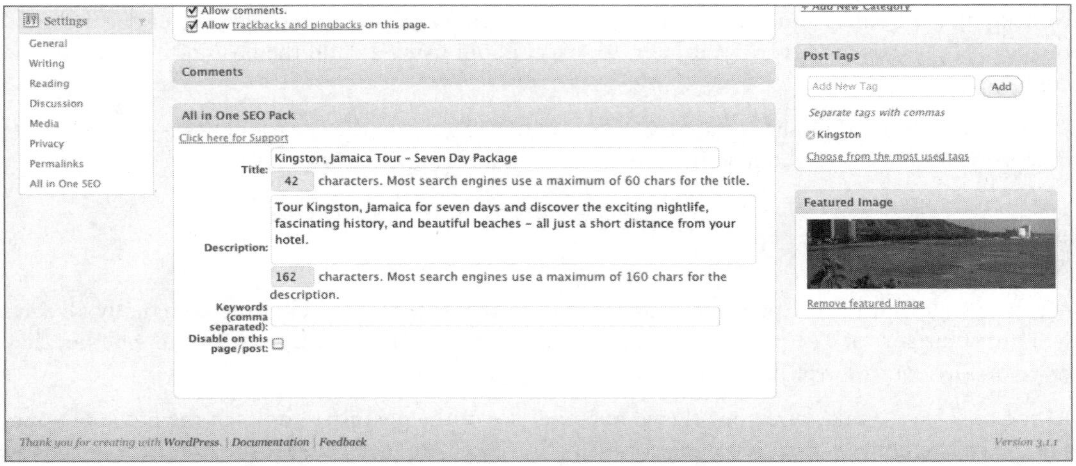

FIGURE 31-4

This is where you can enter an alternative Title tag (different from the title of the post) and a meta description. A running count of the number of characters is provided so you don't get long-winded. There's also a box for the keywords meta tag, which would be better off not being there because it tends to make people use this box rather than using WordPress's tagging feature, which is better for search engines than a keyword meta tag.

In the settings area of All in One SEO Pack, you can control the structure of Title tags for various types of pages, as well as other site-wide parameters (such as the use of canonical URLs or whether to let search engines index category and other types of pages).

One thing that seems handy but should be turned off is the automatic generation of meta descriptions or keywords. As I mentioned before, the keywords meta tag is better left unused (use WordPress's tagging system instead), and meta descriptions should be handcrafted to ensure they meet SEO requirements such as keywords near the start.

At first, there doesn't appear to be much documentation, but if you click the title of any of the settings, it reveals a few sentences to help you understand a bit more about what it's for.

A more powerful recent addition to the SEO plugin category is WordPress SEO by Yoast. Far more settings are available in this plugin (which is good as long as you know what you're doing), but the interface on individual posts and pages is very straightforward (the advanced stuff is hidden), as shown in Figure 31-5.

A very handy feature is the Snippet Preview, which shows you roughly what your page will look like in a search-engine-results listing. And it changes as you change the title and description in the boxes below.

Also very nice is the Focus Keyword function — put in what you think the keywords are for your page and you get an instant analysis of whether they appear in the title, URL, content, and description. It's a great way to quickly tell whether you've actually used the keywords you think you have.

The hidden Advanced tab on each post and page allows you to tell search engines to index or follow, provides a canonical URL that overrides any permalink settings, plus a 301 redirect if you're no longer using the page and want visitors permanently redirected elsewhere.

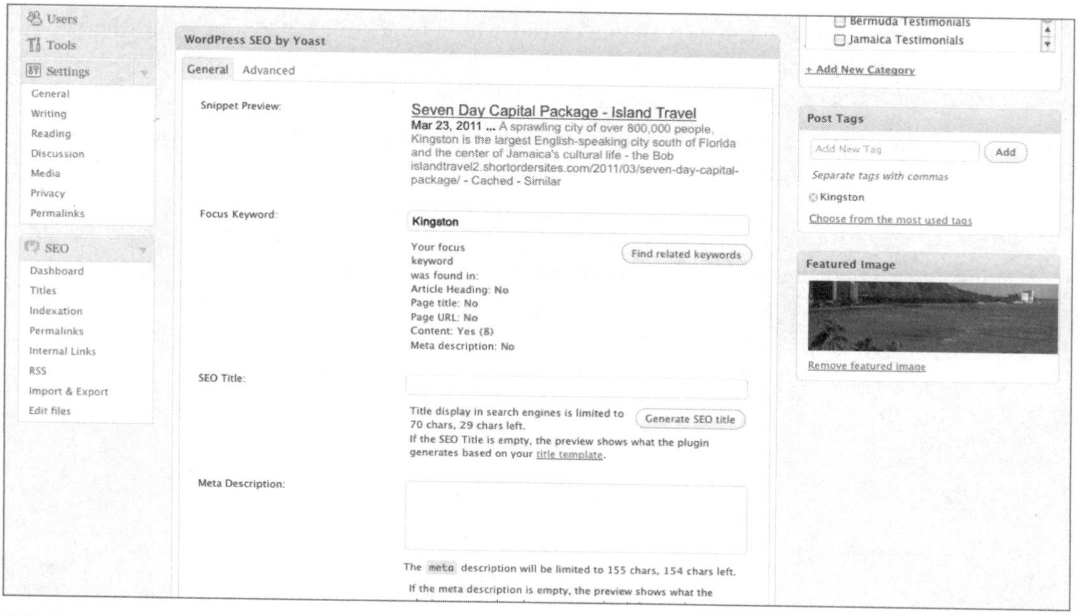

FIGURE 31-5

If you're not sure what any of the preceding paragraph meant, then leave that tab hidden and don't mess with it — the wrong settings can really hurt you.

This is my personal choice of SEO plugin because it's so comprehensive yet user-friendly. Other popular general SEO plugins include Platinum SEO, SEO Ultimate, and Headspace2. If you use the search phrase "compare wordpress seo plugins," you'll find discussions on the merits of these and other contenders.

TRY IT

In this lesson, you check the names of your existing categories for their search engine–friendliness.

Lesson Requirements

At least a few categories for your posts.

Step-by-Step

How to make your category names more search engine–friendly.

1. Go to Posts ➪ Categories.
2. Look over your categories with search engines in mind. Do the category names accurately identify the content you're putting into the categories? Even if a category name is accurate, is that the most likely term people would use to search for that content? Could you separate a category into two or more categories (either at the same level or as subcategories) to better separate the content into topics that people might search for independently?

3. Before changing any category name, consider how long you've had your site, whether you have a lot of people linking to that category, and whether you have a permalink structure that uses category names, because changing the name will change the URL for that category.
4. If you do change a category's name, remember to change the name of the category slug as well (lowercase with dashes between words).

> *To see some of the examples from this lesson, watch the video for Lesson 31 on the DVD with the print book, or watch online at* `www.wrox.com/go/wp24vids`.

SECTION IX
Housekeeping Chores

- ▶ **LESSON 32:** How Is Your Site Doing?
- ▶ **LESSON 33:** Keeping Up to Date
- ▶ **LESSON 34:** Backing Up Your Site

32

How Is Your Site Doing?

Knowing how many people are visiting your site, what they're doing while they're there, and who's linking to your site are all important for tracking the success of your site and knowing how to move forward with it. Some of this is done by WordPress and some of it you'll need outside help with — I cover both in this lesson.

Comments are obviously a very direct way of knowing how people are feeling about your site, and you can use those comments to understand how to improve your site. If you get a lot of comments on a particular topic, that's a pretty sure sign that you should be talking about that topic regularly. Conversely, if a topic is generating few or no comments, then it may not be worth pursuing or might deserve approaching in a different way. No single piece of data is certain, of course, but when you add them all up, they can give you a pretty sophisticated picture of how you're doing and where you should be going in the future.

MONITORING PINGBACKS AND INCOMING LINKS

On the WordPress Dashboard, you'll find two quick ways to find out who's linking to your site: the Comments area showing pingbacks and trackbacks, and the Incoming Links box.

Pingbacks and Trackbacks

In Lesson 25, you learned how to enable pingbacks and trackbacks — two distinct ways of being notified that others are linking to your content. Now, it's time to monitor them.

WordPress treats both as if they're comments. You can moderate pingbacks and trackbacks, including marking them as spam. In the case of trackbacks, you can also edit the excerpt from the other website, just as you can edit the comments that people leave.

How valuable are trackbacks and pingbacks? Aside from the ones that are spam — that's why moderating is important — they each have their advantages for knowing how you're doing. Trackbacks are good because they provide a short snippet of what the other site was saying when it linked to you. Although pingbacks don't show any content, they're considered a bit more reliable because they happen automatically when someone links (a person could create a trackback to your site without actually linking to you).

Incoming Links

If pingbacks and trackbacks tell you someone is linking to your site, what's the purpose of the Incoming Links box highlighted in Figure 32-1?

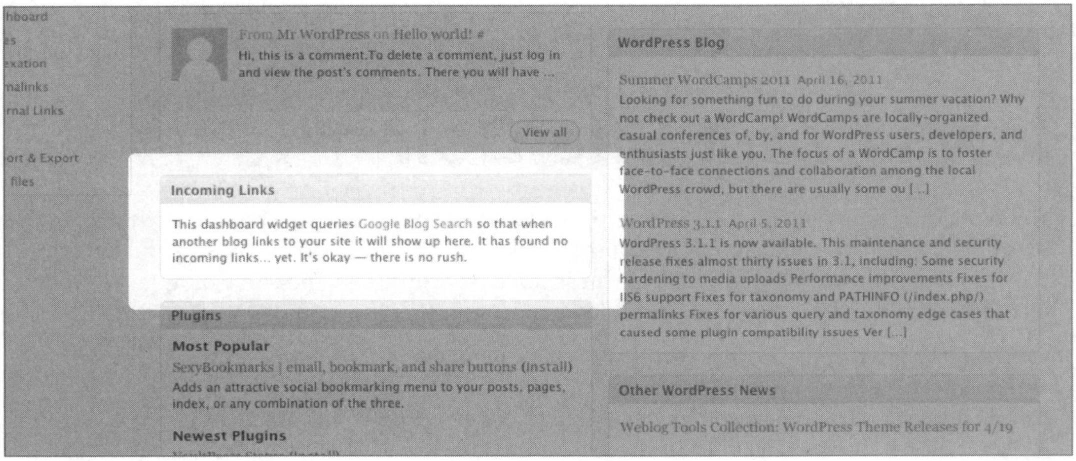

FIGURE 32-1

The answer is that pingbacks and trackbacks work only on individual posts, and only if you and the person linking to you both have the functions turned on. The value of Incoming Links is that it displays a list of who's linking to your site in general, a specific page, or an individual post — whether or not trackbacks and pingbacks are functioning.

By default, the Incoming Links box checks for your website's address on Google Blog Search, but you can change that if you'd prefer to monitor your site in another blog search engine such as Technorati. On the left half of Figure 32-2, you'll see that mousing over the Incoming Links title displays a link called Configure, and clicking that link changes the box to look like the right half of Figure 32-2.

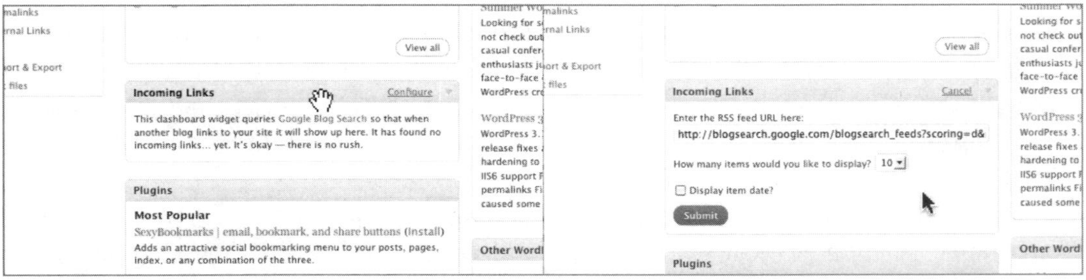

FIGURE 32-2

You'll see the form asking you to enter the RSS feed URL. Just paste it in, choose how many items to display, and click Submit.

Don't be discouraged if nothing is showing in your Incoming Links box when you first set up a site. It will take some time to get people to link to you. This is also one way to monitor if your link-building program is working.

MONITORING SITE STATISTICS

There is no built-in statistics system for WordPress, but you have a number of choices for finding out detailed information on who's visiting your site.

One method is to use the statistics provided by your hosting company. It will have at least one package — such as Webalizer or AWstats — that will give you lots of details about your site visitors. Sometimes, you can access these stats through a URL or you may need to go through your web hosting panel (like Plesk or cPanel). Check the host's knowledge base for instructions on accessing stats.

The disadvantage is that these statistics are more difficult to read and certainly less comprehensive because they're generated by the server logs, which blindly record access to the server. The same person coming back four times in a day could look like four people visiting the site. Other statistics methods use cookies to track the activity of visitors.

The statistics system at WordPress.com — the hosted version of WordPress — uses the cookie method, and you can get the power of this system for your self-hosted site through a plugin called JetPack. This is actually a suite of plugins that makes use of functionality on WordPress.com, among them the statistics package. The statistics package has been available on its own for some time under the straightforward name WordPress.com Stats. That plugin is still available as of the writing of this book, but whether it will continue to be supported on its own isn't clear.

In the video for this lesson, I show you how the newer JetPack statistics work (they show up in your Admin Bar, for example, if you have that turned on). Whether you use JetPack or the stand-alone Stats plugin, you'll need get an account with WordPress.com — you don't need to create a blog, just sign up for the account.

JetPack works by simply signing in to your WordPress.com account through your admin screen. With the WordPress.com username, you can get a special code called the API Key, and that's what you'll need for the WordPress.com Stats plugin.

> *You'll also need this same WordPress API Key to activate the antispam plugin called Akismet (it comes preloaded on all WordPress installations, though of course, you have to activate it yourself). Keep in mind that Akismet is only free for personal use and is a paid service for commercial (moneymaking) sites.*

Some statistics plugins for WordPress keep track of statistics using a database, and though some of them are very good, they're one more thing to maintain on your site. The WordPress.com statistics are all handled for you with no maintenance required.

Whichever of these options you use for statistics, it's a good idea to put Google Analytics on your site as well. This completely free and comprehensive service can be set up very quickly. Even if you don't already have a Google account, signing up for one is fast (at the top-right corner of the Google homepage, click Sign In and look for the Don't Have An Account? link). Then you can create a Google Analytics section of your account, register your site for the service, and then you're given a piece of code that you need to copy.

Many themes now provide a text box in Appearance ➪ Theme Options (or similar wording) where you can paste your Google Analytics (GA) code. The theme template then automatically inserts the code into the HTML. Or some plugins will do this for you as well, such as Google Analyticator. The advantage of a plugin like this is that you know the code is being placed properly, plus it will display some of your statistics right in your WordPress Dashboard.

You'll hear two different stories about where to place GA code: just before the closing `</head>` tag at the top of your HTML or just before the closing `</body>` tag at the bottom of your HTML. Both are correct, depending on the GA code you're using. If it's the recommended asynchronous version (in use since early 2010), then it's best used just before the closing `</head>` tag. Older GA code works better if it's before the closing `</body>` tag.

Don't worry, you don't have to do the placing of the code if you're using a plugin or a theme interface, but if you're using a theme, check the source code of your pages to make sure it's being placed properly.

You'll also need to check your Google Analytics account, where it will tell you that it has verified the placement of the code and everything is working fine (the verification may take up to several hours).

TRY IT

In this lesson, you practice changing the blog search URL for Incoming Links.

Lesson Requirements

No special requirements, just some familiarity with using search engines.

Step-by-Step

How to change the RSS feed monitored in Incoming Links.

1. Go to the Dashboard in WordPress and find the Incoming Links box.
2. Mouse over the right-hand side of the Incoming Links header until you see the link appear.
3. Click Configure and you'll see the configuration form.
4. Go to your favorite blog search engine — such as `http://technorati.com/search/` or `www.icerocket.com`.
5. Do a search for your domain name.
6. Look for the RSS feed link somewhere on the page (it often says Subscribe and shows the orange RSS icon).
7. Right-click the RSS link.

8. Choose Copy Link Location.
9. Back in WordPress, paste the link into the Incoming Links URL field of the Configure box.
10. Choose the number of results you want to show.
11. Decide whether you want to display the date.
12. Click Submit.
13. If you have people linking to your site, the Incoming Links box should now show the most recent ones.

> *To see some of the examples from this lesson, watch the video for Lesson 32 on the DVD with the print book, or watch online at* `www.wrox.com/go/wp24vids`.

33

Keeping Up to Date

Like any software, WordPress is constantly being improved — more features, better speed, increased security, and so on — as are the themes and plugins. Fortunately, keeping them all up to date is pretty straightforward.

Why should you keep up to date? The number-one reason is security. Having access to new features and a better interface are the next-most important reasons. And finally, if you miss a lot of updates, you have a greater chance of problems because over time, the database structure can change significantly, and trying to make all those changes at one sitting may be impossible (at least with an automated update).

On the other hand, rushing to do the very latest update is not always advisable, either. Despite vigorous testing, software, we all know, can still come to market with minor or even major bugs that should be fixed. It isn't until they're released that these problems may present themselves, so it can be wise to wait a few weeks after a new update, unless, of course, the update is a crucial security fix and your site might be at risk.

UPDATING WORDPRESS

WordPress is very clear about the availability of updates. A warning message with a link to perform the update is displayed at the top of every admin screen until the update is completed, as shown in Figure 33-1.

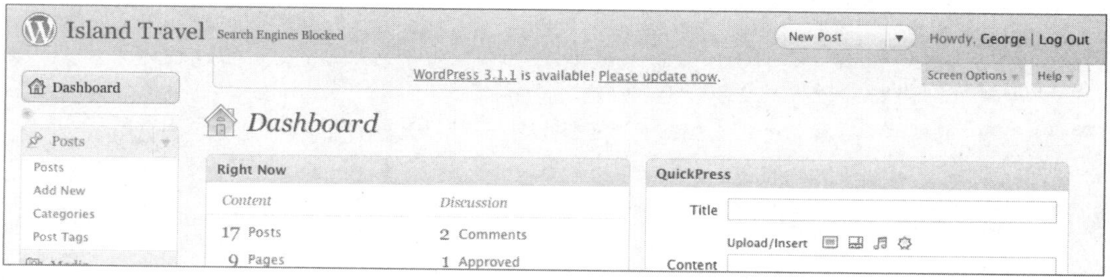

FIGURE 33-1

If you're logged in as any role other than Administrator, the message tells you to notify your administrator of the update. Also, an Update button appears on the Dashboard if there's an update available — it will be next to the name of the version you're running.

If you don't regularly make changes to your site's content, you may not see the update message for many weeks. In that case, it might be good to join the update notifications list at WordPress.org, which you can do from the Downloads page, as highlighted in Figure 33-2.

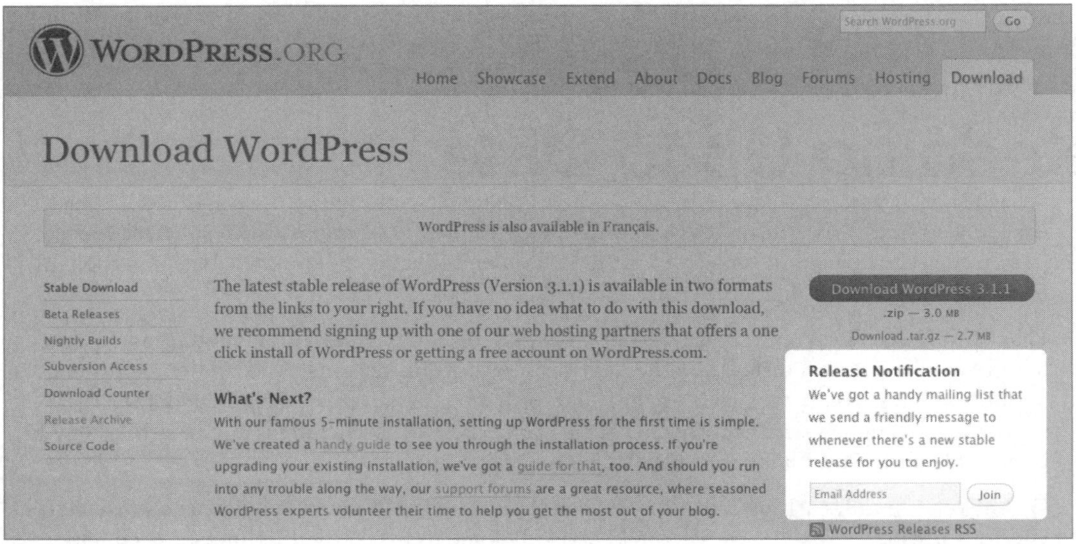

FIGURE 33-2

Automated Update

The key with any update of WordPress is to back up your site before proceeding — the topic of the next lesson. If you're in the habit of regularly backing it up, this may not even be necessary, provided the update is being done very shortly after a backup session. Either way, WordPress reminds you to do the backup before proceeding with the automated update, as shown in Figure 33-3.

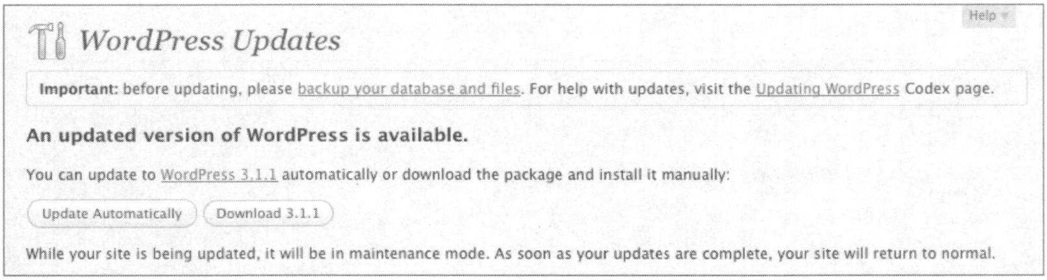

FIGURE 33-3

Once you click Upgrade Automatically, you'll see a list of tasks displayed one by one as WordPress performs them. The whole process usually takes less than 30 seconds. At the conclusion, the screen will look like Figure 33-4.

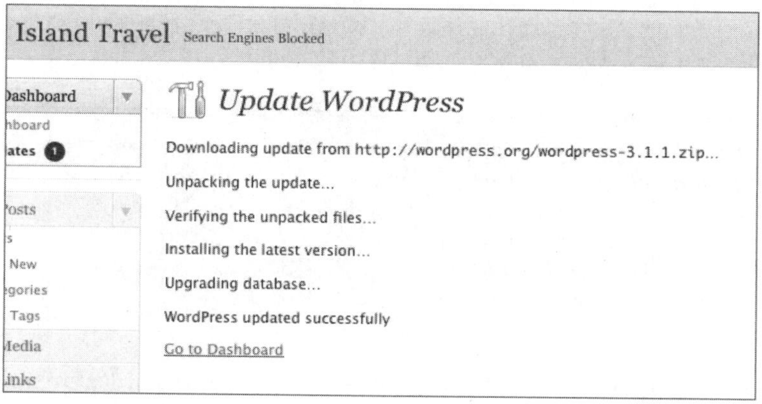

FIGURE 33-4

That last line tells you the update has worked.

Manual Update

It is possible to manually update WordPress as well, and there may be situations in which this is necessary, such as servers not being configured for automatic updates.

There isn't enough room here to go into the details of a manual update because there are a lot of variables. WordPress.org has a handy three-step manual updating process (`http://codex.wordpress.org/Upgrading_WordPress`), but even with that, it warns you that you may need even more details on its extended upgrade instructions page (`http://codex.wordpress.org/Upgrading_WordPress_Extended`).

As with the automated update, it's important to do a backup of both the database and the entire set of WordPress files and folders on your server. Another crucial element of a manual update is to know which files you can't overwrite and which themselves may need to be manually changed, saved, and uploaded again. The WordPress site helps you with all of that. And finally, remember to deactivate all plugins before proceeding.

Troubleshooting WordPress Updates

The two most common problems encountered in the automated update are:

- The server is not configured to allow the automated update.
- There are plugins or themes that are not compatible with the updated version of WordPress.

If you're getting error messages during the update process saying WordPress does not have the correct permissions, you'll either have to change permissions or get your hosting company to do that for you, or you'll need to do the manual upgrade. One way to know if you're going to have this problem is to try installing a plugin. If WordPress asks for your FTP login information, it's like getting the permissions message during an upgrade. It's saying that the WordPress files are not allowed to access the server in the way they need to. Again, talk to your hosting company.

> *On some servers, the FTP details you provide during the installation of a plugin are stored and used for future plugin installs/upgrades as well as the WordPress upgrades. Alternatively, you can put your FTP details into your* `wp-config.php` *file and these will get used instead of having to manually enter them each time. For instructions on altering this file, visit this address:* `http://codex.wordpress.org/Editing_wp-config.php#WordPress_Upgrade_Constants`

If the installation itself goes fine but you have problems with the site — PHP errors or features no longer working — it's likely that one of the existing plugins needs updating or, if there is no update for it, you'll need to disable it for the time being. It's also possible that your theme needs to be updated, which I cover in the final section of this lesson.

In the case of a manual update, a common problem is deleting the `wp-config.php` file. You'll know it's no longer there if you get database connection errors. Simply go to your backup files and reload it via FTP or your hosting control panel.

UPDATING PLUGINS

Just as you receive a warning message that a new version of WordPress is available, you also receive notices for plugins that need updating. The most visible notice from any screen in the admin area is a tiny graphic displayed on your Plugins menu as well as the Updates menu item, as highlighted on the left of Figure 33-5.

The number in the circle tells you how many plugins need updating. The rest of Figure 33-5 shows the Plugins section of the WordPress Updates screen. You can choose to update one or more plugins all at one time.

You can also see which plugins need updating from the Plugins page — a message appears at the bottom of the plugin's listing with an Update Automatically link. You can also view only the plugins that need updating by clicking the Updates Available link on the text menu at the top of the Plugins screen, as shown in Figure 33-6.

If you ever experience a problem after updating a plugin, you at least know that it's likely the plugin causing the problem. Simply deactivate the plugin and see if the problem is resolved. If it is, you can revert to the version of the plugin that was working. If you got it from the WordPress.org directory, simply go to the plugin's page and on the right, in the blue area, you'll see Other Versions. If you got it from somewhere else, hopefully you have a copy on your hard drive or you can get the older version from the site.

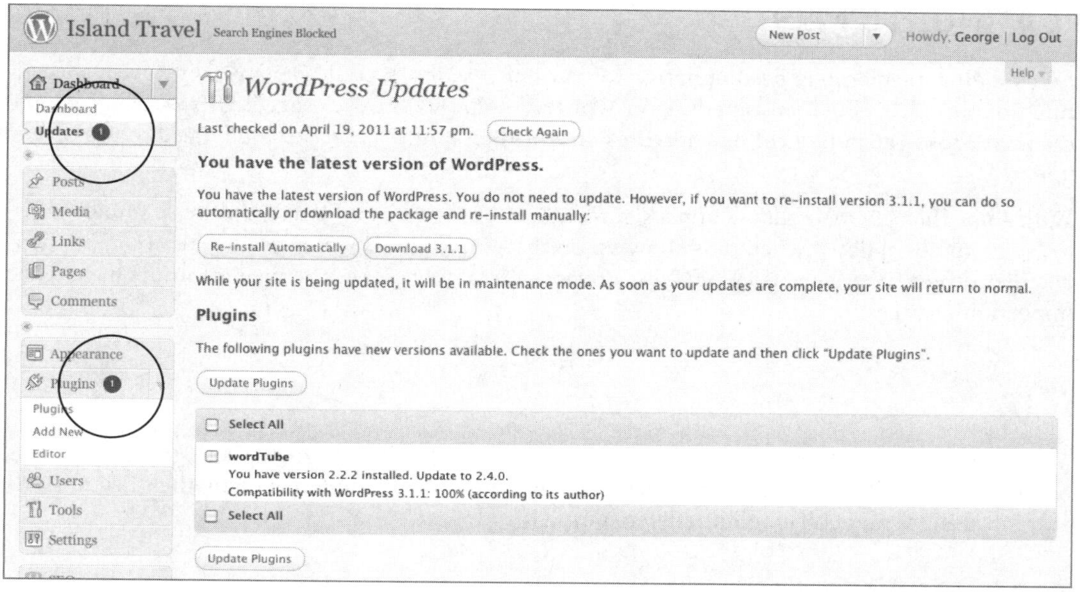

FIGURE 33-5

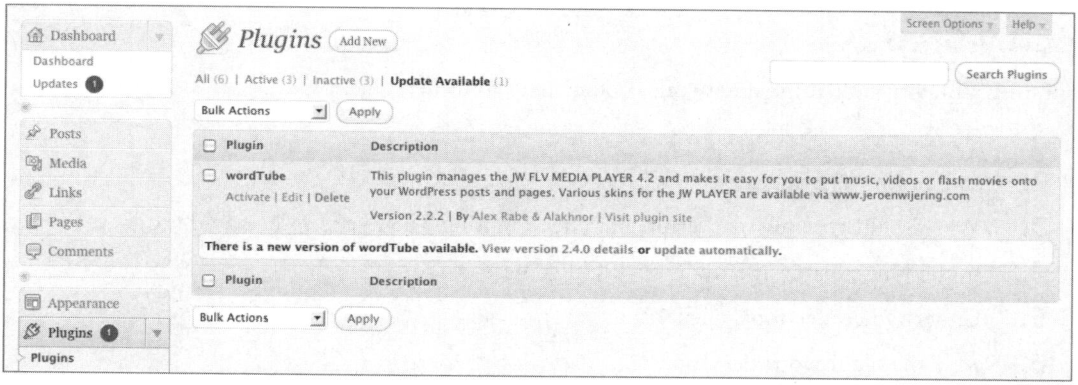

FIGURE 33-6

If you're experiencing problems after a WordPress update, but none of your plugins shows an update available, you may need to troubleshoot by deactivating all plugins, and then reactivate them one at a time until you find the one causing the trouble.

Once you know which plugin it is, you can click through to the plugin's homepage and see if an update was missed. You may find that the plugin author is still working on an update or is no longer supporting the plugin. In either case, you'll need to deactivate the plugin. You can always update and reactivate later if the author makes a new version. Better still, find a new plugin with the same or similar functionality.

UPDATING THEMES

Like plugins, themes may need updating for various reasons. It could be that they have a special functionality that relied on something in WordPress that has now changed. Or the new version of the theme takes advantage of new features in WordPress. In either case, you'll need to perform an update.

With some themes, the update happens automatically when you update WordPress. Others may need to be manually updated when they show up on the WordPress Updates page. This could happen whether or not there's been a WordPress update — it simply means the theme authors have made important changes.

TRY IT

Because you may not have any plugins that need updating, I'll show you how to get one that needs updating. This will give you practice deleting a plugin, downloading one manually, then uploading and installing it manually, and finally, updating it.

Lesson Requirements

No special requirements.

Step-by-Step

Finding a plugin, uploading a new one, updating it, and then deleting it.

1. Go to `http://www.wordpress.org/extend/plugins/`.
2. Search for "fighting the lyrics."
3. You should get only one result, but click Fighting The Lyrics to bring you to its main page.
4. In the blue area on the right, click Other Versions.
5. Under Other Versions, click 1.05.
6. Save the file to your desktop.
7. Go back to your WordPress admin screen.
8. Click Plugins ➪ Add New.
9. On the text menu at the top, click Upload.
10. Click Browse and then select your Fighting The Lyrics zip file from the desktop.
11. Click Install Now.
12. When you see that it's been installed successfully, click the text link "Return to Plugins page."
13. You'll see a light-colored bar on the Fighting The Lyrics listing that tells you there's an automatic upgrade.

14. Click Update Automatically.
15. Once you see the message Plugin Updated Successfully, click the text link "Return to Plugins page."
16. Now mouse over the Fighting The Lyrics listing and you'll see the Delete link.
17. Click Delete.
18. On the Delete Plugin screen, click Yes, Delete These Files and that will remove the plugin completely.

> *To see some of the examples from this lesson, watch the video for Lesson 33 on the DVD with the print book, or watch online at* `www.wrox.com/go/wp24vids`.

34

Backing Up Your Site

There's nothing more devastating in the world of computing than not having a backup of your data when something goes wrong, and the same is true on the Web. Hard drives die on web servers and even the most sophisticated server backup systems are vulnerable to human error or acts of nature.

> *Your hosting company may offer automated backups, but double-check exactly what that means. If it's just your WordPress files, it's only half a backup. If your database* and *all necessary WordPress files are getting backed up, be sure that you can get access to those backups and download a copy to your computer for additional safety.*

A BACKUP ROUTINE

Here's one simple routine for backing up your WordPress site. In the folder on your hard drive where you have anything relating to your site, create a new folder called My Site Backups. Then pick a time each month (more frequently if you're constantly adding new content) when you're going to stop for a moment and back up your site.

Each time you do the backup, create a new folder in My Site Backups using a dating system such as 20110617 (year-month-day). This naming system makes it easy to find, whether you need the latest backup or if you want to restore the site from an earlier time.

Backing up WordPress is a two-step process, so in this 20110617 folder, you're going to have two subfolders: one for the database backup and one for the web server files. The following sections look at how you get the material for each of these.

BACKING UP YOUR WEB SERVER FILES

When you FTP into your web server, what you'll see will vary to some extent depending on what exactly you have on your website. If it's entirely contained within WordPress, you're going to see a file structure much like that shown in Figure 34-1.

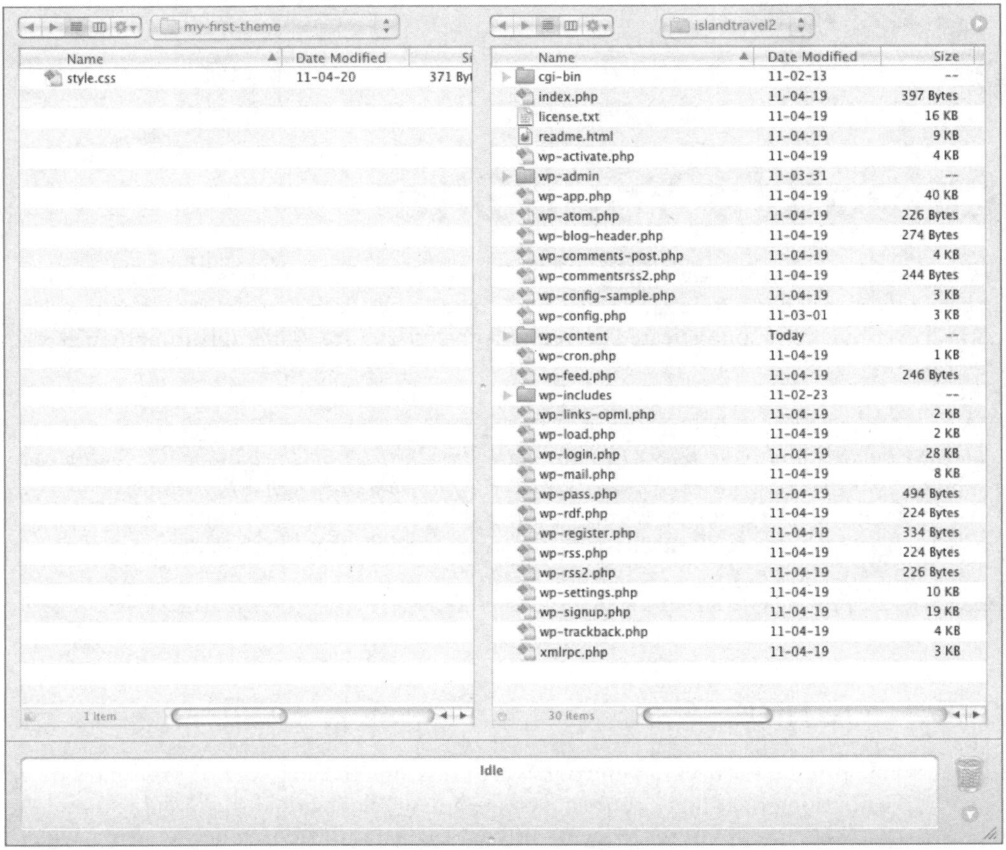

FIGURE 34-1

The simplest routine is to download everything you see in this root directory. Some will argue that you really only need to do this once (unless you upgrade your WordPress, in which case, you'd need to do another download) and then on your regular backup routine, all you need to back up is the folder called `wp-content`. The reason they say this is because it's the `wp-content` folder that contains everything unique to your installation of WordPress: themes, plugins, and media files. WordPress files outside of `wp-content` don't change (the `wp-config.php` file could change if you switch databases or something).

Here's my argument in favor of backing up the entire root directory of your website:

- It doesn't take up much time or space to download all the files.
- A full backup keeps all files together rather than having `wp-content` backups in one place and the core WordPress files elsewhere.
- If you have to move to a new server, it's just simpler to upload everything at once without having to think about anything (except making sure your `wp-config.php` file is accessing the new database with the right passwords, and so on).

It's up to you, but *at the very minimum, you must back up the* `wp-content` *folder* in your backup routine.

BACKING UP YOUR DATABASE

The other half of your backup routine involves the database where WordPress stores your written content and the settings that control, among other things, the relationships between your content (categories and so on). WordPress uses a MySQL database so you can use any method that backs up a database of that type. The most common interface provided by hosting companies is called phpMyAdmin and it provides a pretty user-friendly interface for managing databases, including doing backups.

I won't go into the details of the process here — you can find lots of good resources online if you look up "phpmyadmin backup wordpress database." Always make sure you're reading instructions for your version of phpMyAdmin. Using the Export function, the most important points are to ensure that you're backing up all the database tables, that you choose SQL as the output format, and that you use Save As File. You would save that file to the database folder in the backup folder I talked earlier about creating.

If your hosting company has an automated database backup feature, you can use that, too, again making sure it's backed up in the right way. Have the company e-mail the backup to you, or it may be available on its site for you to download or placed in folder on your site and you can download it from there. Again, you want to have a copy on your computer.

> *Under Tools ⇨ Export, you'll find a feature of WordPress that appears to do what a database backup does, but it's quite different. This feature extracts all the content from your database and preserves elements of the structure in a language called XML, but it is not a full database backup. The file generated is meant to be imported back into a WordPress installation, and as long as the version of WordPress is the same as the one from which you exported, things go pretty smoothly. Still, I wouldn't recommend this as your primary backup, especially not when plugins are available to make full backups very simple.*

SOME DATABASE BACKUP PLUGINS

Simplicity and automation are two advantages to using plugins to manage your WordPress database backups. It's that latter one I find particularly helpful. As easy as the routine is that I just showed you, it's just as easy to forget to do it. Plugins can help by doing the backup at a specified time, over and over again. However, not all plugins perform the same tasks, so you'll want to check out the options. I have a couple of plugin suggestions here, but new ones are always being added at `www.wordpress.org/extend/plugins`.

WP-DBManager is a very powerful database management plugin that has a number of the features you find in phpMyAdmin, and backing up is just one of them. However, the backup function is much simpler and it not only keeps a copy on the server, but it allows you to e-mail any or all of the backups to yourself or some other location. It also has automatic scheduling of backups, e-mailed wherever you want. Another useful feature is the ability to easily restore a backup copy of your database.

WP-DB-Backup is a very straightforward plugin whose only job is to back up your database. By default, the plugin backs up only the core WordPress database tables, but you can choose to include any other tables (it gives you a list) that are used by plugins. There is also a scheduling feature.

As for your `wp-content` files (themes, plugins, images, and so on), if you're not comfortable working with an FTP program, a few plugins are available that automate the backing up of those files, such as *Wordpress* [sic] *Backup*.

BACKUP SERVICES

Complete backup of your entire WordPress site, including the database, is also available using VaultPress. This is a paid service from Automattic, the folks who bring you WordPress. For $20.00 per month, you have automated backups of your full installation every time you make changes to your site. As of this writing, the service is still in beta, but they expect to offer complete site restoration services and more.

A growing number of paid website backup services are also available that store your backups for you or on a server of your choice, such as Amazon's $3.00 storage platform. If you're considering these, just make sure they're backing up both your database and your files.

> *When it comes to backups, it's all about location, location, location — literally. Your data ideally should be in three places at once: on your server, at home on a physically separate hard drive or USB drive (for easy portability), and at a third place (another drive at a friend's place or your office, or on a different server).*

TRY IT

Because many options for database backup exist, in this lesson, you focus on practicing backing up your WordPress files.

Lesson Requirements

FTP program and access to your hosting account.

Step-by-Step

How to back up your WordPress files.

1. Open your FTP program.
2. Log in to your server.
3. In the window showing your computer, find or create your Backups folder and then create a folder with today's date, for example, 20110703, and in that folder, create another folder called WordPress Files.
4. In the server-side window, navigate until you find the `wp-` files (these may be in your root web directory — `www` or `public_html`, for example — or they may be in a subdirectory that you created especially for WordPress).
5. Select all the files in the directory that has the WordPress files (it doesn't matter if some of them aren't part of WordPress — they're part of your site).
6. Click Download (or the down arrow).
7. All the files on the right should now also be in the window at the left (your WordPress Files folder).
8. Disconnect from your server and shut down your FTP program.

To see some of the examples from this lesson, watch the video for Lesson 34 on the DVD with the print book, or watch online at `www.wrox.com/go/wp24vids`.

SECTION X
Adding Functionality Using Plugins

35

Installing and Activating Plugins

There are a lot of things that WordPress doesn't do, and that's a good thing. The simpler the base, the more secure, the more bug-free, and the more efficient it can be. It's also easier to update a simple structure. But you'll probably want WordPress to do more, and that's where plugins fit in, so to speak.

In this lesson, you learn about finding, installing, and activating plugins. Lesson 37 provides a quick guide to help you sort through the more than 15,000 plugins available — during the time I was working on this lesson, more than 150 plugins were added to the directory!

WHAT IS A PLUGIN?

Plugins are scripts that provide additional functionality to WordPress, from simple tasks such as removing the version number of WordPress to creating a full-fledged shopping cart system. The name refers to the simplicity of adding these scripts to WordPress — you just "plug" them in with the click of a mouse. You may have to do some configuration, depending on the complexity of the function, but even then, the vast majority of plugins are meant to be used by novice and expert WordPress users alike. One of the best things about plugins is that you can unplug them. That's important because it helps protect the basic elements of your website, by keeping the plugins separate from the core WordPress files. If something goes wrong with a plugin, either because of a conflict with other plugins or when you update WordPress, or you change your mind and don't want it or want a different plugin, all you have to do is deactivate it.

Plugins are constantly being updated — to keep up with WordPress updates as well as to add new features and security — and as I talked about in Lesson 33, keeping track of those updates is automated for you in WordPress under the Dashboard ➪ Updates area as well as in the Plugins area itself.

Most plugins are open-source and available at no charge from thousands of individuals who often develop a feature for their own site and then share it with the WordPress community, but a growing number of paid plugins also exist. Most authors of free plugins accept donations or have wish lists, and I strongly encourage everyone to send even a few dollars their way to help compensate for the incredible amount of time and talent they devote.

FINDING PLUGINS

The best place to go for plugins is Plugins ⇨ Add New. That's because WordPress has a built-in search function that directly accesses the WordPress.org plugins directory. The handy thing about this directory is that it provides a lot of information about plugins in a consistent way, such as how many people have downloaded a plugin, and users are given a chance to rate the plugin. Plugin authors are also good about updating this directory with the latest versions of their offering.

The search screen on the Install Plugins page offers a whole range of options for finding plugins, as you can see in Figure 35-1.

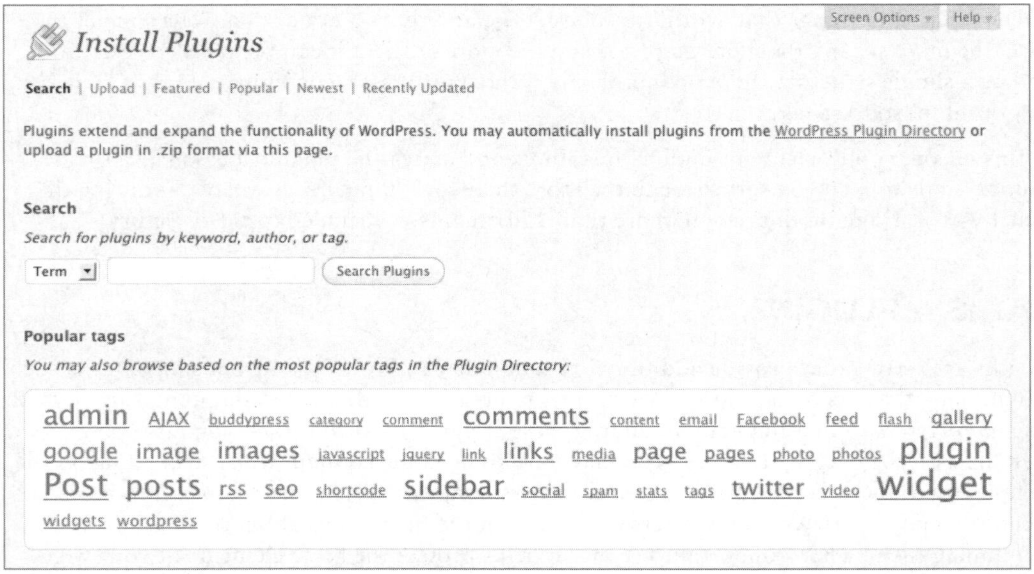

FIGURE 35-1

The menu at the top not only allows you to see a list of Featured, Popular, Newest, or Recently Updated plugins, but you can also upload the zip file of a plugin you've saved to your hard drive.

The search function below that menu enables you to use keywords, author names, or tags to find plugins, and the Popular Tags cloud at the bottom of the screen gives a quick overview of what tags plugin authors have used to describe their contribution.

I'll do a search for "backup" and you can see the results in Figure 35-2.

The data for each plugin on this screen is not quite as detailed as the search results at WordPress .org. In particular, the number of downloads and the date the plugin was last updated are not shown here. However, they are available by clicking Details and getting the popup shown in Figure 35-3.

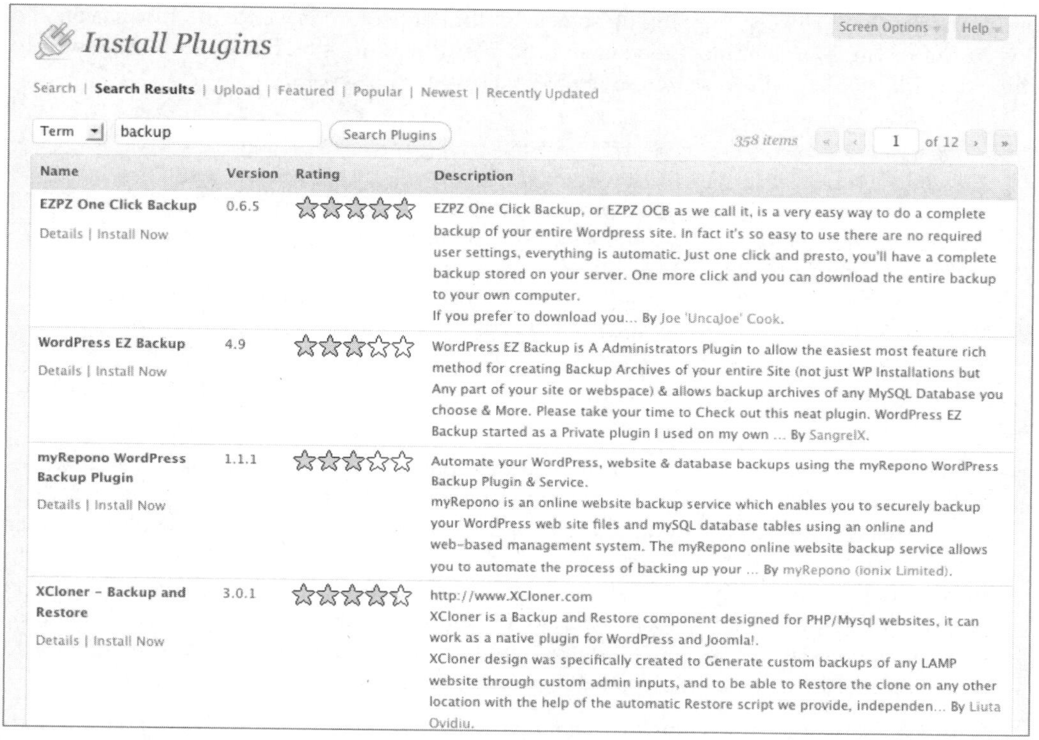

FIGURE 35-2

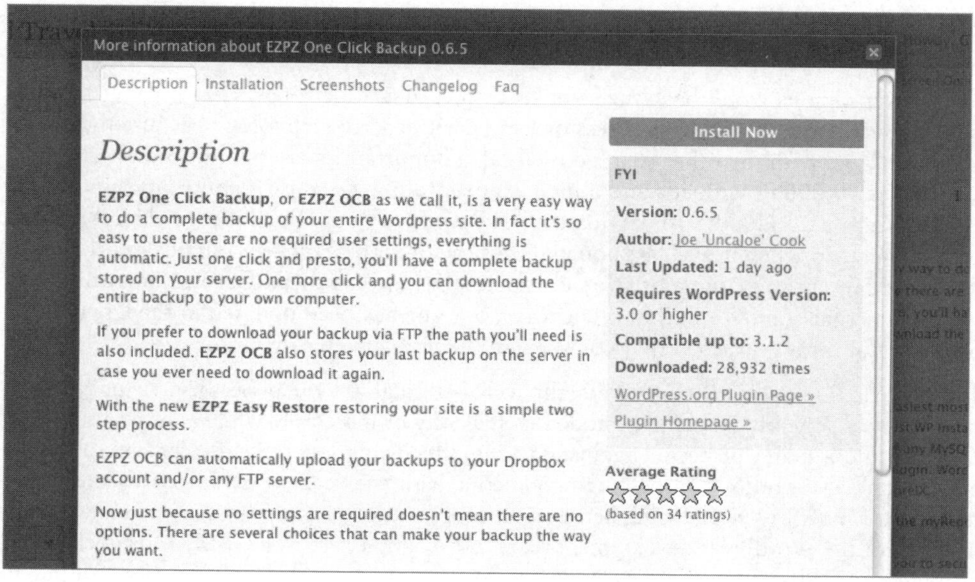

FIGURE 35-3

Still, it means you have to keep popping up screens to find out some very crucial information. That's why, when I'm researching plugins, I tend to use the WordPress.org site, but when I know which plugin I want, I'll use the built-in search in my WordPress admin screen.

> *Whether you search at WordPress.org or through your admin screen, you'll need to be creative with your search terms. A lot depends on how the plugin has been named, tagged, and described by the author (for example, does it contain a keyword you'd use for searching a particular function, such as "backup"). So try several different approaches and don't assume you've found everything the first time.*

Here are some key criteria for deciding which plugin to try when a number of them seem to provide the same function:

- **Number of downloads:** The more people using a plugin, the better the chance that it works well. Of course, you need to keep an eye on the last update of the plugin and whether the downloads continue to be strong. For example, a plugin with 50,000 downloads that tapered off dramatically in 2009 would suggest that it hasn't kept up with WordPress or the developer stopped developing it (you can find the Downloads Per Day chart under Stats on the plugin's page in the WordPress.org directory). Also, the number of downloads does not distinguish between updates and new users — a plugin with a lot of updates will show more downloads. Still, all things being equal, this remains the most important factor in my opinion.
- **Ratings:** Users can rate plugins, but again, you need to be wary of numbers. You can find plenty of plugins with a four- or five-star rating, but you need to look at how many people have rated it, while also factoring in the number of downloads. A four-star rating averaged over 150 people may mean more for a plugin that's been downloaded 5,000 times compared with one with 50,000 downloads.
- **Age:** Newer plugins won't have the same track record as older ones. On the other hand, they may make use of new WordPress or JavaScript or PHP technology because they're new. Combining age with the other two factors is also important: a five-month-old plugin that already has 50,000 downloads and a high average rating based on a couple of hundred ratings would be a good indicator of quality. And age here doesn't just mean when it was first created, but also when it was last updated. I know of many excellent plugins that haven't needed updating for a couple of years or more, so it's not a crucial factor, but if you have two plugins that compare well in other ways, but one has been updated in the last month and the other not for a year, then that could mean the first is better maintained.
- **Author:** Not all plugins are created equally well — though they may perform virtually the same function, one plugin could be coded inefficiently or insecurely while another uses fewer resources and is better protected against hacking. One way to increase the chances of the latter is to look at the author of the plugin. Someone with an excellent track record would tip the scale for me if I were choosing between two substantially equal plugins. Plugins written by members of the WordPress development team, for example, are more likely to be well written — in fact, Automattic itself has lately been getting more involved in the writing of plugins. Researching who's prominent in the WordPress plugin community at large will turn up names like Alex King, Joost de Valk, Viper007Bond, Justin Tadlock, Alex Rabe, and many more.

> *Having mentioned plugin authors, I want to remind you to support free plugins you use by donating to their authors. If you use 20 plugins and donate $5.00 to each of them, think of all the functionality you're getting for only $100.00. You couldn't pay someone to write a single plugin for that. And don't forget to rate it at WordPress.org.*

On top of all this data, you can learn a lot by seeing what others are saying about a plugin in the WordPress forums. On a plugin's page at WordPress.org, over on the right-hand menu, you'll see the most recent forum references, if there are any. Some plugins have their own user forums, and you can find those by going to a plugin's homepage — if one exists, it will be on that same right side menu of the plugin's page in the WordPress directory.

Another excellent source of information is the top plugins lists that bloggers all around the Web love to share. The key here is to look at eight or nine different lists, especially from top WordPress bloggers, to see which plugins appear on all or most of the lists.

And don't forget that on the WordPress Dashboard, there's a box that shows you the latest plugins that have been added to the directory at WordPress.org. It's another way of keeping up with the incredible range of functions that people are making possible with plugins.

Having said all this, in Lesson 37, I mention several plugins in 10 different areas that I think are really valuable, so that will give you a jump start in sorting through a lot of these details (plus I've covered some SEO plugins in Lesson 31 and some backup plugins in Lesson 34). My goal here was to give you some tools when you're on your own looking for a plugin.

INSTALLING AND ACTIVATING PLUGINS

It's important to understand the difference between installing and activating plugins. When you install a plugin, you're really just putting its folder into the plugins directory of `wp-content`. It's easiest to let WordPress do this automatically through the Install Plugins screen but you can do it manually with an FTP program.

Automated installs are as simple as clicking Install next to the plugin you've chosen from the search list. The WordPress installer tells you when you're successful and you can verify that by going to Plugins ⇨ Plugins. The screen shown in Figure 35-4 tells you a number of things at a glance.

White rows are the active plugins, gray are installed but not active, and the colored bar on a row reminds you visually and textually that there's an update available for that plugin, with a link to do the update automatically.

You can also filter what you see on this Plugins screen by using the menu at the top left. You can see All, Active, Recently Active, Inactive, or Upgrade Available (options display only if there are plugins that meet their criteria).

Once you've installed a plugin, activating it is easy: click the Activate link on the text menu below the name of the plugin. Depending on the plugin, you may see new sections on the admin menu, or new choices within existing menu sections, or even a new element on the Admin Bar (if you have it turned on). Some plugins will also show a Settings link under their name or below the description of the plugin.

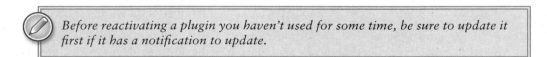

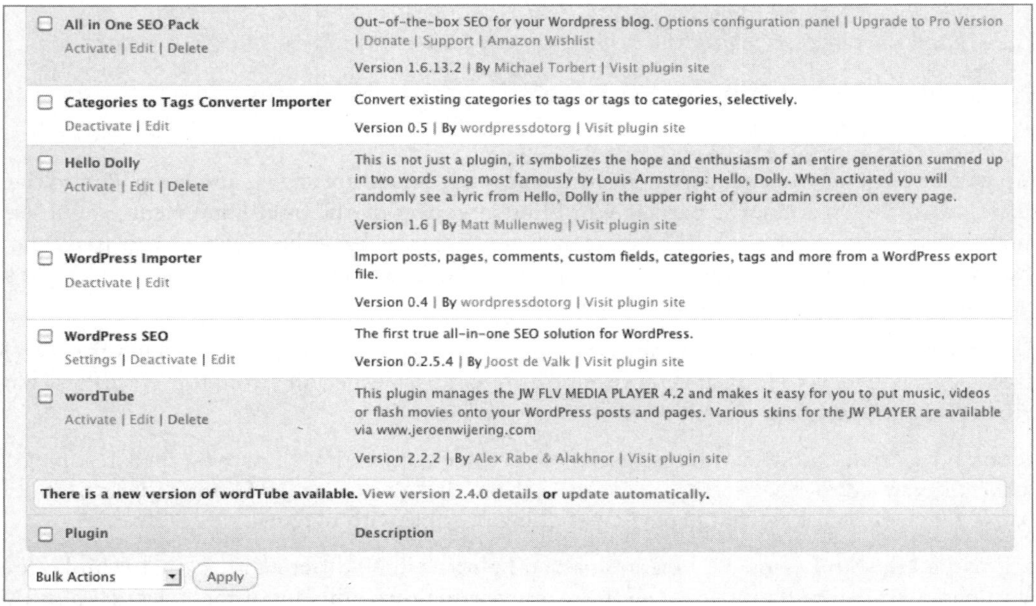

All in One SEO Pack
Activate | Edit | Delete
Out-of-the-box SEO for your Wordpress blog. Options configuration panel | Upgrade to Pro Version | Donate | Support | Amazon Wishlist
Version 1.6.13.2 | By Michael Torbert | Visit plugin site
Categories to Tags Converter Importer
Deactivate | Edit
Convert existing categories to tags or tags to categories, selectively.
Version 0.5 | By wordpressdotorg | Visit plugin site
Hello Dolly
Activate | Edit | Delete
This is not just a plugin, it symbolizes the hope and enthusiasm of an entire generation summed up in two words sung most famously by Louis Armstrong: Hello, Dolly. When activated you will randomly see a lyric from Hello, Dolly in the upper right of your admin screen on every page.
Version 1.6 | By Matt Mullenweg | Visit plugin site
WordPress Importer
Deactivate | Edit
Import posts, pages, comments, custom fields, categories, tags and more from a WordPress export file.
Version 0.4 | By wordpressdotorg | Visit plugin site
WordPress SEO
Settings | Deactivate | Edit
The first true all-in-one SEO solution for WordPress.
Version 0.2.5.4 | By Joost de Valk | Visit plugin site
wordTube
Activate | Edit | Delete
This plugin manages the JW FLV MEDIA PLAYER 4.2 and makes it easy for you to put music, videos or flash movies onto your WordPress posts and pages. Various skins for the JW PLAYER are available via www.jeroenwijering.com
Version 2.2.2 | By Alex Rabe & Alakhnor | Visit plugin site
There is a new version of wordTube available. View version 2.4.0 details or update automatically.
Plugin
Description
Bulk Actions
Apply

FIGURE 35-4

After a plugin has been activated, the text menu below the name changes to show Deactivate and Edit (plus any other menu items created by the plugin itself). There is no Delete option anymore because the plugin is activated.

To deactivate the plugin, of course, you just click Deactivate. You then have the choice of leaving the plugin installed and available for reactivation later, or deleting it. You can leave plugins installed, but rather than clutter up your Plugins screen, think about whether you're ever going to want the plugin again. It's one thing if you're trying out a new plugin and want the old one there in case you want to switch back, but it's quite another to have four-year-old plugins still hanging around.

> *Before reactivating a plugin you haven't used for some time, be sure to update it first if it has a notification to update.*

Deactivating a plugin does not always mean that everything to do with the plugin has been "unplugged." For example, new database tables or stored options are still there — which you want in case you reactivate the plugin. However, deleting (which is uninstalling) may or may not get rid of these leftovers, either. Occasionally, plugins have special instructions or their own way of handling deletion/uninstalling, so keep an eye out for those.

> *Always use the tools in WordPress for deleting or uninstalling a plugin. If you simply delete the plugin folder using your FTP access, especially if the plugin is still active, you could cause problems.*

Manually deleting a plugin or renaming its folder are for emergency measures only — for example, if you can't access the admin screen because of a plugin conflict. If you need an earlier version of a plugin, you can find them archived in the WordPress.org Plugin Directory. Go to the plugin's page and at the top right, under the current version number, you'll find a link to Other Versions. On one occasion, after updating WordPress and all the plugins, I found that one of the plugins wasn't working. Reinstalling an earlier version got it working again.

TROUBLESHOOTING PLUGINS

As I mentioned before, the two most common reasons for having trouble with plugins are:

- Conflicts between plugins
- Conflicts between an updated version of WordPress and a plugin

The great thing is that finding the problem plugin(s) and halting the problems on your live site is made fairly easy by the nature of plugins — you just start deactivating them one at time.

Typically, conflicts between plugins will show up as soon as you've activated a new plugin. If the errors clearly are happening with the functions of one of your existing plugins, you could try deactivating that plugin and see if the problem goes away. You'll also want to research if anyone else is having trouble with these two plugins together and whether a resolution has been found.

> *Sometimes, authors will specify that their plugin does not work with another plugin, so look for that in the WordPress.org directory or the plugin's homepage if one exists.*

Simply deactivate the new plugin and then do some research online to see if anyone's reporting conflicts between that plugin and the ones you already have. Confirm any of those reports by deactivating the older plugin and activating the new one, and hopefully, someone has found an answer that you can use.

If there's no clear indication of what's conflicting with the new plugin, you could try leaving it activated, then deactivate other plugins one by one until the problem goes away, and then start adding back all the other plugins except that last one to confirm that it was the conflicting plugin.

If your problem starts right after updating WordPress, first of all, make sure that you've updated every plugin. One of the reasons for not updating WordPress immediately upon release is that you want to give plugin authors a bit of time to come out with their updates (they're usually pretty good about bringing those out at the same time). With a major update of WordPress, you should see a lot of plugin update notices.

Once all the updates are done, if the problem still persists, check the homepages for any plugins that did not have an update. There may be a notice there saying there's a delay or the plugin is no longer supported, or there may be notices about conflicts with other plugins.

If a plugin is conflicting with a new update of WordPress and you can't find any updates for the plugin, it's time to find a newer plugin offering the same or similar functionality. If you can't find one and you need that functionality, consider hiring a developer to create a plugin for you.

TRY IT

In this lesson, you learn to find a plugin, install it, and activate it.

Lesson Requirements

No special requirements.

Step-by-Step

In the next lesson, one of the plugins I show you in some detail is Contact Form 7, so find, install, and activate it.

1. Go to Plugins ⇨ Add New.
2. Do a search for Contact Form 7. It should come up as the first result or at least very near the top. Look for the author, Takayuki Miyoshi, at the end of the description.
3. Click Install (just below the title on the left).
4. In the resulting popup prompt, click OK.
5. In the Installing Plugin screen, if things are successful, you'll see a link at the bottom to Activate Plugin; click that.
6. You'll be taken to the Plugins screen and you should see Contact Form 7 as a white row, indicating that it's active. Also, on the admin menu, you should see the heading "Contact" near the very bottom of the menu.
7. If you don't want this plugin, you can delete it later, but keep it for the next lesson at least so that you can try out some of the functionality.

> *To see some of the examples from this lesson, watch the video for Lesson 35 on the DVD with the print book, or watch online at* `www.wrox.com/go/wp24vids`.

36

Two Example Plugins

Although every WordPress plugin performs different functions and operates differently, you can get a general sense of how they all operate by seeing a couple in action, and that's what this lesson is about.

I've installed two plugins on the Island Travel site that I think would be useful: NextGEN Gallery to manage photos and Contact Form 7 to help me easily create contact forms. In the next lesson, I cover more uses for plugins and give some recommendations for those as well.

PHOTO GALLERY PLUGIN — NEXTGEN GALLERY

The most popular (more than three million downloads) and the most powerful photo management plugin is called NextGEN Gallery. Developed by Alex Rabe, this highly configurable plugin goes well beyond the image gallery function built into WordPress. I'll barely be able to scratch the surface of its capabilities, but you'll have a good sense of what's possible.

When you activate NextGEN, a special section is created on the admin menu, as you can see at the lower left of Figure 36-1 (immediately above it is a menu section created by the second sample plugin, Contact Form 7, which you will have seen already if you installed that plugin as part of the previous lesson's Try It section).

You can also see from this opening screen of NextGEN that it has its own kind of Dashboard showing you how many images you have, how many galleries and albums (I explain them in a moment), as well as a lot of technical details about your server settings and server graphics capabilities (lower right). You don't need to concern yourself with these details, but they're handy if a technical issue arises and someone on the WordPress forums asks you what your PHP Max Post Size is!

In the top-left box of the NextGEN Gallery Overview, you'll see a button that says Upload Pictures. Clicking this button takes you to the screen shown in Figure 36-2.

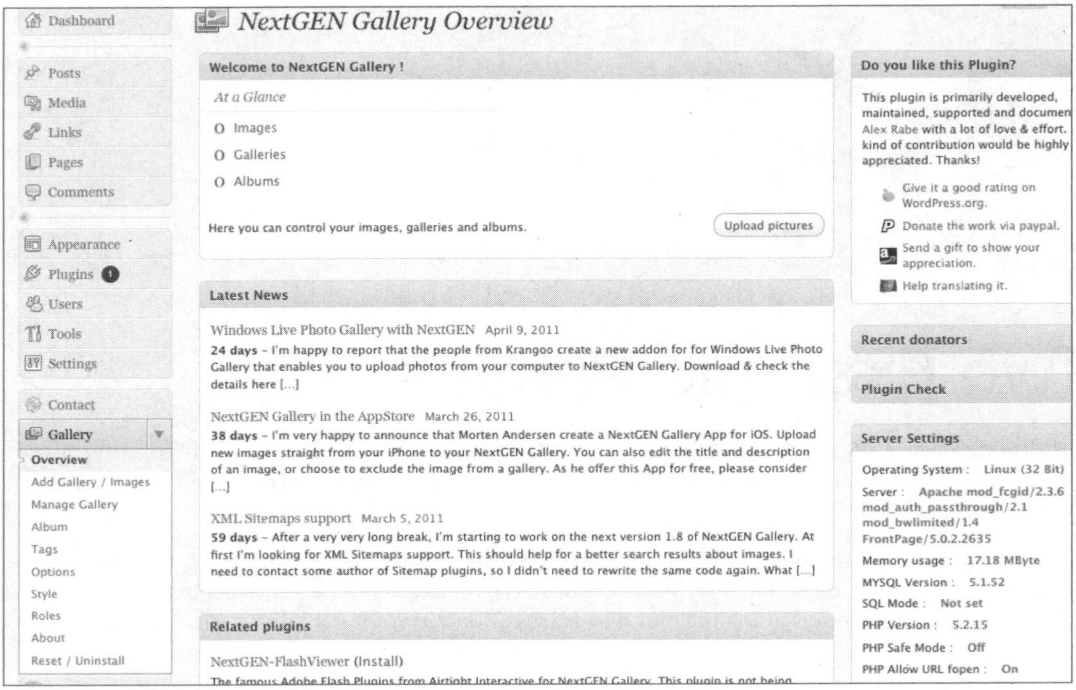

FIGURE 36-1

FIGURE 36-2

> *The first time you use NextGEN, clicking Upload Pictures or Gallery ➪ Add Gallery/Images does not take you to this screen — instead, you're asked to create a gallery. That's because you can only upload images into galleries. After you've created one gallery, these links all lead to the Upload Images screen.*

You can choose multiple files to upload at once, as shown in the top portion of Figure 36-3, or, as the menu says, you can choose a zip file or an image folder.

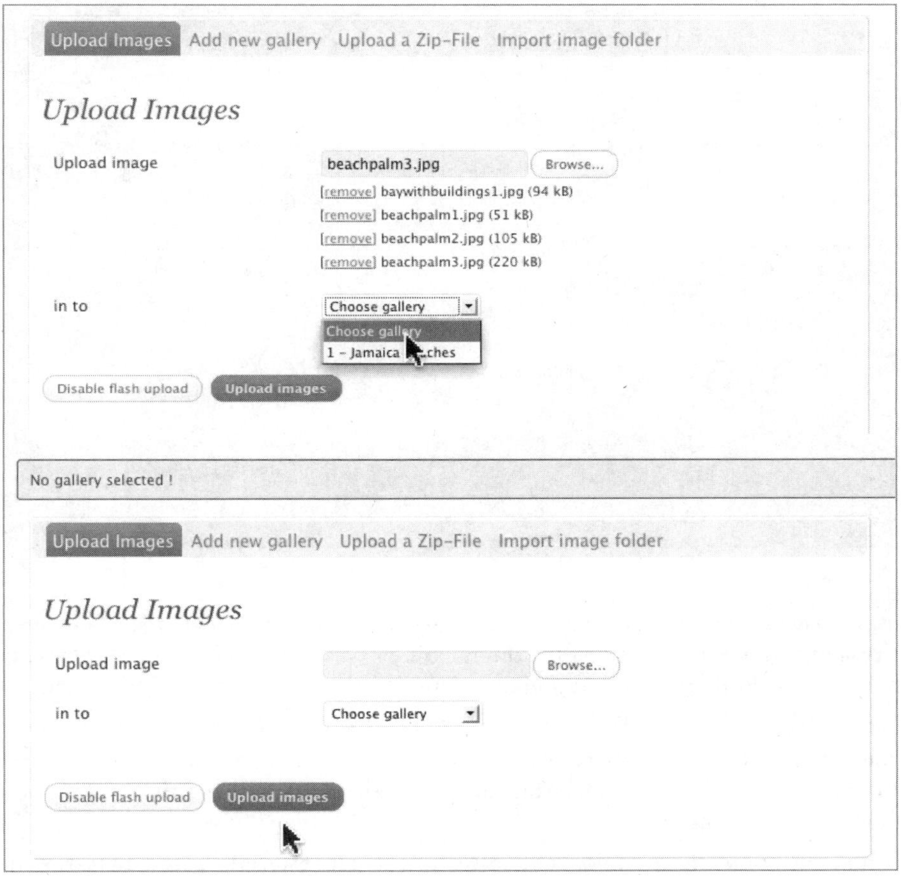

FIGURE 36-3

Notice that I've selected a gallery from the drop-down menu. I recommend that you choose the gallery first and then find your images, because if you try to upload photos without selecting a gallery, you get the error message in the lower portion of Figure 36-3. The error isn't so much an issue as the fact that, as the image shows, you've lost the list of images and you'll need to select them all over again.

As each image uploads, a popup progress bar shows you what's happening, including the creation of thumbnails. When everything is done, you'll get a success message stating how many images were uploaded. Keep in mind that everything I'm doing here is separate from WordPress's Media Library.

Once the images are uploaded to a gallery, there are powerful tools for managing them. After going to Gallery ➪ Manage Gallery, you click the one you want. I've combined a couple of screenshots in Figure 36-4 to show you as many of the features as possible for managing the images in a gallery.

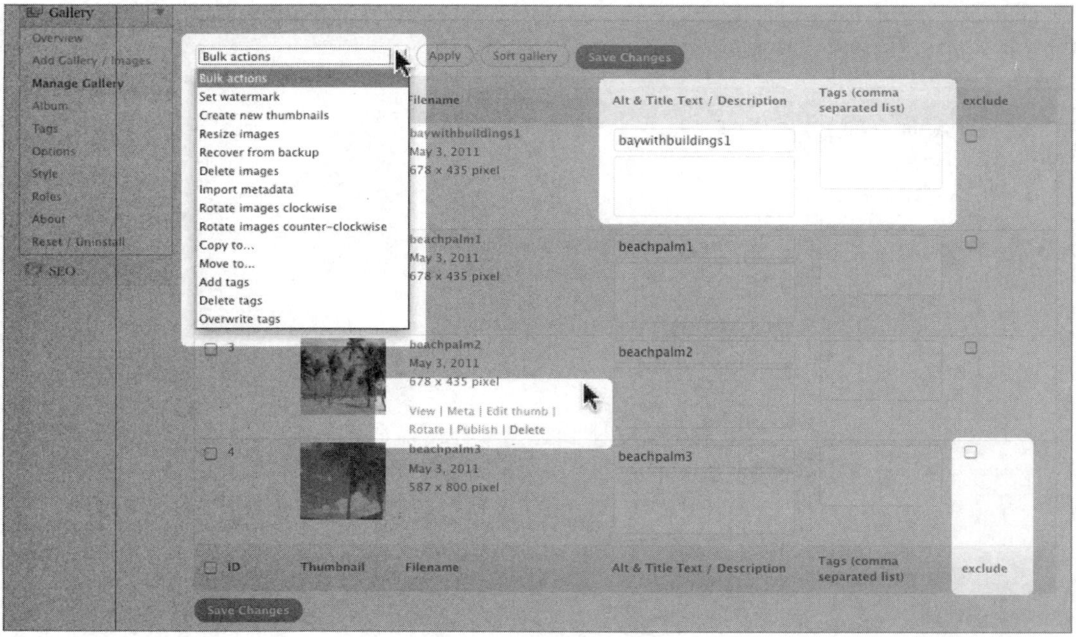

FIGURE 36-4

If you mouse over an image's thumbnail, a text menu appears, allowing you to view the full image, read any metadata contained in the image, edit the thumbnail, or delete the image. There are text fields for you to give the image a title/alternative text and description as well as any tags. There's a checkbox to exclude an image, which means that it won't show when you display the gallery as a whole.

The drop-down menu near the top of the screen shows you the wide range of actions that can be applied to one or many images all at one time. You could copy them to another gallery, give them a watermark, add tags, and much more.

With a gallery created and some images uploaded, here's how to get materials from NextGEN into your posts. The left side of Figure 36-5 shows the button bar in Visual mode of the Text Editor, with the NextGEN button highlighted.

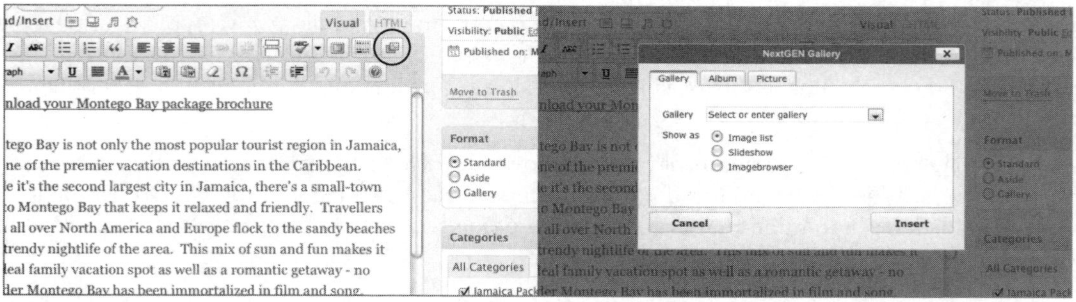

FIGURE 36-5

When you click that button, you get a popup window, as shown on the right side of Figure 36-5. From there, you can choose to insert any picture, gallery, or album from NextGEN.

How exactly do galleries and albums differ in NextGEN? Galleries are the smallest groups of images, whereas albums are ways of grouping several galleries or a mix of galleries and other albums.

So, in the case of Island Travel, I might set up a series of galleries — Kingston, Jamaica Beaches, Jamaica Food — then group them together under an album called Jamaica. I then group the album Jamaica with the album Aruba, and so on, under a single album called Caribbean. Or I could group all beach galleries under a single album called Caribbean Beaches.

You also get a lot of control on the back end of NextGEN, with seven different options screens (the General Options are shown in Figure 36-6) covering everything from the size of thumbnails to how galleries and slideshows work to controlling the watermark option.

| General Options | Thumbnails | Images | Gallery | Effects | Watermark | Slideshow |

General Options

Gallery path	wp-content/gallery/	This is the default path for all galleries
Delete image files	☑ Delete files, when removing a gallery in the database	
Activate permalinks	☐ When you activate this option, you need to update your permalink structure one time.	
Create new URL friendly image slugs	(Proceed now ») Currently not used, prepare database for upcoming version	
Select graphic library	⊙ GD Library	
	◯ ImageMagick (Experimental). Path to the library :	
	/usr/local/bin/	
Activate Media RSS feed	☐ A RSS feed will be added to you blog header. Useful for Coollris/PicLens	
Activate PicLens/Coollris support (Coollris)	☐ When you activate this option, some javascript is added to your site footer. Make sure that wp_footer is called in your theme.	

Tags / Categories

Activate related images	☐ This option will append related images to every post	

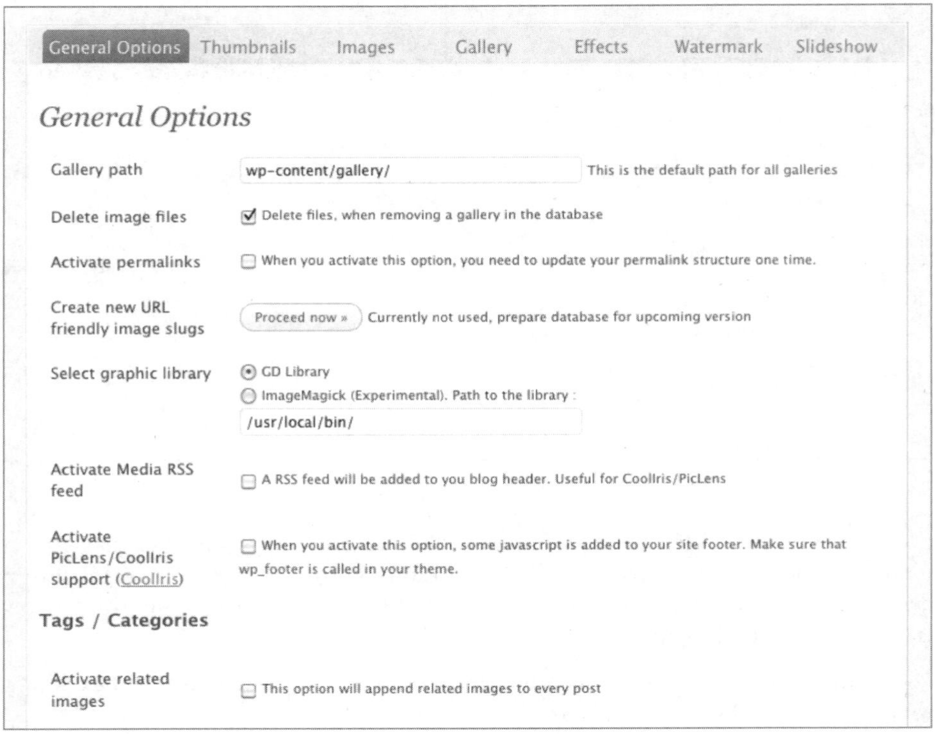

FIGURE 36-6

This range of options, the degree of organizational control, and the ease with which you get fancy JavaScript or Flash slideshows make NextGEN a powerful tool for managing large numbers of images.

FORM CREATION PLUGIN — CONTACT FORM 7

WordPress does not have a form creation tool built in, so a number of developers have made plugins that do the job very nicely. One of the best, I think, is Contact Form 7 by Takayuki Miyoshi. It's not as WYSIWYG as, say, cForms (another popular contact form plugin) but it's not as complex, either, in the coding it adds on to WordPress or in the number of screens the user has to deal with.

You access the plugin from a section of the side admin menu that appears after activation. You can see from Figure 36-7 that it's an extremely simple menu — a single Edit link.

In fact, the entire plugin runs on a single page. If you have more than one form, you'll see them all listed in the menu at the top of the page, where you can also add new forms.

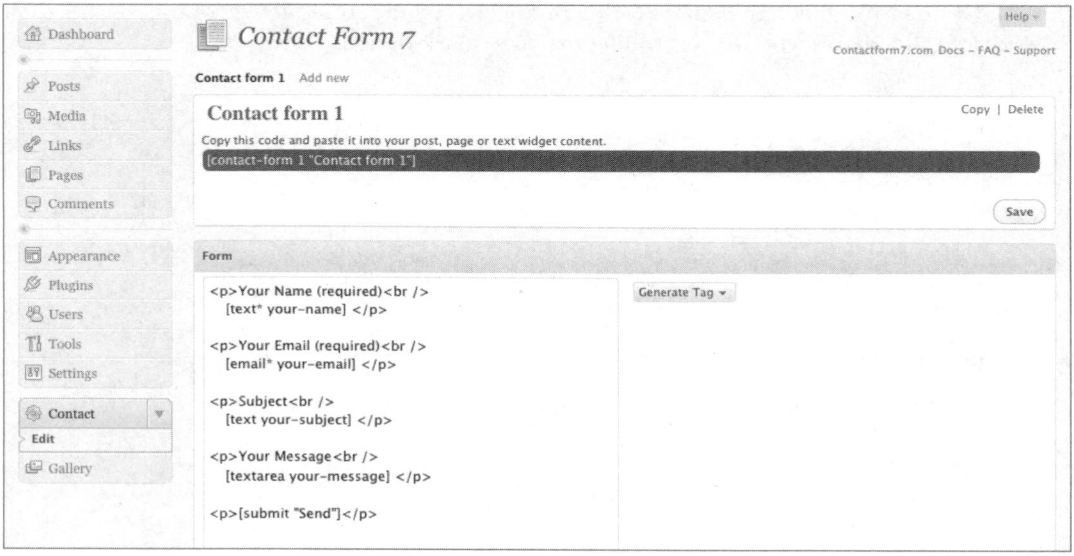

FIGURE 36-7

As I said, this is not a WYSIWYG format, so you see the HTML for the form over on the left. However, generating form elements, such as text fields or radio buttons, is very simple. Just drop down the Generate Tag menu on the right, choose the kind of element you want — in this case, a plain text field — and you get a box like the one in Figure 36-8.

You have lots of options and when you're done, the brown bar at the bottom displays the code you copy and paste into the form HTML on the left.

The bottom half of the Contact Form 7 screen lets you set the e-mail address where the form is sent (by default, it uses your main WordPress e-mail). You can then format the e-mail that's sent, as you can see in Figure 36-9.

Again, you're going to need to do your own copying and pasting, but it's still very straightforward. The items in the square brackets are simply the names of the fields you set up in the top half of the screen. Contact Form 7 has created the most common items for you; you just need to fill in any other customizations you need. For a newsletter signup form, for example, I might want the e-mail to display certain fields that I created for that form. I just copy and paste the correct field names into the message body.

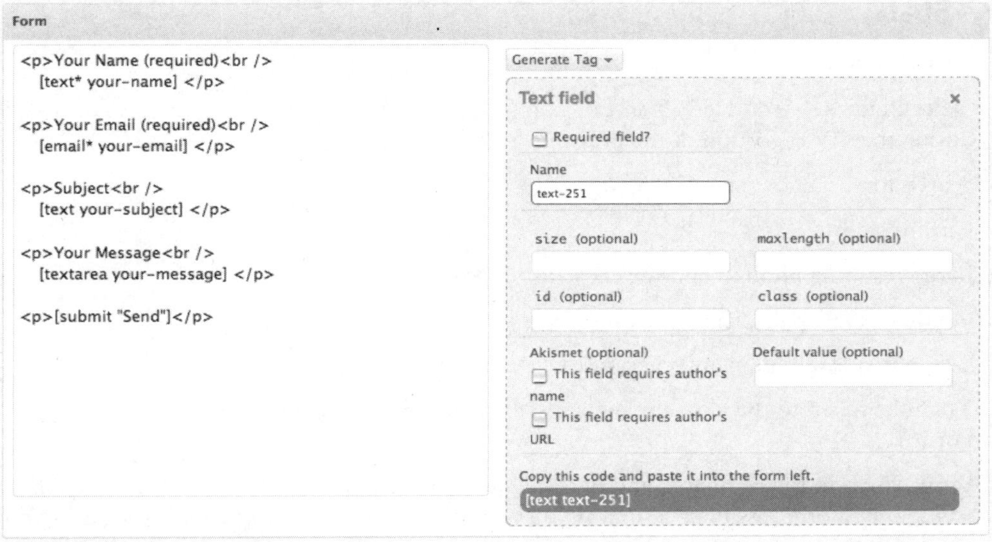

FIGURE 36-8

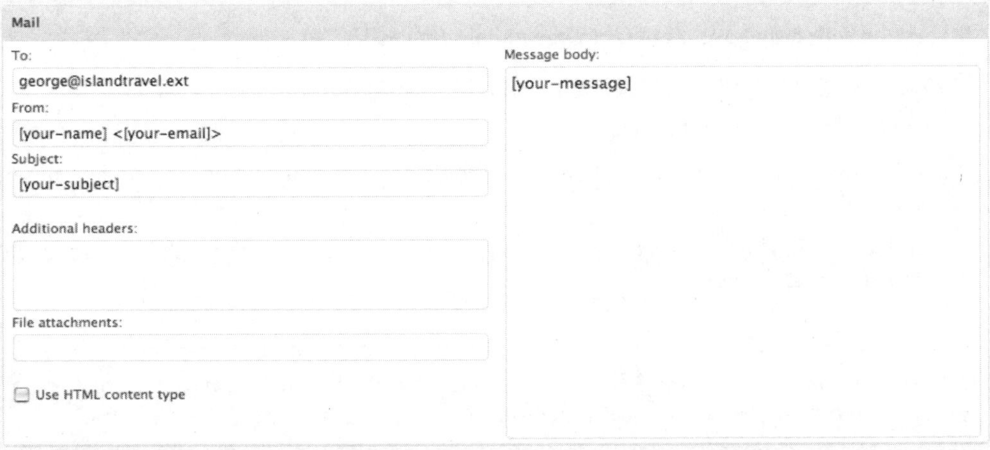

FIGURE 36-9

TRY IT

In this lesson, you walk through the quick creation of a contact form using Contact Form 7.

Lesson Requirements

No special requirements.

Step-by-Step

How to create a simple contact form.

1. Go to Plugins ➪ Add New. You can skip to step 6 if you installed the Contact Form 7 plugin during the Try It portion of the previous lesson.
2. Search for Contact Form 7.
3. Click Install.
4. In the resulting popup window, click Install Now.
5. On the success page, click Activate.
6. On your side admin menu, click the new Contact link.
7. You'll be taken to the Contact Form 7 screen and there's a default form called Contact Form 1.
8. Scroll down to the Mail area and in the To field, you should see the default e-mail address from your WordPress installation. If you want the form to mail to that address, don't do anything; otherwise, enter a new e-mail address.
9. Go back to the top of the screen and just below the title Contact Form 1, you'll see a dark brown bar with some code in it — copy that code.
10. If you don't already have a contact page, create one.
11. In the Text Editor of the contact page, paste the code you copied.
12. Publish or Update the contact page.
13. View the contact page on your site and you should see the form. Fill it out and e-mail yourself a message.
14. If you don't want the form or the plugin, be sure to erase the code from the contact page and then deactivate the plugin.

> *To see some of the examples from this lesson, watch the video for Lesson 36 on the DVD with the print book, or watch online at* `www.wrox.com/go/wp24vids`.

37

Other Common Uses for Plugins

So far in this book, I've talked about plugins that help back up your WordPress site plugins for monitoring site statistics.

This lesson looks at more plugin categories to help you expand your site's functionality and briefly outlines a few specific plugins for each to make it easier when you're searching on the Plugins ➪ Add New page.

SOCIAL NETWORKING

Connecting WordPress to other social media is one of the hottest areas of plugin development these days and it's hard to keep up with new offerings.

Plugins can provide three main functions with respect to social networking:

- Letting you easily display your social media profile or content on your website
- Letting visitors easily use social media to tell others about your site
- Letting you easily repurpose your WordPress content on your social networking accounts

Making it simple for people to connect to your social media profiles is an important feature of websites these days, and many plugins make it simple for you to implement this on your site. Good control over the look and positioning of your site is what you want from plugins of this type: for instance, having graphical interfaces that stay in place while the page scrolls (at the side or the top/bottom of the browser window) is a popular feature. Plugins are available that cater to special social media, such as Facebook, but you're typically going to want a plugin that displays multiple profiles. Some good plugins include *Social Slider* and *Follow Me Plugin*.

Social bookmarking — in the broad sense of enabling visitors to quickly mention your site's content on their social networks — is a great way of sharing information and spreading the word about your site. Make sure the plugins offer e-mailing a friend as well (still a great way to share!). Two basic types of plugins are available for this purpose:

- **Third-party bookmarking tools:** Three of the most popular have plugins for WordPress: *Add to Any*, *ShareThis*, and *Add This*.
- **Stand-alone plugins:** These work from within WordPress and probably the biggest difference between these plugins (and there are a lot of them!) is the way they display the social bookmarking icons. You'll want one that has good-looking icons with options for display (sizing, positioning, and so on). You also want an easy-to-use interface for choosing which bookmarks to display. Some good plugins in this group are *Sociable*, *SexyBookmarks*, *Sociable for WordPress 3.0*, *Simple Social*, *Socialize*, *Social Media Widget* (can only be used in widget areas), and *Jetpack* (this is a plugin pack from Automattic that, among other things, incorporates the old Sharedaddy plugin for bookmarking). Some plugins focus on specific social media bookmarking, such as *TweetMeme Button*, but unless there's a unique functionality you need, the general bookmarking plugins are fine.

Complete Social Media Solutions

Some plugins combine the social profile and social bookmarking functions into a single service. *Share and Follow* is a popular plugin of this type. Although it offers an incredible range of control over the look and positioning of profile and bookmark links, it can be a bit difficult for some users. In its current form, the plugin is one long page of controls, all of which look exactly the same, so it's tough to know sometimes which element you're working with. But once you're past that, it's extremely powerful and consolidates a lot into a single plugin.

BuddyPress

This plugin belongs in a discussion of social media, but instead of connecting visitors to social media, it is a social medium. *BuddyPress* enables you to have your own social network within a WordPress installation: groups, messaging other users, and so on.

This is not a plugin for the faint of heart. You should have or will at some point need to hire someone with the skills to work with template files, PHP, WordPress, and BuddyPress. This complex program is like having a second WordPress core and it's that power which can make it a very valuable tool if you need a way to connect a community of people through your own social medium.

MOBILE

Looking good on platforms like iPhone, iPad, Android, and more is becoming increasingly important, and there's a growing number of WordPress plugins to make a clean mobile view of your site as painless as possible. The key to these plugins is the ease with which you can pick and choose which content to display on the mobile version of your site and how easily you can create your own mobile theme.

At more than two million downloads, *WP Touch* is easily the leader at the moment, and though the latest, more powerful pro edition is a paid plugin, it's well worth the small fee: powerful, flexible, and well supported. There is still a free version, but it's much more limited (no iPad support, no theming). The free edition does work on the latest versions of WordPress.

WordPress Mobile Edition is similar to the free version of WP Touch — it simply detects whether someone is viewing your site on a mobile device and switches them to a built-in theme. It is possible to alter that theme, but there isn't an interface to help you do that.

WordPress Mobile Pack offers a combination of visitor as well as admin interfaces, so you can easily edit your WordPress site from your smartphone. Plus, it has automated features like cached image scaling, splitting posts into multiple pages, and special widgets aimed at mobile users.

> *Here's how fast things change. In the first edition of this book, I recommended a mobile plugin called* WPhone, *which let you administer WordPress through your smartphone. Just a couple of years later and the plugin page at WordPress.org warns people that it doesn't work with new versions of WordPress and that much better plugins are available now that take advantage of all the new features of the iPhone and of Android (which didn't even exist when the plugin was made). Good on the authors for updating their page that way.*

AD MANAGERS

Ad management plugins for WordPress roughly fall into two categories:

- Those that manage ads delivered through networks
- Those that manage both network ads and ones from your own advertisers

If you're interested in running ads only from a single network, such as Google AdSense, then search for plugins using the name of the network. Dozens are available for AdSense, such as *Easy AdSense*, *Quick Adsense* [sic], and *AdSense Now*! If you want to run ads from multiple networks, a plugin like *Advertising Manager* is the way to go. Affiliate marketing fits into this category as well. If you're an affiliate with, say, Amazon, do a search on the name to find plugins that help you manage your offerings. A lot of paid plugins for managing ads exist, but check the ones at WordPress.org first, and above all, do a lot of research about quality and functionality before laying out any money.

If you're looking to manage both network ads and your own advertisers, plugins are available that help you upload the files, and then keep track of impressions and clickthroughs, such as *Ad-minister*, *AdRotate*, or *Random/Rotating Ads V2*.

However, free hosted services like *OpenX.org* also exist. These companies offer powerful ad delivery and tracking functions, and OpenX, in particular, has a great WordPress integration. All the software and ad delivery is done from its servers so you don't have to bother with the technical end of things. You can also run OpenX on your own server.

PHOTO AND GALLERY MANAGEMENT

I showed you a bit about NextGEN, the most powerful and most popular of the WordPress photo plugins, but you have many more to choose from. I've divided them into four common groups based on their functionality:

- **Internal Photo Managers:** Working from within your WordPress installation, plugins like this enable you to upload, organize, and publish images independently of the WordPress Media Library. *NextGEN Gallery* is one example, as is *WP Photo Album Plus*.
- **External Photo Managers:** These plugins make it easy for you to organize and publish images you've uploaded to a third-party site, such as Flickr and Picasa. Popular plugins in this group include *flickrRSS*, *Flickr Gallery*, *WP-SimpleViewer*, and *MudSlideShow*. There are lots of Picasa plugins, but most have not been updated for at least a year or two.
- **Popup Galleries:** These plugins typically use JavaScript (jQuery in particular) to create thumbnails on the web page, and when you click them, a large version pops up and grays out the browser background. You can then browse the images in popup mode without having to return to the thumbnails. Most of these plugins convert existing WordPress galleries into these fancy formats with little or no work (sometimes, you may have to add a class name to each image). There are a lot of these plugins, but some of the most popular are *Lightbox Plus*, *Lightbox 2*, and *Shadowbox JS*.
- **Slideshow/Rotators:** These plugins take the images from posts (or other locations) and rotate them on a page. Many allow you to rotate all kinds of content other than just images. The key to these plugins is that they don't pop up and don't require any visitor interaction to start them going — they're part of the web page. Among the more popular of this type are *Featured Content Gallery*, *Dynamic Content Gallery*, *WordPress Content Slide*, and *WP-Cycle*. Keep in mind that many themes today incorporate content rotators into their homepage templates so you may or may not need a plugin.

There are also plugins that use Flash to create photo galleries, though personally, I find that the effects available through JavaScript libraries such as jQuery are almost as comprehensive as what you can get with Flash...without Flash.

VIDEOS AND PODCASTS

Plugins for video fall under two main groups:

- Playing videos
- Organizing and playing videos

Although WordPress has an auto-embed feature for video — you simply paste in the URL of a third-party video and the system embeds it automatically — it only gives you control over sizing (and if you want individual sizing, you have to use an embed shortcode). Plugins can give you more control, such as *Viper's Video Quicktags* or *Smart YouTube*.

If you're creating your own videos, but aren't using a video sharing site to host them, you'll want a plugin that incorporates one of the popular video players, such as JW Player or Flowplayer. Examples of these plugins include *FV WordPress Flowplayer* or *JW Player Plugin for WordPress*.

If you're going to be working with more than the occasional video on your site, it's well worth installing a plugin that can categorize as well as play videos. *wordTube*, for example, creates its own library through which you can categorize videos into playlists. It also handles audio files and lets you upload your videos as well as pasting URLs from third-party video sites like YouTube. Another very popular plugin that handles both audio and video is *podPress*, which has been updated now to include support for HTML5 media handling. There's also a plugin for Cincopa, which has a limited free media file hosting service if you don't want to run your videos from your own server, but also don't want to use a sharing site like YouTube. As with wordTube, you can create playlists of related videos. *Viper's Video Quicktags* is a popular plugin that creates buttons on your Text Editor for a number of popular video sites, such as YouTube and Vimeo, while giving you lots of customization options for the display of the videos.

> *Many video plugins for WordPress rely on the JW Player (`www.longtailvideo.com`) to display video files. Although this player is available for free, that's only for noncommercial use. If your site is commercial (check the JW Player terms), you'll need to purchase a license. If you have multiple commercial sites, there are generous discounts for multisite licenses. Flowplayer (`www.flowplayer.org`) also has a free version, but it can be used by commercial sites as long as you don't mind their trademark being displayed — a commercial license will remove that.*

GOOGLE MAPS

Displaying maps in your content has become a must in many situations and plugins are available to make this as simple as possible. *MapPress Easy Google Maps* creates a box on your post and page editing screens where you can enter an address and then see the map in real time. You can also edit the maps by dragging markers wherever you want, changing the look of the markers and the popup windows with your HTML editor, adding photos to the popups, and much more.

E-COMMERCE

What a difference a couple of years can make. Before the major changes in WordPress 3.0, there were very few shopping cart plugins; now, there are plenty of contenders. There's not a lot of track record for them yet, and most are paid plugins, but many of them have features that you expect to see on stand-alone shopping cart systems:

- Discounts and gift certificates
- Cross-selling and recommendation features
- Integration with mailing list managers like Aweber and Mail Chimp

- Various shipping options
- Multiple payment gateways
- Order management features
- And much, much more

WP e-Commerce was one of the first shopping cart plugins and continues to be widely downloaded and to be updated. The basic shopping cart is free to use and contains a lot of features. But to get certain kinds of functionality (downloadable products, certain payment gateways), you'll need to purchase add-ons.

eShop is another longtime plugin that is free to use, though it's not quite as comprehensive as most of the others. It uses the WordPress post structure to create its catalog rather than additional database tables. (Not to be confused with *eStore*, a paid shopping plugin.)

Among the paid shopping plugins that have appeared recently are *Shopp*, *Cart66* (formerly PHPurchase), *ShopperPress*, *MarketPress* (from WPMU Dev), and *WordPress Shopping Cart Plugin*.

If you don't need a full catalog/checkout system, there are plugins that make integration with PayPal's shopping cart very simple, such as *WordPress Simple Paypal* [sic] *Shopping Cart*.

And there is also a growing list of WordPress themes geared to shopping sites. Some simply make it easy to display products, while others go even further and include the shopping cart and product management scripting that you find in plugins: for example, *Market Theme*, a premium (paid) theme.

As I say, most of these shopping options for WordPress have only been around since WordPress 3.0 was released, and I haven't personally worked with the newer ones. The first thing to do is assess your needs. For a lot of sites, a simple PayPal integration may be all that's needed.

MEMBERSHIP

Membership sites have become extremely popular over the past couple of years. They're a great way to keep visitors involved in your site by offering free membership or to generate revenue with paid memberships that offer access to your most important material.

Important features to look for in these plugins include the ability to offer free memberships, ease of moving people between membership levels, ease of integration with payment gateways and mailing list managers, ease of specifying which content is open to which members (this should be as fine-grained as allowing part of a post to be visible to nonmembers and the rest to members only), and the ability to automate the release of content to members over a period of time.

Most of the plugins in this category are premium or paid plugins, usually in the $50.00 to $100.00 range for a single site license. They include *WishList Member*, *WordPress Membership*, *Member Wing*, and *wp-Member*. They all have a lot of features, so you'll want to check which one fits your needs best, and then research and ask questions.

If you're simply looking for an easy way to manage free memberships for your site, there are good free plugins for that, including *Role Scoper*, *Members*, and *Member Access*. They'll allow you to restrict content to members only, on a post-by-post basis or within the content of a post (show a teaser to nonmembers).

RANDOM CONTENT

Displaying random content in the sidebar has long been a mainstay of blogging, so lots of WordPress plugins are available to help you randomize content such as posts, comments, and so on: *Random Posts* or *Random Posts Widget* or *Most Popular Posts*.

Plugins are also available that allow you to add content to your site that's outside of the WordPress post/page structure and randomly display it. Typically, these are thought of as random quote generators, but the more sophisticated versions, such as *Stray Random Quotes*, can be used as mini–content management systems, because they enable you to categorize content and then have detailed control of its display. So, for example, on the Island Travel site, I could have interesting facts about Aruba as a category, and then display only those facts, at random, on the pages about Aruba.

RELATED CONTENT

After you start to get some content on your site, it's easy for the older content to get lost in the background. Linking to related content on your site is a huge help to visitors, increases the stickiness of your site, and helps with search engine optimization. The tricky part is remembering which content is relevant. Even the internal linking feature built into the Link button of the Text Editor relies on you looking up related material.

Fortunately, plugins are available that can automate the process for you. The most popular of these is *Yet Another Related Posts Plugin*, and it's also one of the most versatile because it lets you customize the algorithms that weigh such factors as titles, tags, categories, and so on. The plugin used to take up a lot of processing power, though, when it performed this search for related material every time the page was loaded. Newer caching methods have made it more efficient, however.

A newer plugin takes a different approach to finding related material. *Efficient Related Posts* looks for similar content at the time you're saving the post and stores that as metadata.

Images are often a powerful draw for getting visitors to notice something on a site, so related posts plugins exist that will display a thumbnail of the content, such as *Related Posts Thumbnails*. Third-party services also will find related content and the thumbnails, such as *nrelate Related Content*, and one of the advantages here is that they do the work of finding the content so it's less of a drain on your server. However, there may be SEO issues if the linking is going through their server, so you'll want to consider that.

COMMENT ENHANCEMENT

Comments are an important part of the interactivity and sense of community that you're trying to create on a website.

Although WordPress has a good basic commenting system out of the box, a number of plugins are available that will make it even better. *IntenseDebate*, which is created by Automattic, includes features like comment voting, reputation, threaded comments (comments related to one another are kept together), sorting of comments, and much more. *Disqus Comment System* is a plugin that offers similar functionality. Both of these plugins require signing up for an account with their website, but this is free.

Another way to keep your visitors connected to your site is to use a plugin like *Subscribe to Comments*. This popular plugin allows commenters to receive e-mail notification when a new comment is made about the post. They can unsubscribe from individual posts, update their e-mail address, and much more.

To make the editing and management of comments easier, a plugin like *WP Ajax Edit Comments* is very helpful. It even allows comments not placed into moderation to be edited by the commenter for a limited time.

Some plugins will display a list of the most recent comments, for example, the very popular *Get Recent Comments*, whereas others, like *Most Commented*, list the top posts based on how many comments they have.

You can also integrate the commenting features of Facebook with your WordPress comments using a plugin like *Facebook Comments for WordPress*.

SPAM

Spam is annoying and when you have comments open on a site or forms, there's always the danger of spammers taking advantage of that.

By default, WordPress comes with an antispam plugin for comments called *Akismet*. When you activate it, you'll need to enter an API Key and that means signing up for an account with WordPress.com (no need to set up a blog, just get an account). In the settings for that account, you'll find your API key. Akismet works very well, but you should be aware that the plugin is not free for commercial use. Apparently, this has always been true, but until recently, I didn't remember seeing anything about it — now, it's very prominent on the Akismet site.

Akismet is by far the most popular way of reducing the amount of comment spam, but many other plugins are available as well, such as *Bad Behaviour*, which takes the approach of stopping the spammers before they can leave a comment, by looking at their delivery system and other factors as they try to access your site. *WP-SpamFree Anti-Spam* also operates without an API Key or any sort of CAPTCHA challenges (those deliberately hard-to-read letters you see all the time). If you do want a visual CAPTCHA system, lots of plugins do that, but you're best off with one like *SI CAPTCHA for WordPress*, which includes audio for those who can't easily see the images. Other plugins, like *CryptX*, can be used to hide e-mail addresses in your posts so they can't be harvested by spammers.

When it comes to forms, most form-creation plugins will have some type of CAPTCHA to prevent robots from filling them in.

EVENTS

You can manage events listings using WordPress posts, but plugins will make things a lot easier and more powerful. *Events Manager*, for example, automatically integrates Google Maps, has calendars for both pages and widgets, provides a great deal of customization for laying out information, enables you to categories events, and even has an RSVP system if you choose.

Events Calendar is another powerful management tool and it even includes easy integration with Eventbrite, one of the most widely used online event-registration systems.

Some plugins, like *Event Registration*, create an online registration and payment system right in WordPress, using third-party payment gateways like PayPal, Google Pay, and so on.

TRY IT

My best recommendation for trying something in this lesson is to search the WordPress.org plugins directory and get a feel for the variety of functions they can perform.

> *To see a walkthrough of the plugin directory, watch the video for Lesson 37 on the DVD with the print book, or watch online at* `www.wrox.com/go/wp24vids`.

SECTION XI
Taking WordPress Even Further

38

Running Multiple Sites with WordPress

In the past, if you wanted to run several websites using the regular version of WordPress, you needed to install one copy for each site (there was a special version called WordPress MU which could handle multiple sites). With WordPress 3.0, that all changed: there's now just one version and you can administer many sites from a single installation. In multisite mode, a business owner can have a company site and a personal site, families can have a blog for each family member, a group can have a site for itself and each member, schools can have a separate site for each class — the possibilities are endless.

If you're trying to manage the content of two or more sites, it's a real time-saver to have to log in only once, but even if you're just the webmaster for a group of sites, imagine having to update or backup WordPress only once.

> *A new service called ManageWP.com was in beta at the time of this writing and it offers an interesting take on multiple WordPress sites. It provides a single interface from which you can manage sites hosted on different accounts or servers. If you already have a lot of sites, a service like this might be easier than trying to migrate them all to a single WordPress multisite installation.*

ENABLING MULTISITE MODE

By default, WordPress is not installed with multisite mode on — it has to be activated. The process is not overly complex, but it does involve modifying and uploading files, checking how your server is handling certain functions, and setting up an important plugin. This is one of those tasks that I think is best left to the professionals — it will be a lot faster and there are some points at which mistakes can mess things up badly. It won't take a professional long, so the cost should be very reasonable (especially because it gives you peace of mind).

> *It makes a difference whether you're turning on multisite mode during a fresh install of WordPress or if you've already installed WordPress and are converting to be able to host a network of sites. The difference is that in a fresh installation, you'd have a choice whether additional sites use a subdirectory or a subdomain (mydomain.com/newsite vs. newsite.mydomain.com); with an existing installation, you must use subdomains.*

For those who'd like to take the plunge, here are the steps to take if you've already installed WordPress:

1. In your `wp-config.php` file, add the following above the line where it says `/* That's all, stop editing! Happy blogging. */`::

   ```
   define('WP_ALLOW_MULTISITE', true);
   ```

2. Log in to your WordPress admin and you'll now see a Tools ➪ Network link on the admin menu. Click that link.

   You'll get the screen shown in Figure 38-1, which asks for the name of the network and an admin e-mail address — these do not have to be the defaults that get inserted by WordPress based on your installation information.

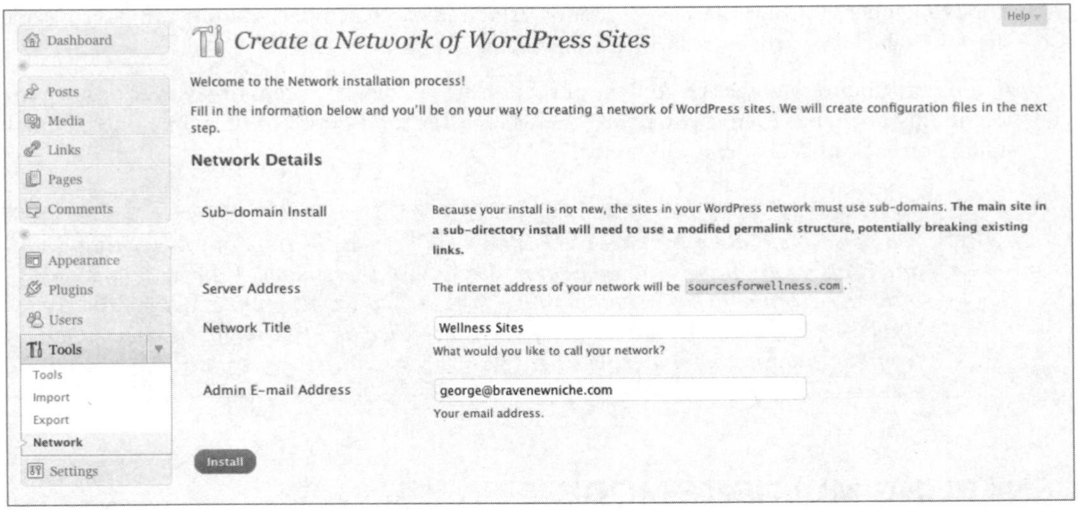

FIGURE 38-1

3. When you're ready, click Install.

You'll get a screen with a series of steps for Enabling the Network, which include creating a new directory in `wp-content` where additional sites will store uploaded media, more coding to add to the `wp-config.php` file, and rules to be added to your `.htaccess` file. This is shown in Figure 38-2.

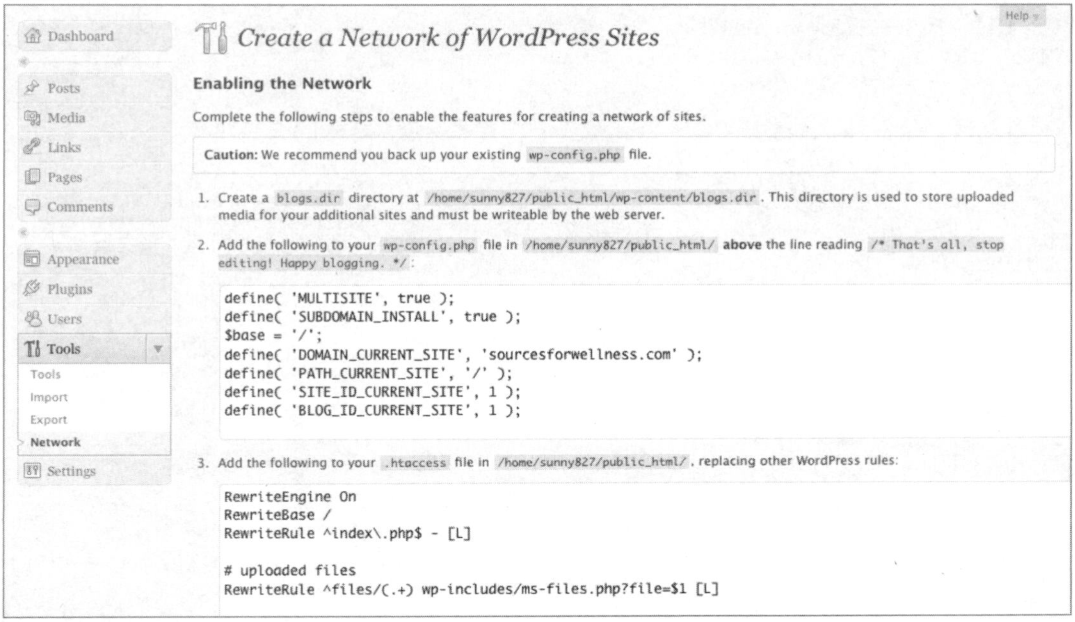

FIGURE 38-2

> *In order for subdomains to work in WordPress multisite mode, you must create a subdomain in your hosting account for each additional site you want. You can do this through your hosting control panel.*
>
> *To avoid having to create a subdomain this way every time you want to add a new site in WordPress, you can set up your hosting account to use wildcard subdomains. What you need to do will vary by host and by hosting control panel. If you're using the popular hosting control panel cPanel, you can simply go into subdomains and add one whose name is just *. Check with your hosting company if you're not sure about any of this.*
>
> *You need to do this before you start creating any additional sites in WordPress (assuming you're using the subdomain method).*

NETWORK ADMIN SCREENS

Once you've completed all the installation steps, you'll need to log back in, at which point Tools ➪ Network disappears, and a new link, Dashboard ➪ My Sites, shows up. This is where you can view and go into the admin screens for each of your sites.

At the top right of the screen is a link to Network Admin. Clicking that produces a Network Admin Dashboard along with a new side menu, as shown in Figure 38-3.

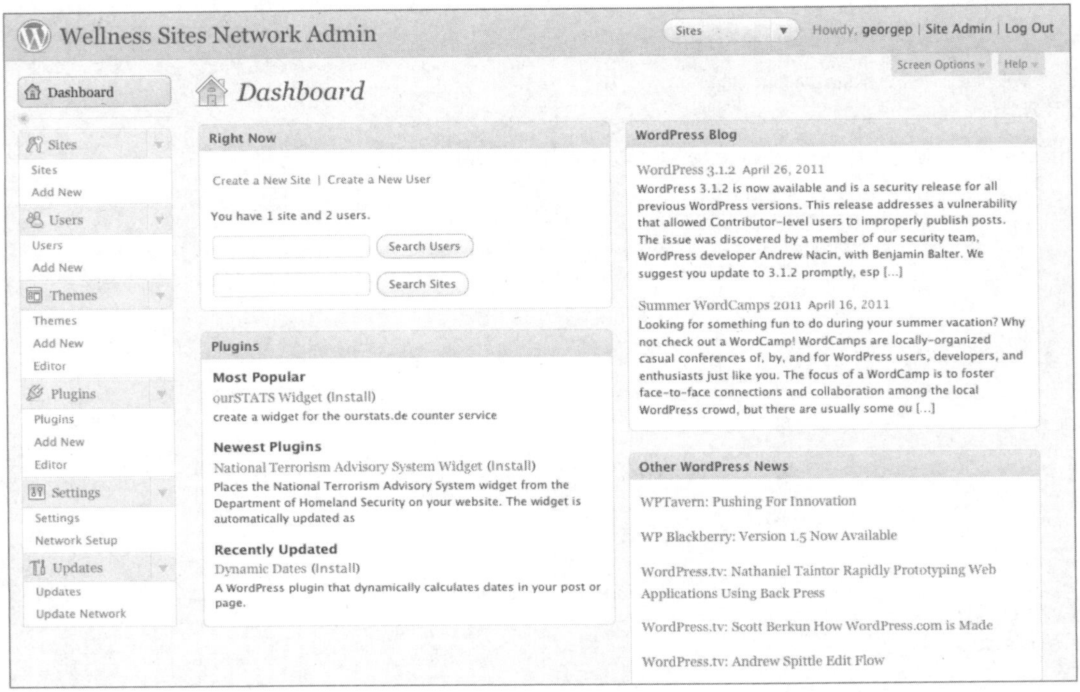

FIGURE 38-3

One of the advantages of this separation of the two admin functions is that you don't mix network menu items with site items.

From this area, you can control everything to do with the network, including:

- Adding or removing sites
- Creating new users
- Adding or removing plugins and themes available across the network
- Updating WordPress and all themes and plugins across the network
- The settings for each individual site
- Overall settings that apply to all sites

When you're ready to return to administering a site, you can either return to the site you were on by clicking Site Admin at the top right or go to Sites, mouse over a site name, and click Dashboard.

MAPPING OTHER DOMAINS TO NETWORK SITES

Depending on how you've activated multisite mode, new websites will be named either `newsite.mydomain.com` or `mydomain.com/newsite`. If you want to use a different domain name for a network site, you'll need a plugin called *WordPress MU Domain Mapping* (MU stands for Multi-User — at one time, WordPress MU was a stand-alone program).

When you've installed and activated the plugin, you'll see two new links on the Settings menu of Network Admin: Domain Mapping and Domains.

If you click Domain Mapping, you'll get a notice telling you to place a file called `sunrise.php` in the `wp-content` folder, and add a `SUNRISE` definition to the `wp-config.php` file.

Using your FTP program, go into `wp-content/plugins` and look in the domain mapping plugin folder. You'll see the `sunrise.php` file there. Download it to your hard drive, then navigate back to the `wp-content` folder and upload `sunrise.php` into there.

You should already have a copy of the `wp-config.php` file on your drive after making the other changes to it as part of the multisite installation. Open it up again and paste in the following above the line where it says `/* That's all, stop editing! Happy blogging. */`:

```
define( 'SUNRISE', 'on' );
```

This tells WordPress to use that `sunrise.php` file you put into `wp-content`. When you've updated the `wp-config.php` file on the server, go back to your Network Admin screen and click Domain Mapping again. You'll see the screen shown in Figure 38-4.

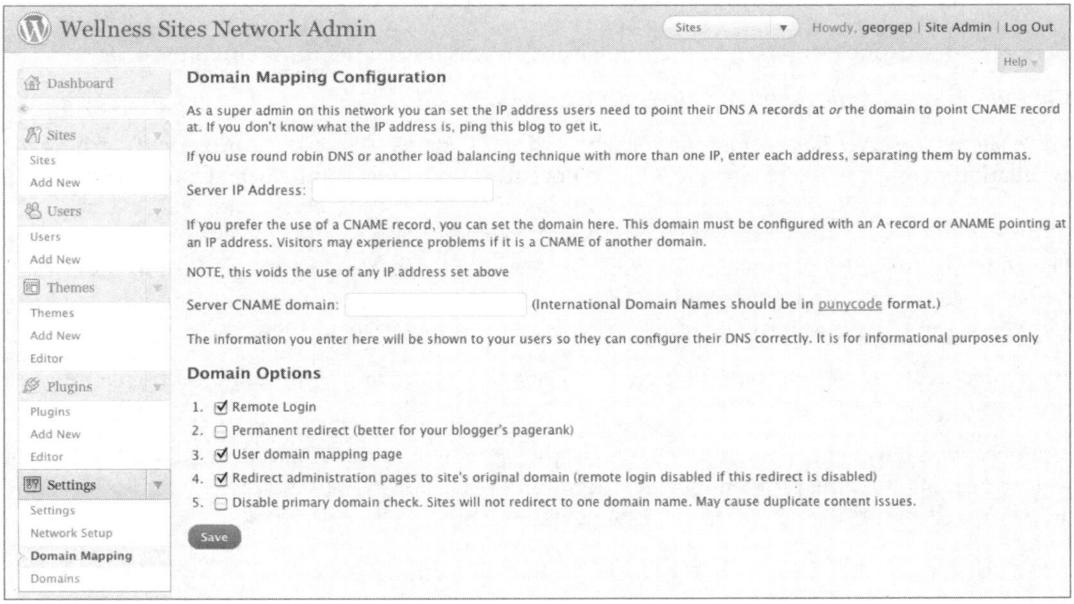

FIGURE 38-4

Here, you can choose between using an IP address or a CNAME record as the place where site owners would point their domain names — it's simplest to use the IP, which is just the IP address of the server where you installed WordPress (if your server uses more than one, separate them with commas).

Of the five Domain Options at the bottom of the screen, you should uncheck Remote Login and Redirect Administration Pages (if these are left checked, then the login for a mapped domain will be redirected to the main site; if unchecked, Super-Admins will still be able to access all sites from a single login), and make sure that Permanent Redirect and User Domain Mapping Page are both checked.

Then click Save and you're ready to map a domain. Click Settings ➪ Domains and you'll see a list of any existing domains and a place to add new ones. What can be a bit confusing is that you're asked for a site ID but nowhere does it list the site IDs. You need to go to your list of sites and mouse over the one to which you're mapping the domain. Down in the status bar of your browser, you'll see a URL with `id=some number` at the end.

Make a note of that number and go back to Settings ➪ Domains, then enter the ID under New Domain along with the domain name. Make sure the Primary check box is checked. Then click Save.

> *Before clicking Save, you must make sure you've pointed the domain name to the IP address you entered in Settings ➪ Domain Mapping. If it's not pointed correctly in your hosting/control panel DNS settings, you're not going to see anything for that domain name.*

TROUBLESHOOTING MULTISITE INSTALLATIONS

Here are a few troubleshooting tips if you have problems during the installation process:

Subdomain sites are not showing up — the page won't load.

Make sure your server has been set up for wildcard subdomains — reread the preceding warning in the installation steps or, if you're not sure what to do, call your hosting company and have them set it up.

Uploaded images won't display.

The code that WordPress provides for your `.htaccess` file will direct requests for images to the proper directory, so you need to make sure you copied the code exactly and updated the `.htaccess` file. You should also check to make sure `mod_rewrite` is on or the file won't be read properly.

I can't access the Domain Mapping page — I keep getting the notice about uploading `sunrise.php` *and so on.*

Assuming you have uploaded `sunrise.php` to the `wp-content` folder and defined `SUNRISE` in your `wp-config.php` file, the problem is that you haven't placed `define( 'SUNRISE', 'on' );` above the `/* That's all, stop editing! Happy blogging. */` line.

TRY IT

There's nothing specific to try from this lesson, since much of it was instructional. One thing to think about if you haven't set up WordPress yet is whether you anticipate needing one or more additional sites in the future. If you do, then it may be worth setting up WordPress in multisite mode when you first install it.

> *No video for this lesson.*

39

Customizing WordPress

The goal of this book was to get you up and running with WordPress and show you the basics of using the software to create content for your site. I also introduced you to the possibilities of extending the functionality of WordPress through plugins. Now, I want to say a little about four important ways you can have your WordPress theme customized to make your site even more powerful and easier to use:

- **Custom templates:** Whether they're page templates, category templates, single post templates, and so on, you can add as many new theme templates as you want to help present your content in different ways.
- **Custom fields:** These additional fields for posts, pages, or any type of content can serve many purposes, but the basic idea is to give you more control over individual pieces of content and make it even easier to enter that content.
- **Custom post types:** Best to think of these as new types of content, different from posts or pages in WordPress. The ability to create and use these types has been a major breakthrough in making WordPress a true content management system.
- **Custom taxonomies:** Like the categories you use for organizing posts, you can create additional ways of classifying your content — each accessible separately from any other taxonomy. Again, this recent development in WordPress has made the system even more flexible.

Learning how to use these features is well beyond the scope of this book, but I think it's important to understand what they can do in a very general way so that you can better imagine what WordPress can do for you. In turn, you'll have a good starting point either for learning more yourself or for intelligently talking about customization with someone who knows how to work with WordPress themes.

CUSTOM TEMPLATES

Did you know that WordPress really only needs a single PHP file in a theme? No theme builder would choose that option because it would be both limiting and complicated to code, but because of a concept called *template hierarchy*, WordPress could, if need be, function with just an `index.php` file (along with a style sheet).

When WordPress goes looking for instructions on how to assemble an HTML page, it has several lists of template files to look for in a particular order. If it doesn't find one, it looks for the next one on the list, and so on. In the end, if none of the files are on the list, it looks for `index.php`. If it doesn't find that, then you're in trouble.

The beauty of this design is that to take advantage of the hierarchy, you just need to drop a properly named template file into your theme folder and WordPress will automatically start using it instead of the next file down the list. For example, if I want all posts in the category Jamaica Packages to display a certain amount of information with a certain look, I just create a template file called `category-jamaica-packages.php` and WordPress will follow the instructions in that file whenever it's displaying posts in that category.

When creating a new page, if you select something other than the default page template, you're making use of the template hierarchy. If you choose the Links page template, what you're telling WordPress is to put `page-links.php` at the top of its list of template files to look for when displaying that page. Suppose `page-links.php` accidentally got erased — no problem, WordPress would simply look for a template file with the page's slug, then for a file with the page's ID, and finally for a template file called `page.php`. If none of those existed, WordPress would look for `index.php`. Aside from being a tool for customization, the template hierarchy is also a kind of fail-safe system that keeps your site displaying in one form or another.

> *Remember that any amount of customization you do to a theme's templates means that if you simply switch themes, you'll lose those customizations. You'll either want to create a child theme, which continues to use those customizations through the parent theme, or if your customizations are part of a child theme, you can either change the design of the child theme or create a new child theme that contains copies of all the customized template files.*

So, what can you do with custom templates? Pretty much anything you want. Maybe you want to have content displayed without a sidebar or a different header or you want the content of a post displayed in a particular way. For example, a list of all posts in your Company News category could be displayed inside their own box with only the date, title, and excerpt.

CUSTOM FIELDS

I briefly showed you the Custom Fields box in Lesson 9 as part of the advanced posts and pages options. I mentioned that it uses two fields: the name and the value of the custom field, as shown in detail in Figure 39-1.

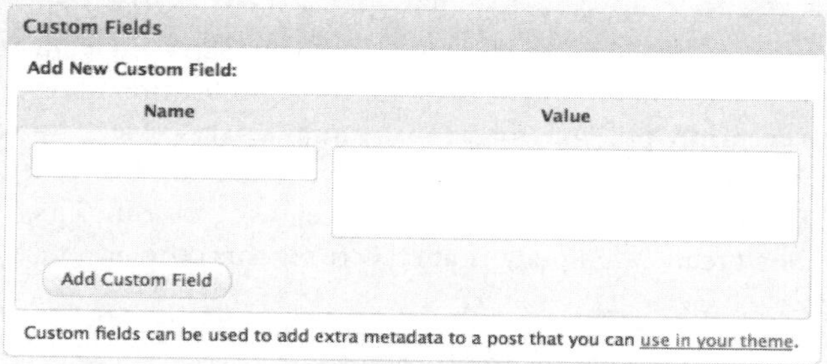
Custom Fields
Add New Custom Field:
Name
Value
Add Custom Field
Custom fields can be used to add extra metadata to a post that you can use in your theme.

FIGURE 39-1

I've talked about the value of customizing theme template files, and one of the most powerful tools for doing that is through the use of *custom fields*. As you may recall from earlier lessons, these are special fields in the WordPress database that you can create yourself by giving them a name (which can be then shared by all other posts or pages) and assigning a value for the particular post.

On the Island Travel site, for example, I could create a set of custom fields for use on destination pages: capital city, population, and average hours of sunshine. For each destination, I enter the particular values for those fields. Keep in mind, however, that the values won't automatically get displayed by WordPress. I would also need to create a custom page template that looks for values in the three fields. If a value is found, the template would print out the information in whatever format I chose, for example, in a box just below the page title.

I could, of course, have simply included these three pieces of information in the Text Editor for each of my destination pages — perhaps as a list. The advantage of having each piece of information as a separate custom field is that I can easily change how the information is displayed (the order, placing them all in a box, moving capital city to its own special place, and so on). I simply change how the custom template outputs the data. If the information were a part of each page's content as a list, I would need to go through every single page and change the order of the list or change the list structure to something else.

Custom fields are also great for setting up conditional situations that can actually produce a different layout of information. Suppose on all travel package posts for Island Travel, I have a custom field called special-offer. I can code a custom category template so that if the field exists and contains a dollar amount, WordPress will display the information in a certain order with a certain look; if not, the post gets displayed in the regular way.

CUSTOM POST TYPES

As I said earlier, the name "post" is a bit misleading because a custom post type is simply a new type of content, different from posts or pages. The name stems from the fact that WordPress stores the content of posts, pages, and custom post types in a database table called `wp_posts`.

A common example of a custom post type is a book. If there were only going to be a few books and no need to classify them, you might just create each one as a WordPress page. But why not just create a category of posts called Books and then have subcategories like Thriller, Murder Mystery, Romance, and so on? It's certainly possible and I did that on Island Travel with Travel Packages.

However, not only can it sometimes be confusing to have regular WordPress posts performing several functions and, as a result, having a complex category structure, but you also may want to have a special way of entering the content. For example, books have authors, publication dates, subtitles, and many more bits of data. It's certainly possible for you to manually style every book post with this data, but what if you change your mind down the road or want to add new information? You'd need to restructure every single post, again by hand. Better to enter author into its own field, subtitle in its own, and so on, and then create a template that structures this content in an easy-to-read way, as shown in Figure 39-2.

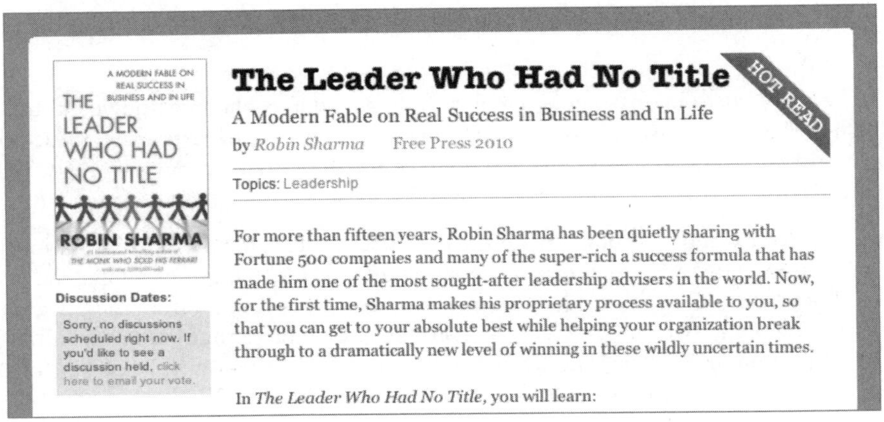

FIGURE 39-2

Change your mind later, and all you have to do is change the template.

Now, if what I just described sounds like using custom fields, you're exactly right. But the advantage of setting up a custom post type with its own custom fields and easy-to-use data-entry screen is that it keeps everything separate from regular posts. In addition, the custom post type "books" can then have its own box in the WordPress admin menu — no need to remember that you enter books under Posts and structure things in a special way. Add to this the fact that it's much easier to have a separate classification system for books — a custom taxonomy — than trying to mix it in with post categories.

In Figure 39-3, you can see the Books menu over on the left and you can see all the specific entry fields below the main Text Editor.

Remember how the default Custom Fields interface in WordPress simply has text fields? Notice here there are check boxes, drop-downs, and so on.

> *When you're talking to a developer about creating custom post types, make sure they're doing it as a plugin. All of functionality can be done through your theme template files, but that means you'll need to keep copying those files into new themes or keep a single parent theme all the time or else you'll lose the functionality. If custom post types are created using a plugin, it's completely theme-independent.*

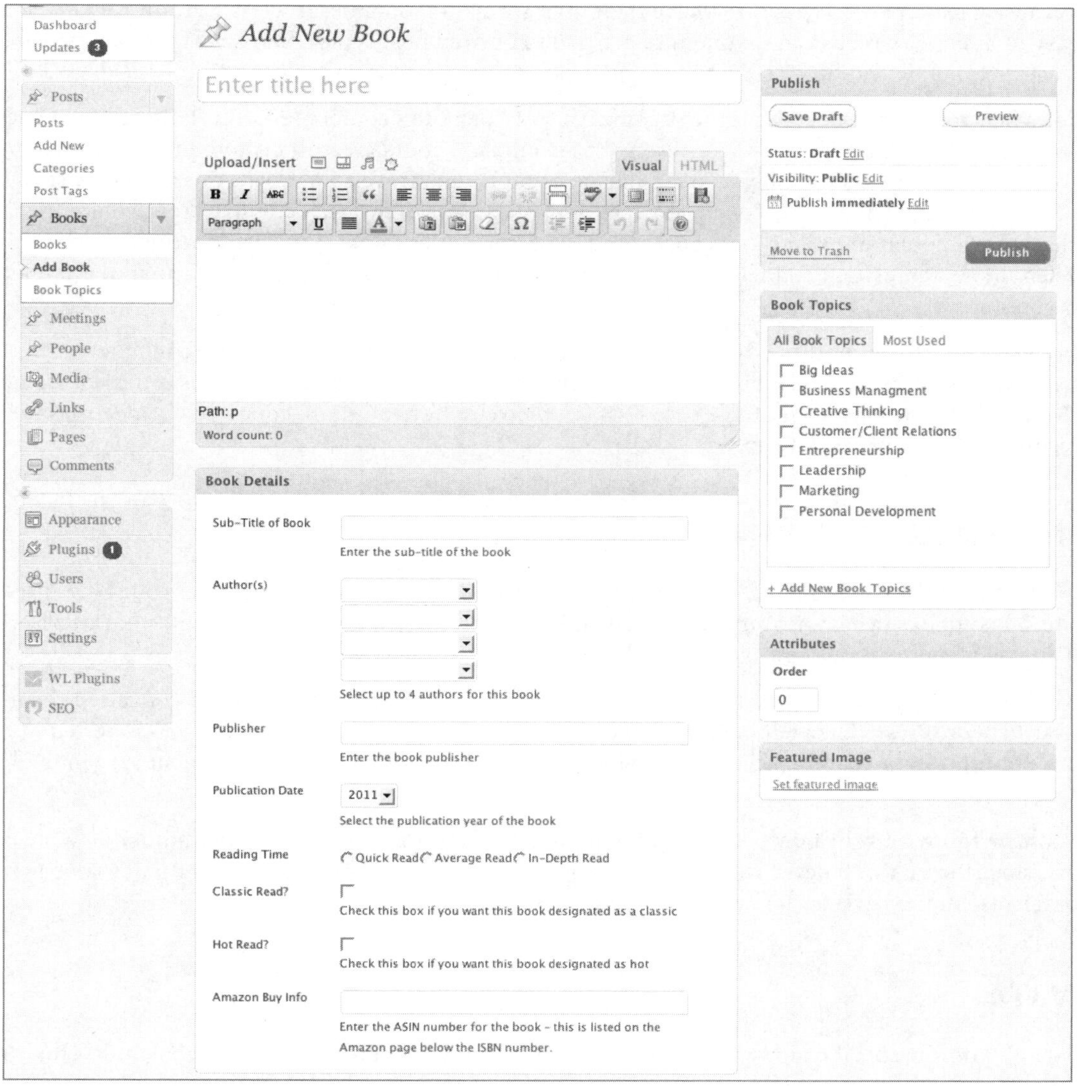

FIGURE 39-3

CUSTOM TAXONOMIES

From what's been said so far, you know that taxonomies are ways of classifying things. WordPress uses three different taxonomies by default: post categories, link categories, and tags. For quite some time, you've been able to create your own custom taxonomies, but for various reasons, it took a great deal of custom code to make use of them. As of WordPress 3.0, that all changed — now, these taxonomies could be hierarchical (have subcategories) and they could be applied to the newly developed custom post types.

Because Custom Post Types often have their own special taxonomies or classification systems, it's easy to assume that custom taxonomies are tied to custom post types, but that's far from the case. Custom taxonomies can be set up for regular posts, links, and even for pages!

So, when you're thinking about the organization of your site's content, don't feel limited by what you see in the default setup of WordPress. For example, I could create a custom taxonomy of countries and cities, and apply it to regular posts on Island Travel. That way, my regular post categories wouldn't need to have separate Testimonial categories for each country. You would just check Testimonial under post categories and Kingston under Jamaica in the Location taxonomy. Then, in my template for Jamaica, I would simply find all Testimonials that are also in the Jamaica taxonomy.

In one sense, there's nothing different going on here — either method allows me to find only those testimonials about Jamaica, but with the custom taxonomy of Location, it makes things easier for the user to enter, plus it's more flexible — I don't have to have all those country subcategories for testimonials, packages, and so on.

SOME FINAL THOUGHTS

I hope this book has been and will continue to be a valuable resource for you and your WordPress site. My aim has been not simply to show you how to do things, but to explain some of the whys and help you to think about new ways to make your WordPress site work for you.

My clients always get very excited about their websites after I've built them in or converted them over to WordPress. They tell me they feel empowered and, as a result, they're more interested in maintaining and expanding their sites, which is exactly what a content management system ought to do.

So, have fun with your new website and don't forget about the tremendous community of WordPress users out there. You'll never want for inspiration or help, and hopefully, you can do the same for others as your experience grows.

TRY IT

There's nothing specific to try from this lesson, but if you've got a site map and content list for your own site, think about ways in which your content might be organized differently using Custom Post Types and Custom Taxonomies.

No video for this lesson.

A

Troubleshooting WordPress

I've tried throughout the book to include small troubleshooting tips with the lesson to which they relate. In this appendix, the goal is help you think through the troubleshooting process.

Consider the variables involved in viewing a web page: what computer you're using, what web browser and what version, what Internet service provider you're using, what type of server the website is on, what version of WordPress you're running, what versions are being run for the dozens of software packages required to run a web server, and so on. No wonder, then, that you might have a problem and virtually no one else has exactly the same one.

Addressing particular problems is next to impossible in a few pages, but what I can do is offer some strategies for trying to solve problems, as well as provide some ideas for getting more information online.

TROUBLESHOOTING AN INSTALLATION

Although WordPress installations are straightforward, sometimes issues arise. Here are some suggestions for a few of the most common:

1. **Error connecting to the database:** Check that you correctly entered the database name, username, and password, and that you don't have any stray spaces before or after each variable (that can happen in particular when you're copying and pasting). Reenter the information and try again.
2. **"Headers already sent" error messages:** This is usually caused by the presence of characters or whitespace before a file's opening `<?php` tag or after the closing `?>` tag. You can tell which file is causing the problem by looking for the part of the error message that begins `(output started at /path/`: the PHP file at the end of that path is the culprit. It will also tell you the line number where the problem is occurring. Using a text editor — not Word or any word processor — check that there's absolutely nothing before the opening `<?php` tag or after the closing `?>` tag. Delete any characters or spaces, save the file, and upload again.

> *The two files you'll most likely be altering are* `wp-config.php` *and* `functions.php`*, and both of those have dropped the terminating ?> tag at the end of the file, preventing the possibility of extra spaces there, at least.*
>
> *Also, don't notice the missing terminating tag and think it needs to be put back in!*

3. **500 Internal Server Error:** If you have access to your server logs (through hosting control panels like cPanel or Parallels, for example), you should check there for specific information on the cause of the error. It may be a problem with an `.htaccess` file or from files not having the right permissions, but you really need the log report to point you in the right direction. If you don't have access to the log files, you'll need to contact your hosting company.

TROUBLESHOOTING AFTER INSTALLATION

Once WordPress is up and running, potential problems can be divided into three general categories:

- The entire site is down.
- A particular function (usually a plugin) stops working.
- Specific content is not appearing.

Each category would lead you to look in a very different place for answers. If the site is down completely, there will often be an error message to guide you: no database connection, internal server error, and so on. If a plugin is not working, the answer is likely to do with the set of plugins you have activated (I give some hints about troubleshooting plugins in Lesson 35).

Whatever category of problem you're having, it's usually helpful to remember or find out if anything has changed recently:

- You added a new plugin.
- You made some change in the admin settings.
- You just upgraded WordPress or there was an upgrade and you haven't done it yet.
- There was some problem or change with your hosting provider (it may have upgraded its version of PHP, for example).

Armed with this kind of information, you can narrow down the problem and get closer to an answer.

> *One way to tell if there's been some Web-wide problem is to check the WordPress forums and see if others have suddenly started reporting a similar issue.*

If specific content is not appearing on your site, check that you properly saved the material or that you haven't deleted a category (in which case, all posts from the category will have been moved automatically to the default category). It could be that you accidentally unpublished the item. Remember, unless you physically delete something from WordPress, it will still be in the system, even if it doesn't show on the live site.

FINDING HELP ONLINE

Because problems with WordPress are often very specific to your particular circumstances, searching online for someone who's had the same problem is going to be your best bet. Fortunately, there's a huge community of WordPress users who share their experiences in a variety of ways, and following are some suggestions for finding them.

The WordPress.org Site

The number-one place to start is the Forum section of the WordPress.org website. You'll find a wealth of information about real-world applications of WordPress and helpful solutions, as well as ideas on making WordPress do exactly what you need it to do. I know I've found a lot of inspiration there for customizations I'd never thought of. Although you don't need to register to use the forum, it's well worth it so that you can post problems for which you haven't found a solution.

> *When you think you haven't found an answer to your problem, your first action should be:* search again. *If you still haven't found the answer,* search again! *Of course, I mean use different wording for each search, follow suggested threads in the results you do find, and try to approach the search from different angles.* Be a detective. *You'll save yourself (and other people in the forum) a lot of time and trouble, and you won't clog the forum with repeat questions.*
>
> *I would almost guarantee that your problem has at least been voiced by someone, even if it hasn't been resolved, and you're better off joining that thread than starting a new one.*

On the WordPress.org site, you'll also find a very helpful set of frequently asked questions (`http://codex.wordpress.org/FAQ`) as well as a whole page of tips on how to find help (`http://codex.wordpress.org/Finding_WordPress_Help`).

Using Search Engines

When it comes to searching for help online, the best tip is to be as specific as you can in your search terms. Simply typing *website is broken* or *page crashes* is far too general, but even if you type *menu not showing properly,* that's still less specific than *the sidebar menu is not showing all my categories.* Once you're more specific, be sure to try other wording as well, such as *displaying* instead of *showing* — not everyone uses the same terminology.

Another aspect of being specific is to remember to narrow the search to your specific software. If the issue is with WordPress, be sure to include *+wordpress* (you may have to use Advanced Search to force a term to be in the search) along with whatever other terms you're searching for. Or if it's a problem with PHP, use *+php* to make sure you're focused on the right scripting language.

It's also important to put quotes around phrases: *sidebar widget* is a very different search from "*sidebar widget*" because the first will look for each word separately, whereas the second tells the search engine to find them together as a phrase.

If you're getting an error message, enclose the entire message (or if it's very long, choose what looks like the most relevant part) in quotation marks and do your search on that. Including your operating system in the search, along with your browser, can also get you to your answer faster.

Finding Professional Help

If you can't find an answer online or the answer is difficult to implement, it may be time to hire someone to troubleshoot for you. You can search for phrases like *wordpress developer*. Most likely, some of the people you know are using WordPress for their site — ask for the names of people who have done WordPress customizations for them.

Check sites like Meetup.com and see if there's a WordPress group in your area where you can meet web designers and developers who work with the platform, or check out one of the many WordCamps (`http://central.wordcamp.org/`) held throughout the world. You can also post your needs on sites like CodePoet (`http://codepoet.net`), which is run by Automattic, or WordPress Jobs (`http://jobs.wordpress.net`).

B

Glossary

Activate a plugin The next step after installing a plugin. WordPress displays a list of plugins you've installed, but you need to activate them before they function on your site. You can deactivate a plugin but that still leaves it installed.

Administrator The highest level of WordPress users. Administrators have full access to all administrative functions, as opposed to, say, Editors, who cannot change the theme of a site nor do anything with plugins.

Admin Bar A horizontal menu bar that remains stationary as the page scrolls and is visible to logged-in users of WordPress if they choose. What appears on the bar depends on the user's role and what plugins are being used. By default, the bar is visible while logged in and viewing the live website. Separate controls for visibility on the live site and the administration screens are located on a user's profile page.

Attachment Any file that has been uploaded to a post or page and, as a result, is listed in the gallery for that post or page. Though the file can be used anywhere on the site, that uploading process created a unique relationship to the post or page and, in that sense, the file has been attached to it.

Auto-Embed A feature of WordPress that automatically embeds videos that come from certain video-sharing sites, such as YouTube. Users simply paste the URL of the video on a separate line in the Text Editor and the video will be embedded. For security purposes, the list of allowed sharing sites is set by WordPress, though this can be altered by custom coding.

Avatar A small graphic or image used in WordPress comments to represent the person making the comment.

Backup Saving and storing a copy of any information. Backing up WordPress is a two-step process: backing up the database, and backing up the theme and uploaded files.

Blogroll A list of links. The name comes from that fact that it was originally intended to display favorite blogs or other sites you regularly visit.

Bookmarklet A button on a browser's bookmark bar that allows the user to perform a function quickly and easily. WordPress has a Press It bookmarklet that allows users to instantly blog about something they're viewing in their browser.

Capability A task that a user is able to perform in the WordPress administrative area. Different users have varying degrees of capabilities, with Administrators having all capabilities.

Category Categories are used to group broadly related content in the way that a book has a table of contents (as opposed to tags, which are like the index of a book). WordPress has two types of categories: post categories and link categories. WordPress pages cannot use post or link categories, though it is possible to create custom taxonomies for pages.

Child Theme A WordPress theme that shares files with a parent theme. At the very minimum, a child theme must contain a style sheet file.

Class An attribute in HTML that allows a CSS style to be applied to any part of a web page that has that class. Example: `<p class="importantparagraph">`.

CMS Content management system. A CMS is software that allows users to easily store, organize, and update information, usually for display on the Web.

Comments Responses to your content that are submitted using a form and, if approved, are displayed for other visitors to read. You can choose whether to allow the comment form to appear on all, some, or none of your WordPress content.

cPanel A popular online tool that allows people to easily manage their web-hosting accounts (adding e-mail accounts, setting up databases, and so on).

CSS Cascading style sheets. A style sheet language used to control the look, formatting, and layout of a web page written in HTML. The cascading part refers to the ways in which style rules get applied.

Custom Fields User-generated fields that can be attached to posts, pages, or custom post types. By default, there is a Custom Fields meta box that can be made visible under Screen Options, but more user-friendly boxes can be created that offer more choices than just text fields for data entry.

Custom Post Type Additional types of content, like posts or pages, which can be created by WordPress users.

Dashboard The homepage of the WordPress administrative interface.

Database Software that stores data of various types and enables relationships to be established between the data. WordPress uses a MySQL database.

Deprecated Functions or template tags in WordPress that are no longer supported and eventually will be obsolete.

Domain Mapping In WordPress multisite mode, this is the act of telling WordPress to use a particular domain name for one of the sites on the network.

Draft A post or page that has been saved but not yet published; also, the state of a previously published page that has been unpublished.

Excerpt A short summary of a post that is entered separately in the excerpt field or is auto-generated using the first 55 words of the post.

Featured Image An image that has been specially designated for a particular post or page and that may be used by a theme in various ways. For example, the theme Twenty Ten — the default theme for versions 3.0 and 3.1 — will automatically replace the header image with a post or page's featured image (if the image is a certain size). Featured images can be changed at any time.

Feed A data format used to provide users with frequently updated content. WordPress creates many different feeds of your site's content in a variety of feed types, such as RSS.

FTP File Transfer Protocol. An FTP program is used to transfer files back and forth to your server.

Gallery A list of all files associated with a particular post or page. Also, a display within the body of a post or page showing thumbnails of all image files belonging to a post or page.

Hosting Provider Anyone who runs a server connected to the Internet and provides accounts for people to run their websites and/or e-mail.

HTML Hypertext Markup Language. This is the basic language used to generate pages on the Internet. For example:

```
<p><em>Emphasized text</em> has certain tags around it, while all the text in
this paragraph is surrounded by the opening and closing paragraph tags</p>
```

ID An attribute in HTML that allows a CSS style to be applied to a unique area on a web page. In other words, an ID name can only be used once per page. Example: <p id="best paragraph">.

Install a plugin In order to use plugins — add-on software that extends the functions of WordPress — you must first install them, which means that the file or files for the plugin have been uploaded to a special plugins folder on the server, using either a file transfer protocol (FTP) program or the automated install process in WordPress.

Internal Linking Linking to content on your own website.

JavaScript One of the most popular client-side scripting languages for use on web pages. Client-side means that it runs in the visitor's browser, which allows JavaScript to react to clicks, mouse movements, and so on, producing effects such as menus changing color when you place your mouse over them. Not to be confused with the programming language Java.

The Loop A section of WordPress template files that automatically runs through all possible pieces of content that meet a certain criteria and displays them according to the coding for that loop. For example, WordPress might loop through all posts in Category 6 and display the date, title, and body of each.

Meta Typically used when talking about meta tags, which provide information about a web page, particularly to search engines, such as a description or a list of keywords relating to the page. In WordPress, the term is also used in relation to posts — post metadata — for such information as the date, categories, tags, and other details about the post.

Meta Box A section of a WordPress administration screen, such as Featured Image or Categories or Publish, which contains functions and can be moved around and whose visibility can be toggled on or off.

Multisite A feature of WordPress that enables a single installation to control more than one website or blog.

MySQL One of the most popular open-source databases. SQL stands for Structured Query Language. MySQL is the database used by WordPress.

Network The name for the collection of sites in a WordPress multisite installation. It's also used to distinguish the administrative area of a multisite installation, as opposed to the site administration areas for each of the sites on the network.

Page A WordPress page is often said to be for "static" content. This is meant to be a contrast with posts, which typically are organized by date and time. The history of a company would be material for a page, while a press release would be material for a post. WordPress pages can be organized into hierarchies of parent and child pages, but unlike posts, cannot be categorized or tagged.

Permalink This is short for "permanent link." The idea of a permanent link is to provide a way for others on the Internet to always find a page on your website, even if you change something that could affect that link, such as a post title.

Permissions Attributes of a file or directory (folder) on a web server that determine what action a particular user may take with respect to that file or directory (reading, writing, or executing the content).

PHP This scripting language is one of the most widely used for generating dynamic content on web pages. PHP is a server-side language, which means that it works before reaching the user's browser, as opposed to a language like JavaScript, which functions in the browser. WordPress is written using PHP. Virtually all hosting providers offer PHP, whether on a Windows, Unix/Linux, or Mac platform.

phpMyAdmin A popular open-source interface for managing MySQL databases.

Pingback One type of notification you receive in WordPress to tell you that someone has linked to content on your site. For this to happen, your site must be pingback-enabled, which is set in the admin section.

Plesk/Parallels A popular online tool that makes it easy for people to manage their web hosting accounts (creating e-mail accounts, setting up databases, and so on).

Plugin A file or set of files that provide additional functionality for WordPress, such as suggesting related content to visitors or displaying maps. Plugins must first be installed in WordPress and, in order to work, must be activated.

Post A type of content in WordPress that can be categorized. The order of displaying posts in a category can be controlled according to several parameters such as date published, title, and so on.

Post Format A set of nine possible designations recognized by WordPress and that, when set up by a theme, can be chosen by users when creating a post. The idea of post formats is to recognize certain standard content types that people may want to organize and design differently from other posts, and a post format makes this easy to do through template scripting and CSS.

Post Status Tells you whether a post or page is published, unpublished, in draft mode, or pending review.

Post Thumbnail See Featured Image.

Publish Publishing a post or a page tells WordPress to display it on your site. You can always save them as drafts until you're ready to publish. You can also tell WordPress to automatically publish posts or pages in the future.

RSS Really Simple Syndication. This is a type of feed format (see Feed).

Scheduling By default, publishing a post or page in WordPress — making it live on your site — happens immediately, but you can also schedule it to publish at a future date and time.

Screen Options A hidden area at the top right of most WordPress administrative screens that, when it's displayed, provides the ability to add or remove meta boxes from the screen, change the number of results displayed, and other functions for controlling the look of the screen.

Sidebar The area of a website on the left or right side of the page, where items such as navigation, advertising, and small chunks of content are displayed.

Slug A word or series of words in lowercase lettering and containing no spaces. There are slugs for posts, pages, categories, tags, and authors, and they're used by WordPress to make URLs more descriptive.

Style Sheet A file that contains the CSS used to create the look, formatting, and layout of a web page.

Tag A keyword you assign to posts and which can be shared by other posts. Posts can have multiple tags. Tags are meant to be specific in the way that entries in the index of a book get very detailed (as opposed to categories, which are like a book's table of contents).

Taxonomy A system of classification. Default taxonomies in WordPress include post categories, link categories, and tags. Users are also able to create their own custom taxonomies.

Teaser The portion of a post prior to the point where you've added a More tag to the post.

Template A file in WordPress themes that provides instructions for assembling HTML pages. Templates may use other templates in the assembly process.

Text Editor In WordPress, this refers to the field on post or page editing screens where the content is edited. Also refers to a program on your computer that you should always use when editing WordPress theme files. Text editors (sometimes called plain text editors) do not introduce the extra information that word processors use, and which can cause problems for files on the Internet.

Theme The set of files that controls the layout, look, and certain aspects of the content on the HTML pages generated by WordPress. A theme consists of at least one style sheet and at least one template file.

Theme Editor A text editor built into the WordPress administration area (listed under the Appearance menu section as Editor) that allows theme files to be edited.

Trackback One type of notification you receive in WordPress to tell you that someone has linked to content on your site.

Update To replace the current version of WordPress, a plugin, or a theme with a newer one.

Update (button) When you see this word on a button, it means you must click it in order to save any changes you've made. It's very important to get in the habit of clicking this before you leave a screen, even if you don't remember changing anything.

URL or URI Uniform Resource Locator or Uniform Resource Identifier. Although a URL is a subtype of URIs, the two are commonly treated as the same. A URI is any string of characters that identifies a resource on the Internet, but is most commonly used to refer to the address of a website or web page, such as `www.wordpress.org`.

User Someone who is a registered user on a WordPress site. There are five levels of users with varying degrees of capabilities: Administrator, Editor, Author, Contributor, and Subscriber.

Widget A piece of code that allows you to place chunks of content (for example, a list of categories, recent posts) on your website (typically in the sidebar) using a drag-and-drop interface.

WordPress MU The name of a version of WordPress that allowed for multiple sites to be controlled by a single installation. The MU is commonly referred to as multiuser, although it's actually phonetic for the Greek letter μ. WordPress MU was merged with the regular version of self-hosted WordPress as of version 3.0.

WYSIWYG Stands for What You See Is What You Get. In the WordPress Text Editor, there is a Visual mode, which displays posts in a partly WYSIWYG format (to see them exactly as they will appear on the Web, you need to use Preview), as opposed to HTML mode, which displays the post with all the code used by the browser to display it.

C

What's on the DVD?

You've read about how WordPress can make creating and maintaining a website much easier — time to see it in action. I love working with my clients online or in person to help train them in the use of WordPress, and that's how I've approached this DVD: to be your virtual coach. So let's get started.

This appendix provides you with information on the contents of the DVD that accompanies this book. For the most up-to-date information, please refer to the ReadMe file located at the root of the DVD. Here is what you will find in this appendix:

- System Requirements
- Using the DVD
- What's on the DVD
- Troubleshooting
- Customer Care

SYSTEM REQUIREMENTS

Make sure that your computer meets the minimum system requirements listed in this section. If your computer doesn't match up to most of these requirements, you may have a problem using the contents of the DVD.

- PC running Windows XP or later, or Mac running OSX
- A DVD-ROM drive
- Adobe Flash Player 9 or later (free download from Adobe.com)

Helpful, but not absolutely necessary:

- Internet connection
- Installed version of WordPress (or a blog with WordPress.com)

USING THE DVD ON A PC

To access the content from the DVD, follow these steps:

1. Insert the DVD into your computer's DVD-ROM drive. The license agreement appears.

> *The interface won't launch if you have autorun disabled. In that case, click Start ➪ Run (For Windows Vista, Start ➪ All Programs ➪ Accessories ➪ Run). In the dialog box that appears, type D:\Start.exe. (Replace D with the proper letter if your DVD drive uses a different letter. If you don't know the letter, see how your CD drive is listed under My Computer.) Click OK.*

2. Read through the license agreement, and then click the Accept button if you want to use the DVD.

   The DVD interface appears. Simply select the lesson video you want to view.

USING THE DVD ON A MAC

To install the items from the DVD to your hard drive, follow these steps:

1. Insert the DVD into your computer's DVD-ROM drive.
2. The DVD icon will appear on your desktop; double-click to open.
3. Double-click the Start button.
4. Read the license agreement and click the Accept button to use the DVD.
5. The DVD interface will appear. Here, you can install the programs and run the demos.

WHAT'S ON THE DVD

Nothing beats watching how something is done and that's why I've provided several hours worth of video about how you can use WordPress. Most lessons in the book have an accompanying video, which not only illustrates several of the examples in the lesson, but goes well beyond what can be covered in print. You'll also gain more insight into the creation of the sample website discussed in the book: Island Travel.

If you have an existing WordPress site — a self-hosted version or a blog on WordPress.com — I encourage you to work along in the admin screen. If you don't have a site, you could install WordPress if you have a web hosting account (see Lesson 3) or you could open an account with WordPress.com. The main thing is that you be able to practice what's covered in the book and on these videos.

TROUBLESHOOTING

If you have difficulty installing or using any of the materials on the companion DVD, try the following solutions:

- **Turn off any antivirus software that you may have running:** Installers sometimes mimic virus activity and can make your computer incorrectly believe that it is being infected by a virus. (Be sure to turn the antivirus software back on later.)
- **Close all running programs:** The more programs you're running, the less memory is available to other programs. Installers also typically update files and programs; if you keep other programs running, installation may not work properly.
- **Reference the ReadMe:** Please refer to the ReadMe file located at the root of the CD-ROM for the latest product information at the time of publication.
- **Reboot if necessary:** If all else fails, rebooting your machine can often clear any conflicts in the system.

CUSTOMER CARE

If you have trouble with the CD-ROM, please call the Wiley Product Technical Support phone number at (800) 762-2974. Outside the United States, call 1 (317) 572-3994. You can also contact Wiley Product Technical Support at `http://support.wiley.com`. John Wiley & Sons will provide technical support only for installation and other general quality-control items. For technical support on the applications themselves, consult the program's vendor or author.

To place additional orders or to request information about other Wiley products, please call (877) 762-2974.

INDEX

Numbers

A

B

F

G

H

I

J

K

L

M

Q

R

S

T

X–Y–Z

WILEY PUBLISHING, INC. END-USER LICENSE AGREEMENT

READ THIS. You should carefully read these terms and conditions before opening the software packet(s) included with this book "Book". This is a license agreement "Agreement" between you and Wiley Publishing, Inc. "WPI". By opening the accompanying software packet(s), you acknowledge that you have read and accept the following terms and conditions. If you do not agree and do not want to be bound by such terms and conditions, promptly return the Book and the unopened software packet(s) to the place you obtained them for a full refund.

1. **License Grant.** WPI grants to you (either an individual or entity) a nonexclusive license to use one copy of the enclosed software program(s) (collectively, the "Software") solely for your own personal or business purposes on a single computer (whether a standard computer or a workstation component of a multi-user network). The Software is in use on a computer when it is loaded into temporary memory (RAM) or installed into permanent memory (hard disk, CD-ROM, or other storage device). WPI reserves all rights not expressly granted herein.

2. **Ownership.** WPI is the owner of all right, title, and interest, including copyright, in and to the compilation of the Software recorded on the physical packet included with this Book "Software Media". Copyright to the individual programs recorded on the Software Media is owned by the author or other authorized copyright owner of each program. Ownership of the Software and all proprietary rights relating thereto remain with WPI and its licensers.

3. **Restrictions on Use and Transfer.**

   (a) You may only (i) make one copy of the Software for backup or archival purposes, or (ii) transfer the Software to a single hard disk, provided that you keep the original for backup or archival purposes. You may not (i) rent or lease the Software, (ii) copy or reproduce the Software through a LAN or other network system or through any computer subscriber system or bulletin-board system, or (iii) modify, adapt, or create derivative works based on the Software.

   (b) You may not reverse engineer, decompile, or disassemble the Software. You may transfer the Software and user documentation on a permanent basis, provided that the transferee agrees to accept the terms and conditions of this Agreement and you retain no copies. If the Software is an update or has been updated, any transfer must include the most recent update and all prior versions.

4. **Restrictions on Use of Individual Programs.** You must follow the individual requirements and restrictions detailed for each individual program in the "About the CD" appendix of this Book or on the Software Media. These limitations are also contained in the individual license agreements recorded on the Software Media. These limitations may include a requirement that after using the program for a specified period of time, the user must pay a registration fee or discontinue use. By opening the Software packet(s), you agree to abide by the licenses and restrictions for these individual programs that are detailed in the "About the CD" appendix and/or on the Software Media. None of the material on this Software Media or listed in this Book may ever be redistributed, in original or modified form, for commercial purposes.

5. **Limited Warranty.**

   (a) WPI warrants that the Software and Software Media are free from defects in materials and workmanship under normal use for a period of sixty (60) days from the date of purchase of this Book. If WPI receives notification within the warranty period of defects in materials or workmanship, WPI will replace the defective Software Media.

(b) WPI AND THE AUTHOR(S) OF THE BOOK DISCLAIM ALL OTHER WARRANTIES, EXPRESS OR IMPLIED, INCLUDING WITHOUT LIMITATION IMPLIED WARRANTIES OF MERCHANTABILITY AND FITNESS FOR A PARTICULAR PURPOSE, WITH RESPECT TO THE SOFTWARE, THE PROGRAMS, THE SOURCE CODE CONTAINED THEREIN, AND/OR THE TECHNIQUES DESCRIBED IN THIS BOOK. WPI DOES NOT WARRANT THAT THE FUNCTIONS CONTAINED IN THE SOFTWARE WILL MEET YOUR REQUIREMENTS OR THAT THE OPERATION OF THE SOFTWARE WILL BE ERROR FREE.

(c) This limited warranty gives you specific legal rights, and you may have other rights that vary from jurisdiction to jurisdiction.

6. **Remedies.**

(a) WPI's entire liability and your exclusive remedy for defects in materials and workmanship shall be limited to replacement of the Software Media, which may be returned to WPI with a copy of your receipt at the following address: Software Media Fulfillment Department, Attn.: *WordPress 24-Hour Trainer*, *Second Edition*, Wiley Publishing, Inc., 10475 Crosspoint Blvd., Indianapolis, IN 46256, or call 1-800-762-2974. Please allow four to six weeks for delivery. This Limited Warranty is void if failure of the Software Media has resulted from accident, abuse, or misapplication. Any replacement Software Media will be warranted for the remainder of the original warranty period or thirty (30) days, whichever is longer.

(b) In no event shall WPI or the author be liable for any damages whatsoever (including without limitation damages for loss of business profits, business interruption, loss of business information, or any other pecuniary loss) arising from the use of or inability to use the Book or the Software, even if WPI has been advised of the possibility of such damages.

(c) Because some jurisdictions do not allow the exclusion or limitation of liability for consequential or incidental damages, the above limitation or exclusion may not apply to you.

7. **U.S. Government Restricted Rights.** Use, duplication, or disclosure of the Software for or on behalf of the United States of America, its agencies and/or instrumentalities "U.S. Government" is subject to restrictions as stated in paragraph (c)(1)(ii) of the Rights in Technical Data and Computer Software clause of DFARS 252.227-7013, or subparagraphs (c) (1) and (2) of the Commercial Computer Software - Restricted Rights clause at FAR 52.227-19, and in similar clauses in the NASA FAR supplement, as applicable.

8. **General.** This Agreement constitutes the entire understanding of the parties and revokes and supersedes all prior agreements, oral or written, between them and may not be modified or amended except in a writing signed by both parties hereto that specifically refers to this Agreement. This Agreement shall take precedence over any other documents that may be in conflict herewith. If any one or more provisions contained in this Agreement are held by any court or tribunal to be invalid, illegal, or otherwise unenforceable, each and every other provision shall remain in full force and effect.

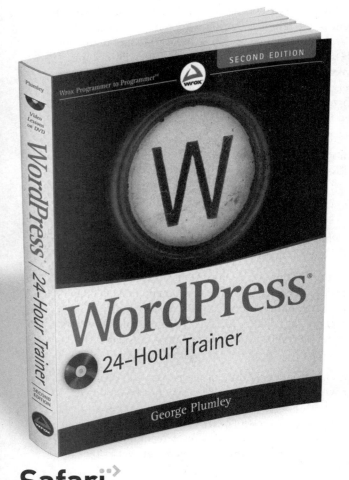